CONTENTS

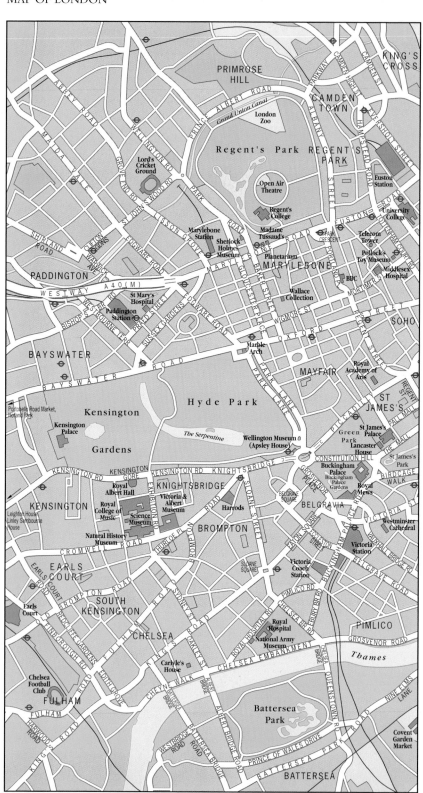

AA

ALL-IN-ONE GUIDE
London

AA Lifestyle Guides

Edited and produced by   AA Publishing

© The Automobile Association 2000. The Automobile Association
retains the copyright in the current edition © 2000 and in all
subsequent editions, reprints and amendments to editions

London Maps produced by   the Cartographic Department of
the Automobile Association.

Typeset by Microset Ltd, Basingstoke, England
Printed and bound by Printer Trento srl, Italy
Cover design by Mike Ballard, Twyford, England
Internal design by PPD, Basingstoke, England

Advertisement Sales   Advertisement Production:
Karen Weeks, ☎ 01256 491545

A CIP catalogue record for this book is available
from the British Library

ISBN 0-7495-2330-1

Published by AA Publishing, which is a trading name
of Automobile Association Developments Limited, whose
registered office is Norfolk House, Priestley Road,
Basingstoke, Hampshire RG24 9NY.
Registered number 1878835

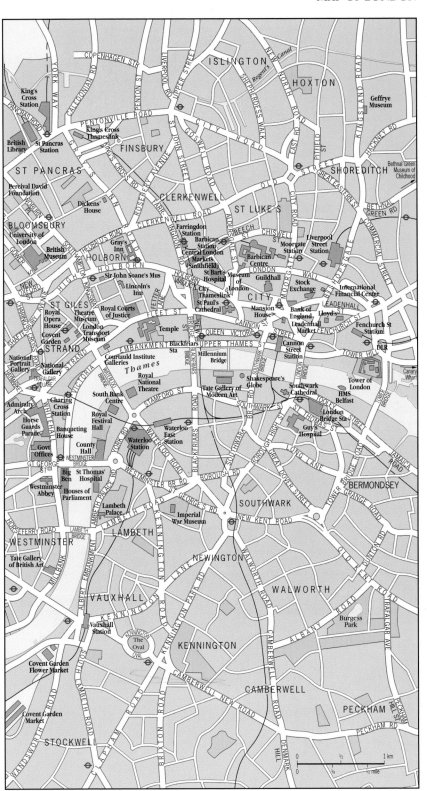

WELCOME TO THE GUIDE

HOW THE GUIDE IS DIVIDED

For the purposes of this guide London has been divided into thirteen areas, with Airports and Excursions sections at the end. For the area maps see the beginning of each area, or consult the key map on pages 4 & 5:

Westminster & Whitehall

St James & The Mall

Mayfair, Piccadilly & Oxford St

Knightsbridge & Chelsea

Kensington, Notting Hill & Hyde Park

Regent's Park & Bloomsbury

Soho & Covent Garden

Camden, King's Cross & Islington

Holborn, The Strand & The South Bank

The City

Docklands

Dulwich & Greenwich

Hampstead

Airports (Heathrow & Gatwick)

Accommodation in Postal Districts

Excursions from London

REGIONAL DIVISIONS

Each region starts with a brief description of the area, followed by a map.
Information is divided into the following sections:

WHERE TO GO AND WHAT TO DO

Our intention has been to include as many attractions as possible to reflect the widest range of interests for the benefit of the reader. This means that entries are necessarily brief, but do include location, a telephone contact number and directions (if applicable and supplied).

The Must See section is generally more informative than the subsequent headings, and is intended to give an overall picture of the best tourist attractions at a glance.

Other interests (see below) have been divided into lists for ease of use. Their descriptions may not be so long , but should always incorporate the address and/or directions and a telephone number (if supplied or applicable). For example, if you are on holiday with the children, the Great for Kids section gives some idea of suitable facilities in the area. If you are looking out for famous buildings or outdoor venues, then Historic & Ancient Sites or Parks and Gardens may be the sections that appeal to you. There is also a wealth of information about entertainment, theatres, concert halls and cinemas, as well as shopping, markets, sports & leisure, etc.

Where an area has a speciality such as Literary Bloomsbury among its places of interest you will find this at the end of the Where to Go, What to Do section. Each section may not have all the sections, and they may be in modified order depending on the strengths and weaknesses of a particular region, but you can expect to see most of these in each area.

MUST SEE

CINEMAS

GREAT FOR KIDS

ENTERTAINMENT & NIGHTLIFE

HISTORIC & ANCIENT SITES

MARKETS

MUSEUMS & ART GALLERIES

PARKS & GARDENS

PLACES OF WORSHIP

SHOPPING

SPORT & LEISURE

THEATRES, & CONCERT HALLS

Must See

Entries include the very best or most interesting places to go in that part of London. These could include any of the Where to Go and What to Do categories. The entries could range from the most famous tourist attractions – for example, Buckingham Palace – to something small that captures the essence of the area. Not all Must Sees are open to the public.

Cinemas

London is one of the best places in Britain to see movies. For example, Leicester Square has some of the biggest and most luxurious cinemas in Europe, and these are often the scene of star-studded premieres and challenging film festivals.

Great for Kids
Many of the big tourist attractions are geared towards children with special exhibitions, audio-visual presentations and the like. The entries in this heading may include some, or none of these, depending on what else is available in the area. Expect to find children's farms, local activities, leisure centres and eating options that are children-friendly.

Entertainment & Nightlife
Nightclubs, discos, etc. Due to the ever-changing and fashion-heavy nature of nightclubs, this section is often rather sparse. The capital has a wealth of free newspapers and magazines which explore in depth the incredible array of possibilities. They will be of much more use to the potential clubber than this book.

Historic & Ancient Sites
London has hundreds of famous buildings and landmarks, some open to the public, some, like Nelson's Column, simply to be viewed from the street.

Markets
One of London's most enduring institutions is its street market. From Portobello Road to Camden Market, visitors can sample all kinds of goods, atmospheres and London life.

Museums & Art Galleries
Museums of every type and size plus art galleries. The lists may be split if there are sufficient numbers to warrant it.

Parks & Gardens
London has many Royal and public parks, from Regent's Park in North West London to Hyde Park, St James's Park, and Green Park in the heart of the capital. They are refreshing places to stroll and picnic, and some, like Hyde Park and Kensington Gardens, have open-air theatre and concerts in the summer.

Places of Worship
London is home to thousands of churches, from St Paul's Cathedral to tiny Spiritualist meeting rooms. In this section we have listed a few of the most significant places of worship.

Shopping
Some areas, like Knightsbridge, are internationally famous for shopping. This section contains information on shopping areas and the sort of thing you will find there.

Sport & Leisure
A wide range of activities is available in London, including swimming pools, sports centres, football, cricket and so on.

Theatres & Concert Halls
Plays, musicals, and live music. London has plenty of all three. Here is just a small selection of the best and best-known.

WHERE TO STAY
Wide range of accommodation
All AA recommended accommodation from 5-star hotels to small bed & breakfast establishments are included in this guide, either in the area directories or in the reference lists at the end of the book.

Quality Assured
When hotels and other guest accommodation apply to join the AA scheme they are visited anonymously by the AA's professional Hotel Inspectorate and are inspected and assessed for facilities and the quality of what they provide. This assessment reflects the quality of the accommodation and services provided by each establishment. Hotels are awarded from one to five stars on a rising scale, and other accommodation is awarded from one to five ♦s for its quality.

Only after testing the accommodation and services and having paid their bill do inspectors introduce themselves in order to make a thorough inspection of the entire premises.

PRICE SYMBOLS
The £ symbol has been used as a price guide. The categories below indicate the price of a single room. Prices are per night and are indications only. The information is the most up-to-date available to us at the time of going to press, but prices can and do change without warning during the currency of a guide, so it is essential to check before booking. If the establishment is in the Bed & Breakfast Accommodation section, then the room price will almost certainly include breakfast. Some establishments offer free accommodation to children up to a certain age, provided they share the parents' room. Check for availability of family rooms and terms and conditions.

£	up to £40
££	£41 - £70
£££	£71 and over

THE RATING SYMBOLS
The Hotel Star Rating
Star classification is a quality scheme at five levels. The assessment rises from one star, denoting hotels with the simplest range of facilities, to five stars, denoting large, luxury hotels with a range of services and facilities that meet the best international standards. The requirements for the five star levels are outlined as follows:

★ Hotels in this classification are likely to be small and independently owned, with a family atmosphere. Services may be provided by the owner and family on an informal basis. There may be a limited range of facilities and meals may be fairly simple. Lunch, for example, may not be served. Some bedrooms may not have en suite bath/shower rooms. Maintenance, cleanliness and comfort should, however, always be of an acceptable standard.

★ ★   In this classification hotels will typically be small to medium sized and offer more extensive facilities than at the one star level. Some business hotels come into the two star classification and guests can expect comfortable, well equipped, overnight accommodation, usually with an en suite bath/shower room. Reception and other staff will aim for a more professional presentation than at the one star level, and offer a wider range of straightforward services, including food and drink.

★ ★ ★   At this level, hotels are usually of a size to support higher staffing levels, and a significantly greater quality and range of facilities than at the lower star classifications. Reception and the other public rooms will be more spacious and the restaurant will normally also cater for non-residents. All bedrooms will have fully en suite bath and shower rooms and offer a good standard of comfort and equipment, such as a hair dryer, direct dial telephone, toiletries in the bathroom. Some room service can be expected, and some provision for business travellers.

★ ★ ★ ★   Expectations at this level include a degree of luxury as well as quality in the furnishings, decor and equipment, in every area of the hotel. Bedrooms will also usually offer more space than at the lower star levels, and well designed, co-ordinated furnishings and decor. En suite bathrooms will have both bath and fixed shower. There will be a high enough ratio of staff to guests to provide services like porterage, 24-hour room service, laundry and dry-cleaning. The restaurant will demonstrate a serious approach to cuisine.

★ ★ ★ ★ ★   Here you should find spacious and luxurious accommodation throughout the hotel, matching the best international standards. Interior design should impress with its quality and attention to detail, comfort and elegance. Furnishings should be immaculate. Services should be formal, well supervised and flawless in attention to guests' needs, without being intrusive. The restaurant will demonstrate a high level of technical skill, producing dishes to the highest international standards. Staff will be knowledgeable, helpful, well versed in all aspects of customer care, combining efficiency with courtesy.

RED STAR HOTELS

These awards are made annually to a select number of hotels as a recognition of excellence within their star rating. This is the AA's supreme award for hotels and to earn it, they must consistently provide outstanding levels of hospitality, service, food and comfort.

LODGES (e.g. Travelodge, Travel Inn)

Useful budget accommodation for an overnight stay. They have rooms suitable for family use which are often charged at a flat rate regardless of number of occupants. There are several in Central London and they provide a consistent standard of comfortable modern en suite accommodation.

THE GUEST ACCOMMODATION '♦' (QUALITY) SYMBOL (Guest Houses, Private Hotels, Inns)

♦ This assessment indicates an establishment with simple accommodation and adequate bathroom facilities.

♦ ♦ This assessment indicates a sound standard of accommodation offering more in terms of decor and comfort and likely to have some bedrooms with en suite bath or shower rooms

♦ ♦ ♦ This assessment indicates well appointed accommodation and a wider range of facilities than a one or two ♦ establishment. Bedrooms may have en suite bath/shower rooms.

♦ ♦ ♦ ♦ This assessment indicates that the accommodation will be comfortable and well appointed, that hospitality and facilities will be of high quality, and that a reasonable proportion of bedrooms will have en suite bath or shower rooms

♦ ♦ ♦ ♦ ♦ This is the AA's highest assessment for guest houses, farmhouses or inns. It indicates an outstanding level of accommodation and service, with an emphasis on quality, good facilities for guests and an exceptionally friendly and hospitable atmosphere.
    The majority of bedrooms will have en suite bath or shower rooms.

HOW TO READ ACCOMMODATION ENTRIES

Hotels are listed in each area of London in alphabetical order within their star rating.
Quality Symbols: all guest accommodation is assessed for quality on a scale of one to five, denoted by the appropriate symbol (see above) and then listed in alphabetical order by '♦' rating.
Name is followed by the address, and postal code of establishment.
Telephone numbers may be changed during the currency of this book in some areas. In case of difficulty, check with the operator.
Fax numbers are given when supplied.

DESCRIPTION OF THE ESTABLISHMENT

Establishments have been described very briefly, but the facilities are shown in italics at the end of each description.

Accommodation details

The first figure shows the number of letting bedrooms.
family - indicates family bedrooms.
No smoking - if the establishment has no-smoking bedrooms, the number of these is indicated.
No children - indicates that children cannot be accommodated. A minimum age may be specified (e.g. No children under 4 yrs = no children under four years old). Although establishments may accept children of all ages they may not necessarily be able to provide special facilities. If you have very young children, check before booking about provisions like cots and high chairs, and any reductions made.

Children's Facilities - a list of accommodation with special children's facilities is in the Quick Reference Accommodation Lists at the back of the book.
Additional facilities - such as lift, night porter etc.
Leisure activities - could encompass tennis, croquet, cycle hire, fishing, golf, sauna, jacuzzi, spa, beauty therapy, horse-riding, swimming pool, snooker.
Parking - a list of accommodation with dedicated parking is at the end of the book in the Quick Reference Accommodation Lists.
Credit cards - the symbol 🖃 indicates that the establishment accepts most or all major credit cards

GUESTS WITH DISABILITIES

Guests with any form of disability should notify proprietors, so that arrangements can be made to minimise difficulties, particularly in the event of an emergency.

NOTES ABOUT ACCOMMODATION
Common to all

Whatever the type of establishment, there are certain requirements common to all, including a well-maintained exterior, clean and hygienic kitchens; good standards of furnishing; friendly and courteous service; access to the premises at reasonable times; the use of a telephone; and a full, cooked breakfast.

CANCELLATION

If you find that you must cancel a booking, let the proprietor know at once, because if the room you booked cannot be re-let, you may be held legally responsible for partial payment. Whether it is a matter of losing your deposit, or of being liable for compensation, you should seriously consider taking out cancellation insurance.

COMPLAINTS

Readers who have any cause to complain are urged to do so on the spot. This should provide an opportunity for the proprietor to correct matters. If a personal approach fails, readers should inform: AA Hotel Services, Fanum House, Basingstoke, Hants, RG21 4EA.

FOOD AND DRINK

If you intend to take dinner at an establishment, note that sometimes the meal must be ordered in advance of the actual meal time. In some cases, this may be at breakfast time, or even on the previous evening. If you have booked on bed, breakfast and evening meal terms, you may find that the tariff includes only the set menu, but, if there is one, you can usually order from the à la carte menu and pay a supplement.

Payment

Most proprietors will only accept cheques in payment of accounts if notice is given and some form of identification (preferably a cheque card) is produced. If a hotel accepts credit or charge cards, this is shown by a global credit card symbol in its directory entry. Please contact establishments directly to check which are accepted.

Prices

Hotels must display tariffs, either in the bedrooms or at reception. Application of VAT and service charges varies, but all prices quoted must be inclusive of VAT.

FIRE REGULATIONS

For safety, you must read the emergency notices displayed in bedrooms and be sure you understand them.

LICENCE TO SELL ALCOHOL

Unless otherwise stated, all hotels listed are licensed. Hotel residents can obtain alcoholic drinks at all times if the owner or responsible manager is prepared to serve them. Non-residents eating at the hotel restaurant can have drinks with their meals.

CODES OF PRACTICE

The Hotel Industry Voluntary Code of Booking Practice was revised in 1986, and the AA encourages its use in appropriate establishments. Its prime object is to ensure that the customer is clear about the precise services and facilities s/he is buying and what price will have to be paid, before entering into a contractually binding agreement. If the price has not been previously confirmed in writing, the guest should be handed a card at the time of registration, stipulating the total obligatory charge.

Some guest houses offer bed and breakfast only, so guests must go out for the evening meal. It is also wise to check when booking if there are any restrictions to your access to the house, particularly in the late morning and during the afternoon.

However, many guest houses do provide an evening meal. They may only be able to offer a set meal, but many offer an interesting menu and a standard of service that one would expect in a good restaurant. You may have to arrange dinner in advance, so you should ask about the arrangements for evening meals when booking. Many places have a full licence, or at least a table licence and wine list.

BOOKING

Book as early as possible, particularly for the peak holiday period from the beginning of June to the end of September, and may also include Easter and other public holidays.

Although it is possible for chance callers to find a night's accommodation, it is by no means a certainty, especially at peak holiday times and in popular areas, so it is always advisable to book as far in advance as possible. Some may only accept weekly bookings from Saturday. Some establishments will require a deposit on booking.

Only brief descriptions appear about each establishment, so if you require further information, write to, telephone or fax the establishment itself. Do remember to enclose a stamped addressed envelope, or an international reply coupon if writing from overseas, and please quote this publication in any enquiry. Although we try to publish accurate and up to date information, please remember that any details, and particularly prices, are subject to change without notice and this may happen during the currency of the guide.

WHERE TO EAT
There are two distinct sections in the Where to Eat section.

AA Recommended Restaurants
The first is AA recommended restaurants and hotel restaurants; these are awarded rosettes for the standard of cooking, the highest being five rosettes.

Pubs, Inns & Other Places
The second section includes a range of pubs, and quick bite places. Names, addressess and telephone numbers are supplied, plus a short description. These do not have a price guide, and have not necessarily been AA-inspected.

HOW AA ROSETTES ARE AWARDED
The AA's rosette award scheme is the only home-grown, nationwide scheme for assessing the quality of food served by restaurants and hotels. The rosette scheme is an award scheme, not a classification scheme and although there is necessarily an element of subjectivity when it comes to assessing taste, we aim for a consistent approach to our awards throughout the UK. It is important, however, to remember that many places serve enjoyable food but do not qualify for an AA award.

Our awards are made solely on the basis of a meal visit or visits by one or more of our hotel and restaurant inspectors who have an unrivalled breadth and depth of experience in assessing quality. They award rosettes annually on a rising scale of one to five. Rosette awards are made or withdrawn only on the basis of our own inspectors' meal visits.

All the entries have been written from reports filed by AA inspectors. Although our inspectors are a highly trained and very experienced team of professional men and women, it must be stressed that the opinions expressed are only opinions, based on the experience of one or more particular occasions. Assessments are therefore to some extent necessarily subjective. AA inspectors are experienced enough to make a balanced judgement, but they are not omniscient.

Vegetarian: almost all restaurants featured will prepare a vegetarian dish or accommodate a special diet if given prior notice.

Smoking: establishments that do not allow smoking in the dining room may allow it elsewhere, in a lounge of bar, for instance. If you are a smoker, it is worth checking beforehand.

What the rosettes signify:

At the simplest level, one rosette, the chef should display a mastery of basic techniques and be able to produce dishes of sound quality and clarity of flavours, using good, fresh ingredients.

To gain two rosettes, the chef must show greater technical skill, more consistency and judgement in combining and balancing ingredients and a clear ambition to achieve high standards. Inspectors will look for evidence of innovation to test the dedication of the kitchen brigade, and the use of seasonal ingredients sourced from quality suppliers.

This award takes a restaurant into the big league, and, in a typical year, fewer than 10 per cent of restaurants in our scheme achieve this distinction. Expectations of the kitchen are high, and inspectors find little room for inconsistencies. Exact technique, flair and imagination will come through in every dish, and balance and depth of flavour are all-important.

This is an exciting award because, at this level, not only should all technical skills be exemplary, but there should also be daring ideas, and they must work. There is no room for disappointment. Flavours should be accurate and vibrant.

This is the ultimate award, given only when the cooking is at the pinnacle of achievement. Technique should be of such perfection that flavours, combinations and textures show a faultless sense of balance, giving each dish an extra dimension. The sort of cooking that never falters and always strives to give diners a truly memorable taste experience.

Price Guidelines For AA Recommended Restaurants
ALC is the cost of an à la carte meal for one person, including coffee and service but not wine. **Fixed L** or **Fixed D** shows the approximate price guide for a fixed-price lunch or dinner. The prices quoted are a guide only, and are subject to change without notice.

£	up to £20
££	£21 - £30
£££	£40 and upwards

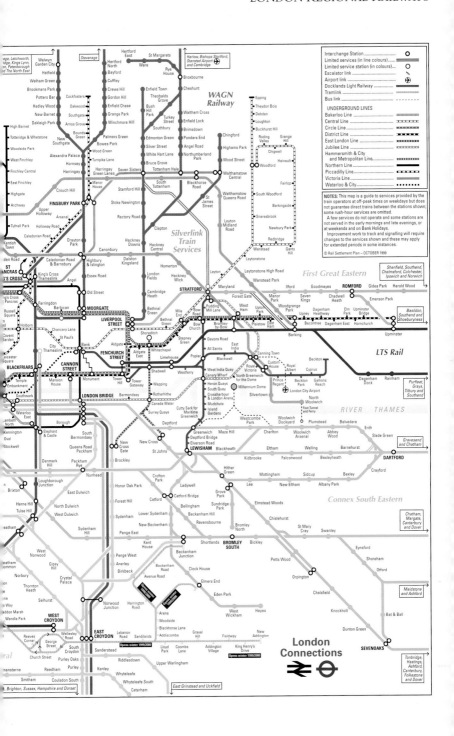

ESSENTIAL INFORMATION

To get the most out of a trip to London, it is important to have practical information so that if you need help or advice you know where to go.

TOURIST INFORMATION

There are a number of tourist information centres approved or run by the London Tourist Board. They are listed below. All should be willing to supply a free map of London. Recorded information is available from Visitorcall on
☎0839 123456
Or telephone the London Tourist Board, ☎020 7932 2000
Their website is at www.londontown.com

HEATHROW TERMINALS 1, 2 AND 3
Heathrow Airport Underground station

LIVERPOOL STREET UNDERGROUND STATION, EC2

SELFRIDGES, Basement, Selfridges, 400 Oxford Street, W1

VICTORIA STATION FORECOURT, SW1

WATERLOO INTERNATIONAL TERMINAL, Arrivals, SE1

BRITAIN VISITOR CENTRE, 1 REGENT STREET, SW1Y 4NS

BRITISH TRAVEL CENTRE, 12 Lower Regent Street, SW1

HELPLINES
CAPITAL HELPLINE ☎020 7388 7575
Run by Capital Radio, they will try and answer anything, and if they can't, they'll find someone who can.

NATIONAL ASSOCIATION OF CITIZENS' ADVICE BUREAUX
136-44 City Road, EC1 ☎020 7251 2000
Citizens' Advice Bureaux are nationwide and offer advice on legal, financial and personal matters.

TELEPHONE
To telephone London from outside the UK, dial the international code followed by 44 and then the ten digit number omitting the first 0. To call abroad from London, dial 00 and the country code. Dial 100 for the operator, 155 for international enquiries and 192 for directory enquiries (national).

POST CODES
London address codes take some getting used to. All codes (such as WC2 and SE16) have letters, which refer to whether they are north, south, west etc, and numbers (from

1 to about 20), which refer to the distance from the centre of London (measured from the City). 'EC' stands for East Central, and 'WC' for West Central.

CLIMATE
Britain's meteorologists have a challenging time trying to predict the weather! It is extremely unpredictable, and can be sunny and warm one day, cold and snowy the next, or even both in the same afternoon. However, as a general rule spring brings rain and winds, summer is a mixture of rain, shine and cloud (some recent summers have been very pleasant), autumn is mild turning to cold, and winter is pretty chilly, with the odd clear, blue day. You just have to take your chances! Luckily, there's no shortage of things to do indoors.

CUSTOMS
Non-EU citizens must follow these limits: 200 cigarettes or 100 cigarillos or 50 cigars or 200g tobacco; 2 litres table wine plus 1 litre spirits or 2 litres fortified wine or other liqueurs; 60cc/ml perfume; 250cc/ml toilet water; other goods to the value of £145 for personal use. The import of meat, fruit, plants, flowers and protected animals is restricted or forbidden. EU citizens can bring in 800 cigarettes or 400 cigarillos or 200 cigars or 1kg tobacco; 10 litres spirits; 20 litres fortified wine; 90 litres wine; 110 litres beer.

FOOD AND DRINK
Britain, like any country, has its traditional dishes, and in London you are likely to find most of them. Roast beef, Yorkshire pudding, roast potatoes and vegetables is served for traditional 'Sunday lunch', which you'll find in pubs and restaurants all over the capital. Other favourites are fish and chips, again, to be found all over the capital, jellied eels and whelks, mostly around the East End, and puddings such as trifle, spotted dick and custard and lemon meringue pie. Old traditional dishes are making a comeback, such as jugged hare and potted shrimps. See the 'Restaurant' section for further details.

TRANSPORT
Britain has a relatively good public transport system, although the privatisation of the railways in 1997, resulting in several private lines instead of the former government-run British Rail, has not had a

smooth transition, with many complaints about late and sub-standard trains. However, London relies more on its buses, underground and taxis than on overground trains.

AIRPORTS
London has four major airports: Heathrow (15 miles west), Gatwick (27 miles south), Stansted (37 miles north) and London City (10 miles east). Gatwick and Heathrow handle by far the most international flights. A special section listing accommodation and restaurants around these two is toward the end of this book.

HEATHROW
☎020 8759 4321
Direct lines to Piccadilly underground, Airbus A1 or A2 to Central London. A taxi will cost around £30.

GATWICK
☎0900 30 15 30
Direct link to London by train, Flightline 777 to Victoria Coach Station. A taxi will cost around £40.

STANSTED
☎01279 680500
Direct links with train services and National Express bus service to London. A taxi will cost around £35.

LONDON CITY
☎020 7474 5555
In the Docklands area of London, links to London via overground train or the Docklands Light Railway. A taxi will cost around £20.

CAR HIRE
You must have at least 1 year's driving experience and a full current driving licence. There are many companies, all of whom include insurance in their fees. Here are the top three.

AVIS
☎020 8848 8765

BUDGET
☎0800 181181

HERTZ
☎0990 996699

CAR PARKING
The best way to avoid a parking fine is to leave the car at home.

London is already a crowded city, and your car is an unnecessary addition. If you do drive, don't park on a double yellow line or areas reserved for permit holders - you will be wheelclamped (an expensive fine and lengthy wait for it to be removed) or towed away (head for one of the car pounds to retrieve your vehicle - very expensive). A single yellow line means you can park there after 6.30pm and on weekends (but check the sign nearby). Carry plenty of change to feed the parking meters, which are usually free after 6.30pm, after 1.30pm on Saturday and all day Sunday.

CYCLE HIRE

Cycling is definitely the easier and fastest way to get around the city, although somewhat unpleasant due to the fumes and risk from cars.

LONDON BICYCLE TOUR COMPANY
1a Gabriels' Wharf, 56 Upper Ground, SE1
☎ 020 7928 6838

TRAINS

Since the privatisation of the train network, there are different companies now operating into Central London from all over the country. London is included in the regional service known as Network SouthEast. Connections are generally good. The cheapest way to travel is to buy a Travelcard (available after 9am), which gives you unlimited travel on the trains, buses and underground for a set price for 1 day, 1 week, 1 month or longer.

BUSES

The famous red double-decker buses are still a common sight around London, although now there are also single-decker 'hoppa' buses which cover shorter routes and are very convenient. The buses are a much better way of seeing the city than the underground (for obvious reasons!), although traffic congestion means that it's best not to be in a hurry. Nightbuses cover central London from midnight to 6am, and most pass through Trafalgar Square. They have the letter 'N' before the number. On both kinds of bus you must pay the driver when you get on at the front of the bus.

UNDERGROUND

Known as the 'tube', the underground network covers the city comprehensively with over 300 stations and 12 lines. The lines are colour coded and there are maps at every station. Connecting services

are well marked and trains are frequent. Fares are divided into zones (Zone 1 is central London).

TAXIS AND MINICABS

London's familiar 'black cabs' (although many carry garish advertising and are far from black) are like large ants crawling all over the city. Their drivers are required to know London like the back of their hand - called 'The Knowledge'. They have meters which show you exactly how much you owe them at the end of the journey (fares go up after midnight). Mini-cabs are normal vehicles with a licence to serve as a taxi. Set the fare with the driver before you start your journey, even though some are metered. There are taxi and mini-cab ranks at most stations. If you're lucky, the cabbie will regale you with classic tales of celebrities they've driven.

EMERGENCIES

EMERGENCY SERVICES

Dial 999 (free) for police, ambulance, or fire brigade.

CAR BREAKDOWN

THE AUTOMOBILE ASSOCIATION (AA)
☎ 0800 887766
To obtain help from the AA you must be a member, or have membership of your own national automobile club with reciprocal arrangements.

THEFT/CRIME

You can feel fairly safe in London, compared with other world capitals, but here are a few tips:
• keep your money out of sight. Don't keep your wallet in your back pocket.
• don't leave any valuables unattended, especially at the airports, in pubs, cinemas, department stores and in crowds
• don't leave your bag on the back of your chair
• don't wear expensive jewellery
• avoid parks and commons after dark

24-HOUR CASUALTY DEPARTMENTS

CHELSEA AND WESTMINSTER HOSPITAL
369 Fulham Road, W6
☎ 020 8746 8080

GUY'S HOSPITAL
St Thomas Street, SE1
☎ 020 7955 5000

ST THOMAS'S
Lambeth Palace Rd, SE1
☎ 020 7928 9292

UNIVERSITY COLLEGE HOSPITAL
Grafton Way, WC1
☎ 020 7387 9300

LOST PROPERTY

Always inform the police if you lose anything, and also your embassy if you have lost your passport. All four major airports, as well as most major stations have lost property offices.

HEALTH AND INSURANCE

Free medical health is available under the NHS to European Union nationals and those from many other countries. If you are in doubt, contact your embassy or high commission. It is important to have medical insurance if your country does not have a reciprocal arrangement with Britain as regards free medical treatment.

LEFT LUGGAGE

GATWICK AIRPORT
☎ 01293 505121 & 569900

HEATHROW AIRPORT
☎ 020 8745 5301

LONDON CITY AIRPORT
☎ 020 7474 5555

STANSTED AIRPORT
☎ 01279 680500

VISITORS WITH DISABILITIES

London has improved its facilities for those with disabilities, so that accessibility to events and sights for those in wheelchairs, people who are blind or deaf, or people with other disabilities are catered for as much as possible. Tourist agencies have full details. Contact Artsline in London (020 7388 2227) for information about art and entertainment venues in London.

EMBASSIES AND CONSULATES

AMERICAN EMBASSY
24 Grosvenor Square, W1
☎ 020 7499 9000

AUSTRALIAN HIGH COMMISSION
Australia House, Strand, WC2
☎ 020 7379 4334

FRENCH EMBASSY
58 Knightsbridge, SW1
☎ 020 7838 2000

JAPANESE EMBASSY
101-104 Piccadillly, W1
☎ 020 7465 6500

NEW ZEALAND HIGH COMMISSION
80 Haymarket, SW1
☎ 020 930 8422

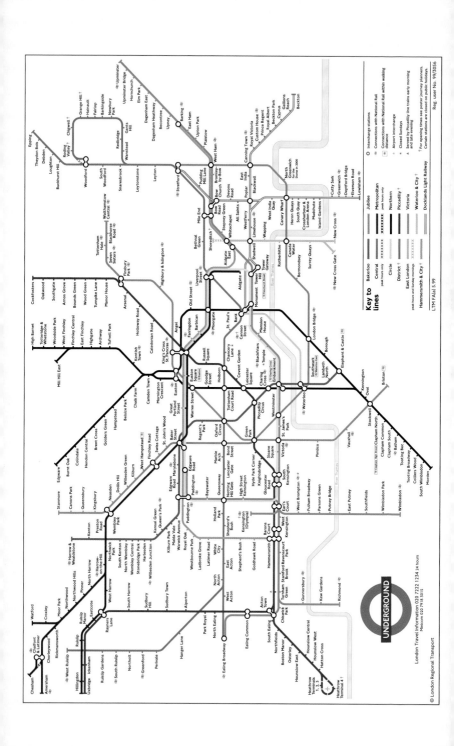

AA Hotel Booking Service

AA

The AA Hotel Booking Service - Now you have a free, simple way to reserve a place to stay for a week, weekend, or a one-night stopover.

Do you want to book somewhere in the Lake District that has leisure facilities; a city-centre hotel in Glasgow with parking facilities, or do you need accommodation near Dover which is handy for the Eurotunnel?

The AA Booking Service can take the hassle out of booking the right place for you.

And if you are touring round the UK or Ireland, simply give the AA Hotel Booking Service your list of overnight stops, and from one phone call all your accommodation can be booked for you.

Telephone
0870 5050505

Office hours
Monday-Friday 9am-6pm
Saturday 9am-1pm
Not available Sundays or Bank
Holidays

Full listings of AA recognised accommodation available through the Hotel Booking Service can be found and booked at the AA's Internet Site:

http://www.theaa.co.uk/hotels

 **www.theaa.co.uk**

Find the "Where to Stay, Where to Eat" pages at www.theaa.co.uk/hotels

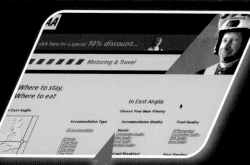

Search for...

a town or establishment name, by region or across the whole of Britain & Ireland

Where to stay,
Where to eat

in East Anglia

Search for:

○ This region
○ Whole site

Book Now
Locate on map

Select region
Select Priority

♦♦♦♦♦
Lavenham Priory
Water Street
LAVENHAM
Sudbury
England
CO18 9RW

Telephone: 81787 247484
Facsimile: 81787 248472
Email: tim.pitt@btinternet.com
Website: www.btinternet.com/~lavpriory

Lavenham Priory, Lave

 Locate

Locate your chosen B&B on a road map

Use the contact details or hotlink to get more information or make a booking direct

Book Now

Booking online is easy with the AA online booking service

WESTMINSTER
AND
WHITEHALL

Whitehall is a broad avenue that connects Trafalgar Square with Parliament Square. The name evokes images of power, intrigue and pomp, and not without good reason. The original Whitehall Palace was the official London residence of the monarch for over a century. Henry VIII confiscated it from the Archbishop of York, after a fire at Westminster in 1512. When Henry died there in 1547, it was over half a mile long and had over 2,000 rooms. The Palace was later home to Cromwell – who died there in 1658 – as well as Charles II, James II, and William and Mary. The monarch's seat shifted to St James's after 1698 when Whitehall was decimated by fire. All that now remains of this once great edifice are Cardinal Wolsey's wine cellars, which are under the Ministry of Defence, and the Banqueting House which witnessed the execution of Charles I in 1649.

The area is currently better known as the home of nearly all Britain's most important government ministries, including the Treasury, the Admiralty and the Foreign and Commonwealth Office. The area positively reeks of government business, and is surrounded by gentleman's clubs, statues and imposing buildings with an air of intrigue. Downing Street, which turns off Whitehall between the Treasury and Foreign Office, is home to the official residences of the Prime Minister and Chancellor of the Exchequer.

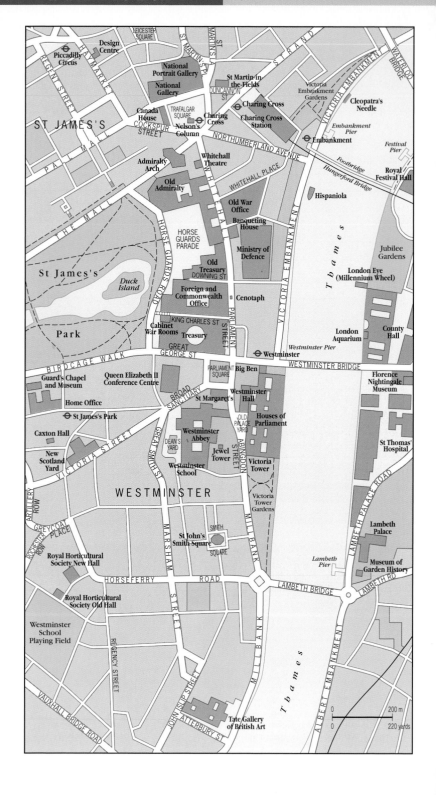

Whitehall descends from Trafalgar Square, with its world-famous tribute to Lord Nelson, to Parliament Square, the Houses of Parliament and Westminster Abbey. Trafalgar Square is the more lively end of the street, with easy access to the National Portrait Gallery, the National Gallery, and the splendid church of St-Martin-in-the-Fields, which has a restaurant in its catacombs. Through the centuries, ordinary people and non-mainstream political groups of many kinds have used the Square to bring their grievances into the heart of government power. Demonstrating groups have included the Chartists in 1848, Oswald Mosley's fascists in the 1930s, and a variety of nuclear disarmament, pro-health service and anti-apartheid groups in the 1980s. The square also saw the worst rioting in London for centuries after an anti-poll tax demonstration in 1990.

Westminster Square was set out in 1868 and is surrounded by statues of political celebrities including Abraham Lincoln, Jan Smuts, Winston Churchill and Benjamin Disraeli. Opposite stands the Houses of Parliament, the "mother of all parliaments", which houses both the House of Commons and the House of Lords, as well as numerous committee rooms, and is essentially the place where British law is written. Big Ben, its giant clock, visible and audible for miles around, still keeps good time, and is one of London's most memorable sights.

MUST SEE

WESTMINSTER ABBEY
Dean's Yard, SW1
☎ 020-7222 5152

Since William the Conqueror had himself crowned here in 1066, Westminster Abbey has been the venue for every coronation of a British monarch save two. Edward the Confessor built a large church on this site in the 11th century, but the structure that stands now was really begun in 1245 by Henry III. Over the centuries additions have included the Lady Chapel in the 15th century, and Nicholas Hawksmoor's quasi-Gothic twin towers, which were completed in 1745. The most recent addition was a series of ten statues depicting 20th-century Christian martyrs, unveiled in 1998. Among the statues that stand over the west door, are Martin Luther King, Oscar Romero, Dietrich Bonhoeffer and Elizabeth of Hesse-Darmstadt.

As well as coronations, the abbey has seen many royal funerals. Nearly every monarch between Henry III and George II is buried here. More recently, Princess Diana's funeral was held at the Abbey in September 1997, as well as a service for the happier occasion of Queen Elizabeth II and the Duke of Edinburgh's 50th wedding anniversary in November of that year. The interior has dozens of monuments to statesmen (Chamberlain, Churchill, Gladstone, Pitt the Edler), musicians (Elgar, Purcell, Vaughan Williams) and poets (Chaucer, Ben Jonson, Blake). The last person to be buried here was Sir Laurence Olivier in 1989, and the strangest burial was that of David Livingstone, whose internal organs are buried under a tree somewhere in Africa. The Tomb of the Unknown Warrior is a simple and moving grave containing the body of an anonymous soldier, a symbol of over 1 million Britons who gave their lives in World War I.

TATE GALLERY
Millbank, SW1
☎ 020-7887 8000

International modern art and the national collection of British paintings are featured in what is surely Britain's most important gallery, founded in 1897 with money provided by Sir Henry Tate of sugarcube fame. Since then it has been a major tourist attraction as well as an undoubted influence on British painters. It has even become a "chain gallery" with branches in Liverpool and St Ives. Inside, the atmosphere is refreshingly informal and young artists making notepad sketches are commonplace.

Westminster Abbey

The adjoining Clore Gallery houses over 20,000 works by JMW Turner, who died in 1851 and remains one of Britain's best known painters, chiefly of landscapes. By way of contrast, ArtNow is a recently opened space dedicated to the work of young contemporary artists.

In an attempt to get more of its 5,000 pictures hung, the Tate have used a sizeable National Lottery grant to aquire the Bankside Power Station in Southwark. This will house the Tate Gallery of Modern Art, scheduled to open in May 2000.

At the Tate works are changed every year, but some artists are always represented. These incude Williams Hogarth and Blake,

Henry Moore, Francis Bacon, Hockney, Gainsborough, Reynolds, George Stubbs, Magritte, Ernst, Dali, Picasso and Matisse.

HOUSES OF PARLIAMENT
Parliament Sq, SW1
☎ 020-7219 4272 Commons information
☎ 020-7219 3107 Lords information

Edward I (the Confessor) built the first Palace of Westminster on this site in 1049, and although none of the building remains, it was the monarch's residence here that gave rise to the location of the present Parliament. Westminster Hall is the only surviving part of the palace commissioned by William the Conqueror's son, William Rufus in the 11th century. The palace was one of the monarch's main residences during the Middle Ages and led to the congregation of government institutions there. Both the Lords and the Commons started life at the palace, but the Commons did not have a fixed home, often meeting in the Chapter House of Westminster Abbey until the monarch moved to Whitehall, leaving plenty of space for the machinery of government. The palace burned down in 1834 and was rebuilt in neo-Gothic style by Charles Barry and Augustus Pugin in 1852. Inside are 1,100 rooms, 100 staircases, and over three miles of passages. The Clock Tower is affectionately known as 'Big Ben', although the nickname really refers to the Great Bell which tolls the hour and weighs 13 tons. Visits to Parliament are by permit only. British residents must apply to their MP, and foreign nationals should apply to the Parliamentary Education Office.

NATIONAL GALLERY
Trafalgar Square, SW1
☎ 020-7747 2885

Founded in 1824 with just 38 pictures purchased for £57,000, the gallery now has over 2,000 western European paintings from the mid-13th to late-19th centuries. The current gallery was completed in 1838, and the collection was built up partly through the efforts of shrewd gallery

The Tate Gallery

Rubens' ceiling at the Banqueting Hall in Whitehall

directors who went to Europe and bought pictures by temporarily unfashionable painters. A recent addition is the Sainsbury wing which houses great Renaissance works in a stylised Italian palazzi setting. Among the artists represented at the gallery are: Piero della Francesca, Titian, Constable, Seurat, da Vinci and Arnolfini.

NATIONAL PORTRAIT GALLERY
2 St Martin's Pl, WC2
☎ 020-7306 0055
Founded in 1856, the gallery houses nearly 10,000 paintings, drawings, sculptures and photographs of the famous in British history, from royalty to scientists and the arts (take a look at Helen Mirren, John Gielgud, Shakespeare, Jane Austen and Dorothy L Sayers). The portraits are generally arranged chronologically from the top floor, starting with the Tudors, down to the ground floor which is concerned with the late 20th century and usually excellent temporary exhibitions. The works are collected on merit of the subject, although several important artists are represented including Holbein, Hockney and Gainsborough.

HISTORIC AND ANCIENT SITES

TRAFALGAR SQUARE
WC2
This is the centre of London - a bronze plaque in the pavement behind Charles I's statue says so. Nelson's Column, raised in

1843, is the focal point - a 5m high statue on a 53m Corinthian column. Around the base are four friezes depicting Nelson's most important victories. They were cast using metal from cannon captured at the Battle of Trafalgar itself. The square was laid out in 1829 to commemorate Nelson's victory over Napoleon in 1805. The four lions, by Sir Edwin Landseer,

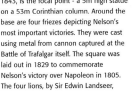

Middlesex Guildhall, Parliament Square

were added in 1868. Other statues include Victorian generals Napier and Havelock, and a horseback statue of George IV. Trafalgar Square is also famous for its pigeons (birdfeed is available if you really want to be smothered by them), and New Year's Eve revellers.

JEWEL TOWER
Old Palace Yard, SW1
☎ 020-7222 2219
Built in 1366 to house Edward III's gold and jewels, the moated Jewel Tower is a survivor of the Palace of Westminster. Restored in 1956 after suffering bomb damage, it now has an exhibition tracing English parliament up to the present day.

ST MARGARET WESTMINSTER
Parliament Sq, SW1
☎ 020-7222 5152
Since 1614, this has been the parish church of the House of Commons. Samuel Pepys married here in 1655, John Milton in 1656, and Winston Churchill in 1908. The east Crucifixion stained-glass window was commissioned by Ferdinand and Isabella of Spain in 1500 for the marriage of their daughter, Catherine of Aragon. More modern windows depict printing pioneer William Caxton, buried here in 1491, explorer Sir Walter Ralegh, also buried here, and John Milton, author of *Paradise Lost*.

ST JOHN'S SMITH SQUARE
Smith Sq, SW1
☎ 020-7222 1061
Built between 1713 and 1728, St John's church is a bold example of English baroque architecture. It is known as 'Queen Anne's Footstool' due to the story that Queen Anne turned over her footstool when asked how she wanted the church to look. Today it is famous as a concert hall offering chamber music and solo recitals that are often broadcast by the BBC.

CLEOPATRA'S NEEDLE
Victoria Embankment, WC2
Although this 180 ton needle was originally erected in Heliopolis in 1475 BC, it actually has nothing to do with Cleopatra at all. The monument was brought to London in 1878 as a gift from Egypt. Beneath it are buried some 'items of the day' including pictures of Britain's prettiest women.

The base of Nelson's Column

MUSEUMS

CABINET WAR ROOMS
Clive Steps, King Charles St, SW1
☎ 020-7930 6961
A labyrinth of underground rooms covering over six acres, which was used as the HQ of Winston Churchill, the War Cabinet and the Chiefs of Staff during WW2. Only a few of the 21 rooms are open to the public, but that's enough to get a good impression of the cramped and claustraphobic conditions under which major decisions were made. Visitors can see Churchill's office, the Map Room, and the Telephone Room where Churchill would discuss plans with the American President, Franklin D Roosevelt.

HORSE GUARDS' PARADE
Whitehall, SW1
Throughout its long history (it was completed in 1760), Horse Guards' Parade has been associated with ceremony and parades. Today, Trooping the Colour and the floodlit Beating the Retreat take place here.

Horse Guard outside Whitehall

ENTERTAINMENT AND NIGHTLIFE

ST JOHN'S SMITH SQUARE
Smith Sq, SW1
☎ 020-7222 1061
Lunchtime music concerts in an atmospheric setting.

St-Martin-in-the-Fields

THE CENOTAPH
Whitehall, SW1
This elegant monument honours the dead of both World Wars. The Remembrance Sunday service is held every year at the eleventh hour of the eleventh day (or nearest Sunday) of the eleventh month, to commemorate the armistice day of World War I. Designed by Edwin Lutyens in 1919 it was plaster and wood at first, but rebuilt in Portland Stone the following year.

THEATRES

WHITEHALL THEATRE
Trafalgar Sq, SW1
☎ 020-7369 1735
Musicals, light entertainment and farce.

PARKS AND GARDENS

VICTORIA TOWER GARDENS
Millbank, SW1
With a view across the Thames to Lambeth Palace, these riverside gardens are small but perfectly formed. The statue is of the suffragette, Emmeline Pankhurst. There is also a cast of Rodin's Burghers of Calais and an impressive Gothic drinking fountain.

GREAT FOR KIDS

There are lots of festivals and events in this area which children will enjoy, such as Changing the Guard, Trooping the Colour, the Lord Mayor's New Year's Day Celebration, Beating the Retreat and Christmas Carol Concerts.

WESTMINSTER BOATING BASE
Dinorvic Wharf, 136 Grosvenor Rd, SW1
☎ 020-7821 7389
Sailing and canoeing courses are run here for both children and adults.

PLACES OF WORSHIP

ST-MARTIN-IN-THE-FIELDS
Trafalgar Square
Built between 1721 and 1726 by James Gibbs, St Martin's has a spire that, at 56m (185ft) rivals Nelson's Column. The church has many connections with royalty (Charles II was christened here) and the Admiralty, whose offices are in Whitehall. At the other end of the social scale, the church has done a lot of work for the homeless since vicar Dick Sheppard opened the vaults to the unemployed and destitute ex-soldiers after World War I. Today, visitors can browse the bookshop, take a meal, do some brass rubbing and visit the craft market. Free lunchtime concerts are also a regular feature.

METHODIST CENTRAL HALL
Storey's Gate, SW1
The first assembly of the United Nations was held here in 1948. It is known as the 'Cathedral of Methodism', but is now mainly used for political meetings.

SPORT AND LEISURE

QUEEN MOTHER'S SPORTS CENTRE
223 Vauxhall Bridge Rd, SW1
☎ 020-7630 5522
A fine sports centre with plenty of activities for everyone, including swimming, football and gymnastics.

SHOPPING

CORNUCOPIA
12 Upper Tachbrook St, SW1
☎ 020-7828 5752
A large selection of second-hand, 20th-century womenswear, plus a wide choice of ornamental jewellery.

WHERE TO STAY

HOTELS

AA RECOMMENDED

★★★★ THE ROYAL HORSEGUARDS
Whitehall Court SW1A 2EJ
☎ 020 7839 3400 📠 020 7925 2263
Government buildings are all around this hotel, which is close to the Palace and the River Thames. Major refurbishment has transformed the accommodation which is now very smart and spacious. There is an alliance with the magnificent meeting facilities of the adjacent One Whitehall, owned by the same company.
280 rooms (189 non smoking) / International Cuisine / Gym / Lift, Night porter, Air cond / No dogs

★★★ QUALITY ECCLESTON
82-83 Eccleston Square SW1V 1PS
☎ 020 7834 8042 📠 020 7630 8942
Set in a quiet location, the Eccleston is popular with tourists and business guests. Bedroom sizes vary, with Premier Plus providing the greatest comfort and additional facilities. Public rooms include coffee shop, foyer bar, fitness room and various types of meeting room.
115 rooms (30 non smoking) / English & Continental Cuisine / Lift, Night porter Price band £££

> Call the AA Hotel Booking Service on
> **0870 5050505** to book at AA recognised
> hotels and B&Bs in the UK,
> or through our internet site:
> **http://www.theaa.co.uk/hotels**

BED & BREAKFAST

AA RECOMMENDED

Windermere Hotel

♦♦♦♦ WINDERMERE HOTEL
142/144 Warwick Way, Victoria SW1V 4JE
(from the coach stn on Buckingham Palace Rd - opposite the stn turn left onto Elizabeth Bridge, then 1st right, hotel at end of road)
☎ 020 7834 5163 & 834 5480
📠 020 7630 8831
A fine example of early Victorian classical design, this family-run hotel is relaxed and

informal. Bedrooms are well equipped, and evening meals are served in the dining room, which has a small, well stocked bar.
22 rooms (3 family & 7 non smoking) / No dogs (ex guide dogs) / Price band £££

♦♦♦ MELBOURNE HOUSE HOTEL
79 Belgrave Rd, Victoria SW1V 2BG
(from Pimlico tube stn on Lypus St, turn right into St George's Sq which continues into Belgrave Rd)
☎ 020 7828 3516 📠 020 7828 7120
A family run private hotel. The bedrooms have all been re-furbished in a modern style and most have en suite bathrooms. Some family rooms are also available. A choice of breakfast is offered and this is included in the tariff.
14 rooms (2 family) / No dogs Price band ££

♦♦♦ VICTORIA INN
65-67 Belgrave Rd, Victoria SW1V 2BG
☎ 020 7834 6721 & 7834 0182
📠 020 7931 0201
Two fine Victorian houses that cater well for both business and tourist clientele. Bedrooms are comfortably appointed and provide many modern amenities. A choice of English, for which an extra charge is made, and continental breakfast is served in the newly decorated dining room. There is also a small lounge available to guests.
41 rooms (1 family) / No dogs / No coaches Price band ££

♦♦♦ WINCHESTER HOTEL
17 Belgrave Rd SW1V 1RB
(3min from Victoria Station)
☎ 020 7828 2972 📠 020 7828 5191
The Winchester Hotel is privately owned and family-run, offering comfortable rooms that all benefit from en suite facilities. Full English and continental breakfast is included in the tariff, and staff are happy to recommend places to dine in the evening.
18 rooms (2 family) / No dogs / No children under 10 years / No coaches

Victoria Inn

WHERE TO EAT

RESTAURANTS

AA RECOMMENDED

⊛ ⊛ BOISDALE
15 Eccleston Street SW1W 9LX
☎ 020 7730 6922 📠 020 7730 0548
Upmarket Scottish restaurant with deep red walls, lots of pictures and bistro-type tables and chairs. Cock-a-leekie soup is the traditional rendition with prunes, leeks and a strong, clear broth. Main courses might include fishcakes (made from cod), smoked haddock and Orkney salmon or game in season. A back tobacco bar, strong on cigars, suits the Sloaney, cashmere-Crombie-clad clientele down to the ground. Service is good, if at times bordering on the condescending.

⊛ ⊛ SHEPHERDS
Marsham Court Marsham Street SW1P 4LA
☎ 020 7834 9552
📠 020 7233 6047
Shepherds works to a tried-and-tested formula - one which certainly finds favour with the inhabitants of Pimlico and Westminster. Neither the decor nor the menu follow current fashion trends - the latter being rather long by today's standards - but it is thoroughly British in the old-fashioned sense with steak and kidney pudding, roast beef and Yorkshire pudding, and haunch of venison with chestnuts and port sauce as typical examples.
Fixed L/D £

⊛ ⊛ SIMPLY NICO
48a Rochester Row SW1P 1JU
☎ 020 7630 8061 📠 020 7828 8541
This, the original Simply Nico, is the pick of a bunch of a chain owned by the Restaurant Partnership; it remains closest to the precept laid down by Nico Ladenis - who has severed all connections with the new owners. The setting is pleasant, with slick, friendly staff, straightforward (and good-value) pricing, and sound, uncomplicated French cooking that largely sticks to tried-and-trusted combinations.
Fixed D £ £

PUBS, INNS & OTHER PLACES

THE CLARENCE
55 Whitehall SW1A 2HP
☎ 020 7930 4808
Haunted pub, situated five minutes' walk from Big Ben and Trafalgar Square, with leaded windows and ancient ceiling beams from a Thames pier. Traditional fare is served, such as fish and chips, chicken and mushroom pie, and Sunday roast.

WESTMINSTER ARMS
9 Storey's Gate SW1
☎ 020 7222 8520
The division bell calls MPs to the House from this Edwardian pub close to Westminster Abbey.

THE ALBERT
52 Victoria Street SW1H 0NP
☎ 020 7222 5577
The Albert also has a division bell as well as a collection of prime minister pictures. No wonder, as it's only 500 yards from the Houses of Parliament and Whitehall. A great place to spot celebrities, from cabinet ministers to theatre stars.

THE BUCKINGHAM ARMS
62 Petty France SW1H 9EU
☎ 020 7222 3386
Elegant and busy pub situated close to the Passport Office and Buckingham Palace. Popular with tourists, business folk and real ale fans alike, it offers a good range of simple pub food, including the 'mighty' Buckingham burger, nachos with chilli, shepherd's pie, and lasagne. The long bar has some attractive etched mirrors.

FINNEGAN'S WAKE
2 Strutton Ground
☎ 020 7222 7310
Not famous as one of James Joyce's watering holes, but rather as the place where 1950s radio comedy team The Goons was born. Harry Secombe, Spike Milligan, Peter Sellers, Jimmy Grafton and Michael Bentine planned their surreal takeover of BBC Radio in the upstairs front room.

ADAM & EVE
81 Petty France SW1
☎ 020 7222 4575
Scottish & Newcastle real ale pub, not far from Buckingham Palace.

PAVIOUR'S ARMS
Page Street SW1
☎ 020 7834 2150
Thai food is available at this nice Art Deco pub close to the Tate Gallery.

ST JAMES'S AND THE MALL

If Westminster is the seat of government, then its neighbour, St James's, is the seat of the British monarchy. The Mall leads south-west from Trafalgar Square to Buckingham Palace and is one of the widest avenues in London. Laid out in 1660 as part of the Restoration, The Mall was later vastly reworked as a tribute to Queen Victoria, who had made Buckingham Palace the offical royal residence when she came to the throne in 1837. The present Royal Family also use "Buck House" as their main London residence, with the Queen and the Duke of Edinburgh having private apartments there. The Queen Mother also lives nearby, at Clarence House by St James's Palace. The Mall is best known as the formal route taken by the Royal Family on state occasions such as Trooping the Colour and the State Opening of Parliament.

On either of side of The Mall is some lovely royal parkland which was originally used for regal hunting. St James's Park is the oldest royal park, first used by Henry VIII, then opened to the public by Charles II. In 1828 the park was landscaped by John Nash, the influential architect who also remodelled Regent's Park, Regent's Street and Buckingham Palace. The Park is still a haunt of the inhabitants of Whitehall, although they are now office workers rather than royalty. Ducks, geese and pelicans (descended from a pair given to Charles II by the Russian ambassador in the 17th century) live on the meandering lake.

Due to its associations with royalty, the area has long displayed an air of wealth and privilege, and is home to a variety of firms that produce some of the finest goods that money can buy. For example, Jermyn Street is well known for bespoke tailoring, especially the firms of Turnbull & Asser and Hilditch & Key. The street can also supply the best (and most expensive) in hats, pipes, antiques, perfumes and shoes. It's no surprise to learn that the Queen Mother buys her provisions from Paxton & Whitfield at No 93.

Pall Mall is lined with gentlemen's clubs such as the Institute of Directors, a club for business leaders; the Reform Club, created by supporters of the 1832 Reform Act; and the Athenaeum, named after Athena, Greek Goddess of Wisdom, and frequented by writers and artists. Many were founded in the 18th century and flourished as a second home for aristocrats, who spent many an evening throwing away fortunes on a game of cards. Women were excluded for many years, and in fact still are from some of the clubs, while at others they have to enter by the back stairs.

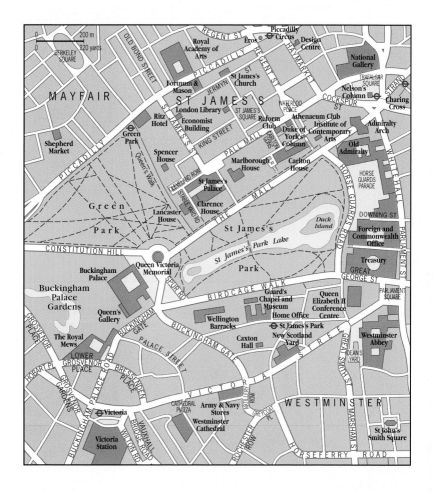

MUST SEE

Buckingham Palace

BUCKINGHAM PALACE
The Mall, SW1
☎ 020-7839 1377
☎ 020-7930 9625

In 1837 Queen Victoria moved into Buckingham Palace, and it remains the main royal residence today. The Royal Standard flies when the Queen is in residence. Buckingham House was built in 1705 for the Duke of Buckingham, and sold to George III in 1762. The present façade was remodelled in 1913 by Aston Webb, in time for George V's coronation. It has over 600 rooms, although the Queen and the Duke of Edinburgh only occupy a small number. For eight weeks during the summer, the State Apartments are open to the public (begun in order to raise funds to rebuild Windsor Castle, badly damaged by fire in 1992 but now beautifully restored). You can see the Throne Room, State Dining Room, drawing rooms and the Music Room. The Queen's Gallery and Royal Mews are both worth a visit. One of London's most popular daily events, the Changing of the Guard, takes place here.

ST JAMES'S PALACE
Pall Mall and St James's St, SW1

A red-brick Tudor palace, St James's was built in the 1530s by Henry VIII for Anne Boleyn, mother of Queen Elizabeth I. It was the main royal residence after Whitehall Palace burned down in 1698, until Queen Victoria moved to

Buckingham Palace in 1837. All major state functions took place here, and foreign ambassadors are still officially accredited 'to the Court of St James's'. The Palace is not open to the public, although you can visit the Chapel Royal which has a colourful history, including an impressive list of royal marriages: William and Mary, George III and Queen Charlotte, Victoria and Albert, and George V and Queen Mary. The Chapel also saw Charles I take communion on the morning of his execution. Sunday services are held from October to Easter.

ST JAMES'S PARK
SW1

One of the most attractive of London's parks, St James's affords splendid views of the Government Offices to the east. Sir George Gilbert Scott's byzantine architecture framed by weeping willows creates a scene more reminiscent of Eastern Europe than central London. The classical façade of Buckingham Palace is visible to the west. Under Henry VIII it was a deer park, Charles II introduced wildfowl, and under George IV John Nash created the fine meandering lake. Running alongside the park is Birdcage Walk, where James II had aviaries built. The park is a very popular place with nearby office workers for lunchtime relaxation in summer. There is a playground at the end nearest Buckingham Palace.

WESTMINSTER CATHEDRAL
Ashley Pl, SW1
☎ 020-7798 9055/6
Service Times: ☎ 020-7998 9097

This is the headquarters of the Catholic Church in Britain, and seat of the Archbishop of Westminster. The building has many similarities to the Basilica of St Mark in Venice, as well as Hagia Sophia in Istanbul. Its 83m campanile is built from red brick alternating with Portland Stone, and offers some stunning views of London. The cathedral was begun in 1895

Changing Guard at Buckingham Palace

but remains unfinished. The money ran out before the interior could be fully lined with mosaics and marble, although what was completed is magnificent. The artwork includes Eric Gill's 14 Stations of the Cross, which was carved during World War I. The side chapels, with their rich use of different marbles, give an impression of what the cathedral would have looked like if it had been completed.

HISTORIC AND ANCIENT SITES

CLARENCE HOUSE
Stable Yard Gate, SW1

Clarence House is the home of Queen Elizabeth, the Queen Mother, and is where the beleaguered Lady Diana Spencer took refuge during the final days of her engagement to Prince Charles. The

Westminster Cathedral

Institute of Contemporary Arts (ICA)

MUSEUMS

GUARD'S MUSEUM
Wellington Barracks, Birdcage Walk, SW1
☎ 020-7414 3271
Exhibits honour the Guards regiments, which were founded during the 17th century. On display are uniforms and paintings from Oliver Cromwell to present day. Also open to the public is the Guards' Chapel, a modernistic 1960s rebuilding of the original chapel which was hit by a V-1 rocket in 1944 killing 121 people.

ART GALLERIES

INSTITUTE OF CONTEMPORARY ARTS (ICA)
Nash House, The Mall, SW1
☎ 020-7930 3647
Opened in 1948, this gallery was intended to be an alternative to the many traditional galleries in the capital. It has kept its word, and plays host to a wide variety of contemporary art exhibitions, performances, and film. Picasso, Henry Moore and Damien Hurst are among the artists who had their first London exhibitions here. The bar stays open until 1am, and there is also a good Italian café/restaurant.

Princess Royal (Princess Anne) was born here. There is no public access, but you can see the sentries on duty outside.

SPENCER HOUSE
27 St James's Pl, SW1
☎ 020-7499 8620
Built between 1756 and 1766 for the Spencer family, ancestors of Diana, Princess of Wales. Among its designers

CARLTON HOUSE TERRACE
SW1
This grand, sweeping frontage was built in 1832 to the designs of John Nash, who was also responsible for much of the architecture around Regent's Park. The Royal Society is at No 6. This influential scientific society was founded in 1660 by Charles II. Wren, Newton and Pepys were among its early presidents, and numerous

QUEEN'S GALLERY
Buckingham Palace, The Mall, SW1
☎ 020-7839 1377
Recorded Information: 020-7799 2331
Once the palace chapel, this gallery was converted for Queen Elizabeth II in 1962, and is usually open all year round. Unfortunately, it will be closed from October 1999 for remodelling. Its re-opening is scheduled for 2002, which will be the Queen's Golden Jubilee. The royal collection is one of the largest private collections in the world, and includes Rembrandt, Rubens and Canaletto, as well as Sèvres porcelain and watercolours painted by Queen Victoria.

Queen Victoria Memorial

were James Stuart, James Vardy and Robert Adam, who created one of his famous 'Adam ceilings' in the Great Room. On Sunday there are guided tours around the state rooms. The house is currently leased by the Rothschilds, who have spent a considerable amount of money on restoration.

QUEEN VICTORIA MEMORIAL
Queen's Gardens, Buckingham Palace, SW1
Created in 1911 by Thomas Brock, this is an impressive memorial to Queen Victoria, Britain's longest-reigning monarch. The 4m statue is the best of many of the extraordinary queen in the city.

NEW SCOTLAND YARD
Victoria St, SW1
This is the headquarters of the London Metropolitan Police, so behave while you walk past! Home of the famous rotating sign that has graced so many TV police dramas.

Nobel Prize winners are among its members. No 12 is the Institute of Contemporary Arts, home to some innovative and often contraversial art. By way of contrast, No 17 is the gallery of the Federation of British Artists, which tends to display altogether more traditional landscapes, water colours and portraits.

Changing the Guard

CINEMAS

ICA CINEMA
Nash House, The Mall, SW1
☎ 020-7930 3647
Part of the Institute of Contemporary Arts
(see above), there are two screens
showing avant-garde films and
documentaries.

THEATRES

VICTORIA PALACE
Victoria St, SW1
☎ 020-7834 1317
Home to musicals and variety shows.

APOLLO VICTORIA
Wilton Rd, SW1
☎ 020-7416 6042
This theatre underwent a major structural
renovation in order to stage Andrew Lloyd
Webber's rollerskating musical, Starlight
Express, which is still playing to packed
houses.

SHOPPING

*St James's is a great place for shopping,
if you have a flexible accountant. Expect
to empty your bank account in any of
these exclusive establishments.*

ARMY & NAVY STORES
Victoria St, SW1
☎ 020-7834 1234
A quality department store.

JJ FOX (ST JAMES'S)
19 St James's St
☎ 020-7930 3787
Cigar and pipe shop.

JAMES LOCK
6 St James's St, SW1
☎ 020-7930 5849 & 020 7930 8874
Milliners to the rich and famous since
1686

Feeding the Ducks in St James's Park

HILDITCH & KEY
73 Jermyn St, SW1
☎ 020-7930 5336
One of several eminent shirtmakers along
this venerable old street.

TURNBULL & ASSER
71 Jermyn St, SW1
☎ 020-7808 3000
Bespoke shirtmakers for women. The
men's branch is at 23 Bury St, SW1.

FLORIS
89 Jermyn St, SW1
☎ 020-7930 2885
Upmarket perfumier in business since
1730.

PAXTON & WHITFIELD
93 Jermyn St, SW1
☎ 020-7930 0259
A very exclusive place for many different
varieties of cheese, as well as traditional
picnic treats such as chutneys and hams.

BERRY BROS & RUDD
3 St James's St, SW1
☎ 020-7396 9600
A well respected wine merchant.

JOHN LOBB
88 Jermyn St, SW1
☎ 020-7930 8089
A stylish, traditional shoemakers. Money
no object.

GREAT FOR KIDS

*There are loads of Festivals and Events
throughout the year in London which
children will love - See Festivals and
Events.*

CHANGING THE GUARD
Buckingham Palace and St James's Palace,
SW1
The Queen's Guard is changed daily at
11.30am at Buckingham Palace.

ROYAL MEWS
Buckingham Palace Rd, SW1
☎ 020-7839 1377
Recorded info: 020-7799 2331
These traditional mews, built in 1824,
house the carriage horses, royal cars and
carriages of the royal family. The Gold
State Coach is the highlight, used for
coronations, the Glass State Coach carries
foreign ambassadors to the Queen. The
open-top landau was used for the
spectacular but ill-fated weddings of the
Prince and Princess of Wales in 1981 and
the Duke and Duchess of York in 1986.

GUARDS' CHAPEL
Wellington Barracks, Birdcage Walk, SW1
The new chapel, completed in 1963,
replaced the original one which was all
but destroyed in 1944 by a flying bomb
which killed over 120 people. It is also
known as the Royal Military Chapel.

THE QUEEN'S CHAPEL
St James's Palace, Marlborough Rd, SW1
This charming chapel was begun for the
Infanta of Spain, who was then betrothed
to Charles I. It was designed by Inigo
Jones and completed in 1626.

Spencer House

WHERE TO STAY
HOTELS
AA RECOMMENDED

★★★★ ⑱ THE CAVENDISH
81 Jermyn St SW1Y 6JF
(follow signs for Marble Arch along Park Lane to Hyde Park Corner left to Piccadilly. Past Ritz hotel right down Dukes St Behind Fortnum and Mason)
☎ 020 7930 2111 🖷 020 7839 2125
Close to both Piccadilly and Green Park this modern hotel is particularly popular with business guests. The Sub Rosa Bar is a cosy, club-like venue off the lobby, and there is a spacious, well maintained lounge on the first floor. '81' Restaurant offers a Mediterranean-style menu with hints of Spanish influence.
251 rooms (195 no smoking) / Mediterranean Cuisine / Lift, Night porter Price band £££ 🍷

The Cavendish

★★★★ ⑱ THE STAFFORD
16-18 St James's Place SW1A 1NJ
(turn off Pall Mall into St James's Street, take second left turn into St James's Place)
☎ 020 7493 0111 🖷 020 7493 7121
The Stafford has elegant, individually designed bedrooms, which include a superb new studio courtyard suite. Public rooms include a drawing room and the bustling American Bar, famous for its collection of caps and ties. In the restaurant, menus balance traditional grills with more creative dishes. Service throughout the hotel demonstrates a serious commitment to customer care. Ask the sommelier for a tour of the 350-year-old cellars.
81 rooms / Fitness Club / Lift, Night porter, Air cond / No dogs / No coaches Price band £££ 🍷

22 JERMYN STREET
St James's SW1Y 6HL
☎ 020 7734 2353 🖷 020 7734 0750
An elegant town house in an equally elegant street just off St James's and behind Piccadilly. Bedrooms offer very high standards of comfort, and are provided with bathrobes, slippers, fruit, flowers and good toiletries. There is also a wide range of office services for the business guest, 24-hour room service and a mini-bar.
18 rooms (13 family) / Lift, Night porter, Air cond / No coaches Price band £££ 🍷

WHERE TO EAT
RESTAURANTS
AA RECOMMENDED

⑱ THE AVENUE
7-9 St James's Street SW1
☎ 020 7321 2111 🖷 020 7321 2500
Bright, modern glass-fronted restaurant in St James. A brasserie-style menu draws the crowds, offering choices such as a smoked haddock fishcake with Welsh rarebit and chocolate orange tart.

⑱ CAFÉ FISH
36-40 Rupert Street W1
☎ 020 7930 3999 🖷 020 7839 4880
Bustling two-storey seafooder just off Shaftesbury Avenue, with a simple approach from the kitchen, backed up by friendly service. The crustacea is ever popular.

⑱ ⑱ ⑱ LE CAPRICE
Arlington Street SW1A 1RT
☎ 020 7629 2239 🖷 020 7493 9040
London classic with exemplary service - a place to see and be seen. The stark black and white decor might have something of retro chic to it, but here it feels like a design classic when in lesser places it would just seem dated. To say that the menu has evolved hardly at all is no criticism, as the whole style is pretty timeless; the old classics still there in the form of Caesar salad, dressed crab, eggs Benedict and salmon fishcakes, but chargrilled squid with crispy pancetta and a rocket and red pepper salsa shows the kitchen working in modern idiom. Pitchers of Buck's Fizz show up on the popular Sunday brunch menu, and there's a decent choice of wines by the glass.
ALC £££

⑱ THE CAVENDISH
81 Jermyn Street SW1Y 6JF
☎ 020 7930 2111 🖷 020 7839 2125
Large, modern hotel with a good range of amenities that includes the smart 81 Restaurant. Here a Med-style menu with strong Spanish flavours also takes in the likes of mussels with garlic cream, wild boar cutlet with chive and leek mash, Puy lentils and port sauce, and cod fillet with pepper sauce.
Fixed L/D £ ALC £

⑱ ⑱ GREEN'S RESTAURANT & OYSTER BAR
36 Duke Street SW1Y 6DF
☎ 020 7930 4566 🖷 020 7491 7463
A long-established restaurant with the feel of an exclusive dining club. The style is modern without going over the top -

expect dishes along the lines of black leg chicken breast with wild mushrooms, as well as simple offerings such as corned beef hash with fried egg. As you'd expect, fish and shellfish make a strong appearance: smoked eel salad, and potted shrimps with toast for example, while main dishes range from roast halibut with mussel stew to whole Canadian lobster, served cold.
Fixed D £££ ALC £££

⚜ ⚜ MATSURI
15 Bury Street SW1Y 6AL
☎ 020 7839 1101 📠 020 7930 7010
A good starting point for an introduction to Japanese cuisine. Matsuri means 'festival' in Japanese and lots of touches around the dining room are related to the various (usually religious) festivals held throughout the year in Japan. Staff are particularly helpful and pleased to guide newcomers around the menu. Dessert is irrelevant, fresh fruit only is offered.
Fixed L £ ALC £££

⚜ ⚜ L'ORANGER
5 St James's Street SW1A 1EF
☎ 020 7839 3774
📠 020 7839 4330
Stylish modern restaurant in an upscale Mayfair street. Natural light streams into the restaurant through a skylight, creating a bright, warm setting. The modern carte kicks off with starters ranging from braised Swiss chard in a veal broth, to ravioli of beef Monegasque with Parmesan, and goes onto roasted loin of veal wrapped in bacon and sage and served with creamy wild mushrooms on a bed of spinach. The wine list is focused on the old world, and is particularly strong in its selection from Burgundy.
Fixed L £ ALC ££

⚜ ⚜ ⚜ PÉTRUS
33 St James's Street SW1 1HD
☎ 020 7930 4272 📠 020 7930 9702
This is an ambitious enterprise, with a kitchen that's strong on precision and presentation delivering food that's big on flavour. Typical of the currency are rabbit

Wiltons

terrine with cabbage, pickled onions and sliced leeks, halibut braised with asparagus and lettuce served with Sauternes sauce and grapefruit, and pan-fried sweetbreads on sautéed ceps in a light veal jus. Wines are kept in a 'cellar' that's visible, the list concentrating on the eponymous Château Pétrus at prices that corroborate that this is one of the costliest wines in the world; house wines, very drinkable and full of character, are more easily attainable.
Fixed L £ ALC ££

⚜ QUAGLINO'S
16 Bury Street St James's SW1Y 6AL
☎ 020 7930 6767 📠 020 7839 2866
Landmark restaurant with great sense of style. The emphasis is on enjoyment, and there are plenty of taste sensations on the easy-reading menu - pan-fried foie gras with spiced pear and rocket, followed by sea bream saltimbocca with lemon and sage.
Fixed L/D £ ALC ££

⚜ ⚜ THE STAFFORD
16-18 St James's Place SW1A 1NJ
☎ 020 7493 0111 📠 020 7493 7121
Luxury is the trademark of this 18th-century town-house hotel. The restaurant, strong on the comfort factor, occupies a large, well-proportioned room. The kitchen weaves its own distinctive course between the traditional, the classical and the

fashionable, from roast chicken with roast potatoes, cabbage and chopped carrots, through Dover sole meunière, to roast veal cutlet topped with tomato, Parma ham and a Parmesan biscuit with fried polenta and chargrilled marinated aubergine.
Fixed L £ ALC £££

⚜ ⚜ SUNTORY RESTAURANT
72 St James's Street SW1A 1PH
☎ 020 7409 0201 📠 020 7499 0208
The oldest Japanese restaurant in London. Now entering its twenty fourth year, Suntory has built up quite a fan base. They offer some of the most reasonably priced Japanese food in London, especially at lunch, but the sky can also be the limit, so choose conservatively to stay within budget. The cooking is good, sake is worth ordering.

⚜ ⚜ WILTONS
55 Jermyn Street SW1Y 6LX
☎ 020 7629 9955 📠 020 7495 6233
The plush green interior is in keeping with the St James location. A series of connected rooms with secluded booth seating provides a discreet atmosphere in which Wilton habitués can talk business, conduct affairs of state or swop shooting stories. Traditional British cooking rules OK, with raw ingredients that are second to none. The emphasis is on fish and game, although there are also steaks, sausages and grilled lambs' kidneys.

PUBS, INNS & OTHER PLACES

RED LION
Duke of York Street
SW1
The Victorian atmosphere of this gin palace is helped out by its lack of TV, music, and video games. It also seems to have no phone!

THE TWO CHAIRMEN
1 Warwick House Street
☎ 020 7930 1166
Just off Pall Mall close to Trafalgar Square, this quiet pub is named after the sedan taximen of old London.

RED LION
Crown Passage
☎ 020 7930 4141
Small timber-fronted pub in a tiny alley opposite St James's Palace. Owner of the second oldest beer licence in London.

AA Hotel Booking Service

The AA Hotel Booking Service - Now you have a free, simple way to reserve a place to stay for a week, weekend, or a one-night stopover.

Do you want to book somewhere in the Lake District that has leisure facilities; a city-centre hotel in Glasgow with parking facilities, or do you need accommodation near Dover which is handy for the Eurotunnel?

The AA Booking Service can take the hassle out of booking the right place for you.

And if you are touring round the UK or Ireland, simply give the AA Hotel Booking Service your list of overnight stops, and from one phone call all your accommodation can be booked for you.

Telephone 0870 5050505

Office hours
Monday-Friday 9am-6pm
Saturday 9am-1pm
Not available Sundays or Bank Holidays

Full listings of AA recognised accommodation available through the Hotel Booking Service can be found and booked at the AA's Internet Site:

http://www.theaa.co.uk/hotels

MAYFAIR, PICCADILLY AND OXFORD STREET

Although these three areas are very close together, they all have very different characters, demonstrating how much variety and diversity there is in central London.

Mayfair has enjoyed the patronage of the aristocracy since the 18th century, when the big names of the day moved away from Covent Garden and Soho. Today is no different. Here are some of London's most elegant houses, set around leafy squares laid out by big landowners, and generally inhabited by foreign embassies and multi-millionaires. The names conjure up images of wealth and sophistication: Berkeley Square, Hanover Square and Grosvenor Square. The area also boasts some of the country's most prestigious hotels, including Claridge's, The Dorchester, The Ritz and The Connaught. Shepherd Market, just off Piccadilly, is also worth a look. It is situated on the site of the raucous 17th-century May Fair, which gave the area its name. Along Piccadilly from Mayfair is Green Park, a delightful oasis of green.

Piccadilly Circus is known to most tourists as the 'heart of London' and certainly serves well as a meeting place, judging by the number of backpackers who congregate under the statue of Eros. It seems that London dandies gathered in this area in the 17th century. Their ruffled sleeves were known as 'pickadills.' Robert Baker, a tailor who made a fortune through the manufacture of these sleeves, built Piccadilly House, thus giving the area its name. Nowadays the multi-coloured, flashing neon advertisements almost cover one side of Piccadilly Circus, a name which has come to be used to describe anything chaotic or disordered. Along Piccadilly you'll find Hatchard's bookshop, opened in 1797, Fortnum & Mason, London's foremost supplier of very fine foods and the Royal Academy of Arts in Burlington House.

From Piccadilly it is a short but very interesting journey up Regent Street to reach Oxford Street. Regent Street was designed by Sir John Nash in the early 1800s to complement Carlton House, the Prince Regent's residence at the time. It was also intended to create a barrier between the gentry of Mayfair and the riff-raff of Soho, an intention which seems to have been successful. Today it is a thriving shopping street, packed with expensive clothing stores such as Burberry's, Dickins & Jones, and Liberty, as well as top jewellers Garrard & Co. Carnaby Street, off Regent Street, was a major component of the 'Swinging London' scene in the 1960s. Today it is a much less influential

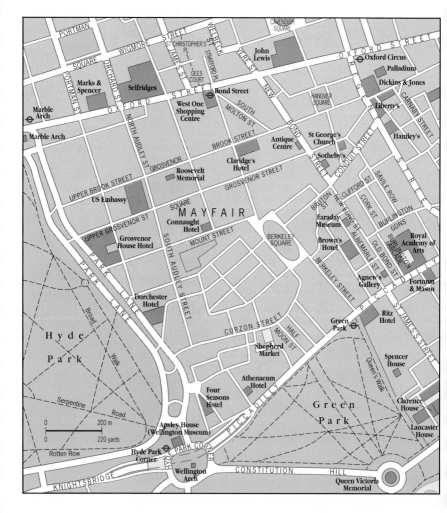

area, consisting mainly of tourist traps selling cheap t-shirts, with the odd worthwhile shop still trading.

Oxford Street is a shopper's paradise, with all the major high-street chains, plus department stores like Selfridges, Debenhams and John Lewis and many more boutiques, souvenir shops and gift shops. In the 18th century, as Mayfair became more fashionable, Oxford Street replaced Cheapside as the premier shopping street of London. It now stretches for 2 miles between Marble Arch and Tottenham Court Road, bisected half way along by Regent Street. The department stores are mainly at the Marble Arch end, where Oxford Street itself becomes smarter and more impressive.

Between Oxford Circus and the Park Crescent that leads into Regent's Park, there are Langham Place and Portland Place, which was once the widest street in London. The walk from here to the park will take you past the impressive bulk of BBC Broadcasting House, John Nash's All Saints Church, the Chinese Embassy and the Royal Institute of British Architects. In a marked contrast to its current gentility, the area between Oxford Street and Regent's Park was once the site of two of London's most notorious districts, Lileston and Tyburn. The second of these was home to Tyburn Hill where the infamous gallows despatched lawbreakers from 1388 to 1783. A plaque near Marble Arch marks the spot.

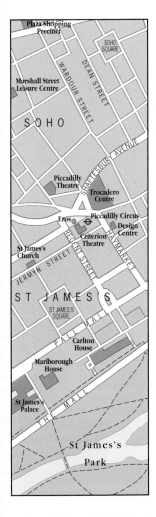

MUST SEE

OLD AND NEW BOND STREETS
W1

Together, Old and New Bond streets cut through the centre of Mayfair. Both are dedicated to exclusive shops offering clothing, art, jewellery, silver and antiques. Those to look out for include Gianni Versace, Asprey & Co (jewellery), and Bond Street Silver Galleries. For an Antiques Roadshow-style experience, take a family heirloom along to Sotheby's and get a genuine valuation from one of their staff.

GREEN PARK

A very aptly-named park - it provides uninterrupted grass and trees across its 22 hectares (53 acres). A fireworks display was given here in 1749 to commemorate the Peace of Aix-la-Chapelle. Over 10,000 fireworks were let off, but in a nightmare

The Gates of Green Park

scenario worthy of the most frightening public information film, the Temple of Peace was set alight and three people were killed. Handel immortalized the fireworks in his famous work Music for the Royal Fireworks.

PICCADILLY
W1

Marking the junction of five major streets, Piccadilly Circus is famous for its illuminated advertising signs and Sir Alfred Gilbert's figure of a winged archer, which has long been mistaken for Eros. Its title is in fact, Angel of Christian Charity, and it was unveiled in 1893 as a tribute to the 7th Earl of Shaftesbury, who campaigned against the use of child labour in the 19th century. This is a popular meeting place for backpackers, who must be slightly disappointed in thinking this is the heart of London. The area is a traffic nightmare. Attractions nearby include the Trocadero and Rock Circus.

THE RITZ HOTEL
150 Piccadilly, W1

☎ **020-7493 8181** 📠 **020-7493 2687**

Founded by Cesar-Ritz in 1906 the interior of this famous hotel is in Louise XVI style with rich gold-leaf finish. The restaurant has a 1920s and 30s theme, and the really popular (and cheapest) way to visit is to take afternoon tea in the Palm Court (book in advance).

WELLINGTON MUSEUM (APSLEY HOUSE)
149 Piccadilly, W1

☎ **020-7499 5676**

Occupied by the Duke of Wellington (who defeated Napoleon at the Battle of Waterloo) from 1817 until his death in 1852, Apsley House was once called 'Number One, London'. It was designed by Robert Adam in the 1770s, and is still a private home, but also exhibits a wonderful collection of paintings, sculpture and ceramics which were gathered by the 'Iron Duke'. Among the most interesting exhibits are a 3m statue of the diminutive Napoleon (naked except for a figleaf) by Canova, and Goya's Equestrian Portrait of Wellington. It has been proved that this was originally a portrait of Joseph Bonaparte, Napoleon's brother, who was also defeated by Wellington in the Battle of Vittoria, and that Goya must have quickly painted Wellington's head over Joseph's!

ROYAL ACADEMY OF ARTS
Burlington House, Piccadilly, W1

☎ **020-7300 8000**

Founded in 1768 by a group of painters that included Thomas Gainsborough and Joshua Reynolds, the prestigious RA's members include many well-known British artists and architects (Constable and Turner studied here). It is used for major art exhibitions, and is also famous for its Summer Exhibition, when thousands of paintings, ranging from the brilliant to the inept, are on public view.

HISTORIC AND ANCIENT SITES

BURLINGTON ARCADE
off Piccadilly, W1

Built in 1819 by Lord George Cavendish to prevent rubbish being thrown in his garden, this was one of England's first shopping precincts. In pure Regency style and atmosphere, it houses exclusive shops watched over by Beadles, known as 'Burlington Berties', in top hats and great coats, who forbid 'singing, carrying open umbrellas or large parcels, or running'.

SHEPHERD MARKET
off Piccadilly, W1

Built by Edward Shepherd in 1735, this jumble of narrow streets and alleys is on the site of the ancient May Fair that gives the district its name. Among the shops and restaurants is *The Bunch of Grapes*, a Victorian pub.

HANOVER SQUARE

Until it was demolished in 1900 the Hanover Square Rooms was a hotbed of musical innovation, playing host to performances by Bach, Haydn, Liszt and the fiery violinist, Paganini. The square was set out in 1717 and named after the Elector of Hanover, better known as King George I. In St George's Street, and built around the same time as the square, is St George's Church where Percy and Mary Shelley, Disraeli, and Teddy Roosevelt were married. Contains some lovely 16th-century stained glass.

SOTHEBY'S
34-35 New Bond St, W1

☎ **020-7493 8080**

The famous auctioneers' house offers antiques including paintings, ceramics, jewellery, furniture, glass, silver, books and manuscripts. There are up to three sales a day (telephone for details). The doorway is topped by an Egyptian statue that dates from the 17th century BC, making it the oldest outdoor sculpture in the city.

SAVILE ROW
W1

Parallel with New Bond Street, Savile Row is world famous as the major place for fine gentlemen's tailoring. Here you'll find Gieves & Hawkes, Dege, Henry Poole & Co, and Hardy Amies. In the late 60s, No. 3 was home to the Beatles' own record label and studio, Apple. Their final public performance was given on the roof of the studio in 1969, and captured on film for *Let It Be*.

CARNABY STREET
W1

In the 1960s Carnaby Street was the epitome of 'Swinging London' cool.

Berkeley Square

Fashion boutiques, hairdressers and shoe shops (some owned by celebrities like The Beatles) made this area the heart of London's 'mod' culture. It is now lined with less innovative shops and cafés and has lost a lot of its former glory. Very popular with tourists. For more exciting fashion innovation, try nearby Newburgh Street.

BROWN'S HOTEL
30 Albemarle St, W1
☎ 020-7493 6020 **📠 020-7493 9381**
A fine example of elegant English life, Brown's has managed to maintain a relaxed and calm atmosphere, and serves an excellent afternoon tea. Rudyard Kipling, Agatha Christie and Alexander Graham Bell have all stayed here. In fact, Bell made the first successful phone call from here in 1876.

CLARIDGE'S HOTEL
Brook St, W1
☎ 020-7629 8860 **📠 020-7499 2210**
Choose from art-deco or Victorian surroundings in this dignified and charming hotel. A firm favourite with statesmen, royalty and international celebrities. Eisenhower was a guest here, and it also seems to have been used by the OSS (precursor to the CIA) during the war.

GROSVENOR SQUARE
Grosvenor Square is something of an American home-from-home. Eisenhower ran the D-Day campaign from here, and a statue commemorates his role. There's also a Roosevelt Memorial, and the Grosvenor Chapel is attended mainly by London's American community. The scene of political demonstrations for decades, including major protests against the Vietnam war in the 1960s, the US Embassy is a daunting mass that takes up one side of the square. Designed by Finnish-American architect and furniture

Christie's

designer, Eero Saarinen, the embassy is guarded by a giant eagle and heavily armed police.

HYDE PARK CORNER
SW1
Joining Knightsbridge to Piccadilly, Hyde Park Corner was originally intended to be an imposing feature to enjoy en route from Buckingham Palace to Hyde Park.

Today it shudders under the weight of traffic and pedestrians swarming under and around it. The statues are worth a look though, and include the Duke of Wellington, Peace and her four winged horses, and two grand war memorials.

BERKELEY SQUARE
Argyll St, W1
At the heart of Mayfair is Berkeley Square, made famous by the song *A Nightingale Sang in Berkeley Square*. You have to be seriously rich to actually live here, but it's worth wandering around to get a glimpse of the chandeliered luxury.

MUSEUM OF MANKIND
6 Burlington Gdns, W1
☎ 020-7323 8044
This is the British Museum's ethnographic collection, and contains a massive collection of domestic, religious and figurative items from all over the world, apart from Western Europe. The policy is to mount a stream of temporary exhibitions rather than any kind of permanent display.

ART GALLERIES

There are many commercial art galleries around the West End, particularly in Cork Street and the surroundings streets. Bond Street galleries sell pictures too, but they are mainly older works being sold on.

BERNARD JACOBSON
14a Clifford St, W1
☎ 020-7495 8575
British painters, both abstract and more traditional.

BOUKAMEL CONTEMPORARY ART (BCA)
9 Cork St, W1
☎ 020-7734 6444
International figurative painting and large sculptures are BCA's speciality.

ENTWISTLE
6 Cork St, W1
☎ 020-7734 6440
Specialises in young British and American artists.

The Duke of Wellington at Hyde Park Corner

HELLY NAHMAD
2 Cork St, W1
☎ 020-7494 3200
Exhibitions here have included works by
Picasso, Monet, Dali, Magritte and Miró.

MARLBOROUGH FINE ART
6 Albemarle St, W1
☎ 020-7629 5161
Part with your money for a modern British
masterpiece. Often features one-person
shows.

VICTORIA MIRO
21 Cork St, W1
☎ 020-7734 5082
Modern art in minimalist surroundings.

HAMILTON'S
13 Carlos Pl, W1
☎ 020-7499 9493
Photography by David Bailey and Helmut
Newton is for sale here - at the right price.
Hamilton's treats its photographs as fine
art, and is appropriately situated in the
midst of Mayfair's fine-art galleries.

Selfridges

CINEMAS

ABC PANTON STREET
Panton St, W1
☎ 020-7930 0631
Four screens showing latest Hollywood
releases and some more unusual films.

ABC PICCADILLY
Piccadilly, W1
☎ 020-7437 3561
Two screens, slightly shabby auditorium.

ABC SHAFTESBURY AVENUE
Shaftesbury Ave, W1
☎ 020-7836 8606
Two screens and pleasant auditorium.

CURZON SOHO
Shaftesbury Ave, W1
☎ 020-7734 2255
International films and off-beat American
movies.

ABC SWISS CENTRE
Swiss Centre, Leicester Sq, W1
☎ 020-7439 4470
Four screens offering mostly foreign films.

CURZON MAYFAIR
Curzon St, W1
☎ 020-7369 1720
Luxury surroundings means luxury prices.
Mostly arty films.

METRO
Rupert St, W1
☎ 020-734 1506
Two screens, showing quirky US films and
regular Chinese and Asian features.

ODEON HAYMARKET
Haymarket, SW1
☎ 0870 505 0007 (Film info line)
One screen, showing quality films.

ODEON MARBLE ARCH
10 Edgware Rd, W1
☎ 01426 914501
Multi-screen complex showing Hollywood
releases. Home to the city's biggest screen.

PLAZA
Lower Regent St, W1
☎ 020-7437 1234
Five screens, latest releases.

VIRGIN HAYMARKET
Haymarket, W1
☎ 0870 907 0712
Multi-screen complex showing the very
latest releases.

THEATRES

HER MAJESTY'S
Haymarket, SW1
☎ 020-7494 5000/5004
A longstanding theatre whose stage has
been occupied by Andrew Lloyd Webber's
The Phantom of the Opera for over a
decade.

LONDON PALLADIUM
Argyll St, W1
☎ 020-494 5020
Top variety shows are staged here, as well
as the Royal Command Performance. A
legendary venue.

THEATRE ROYAL, HAYMARKET
Haymarket, W1
☎ 020-7930 8800
Long-established drama venue which
boasts a Corinthian portico. Designed by
John Nash.

ENTERTAINMENT AND NIGHTLIFE

COMEDY STORE
Haymarket House, Oxendon St, SW1
☎ 01426 914 433 (info line)
Possibly the best comedy venue in the
land. Many household names started out
here, including *Whose Line is it Anyway?*
stalwarts Paul Merton, Greg Proops and
Josie Lawrence. The Comedy Store Players
perform on Wednesday and Sunday
evenings.

100 CLUB
100 Oxford St, W1
☎ 020-7636 0933
A longstanding tradition of staging jazz
and blues still continues in this hot and
smoky basement club. Also home to many
of London's first punk rock concerts in the
mid-70s. Punk dinosaurs like the U.K.Subs
still crash through their hits here on a
regular basis.

CAFÉ DE PARIS
3 Coventry St, W1
☎ 020-7734 7700
A glamorous and stylish dance hall which
was once the haunt of Noel Coward and
Marlene Dietrich. Plenty of variety in the
music.

THE EMPORIUM
62 Kingly St, W1
☎ 020-7734 3190
Well-established nightspot, and a favourite
with celebs about town.

LEGENDS
29 Old Burlington St, WC2
☎ 020-7437 9933
Small and intimate and very popular with
the image conscious people of London -
passers-by can look through a large
window into the club.

SHOPPING

*Mayfair, Piccadilly and Oxford Street
all mean shopping, yet each has a
different angle. Piccadilly has exclusive
and high street shopping along Regent's
Street and around Piccadilly Circus,
Oxford Street offers high-street chains,
cheap clothing and electrical goods and
tourist souvenirs, and Mayfair is the
place for exclusive boutiques and
antiques along Bond Street. Brave the
crowds and get rid of some of that
disposable income, but watch your wallet
or handbag, pickpockets are common
here.*

OXFORD STREET

SELFRIDGES
400 Oxford St, W1
☎ 020-7629 1234

This vast and impressive store competes with Harrods as the largest and best-stocked London department store, covering fashion, food, household goods, toys, sports, electrical goods - you name it. Opened in 1909 by American millionaire, Harry Gordon Selfridge, who became a British citizen in 1937.

JOHN LEWIS
278-306 Oxford St, W1
☎ 020-7629 7711

An excellent department store offering very good quality merchandise at reasonable prices. Their motto is 'never knowingly undersold'. The homeware and haberdashery departments are the best, but there is also fashion and foods in the form of Waitrose supermarkets. Branches outside London.

DEBENHAMS
344 Oxford St, W1
☎ 020-7580 3000

Kitchen-ware, lingerie, cosmetics and hosiery as well as fashion for men, women and children. Branches all over London and countrywide.

DH EVANS
318 Oxford St, W1
☎ 020-7629 8800

Part of the House of Fraser chain - one with an excellent reputation. Excellent fashion departments as well as perfumery, furniture and household goods.

MARKS & SPENCER
458 Oxford St, W1
☎ 020-7935 7954

Good value, reliable and a British institution that was once a chain of penny bazaars in 19th-century Yorkshire. Their motto then was "Don't ask the price - it's a penny". Shoppers would be well advised to take a little more into the store these days.

Burlington Arcade

PLAZA SHOPPING PRECINCT
Oxford St, W1

Full of the major high-street chains and some one-off boutiques and jewellery stores.

WEST ONE SHOPPING CENTRE
corner Oxford St and South Molton St, W1

A big and modern centre next to the more exclusive South Molton Street shops, with all the regular chains and a few independent stores.

HMV
150 Oxford St, W1
☎ 020-7631 3423

Huge store of this multi-branch high-street chain. All kinds of music, from the current pop sensation to obscure ethnic jazz. Branches at 363 Oxford Street and in the Pepsi Trocadero, Coventry Street.

VIRGIN MEGASTORE
14 Oxford St, W1
☎ 020-7631 1234

CDs, cassettes, videos, computer games and books in this Branson commercial flagship store.

JJB SPORTS
301 Oxford St, W1
☎ 020-7409 2619

A chain of sports shops offering a wide range of equipment and clothing.

OSPREY
11 St Christopher Pl, W1
☎ 020-7935 2824

Not only jewellery, but also top-quality handbags and belts.

THE SWATCH STORE
313 Oxford St, W1
☎ 020-7493 0237

For those fans of eccentric and colourful watches, this is the place to come to choose from the entire range of Swatch watches.

DIVERTIMENTI
45-47 Wigmore St, W1
☎ 020-7935 0689

Everything you could need for the kitchen - plus several other things you've never thought of. A great place for gifts.

NELSON'S HOMEOPATHIC PHARMACY
73 Duke St, W1
☎ 020-7629 3118

Homeopathic and other remedies, including the full range of Bach Flower remedies. Knowledgeable staff.

PICCADILLY AND REGENT STREET

DICKINS & JONES
224-244 Regent St, W1
☎ 020-7734 7070

Four floors of stunning department store dedicated to the beauty and clothing of women. Prepare to be pampered.

LIBERTY
214-220 Regent St, W1
☎ 020-7734 1234

Famous for their Liberty print scarves and other merchandise, a Tudor-style design. Housed in a mock-Tudor building on busy Regent Street, Liberty's offers fabulous fashion and household accessories. Very popular with Londoners and tourists alike.

SIMPSON
203 Piccadilly, W1
☎ 020-7734 2002

Very high quality clothing for men and women. This is a long-established store with old-fashioned service.

Asprey's & Co, New Bond Street

41

Sotheby's

GIEVES & HAWKES
1 Savile Row, W1
☎ 020-7434 2001
Bespoke tailors situated on 'bespoke-tailor-street'. Shirts and suits that fit like a glove.

HENNES
261 Regent St, W1
☎ 020-7495 4003
Very good lower-priced clothing from Sweden. Also good for children's clothing. Branches on Oxford Street and Kensington High Street.

HATCHARDS
187 Piccadilly, W1
☎ 020-7439 9921
An 18th-century frontage hides a vast selection of books within. This is a venerable bookshop well loved by all its patrons.

TOWER RECORDS
1 Piccadilly Circus, W1
☎ 020-7439 2500
Massive choice of music - the biggest in London. Several floors of everything from the latest Top 40 to easy listening exotica and the Japanese avant-garde.

LILLYWHITES
24-36 Lower Regent St, W1
☎ 020-7930 3181
Vast range of sporting equipment, including clothing, bats, racquets, sticks etc.

BOOSEY & HAWKES
295 Regent St, W1
☎ 020-7580 2060
A vast range in classical sheet music, for those who play an instrument.

BOND STREET
Bond Street is famed for its exclusive stores.

Fortnum & Mason - by Appointment

GARRARD & CO
165 New Bond St, W1
☎ 020-7493 6767
One of the top jewellers in London. Very courteous service and re-mortgages necessary for many purchases.

FENWICK
63 New Bond St, W1
☎ 020-7629 9161
A very stylish store on four floors, with everything a woman could need from underwear to fake furs.

BROWNS
23-27 South Molton St, W1
☎ 020-7491 7833
There are many branches of this well-established fashion emporium. Along South Molton Street are several affiliated Brown's shops, such as hairdressers, shoes etc.

COMME DES GARÇONS
59 Brook St, W1
☎ 020-7493 1258
Very very fashionable clothing and of course, their own scent.

DONNA KARAN
19 New Bond St, W1
☎ 020 7495 3100
Glamorous understatement with a high price tag.

DKNY
27 Old Bond St, W1
☎ 020-7499 8089
In case you didn't know, the DKNY stands for Donna Karan New York. If you're a woman at work in London, this is how you're supposed to look.

JOSEPH
23 Old Bond St, W1
☎ 020-7629 3713
Gorgeous sweaters, suits and jackets for men and women, very beautifully made. Branches all over London.

NICOLE FAHRI
158 Old Bond St, W1
☎ 020-7499 8368
The classic look is favoured here, although it is comfortable and fairly reasonably priced. Branches all over central London.

VIVIENNE WESTWOOD
6 Davies St, W1
☎ 020-7629 3757
Eccentric British couture. Westwood is famous among music fans for dressing the

Hamleys Toy Shop

Sex Pistols and Bow Wow Wow. Also responsible for popularising pre-revolutionary French chic. There's another branch at 430 King's Rd.

ELECTRUM GALLERY
21 South Molton St, W1
☎ 020-7629 6325
Modern jewellery galore.

MAGGS BROTHERS
50 Berkeley Sq, W1
☎ 020-7493 7160
A wide range of secondhand and antiquarian books available.

MARKETS

GRAY'S ANTIQUE MARKET
58 Davies St, W1
☎ 020-7629 7034
An impressive market run by knowledgeable people. Have a look at the varied pieces, from jewellery to oriental artefacts.

GREAT FOR KIDS

There are loads of Festivals and Events throughout the year in London which children will love - See Festivals and Events.

PEPSI TROCADERO
Piccadilly Circus, W1
☎ 0891 881100
The Trocadero (formerly a music hall) has been given an expensive facelift, and is now Adrenalin Zone, Europe's largest indoor entertainment facility, offering masses of chrome and neon lights. Included in the fun are The Emaginator, where the cinema seats move, giving the viewer the impression of being in space or hurtling through a pinball machine. The Pepsi IMAX 3D Cinema shows 3D films on a huge screen to an audience wearing headsets with 'surround sound'. Segaworld offers high-tech adventure, and will undoubtedly be the place to pick up all the top gear for the new Dreamcast console. And if you get dazzled by the choice, you can always sit in the electric chair on Level 2 to help jolt you into a decision!

ROCK CIRCUS
London Pavilion, Piccadilly Circus W1
☎ 0171-734 7203
Madame Tussaud's wax models of rock stars tell the tale of rock, and even put on a 'live' show at the end. Always stuffed with tourists wearing headphones and looking bemused. If you're a serious music fan, then the Rock Circus will probably drive you mad.

HAMLEY'S
188 Regent St, W1
☎ 020-7734 3161
One of the world's largest toy stores, with seven floors of entertainment and fun, and over 40,000 things to buy. One of those places where you don't need to spend any money to have a good time. You also don't need to have any children with you. There's enough to entertain any adult. The toy demonstrations are very entertaining. The window displays are always fun and inventive, especially at Christmas.

CHILDREN'S RESTAURANTS

ROCK ISLAND DINER
London Pavilion, W1
☎ 020-7287 3500
Perfect for after a visit to the Rock Circus, and very good value if you come here between 12 noon and 5pm on Saturday or Sunday - the kids eat for free. Always has a lively atmosphere and favourite children's food.

PLANET HOLLYWOOD
13 Coventry St, W1
☎ 020-7287 1000
Owned by Hollywood stars, Bruce Willis, Arnold Schwarzenegger and Sylvester Stallone, there are branches of this chain all over the world. It is a 'movie experience', with burgers and fries and

Lubbock's finest, Buddy Holly, welcomes visitors to the Rock Circus

plenty of Hollywood memorabilia. But don't expect to see the great men themselves, and watch out for the prices in the souvenir shop.

RAINFOREST CAFÉ
20 Shaftesbury Ave, W1
☎ 020-7434 3111
A hot and steamy replica of a Brazilian jungle awaits you here. You can eat Cajun and Jamaican dishes (as well as straight burgers) to the sound of parrots and other jungle birdlife. Or take a trip on the virtual safari and meet elephants and gorillas. The bar stools downstairs are shaped like the back end of various animals eg a giraffe, an elephant and a zebra.

SMOLLENSKY'S BALLOON
1 Dover St, W1
☎ 020-7491 1199
A really children-friendly restaurant with burgers and fries and delicious puddings. Loads of entertainment at weekends for the children including puppets, clowns and storytellers.

HARD ROCK CAFÉ
150 Old Park Lane, W1
☎ 020-7629 0382
A worldwide chain with rock memorabilia that's exchanged around the world, the Hard Rock is legendary for its burgers, loud music and rock and roll.

BASKIN-ROBBINS ICE-CREAM
Plaza Cinema, Lower Regent St, W1
Delicious American full-cream ice-cream in loads of different flavours.

McDonald's and Burger King are plentiful in this area.

CHILDREN'S SHOPPING

BABY GAP/GAP KIDS
146-148 Regent St, W1
☎ 020-7287 5095
Wonderful colourful clothing for children and babies, often to complement the adult versions. Many branches throughout London.

BUCKLE MY SHOE
19 St Christopher's Pl, W1
☎ 020-7935 5589
Stacked with children's shoes in a wide variety of styles and sizes.

PLEASE MUM
69 New Bond St, W1
☎ 020-7493 5880
For ultra-discerning children only - and of course their parents. Mostly designer labels.

THE DISNEY STORE
140-141 Regent St, W1
☎ 020-7287 6558
Everything in this store is connected to a Disney film or character. There are hundreds of toys and Disney-imprinted gifts.

WARNER BROTHERS STUDIO STORE
178-182 Regent St, W1
☎ 020-7434 3334
Believe it or not, another theme store right along from The Disney Store. This time it's

St James's Church, Piccadilly

Bugs Bunny, Yosemite Sam and the like to tempt you.

PLACES OF WORSHIP

ST JAMES'S CHURCH
197 Piccadilly, W1

Originally built by Sir Christopher Wren, and his personal favourite, St James's was destroyed in 1940 and then immaculately restored. Today it is more than a church, it also has an extremely popular café to the rear (35 Jermyn St), with works of art for sale on the walls. Baroque music recitals are held at lunchtimes, and there's a craft market in the courtyard on Friday and Saturday.

ALL SAINT'S
Margaret St, W1

A Gothic Revival church with a rather gloomy interior, although the decoration and stained glass windows are beautiful. Built in the 1850s by William Butterfield, whose other works include Keble College, Oxford and the quadrangle of Rugby School, it serves as a clergy house and choir school as well as a church.

CHURCH OF THE IMMACULATE CONCEPTION
114 Mount St, W1

Headquarters of the Jesuit Order in Britain. Tours by appointment only.

SPORT AND LEISURE

DANCEWORKS
16 Balderton St, W1
☎ 020-7629 6183

After learning the finer points of tap, contemporary dance, ballet and reggae (among others), relax in the capable hands of Natureworks, who will soothe away your aches and pains with aromatherapy, massage, or, if things have gone really wrong, physiotherapy.

MARSHALL STREET LEISURE CENTRE
14 Marshall St, W1
☎ 020-7287 1022

A swimming pool, among other facilities.

SEYMOUR LEISURE CENTRE
Seymour Pl, W1
☎ 020-7723 8019

Aerobics and step classes, plus a steam room, sauna and swimming pool to help you get fit and chill out.

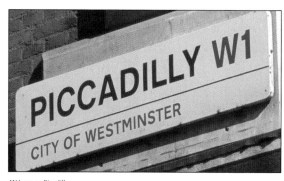

Welcome to Piccadilly

EXCLUSIVE MAYFAIR

You'll often see a celebrity or two wandering around the expensive and beautiful shops in Mayfair. Antiques, jewellery, Persian carpets and gifts are all stocked with loving care and service is likely to be extremely attentive.

TIFFANY & CO
25 Old Bond St, W1
☎ 020-7409 2790

An exciting range of jewellery for those with money to burn. Famous as Audrey Hepburn's ultimate wish in the film *Breakfast at Tiffany's.*

BOND STREET ANTIQUES CENTRE
New Bond St, W1
☎ 020-493 1854

Rare antiques on sale at this serious antiques centre.

BOND STREET SILVER GALLERIES
111 New Bond St, W1
☎ 020-7493 6180

Browse among the antique silver, objets d'art and second-hand jewellery.

CHARBONNEL ET WALKER
28 Old Bond St, W1
☎ 020-7491 0939

Exquisite and luxuriously presented chocolates.

HERBERT JOHNSON
55 James St, W1
☎ 0171-408 1174

Hats and accessories by one of the master makers.

CHRISTIE'S
8 King St, W1
☎ 020-7839 9060

A major auction house, telephone for details of the time and subjects of sales.

PHILLIPS
101 New Bond St, W1
☎ 020-7629 6602

A famous and long-established auctioneers. Telephone for details.

FORTNUM AND MASON
181 Piccadilly, W1
☎ 020-7734 8040

Founded in 1707 by William Fortnum and Hugh Mason, the store offers exclusive furniture, clothes and the foods that go into Fortnum & Mason hampers - all under cover of chandeliers. 1964 saw the addition of a rather special clock on the front of the building. Models of Mr Fortnum and Mr Mason bow to each other on the hour, while the clock plays the Eton school anthem. Customers can relax in the splendid tearooms.

SOTHEBY'S
34-35 New Bond Street, W1
☎ 020-7293 5000

Founded in 1745, Sotheby's is one of Britain's best known auction houses. Worth a visit to catch a potential glimpse of a famous painting or sculpture. Remember not to catch the auctioneer's eye or wave your hands around, or you may find yourself going home with a Gainsborough and a big bill.

WHERE TO STAY

HOTELS

AA RECOMMENDED

★★★★★◉ ◉ **CHURCHILL INTER-CONTINENTAL**
30 Portman Square W1A 4ZX
☎ 020 7486 5800 📠 020 7486 1255
Overlooking Portman Square, this impressive hotel provides luxury accommodation with such modern amenities as dual voltage plugs, and Internet and fax connections. Public areas display a wealth of marble, pillars and chandeliers, and afternoon tea is served in the Terrace. The Churchill Bar and Cigar Divan has a gentleman's club atmosphere, perfect for a pre-dinner drink before dining in Clementine's Restaurant, an attractive setting for Mediterranean-inspired cooking.
440 rooms (135 no smoking) / Tennis / Live entertainment / Lift, Night porter, Air cond / No dogs (ex guide dogs)
Price band £££ 🍷

★★★★★◉ ◉ **CLARIDGE'S**
Brook St W1A 2JQ
(Between Grosvenor Square and New Bond Street parallel with Oxford Street)
☎ 020 7629 8860 📠 020 7499 2210
An expensive and expansive refurbishment has blended state-of-the-art modern design and technology into a traditional setting, and the 7th-floor penthouses are particularly impressive. Reception rooms and public areas are best described as opulent, giving an overall impression that is simply majestic. In addition to the famous restaurant, refreshments are also served in the lounge and reading room.
197 rooms (18 no smoking) / International Cuisine / Sauna, Gym, Tennis / Live entertainment / Lift, Night porter, Air cond / No dogs (ex guide dogs) / No coaches
Price band £££ 🍷

★★★★★◉ ◉ **CONNAUGHT**
Carlos Place W1Y 6AL
(Situated between Grosvenor Square and Berkeley Square in Mayfair)
☎ 020 7499 7070 📠 020 7495 3262
The Connaught, one of London's great hotels, continues to offer measured service and quiet comfort. The unhurried atmosphere is sustained by bans on both mobile telephones and business meetings. The Restaurant and The Grill Room share the same impeccable service and exhaustive menu, offering classical cuisine.
90 rooms / English & French Cuisine / Health & beauty facilities available at sister hotels / Lift, Night porter, Air cond / No dogs / No coaches
Price band £££ 🍷

Grosvenor House

★★★★★◉ ◉ ◉ **THE DORCHESTER**
Park Ln W1A 2HJ
(half way along Park Lane between Hyde Park Corner & Marble Arch, overlooking Hyde Park on corner of Park Lane & Deanery St)
☎ 020 7629 8888 📠 020 7409 0114
One of London's best-known hotels, the Dorchester is sumptuously decorated in every department. Bedrooms are individually designed, beautifully furnished, and the luxurious bathrooms have huge baths that are a Dorchester hallmark. The Promenade serves afternoon tea or drinks, and in the evening there is live jazz in the bar. The Grill is a restaurant in the traditional style and there is also an acclaimed Cantonese restaurant, the Oriental.
248 rooms (24 no smoking) / Sauna, Solarium, Gym, Jacuzzi / spa, The Dorchester Spa Health club / Live entertainment / Lift, Night porter, Air cond / No dogs (ex guide dogs) / No coaches
Price band £££ 🍷

★★★★★◉ ◉ **FOUR SEASONS**
Hamilton Place, Park Ln W1A 1AZ
☎ 020 7499 0888 📠 020 7493 6629
The grand foyer sets the tone for this elegant but friendly hotel. Accommodation offers excellent standards of comfort, and in addition to the standard rooms, there are suites and impressive 'conservatory' rooms, with extra touches of luxury. Lanes Restaurant looks out on one side to Park Lane and serves up some interesting modern food.
220 rooms (72 no smoking) International Cuisine / Gym, Fitness club / Live entertainment / Lift, Night porter, Air cond / No dogs (ex guide dogs) / No coaches
Price band £££ 🍷

★★★★★◉ ◉ ◉ ◉ **GROSVENOR HOUSE**
Park Ln W1A 3AA
(Marble Arch, halfway down Park Lane)
☎ 020 7499 6363 📠 020 7493 3341
Majestically positioned on Park Lane, this internationally recognised hotel, with its Lutyens' façade, offers thoughtfully equipped accommodation. Some of the suites enjoy views of Hyde Park, while the Crown Club rooms have the advantage of a range of extra services and facilities. The public areas include a wide range of banqueting, function and private dining rooms, and the leisure centre has been completely overhauled. Guests have the choice of eating at Chez Nico, Café Nico, or the hotel's own Italian Restaurant.
453 rooms (70 no smoking) / English, French & Italian Cuisine / Indoor swimming pool (heated) / Sauna, Solarium, Gym, Jacuzzi/spa, Health & Fitness centre / Live entertainment / Lift, Night porter, Air conditioning / No dogs (ex guide dogs)
Price band £££ 🍷

★★★★★◉ ◉ ◉ ◉ **LE MERIDIEN PICCADILLY**
21 Piccadilly W1V 0BH
(100mtrs from Piccadilly Circus)
☎ 020 7734 8000 📠 020 7437 3574
Within whistling distance of Piccadilly Circus, this well established hotel is possibly the closest to the capital's hub. The comfortable bedrooms enjoy traditional decor and the expected amenities. Renowned chef Marco Pierre White runs the hotel's ever popular Oak Room restaurant as a separate entity, while the Terrace offers a more informal setting for all day dining and afternoon teas. Champney's health club offers

luxurious pampering in smart surroundings.

267 rooms (19 family & 91 no smoking) / British & French Cuisine / Indoor swimming pool (heated) / Squash, Sauna, Solarium, Gym, Jacuzzi/spa, Beauty treatments Aerobics Massage / Lift, Night porter, Air cond / No dogs (ex guide dogs) Price band £££ 🍽

See advert on page 239.

★★★★★ ◉ MAY FAIR INTER-CONTINENTAL LONDON
Stratton St W1A 2AN
(from Hyde Park Corner/Picadilly turn left onto Stratton St & hotel is on left)
☎ 020 7629 7777 📠 020 7629 1459
This friendly, welcoming hotel has an intimate atmosphere and congenial surroundings. Public areas offer a choice of restaurants, bars, a manned business centre and a conference auditorium. Air-conditioned bedrooms of varying sizes have a useful range of extra amenities. The Opus 70 restaurant is a showcase for the hotel's excellent modern British cuisine.

290 rooms (14 family & 148 no smoking) / English, American & French Cuisine / Indoor swimming pool (heated) / Sauna, Solarium, Gym, Hair & Beauty salon / Live entertainment / Lift, Night porter, Air cond / No dogs (ex guide dogs) / No coaches Price band £££ 🍽

★★★★★ PARK LANE
Piccadilly W1Y 8BX
(On Piccadilly opposite Green Park)
☎ 020 7499 6321 📠 020 7499 1965
Examples of this fine hotel's stylish and sophisticated public areas include the art-deco ballroom and period-style Palm Court, the perfect setting for a fine afternoon tea with harp accompaniment. The French-style Brasserie on the Park offers guests an interesting range of modern dishes. Other facilities include hairdressing, a small gym, a business centre and garage.

305 rooms (20 family & 116 no smoking) / English Mediterranean & French Cuisine / Gym / Live entertainment / Lift, Night porter / No dogs (ex guide dogs) Price band £££ 🍽

★★★★★ ◉ ◉ THE RITZ
150 Piccadilly W1V 9DG
(from Hyde Park Corner travel E on Piccadilly. The Ritz is the first building on the right immediately after Green Park)
☎ 020 7493 8181 📠 020 7493 2687
One of the world's great metropolitan hotels, the Ritz has become a byword for magnificent decor. Bedrooms are furnished in Louis XVI style and have fine marble bathrooms. Elegant reception rooms include the Palm Court, with its famous afternoon-teas, and the sumptuous Ritz Restaurant with its gold

Park Lane

chandeliers and extraordinary trompe l'oeil decoration.

131 rooms (20 no smoking) / International Cuisine / Gym / Live entertainment / Lift, Night porter, Air cond / No dogs (ex guide dogs) / No coaches Price band £££ 🍽

★★★★ ◉ ATHENAEUM
116 Piccadilly W1V 0BJ
(located on Piccadilly, overlooking Green Park)
☎ 020 7499 3464 📠 020 7493 1860
An elegant hotel overlooking Green Park, the Athenaeum is prized for its high standards of service and welcoming atmosphere. Dining in Bullochs Restaurant from the menu of modern classics is a highlight of any visit. Afternoon tea and other refreshments are served in the Windsor Lounge and there is also a clubby, panelled bar.

156 rooms (50 no smoking) / International Cuisine / Sauna, Gym, Jacuzzi/spa, Massage & treatment rooms / Live entertainment / Lift, Night porter, Air conditioning / No dogs (ex guide dogs) / No coaches Price band £££ 🍽

★★★★ THE BERNERS HOTEL
Berners St W1A 3BE
☎ 020 7666 2000 📠 020 7666 2001
Well positioned in the heart of London's West End, just off Oxford Street, this traditional hotel has a classical marble-columned foyer with a comfortable lounge - popular for afternoon tea - and attractive

restaurant. Bedrooms are all equipped with modern comforts.

217 rooms (100 no smoking) / English & French Cuisine / Lift, Night porter Price band £££ 🍽

★★★★ ◉ ◉ BROWN'S
Albemarle St, Mayfair W1X 4BP
(from Green Park Underground Station on Piccadilly, take third left into Albemarle Street)
☎ 020 7493 6020 📠 020 7493 9381
Brown's is famous for its English country-house style and traditional emphasis on comfortable furnishings. Accommodation is of good quality and there is a smartly decorated restaurant with an imaginative menu. The hotel is a popular venue for afternoon tea.

118 rooms (15 family) / French Cuisine / Live entertainment / Lift, Night porter / No dogs (ex guide dogs) / No coaches 🍽

★★★★ ◉ THE CHESTERFIELD
35 Charles St, Mayfair W1X 8LX
(Hyde Park corner along Piccadilly, turn right into Half Moon St. At the end turn left and first right into Queens St, then turn right onto Charles St)
☎ 020 7491 2622 📠 020 7491 4793
Quiet elegance and an atmosphere of exclusivity appropriate to its prestigious Mayfair address characterise this privately owned hotel. The lobby with its marble floor, glittering chandelier and fluted pillars leads into a library lounge and club-style bar. The restaurant, although traditional in decor, provides a modern menu.

Brown's

Bedrooms are stylish and amenities include direct Internet access via the TV.
110 rooms (4 family & 16 no smoking) / Live entertainment / Lift, Night porter / No dogs (ex guide dogs) / No coaches Price band £££

★★★★ CLIFTON-FORD
47 Welbeck St W1M 8DN
☎ 020 7486 6600 ☎ 020 7486 7492
This well managed and friendly hotel is popular for business and conference use, as well as keeping its appeal for holidaymakers. Accommodation offers high standards of modern comfort, especially in the private suites. A marbled lobby, where guests may enjoy complimentary sherry and canapés during the cocktail hour, leads into an intimate lounge. There is also a cocktail bar and a brasserie.
*186 rooms (7 family)
Price band £££*

★★★★ THE CUMBERLAND
Marble Arch W1H 8DP
(M4 to central London. At Hyde Park Corner take Park Lane to Marble Arch. Hotel is above Marble Arch tube station.)
☎ 020 7262 1234 ☎ 020 7724 4621
Convenient for shopping and Hyde Park, the Cumberland's position is excellent. The vast range of eating and drinking options includes cafés, oriental dining in Sampans, the ever popular Carvery, and Callaghan's bar and restaurant for fresh Irish fare and nightly musical entertainment. Bedrooms are comfortably furnished and up-to-date and guests have the option of upgrading to the Premier Club for extra comfort and amenities.
917 rooms (21 family & 480 no smoking) / English Mediterranean Chinese & Carvery Cuisine / Live entertainment / Lift, Night porter / No dogs (ex guide dogs)

★★★★ ® ® LONDON MARRIOTT
Grosvenor Square W1A 4AW
(M4 east to Cromwell Rd through Knightsbridge to Hyde Park Corner, Park Lane right at Brook Gate onto upper Brook St to Grosvenor Sq/Duke St)
☎ 020 7493 1232 ☎ 020 7491 3201
Situated in the heart of Mayfair, this popular hotel offers comfortable, well equipped accommodation in a variety of room sizes, all with a good range of facilities. Light refreshments are served all day in the Regent Lounge and a full menu is offered in the Diplomat Restaurant, where an impressive breakfast buffet is also laid out.
*221 rooms (26 family & 120 no smoking) / Gym, Exercise & fitness centre / Lift, Night porter, Air cond / No dogs (ex guide dogs) / No coaches
Price band £££*

★★★★ LONDON MARRIOTT HOTEL MARBLE ARCH
134 George St W1H 6DN
(from Marble Arch turn into the Edgware Road then take 4th turning on right into George St. Turn immediate left into Forset Street for main entrance)
☎ 020 7723 1277 ☎ 020 7402 0666
This modern hotel offers a good standard of accommodation. Bedrooms are well equipped and furnished with quality fittings. Executive rooms have their own lounge on the top floor, where breakfast and special check-out facilities are available. Public lounge and bar areas, although not spacious, are comfortable and the hotel also benefits from a leisure centre and car parking.
*240 rooms (100 family & 120 no smoking) / English & American Cuisine / Indoor swimming pool (heated) / Sauna, Solarium, Gym, Jacuzzi/spa / Lift, Night porter, Air cond / No dogs (ex guide dogs)
Price band £££*

★★★★ ® ® MILLENNIUM BRITANNIA MAYFAIR
Grosvenor Square W1A 3AN
☎ 020 7629 9400 ☎ 020 7629 7736
The extensive range of facilities at this professional hotel includes a cocktail bar and piano bar, plus a choice of two restaurants. The Shogun earns Two AA Rosettes for its Japanese fare. The hotel also boasts a fine ballroom, equipped with state-of-the-art communications. A 24-hour business centre and fitness room are available. Services include valet and 24-hour room service.
*316 rooms (60 no smoking) / English, American, French, Italian & Japanese Cuisine / Gym / Live entertainment / Lift, Night porter, Air cond / No dogs (ex guide dogs)
Price band £££*

★★★★ ® ® THE MONTCALM-HOTEL NIKKO LONDON
Great Cumberland Place W1A 2LF
☎ 020 7402 4288 ☎ 020 7724 9180
Named after the 18th-century French General Montcalm, defeated by Wolfe at Quebec, this Japanese-owned hotel offers extremely comfortable accommodation, ranging from standard to duplex, 'junior' suites and penthouse suites. Japanese guests appreciate "the best Japanese breakfast outside Japan". Staff are really charming and low key in their approach. The Crescent Restaurant has a good reputation for modern cooking, with an inexpensive lunch.
*120 rooms (18 no smoking) / Lift, Night porter, Air cond / No dogs (ex guide dogs) / No coaches
Price band £££*

★★★★ ® ® RADISSON EDWARDIAN BERKSHIRE
Oxford St W1N 0BY
☎ 020 7629 7474 ☎ 020 7629 8156
Situated almost directly opposite Bond Street Tube station in Oxford Street, this is

an ideal hotel for shoppers, and also attracts an international business clientele. Bedrooms, though not over-large, are stylishly decorated. Public rooms are intimate in scale, and include an elegant drawing room, cocktail bar and first-floor restaurant.
*147 rooms (2 family & 44 no smoking) / English & French Cuisine / Lift, Night porter, Air cond / No dogs (ex guide dogs)
Price band £££*

★★★★® ® RADISSON SAS PORTMAN
22 Portman Square W1H 9FL
(100mtrs N of Oxford St and 500mtrs E of Edgware Rd)
☎ 020 7208 6000 ☎ 020 7208 6001
Guests can choose from four distinct styles of bedroom: Oriental, Scandinavian, British and Classic. Some rooms, with fax and modem points, are designated 'business class'. The intimate Library Restaurant claims to be the smallest hotel dining room in London, and offers a sophisticated menu. Portman Corner is the more informal restaurant, and afternoon tea is served in the lobby lounge.
*280 rooms (21 family & 129 no smoking) / International Cuisine / Tennis (hard) / Sauna, Solarium, Gym / Live entertainment / Lift, Night porter, Air cond / No dogs (ex guide dogs)
Price band £££*

★★★★ THE SELFRIDGE
Orchard St W1H 0JS
(behind Selfridges Department store)
☎ 020 7408 2080 ☎ 020 7409 2295
Situated in the heart of shopping land, this elegant hotel is very popular. Most of the bedrooms have been refurbished and although on the small side, they are very smartly decorated and equipped. The first floor is a peaceful retreat from the hustle and bustle with a lounge, rustic-themed bar and informal restaurant.
*294 rooms (98 no smoking) / European Cuisine / Lift, Night porter, Air cond / No dogs (ex guide dogs)
Price band £££*

★★★★ THISTLE MARBLE ARCH
Bryanston St, Marble Arch W1A 4UR
☎ 020 7629 8040 ☎ 020 7499 7792
Just off Oxford Street, this very popular hotel offers some of the most spacious, elegant and thoughtfully equipped bedrooms in London with extras such as voice mail, American power outlets, and climate control. Guests may dine in The Charleston restaurant, or from the 24-hour room service menu. The hotel offers a business centre and executive lounge facilities.
689 rooms (12 family & 331 no smoking) / International Cuisine / Live entertainment / Lift, Night porter / No dogs (ex guide dogs)

The Westbury

foreign visitors. There are also good business and conference facilities. Oceana Restaurant offers inventive, up-market cooking, and there is another all-day restaurant and a pub serving bar food.

165 rooms (30 no smoking) / International Cuisine / Lift, Night porter / No dogs (ex guide dogs)

Price bands £££ 🍷

★★★ MOSTYN
4 Bryanston St W1H 8DE

☎ 020 7935 2361 📠 020 7487 2759

Close to Oxford Street and Marble Arch, this Georgian hotel has well equipped bedrooms with good quality furnishings and smart marble bathrooms. For meals, guests may choose to dine in the Spanish Tío Taberna or in the Bistro, with its range of provincial French dishes. There are two car-parks within a short walk.

121 rooms (15 family & 54 no smoking) / Spanish Brasserie & French Cuisine / Lift, Night porter / No dogs (ex guide dogs) / No coaches

Price £££ 🍷

⌂ THE LEONARD
15 Seymour St W1H 5AA

☎ 020 7935 2010 📠 020 7935 6700

The Leonard is a townhouse only two minutes' walk from Oxford Street, and offers bedrooms that are superbly decorated and benefit from every conceivable comfort. There is a compact exercise room, and the lounge and bar are lavishly furnished with some fine antique pieces and fresh flowers. Guests can dine in the café bar or via room service.

28 rooms / English & Italian Cuisine / Lift, Night porter, Air cond / No dogs (ex guide dogs) / No coaches

Price band £££ 🍷

★★★★ ⊛ THE WASHINGTON
5-7 Curzon St, Mayfair W1Y 8DT

☎ 020 7499 7000 📠 020 7495 6172

This smart, Air conditioned modern hotel offers a high standard of accommodation. Bedrooms, furnished in burred oak, range from state rooms and suites with spa baths to equally comfortable twins and doubles. Light refreshments are served in the marbled and wood-panelled public areas, and there is a wide range of business services, a concierge desk and help with car parking.

173 rooms (94 no smoking) / International Cuisine / Live entertainment / Lift, Night porter, Air conditioning / No dogs (ex guide dogs)

Price band £££ 🍷

★★★★ ⊛ ⊛ THE WESTBURY
New Bond St W1A 4UH

(from Oxford Circus south down Regent St turn right onto Conduit St, hotel at junct of Conduit St & Bond St)

☎ 020 7629 7755 📠 020 7495 1163

Set in the heart of London's shopping district, this distinctive property aims to provide accommodation of the highest standards for an international clientele. Reception rooms include the Polo Lounge, and La Méditerranée Restaurant, serving traditional dishes at lunchtime and a more adventurous evening menu.

244 rooms (76 no smoking) / European Cuisine / Complimentary access to nearby Health Club / Lift, Night porter, Air cond / No dogs (ex guide dogs)

Price band £££ 🍷

★★★ MANDEVILLE
Mandeville Place W1M 6BE

(off Oxford Street & Wigmore St near Bond St underground station)

☎ 020 7935 5599 📠 020 7935 9588

The language skills of the reception staff at this quiet hotel have made it popular with

BED & BREAKFAST
AA RECOMMENDED

♦♦♦♦ BRYANSTON COURT
60 Great Cumberland Place W1H 7FD

☎ 020 7262 3141 📠 020 7262 7248

This historic terrace of houses has been converted to a large, elegant guesthouse, close to Oxford Street and Marble Arch. Smart public areas include a club-style lounge and a small breakfast room where a continental spread is provided each morning. A cooked breakfast is available on request. Bedroom sizes vary considerably and are all being steadily upgraded.

54 rooms (3 family) / No dogs / Lift / No coaches

Price band £££ 🍷

♦♦♦♦ 22
W1H 1FD

☎ 020 7224 2990 📠 020 7224 1990

This elegant town house is within walking distance of Oxford Street and very close to

the Tube, so is an ideal base for shopping, theatre-going and sightseeing. A splendid staircase leads up to the bedrooms and first-floor lounge. All rooms are high-ceilinged and beautifully decorated. Continental breakfast is served around a

large table in the open-plan kitchen/dining room.

6 rooms (2 family & all no smoking) / No dogs / No children under 5 years / No coaches

Price band £££ 🍷

Hart House Hotel

♦♦♦ HART HOUSE HOTEL
51 Gloucester Place, Portman Sq W1H 3PE
(just off Oxford St behind Selfridges, nearest
underground is Baker St or Marble Arch)
☎ **020 7935 2288** 📠 **020 7935 8516**
Hart House Hotel is an elegant Georgian
town house which is part of a terrace of
mansions that were home to the French
emigré nobility during the French
Revolution. The building has been restored
to much of its original character, and
offers modern bedrooms with a good
range of facilities. Breakfast is served in
the cosy dining room.
16 rooms (4 family) / No dogs / No coaches
Price band ££

The Regency Hotel

♦♦♦ THE REGENCY HOTEL
19 Nottingham Place W1M 3FF
(A40 into Marylebone Rd, turn right at
Baker St, left into Crawford St which leads
into Nottingham Place)
☎ **020 7486 5347** 📠 **020 7224 6057**
Located close to the West End shops and
theatres, the Regency offers a high
standard of accommodation. The
comfortable bedrooms are very well
equipped with such extras as mini-fridges
and ironing centres. There is an attractive
breakfast room, where guests are offered
a choice of breakfast.
20 rooms (2 family & 2 no smoking) / No
dogs (ex guide dogs)
Price band ££

♦♦♦ WIGMORE COURT HOTEL
23 Gloucester Place W1H 3PB
(turn off A40 onto Baker St, turn right at
George St, turn right at Gloucester Place)
☎ **020 7935 0928** 📠 **020 7487 4254**
A small, family run hotel, the Wigmore
Court offers comfortable accommodation
with well equipped bedrooms. In addition,
a cosy lounge is available, together with a
nicely appointed dining room, where a
choice of English and continental breakfast
is served. Laundry and kitchen facilities are
available on request.
18 rooms (4 family) / No dogs (ex guide
dogs)
Price band ££

♦♦ GEORGIAN HOUSE HOTEL
87 Gloucester Place, Baker St W1H 3PG
(parallel to Baker St, N of Oxford St, short
walk from Marble Arch)
☎ **020 7486 3151** 📠 **020 7486 7535**
This popular hotel provides good value for
money and attracts both business and
leisure guests. Bedrooms are modest but
comfortable and all are spacious and well
equipped. A limited choice of breakfast is
served in the nicely appointed dining
room.
19 rooms (4 family) / No dogs / Lift / No
children under 5 years / No coaches
Price band £££

WHERE TO EAT

RESTAURANTS

AA RECOMMENDED

Bentley's

⊛ ATHENAEUM HOTEL
116 Piccadilly W1V 0BJ
☎ 020 7470 3333 📠 020 7493 1860
Stylish contemporary restaurant with Jerusalem stone floor and natural lighting. The brasserie-type menu reflects international influences with some Cajun, Thai and Italian dishes.
ALC ££

⊛ ⊛ BENTLEY'S
11-15 Swallow Street W1R 7HD
☎ 020 7734 4756 📠 020 7287 2972
Bentley's has been synonymous with seafood since it opened its doors in the middle of the First World War. Eat in the Oyster Bar, or in the old-fashioned surroundings of the first-floor restaurant with its comfortable booth seating, foodie stills and period caricature prints hanging on the walls. This is a place where the traditional and the modern sit side by side: dressed crab and crab risotto with saffron and red peppers, for example. Perhaps surprisingly, red wines are a strong point on the wine list.
Fixed L/D £ ALC ££

⊛ ⊛ BICE
13 Albemarle Street W1X 3HA
☎ 020 7409 1011 📠 020 7493 0081
Downstairs from Donna Karen's DKNY, a fashionable, expensive modern Italian restaurant well worth a visit for the mix of clientele that ranges from fashion victim, through business suits to comfort-clad American tourists. The service has that direct American-style no-nonsense approach - a warm welcome and really means business. For the area, the quality and simplicity of the food is hard to beat. Interesting all-Italian wine list but few bottles under £20.
Fixed L £ ALC ££

⊛ ⊛ BROWN'S, 1837
Albemarle Street Mayfair W1X 4BP
☎ 020 7408 1837 📠 020 7408 1838
Brown's Hotel has become a famous Mayfair institution, and rightly so. Renowned for its wonderful afternoon teas, it is now promoting its restaurant to a wider audience. The walls are oak-panelled and the restaurant is in grand style. Although there are elements of contemporary cooking to be found on the menu, the repertoire is, by and large, a classical French one, with an emphasis on gracious dining. The wine list is impressive with some great vintages, but at a price.
Fixed L £ ALC £££

⊛ CAVIAR HOUSE
161 Piccadilly W1V 9DF
☎ 020 7409 0445 📠 020 7493 1667
Sea-blue and sand colours, crystal mosaics covering mirror frames, waterfalls mounted in picture frames form a striking, fresh, light backdrop. Caviar is the main raison d'être - teamed with a glass of champagne, blinis, sour cream and new potatoes - but excellent-quality raw materials are used in the series of short, modern menus. Dishes are beautifully presented Japanese-style, in small, rich portions. Don't forget you can buy some caviar to take away from the shop at the front.
Fixed L/D ALC £££

⊛ THE CHESTERFIELD HOTEL
35 Charles Street Mayfair W1X 8LX
☎ 020 7491 2622 📠 020 7491 4793
Traditionally luxurious setting in a prestigious Mayfair address. The modern carte brings seared sea bass on a warm salad niçoise, and rosette of English spring lamb on a root vegetable rösti with confit of shallot and garlic.
Fixed L/D £ ALC ££

⊛ ⊛ ⊛ ⊛ CHEZ NICO AT NINETY PARK LANE
90 Park Lane W1A 3AA
☎ 020 7409 1290 📠 020 7355 4877
Nico Ladenis' grand restaurant within the Grosvenor House Hotel remains very much its own boss: immaculate in every sense with great, albeit formal, staff, but with touches of personality from the more senior - the sommelier is particularly good. The stylish, understated room is an antidote to glaring restaurant minimalism - here tables are wide and well-spaced, seats comfortably padded, floor-length tablecloths, carpets and drapes absorb any hard-edged noise. The carte offers an haute cuisine-dominated selection of dishes but there's a directness to Paul Rhodes sophisticated, accomplished cooking.
Fixed L £££ ALC £££

⊛ CHOR BIZARRE
16 Albemarle Street W1X 3HA
☎ 020 7629 9802/7629 8542
📠 020 7493 7756
Cluttered with unusual artefacts and offering a broad range of regional Indian dishes, research is thorough and it pays to be adventurous. More conservative tastes are satisfied with familiar tandooris, tikkas and pakoras. Wines are matched to the food.
Fixed L £ ALC ££

⊛ CHURCHILL INTER-CONTINENTAL
30 Portman Square W1A 4ZX
☎ 020 7486 5800 📠 020 7486 1255
Executive Chef Idris Caldora is one of the country's most respected professionals, and his cooking is always basically simple, stylish and fresh. A signature dish of terrine of foie gras, celeriac and duck confit with herb salad, or roasted onion and garlic soup with goats' cheese croûtons, and grilled yellow fin tuna with Mediterranean vegetable, ragout and tomato dressing give an indication of the style.
Fixed L £ ALC ££

⊛ ⊛ CLARIDGES
Brook Street W1A 2JQ
☎ 020 7629 8860 📠 020 7499 2210
Gloriously grand hotel finally resurfacing from a period of refurbishment. Claridge's Restaurant and The Orangery remain as elegant as ever though subtle changes have been made. There is now a 'Claridge's Centenary' menu available at lunch in addition to the carte, and a 'Menu Sonata' in the evenings. Classical British with a strong French accent sums

up the style. An orchestra entertains dinner-dance guests on Friday and Saturday nights.
Fixed L £££ ALC £££

❀ ❀ COAST RESTAURANT
Albemarle Street W1

☎ 020 7495 5999 📠 020 7495 2999

On the trendy side of modern, but not so avant-garde as to frighten off anyone dressed in M&S. Bright, light and airy with pale green walls. Traditional dishes can make an appearance, ham, egg and chips, for example, albeit given a designer twist in the presentation. Wines aren't cheap but there is plenty of interesting choice by the glass.

❀ ❀ THE CONNAUGHT
Carlos Place W1Y 6AL

☎ 020 7499 0888 📠 020 7495 3262

The service is from the top drawer and so are the prices. Times may be changing, but not at the Connaught where, for a few brief hours, one can be forgiven for thinking the old world remains. It is fitting that Michel Bourdin's style and menu are just so, so classical, and that this is a kitchen that remains proudly and solidly steeped in the past (turn of the century to be exact). The main menu (the same in the restaurant and the grill room) is 'dedicated' to the traditions of Escoffier and had he eaten here, we doubt whether Bourdin would have been reproached.
Fixed L £££ ALC £££

❀ ❀ THE CRITERION
224 Piccadilly W1V 9LB

☎ 020 7930 0488 📠 020 7930 8380

A great place for people-watching. Marco Pierre White's opulent brasserie-style operation at the heart of Piccadilly Circus just heaves from 5.30pm til late. A gold mosaic ceiling glitters down the entire length of the 45 metre long room; semi-precious stones stud the walls. Service is, however, very rapid, perhaps necessarily so for the volume of business the Criterion is doing. Standards, fortunately are good.
Fixed L/D £ ALC ££

❀ ❀ THE DORCHESTER, GRILL ROOM
Park Lane W1A 2HJ

☎ 020 7317 6336 📠 020 7317 6464

Classic hotel with style and service to match. The Grill keeps the flag flying with traditional British food and gentleman's club power-dining on a grand scale. The decor is thoroughly opulent with gold leaf and leather aplenty, staff are immaculate in every sense and there are trolleys for just about everything.
Fixed L ££ ALC £££

❀ ❀ ❀ THE DORCHESTER, THE ORIENTAL
Park Lane W1A 2HJ

☎ 020 7317 6328 📠 020 7409 0114

Great Cantonese cooking served impeccably by tail-coated waiters in first-class, stylishly understated surroundings. The staff are true Dorchester professionals and conduct themselves with the utmost discretion and skill, but without sacrificing any sense of hospitality. As well as the carte, there are several set menus, a page of vegetarian dishes and special chef's recommendations - and it is worth spending some time discussing with your waiter how best to construct a balanced meal - their advice is spot-on.
Fixed L ££ ALC £££

❀ ❀ THE FOUR SEASONS HOTEL
Hamilton Place Park Lane W1A 1AZ

☎ 020 7499 0888 📠 020 7493 1895

The hotel's grand foyer is an elegant introduction to the wood-panelled Lanes Restaurant. Now strikingly revamped the restaurant offers contemporary, cosmopolitan menus matched with a polished but easy style of service. At lunch the menu tends to be lighter; dinner has a more refined style, but both include a pasta section and traditional specialities such as grilled Dover sole.
Fixed L ££ ALC £££

❀ ❀ ❀ LE GAVROCHE RESTAURANT
43 Upper Brook Street W1Y 1PF

☎ 020 7408 0881/7499 1826
📠 020 7409 0939/7491 4387

The setting is comfortable (although the tables may be a little too close together). It may look and feel like a discreet, English gentleman's club but the cooking is French. Michel Roux really hits the mark with dishes such as lobster and stuffed pigs trotter and onion, caper and gherkin sauce, or a cote de veau sur mousseline d'haricots blancs et sauce verte. Lunch is great value with the likes of gratin of crab with penne and Parmesan, or a supreme of chicken teamed with a cep-flavoured risotto noted for their quality. The lengthy wine list remains rooted in France and is not cheap, but don't despair - the sommelier is excellent and will give good advice on what to drink with your meal. Indeed, there are a few bins under £20.
Fixed L £££ ALC £££

❀ ❀ ❀ HOTEL INTER-CONTINENTAL LONDON - LE SOUFFLÉ
1 Hamilton Place Hyde Park Corner W1V 0QY

☎ 020 7318 8577 📠 020 7491 0926

In a prime site on Hyde Park Corner, the Inter-Continental is everything expected of a large, modern, international hotel. Le Soufflé is decorated in pale colours, with upholstered chairs and plenty of elbowroom. There are a number of menus to choose between, from a two-course business lunch, or an innovative set-price organic menu, to the pinnacle of a no-choice eight-course 'Gourmet Menu' at nearly £100, the sommelier's selection of wines thrown in, for those who want to scale the heights. The repertoire is wide-ranging and shows an up-to-the-minute approach with the kitchen brigade a hive of industry. Service, from a mainly young French team, is impeccable, and even those not on expenses will find much of interest on the wine list.
Fixed L ££ ALC £££

❀ ❀ KAI MAYFAIR
65 South Audley Street W1Y 5FD

☎ 020 7493 8988 📠 020 7493 1456

Some of the best Chinese food in the capital. The menu of this elegant, pricy restaurant is more adventurous than most, as well as delightfully descriptive. 'The Enrichment of the Surprised Piglet' - steamed pork dumplings to you and me - for example, or 'Hokkien Opium', a clear soup of salted mustard leaves and beancurd. Service is efficient and well supervised.
ALC £££

❀ ❀ ❀ THE LANESBOROUGH
Hyde Park Corner SW1X 7TA

☎ 020 7259 5599 📠 020 7259 5606

Built in 1828 and named after a country house that once stood on the site, The Lanesborough has been meticulously (and expensively) restored to its original grandeur. The menu takes in tempura vegetables with sticky rice, plum and watercress, and Szechuan pepper-crusted duck with lime and ginger, but the kitchen is not stuck out East, for it also encompasses Moroccan carrot soup with chermoula, and rosette of venison with red cabbage, chestnuts and wild mushrooms. And, as befits a chef who's at the cutting edge of vegetarian cooking, there's an exclusively vegetarian menu.
Fixed L £ ALC £££

❀ ❀ ❀ LONDON HILTON ON PARK LANE
22 Park Lane W1Y 4BE

☎ 020 7493 8000 📠 020 7208 4142

The top-floor Windows Restaurant, with its sweeping views, is the place to head for at the London Hilton. Business lunches see a weekly-rotating joint of meat carved at table from a trolley but the carte is based firmly in Jacques Rolancy's homeland, the style described as 'French cuisine bourgeoise'. Tournedos of salmon with a bean salad and balsamic vinaigrette, fillet of venison in a parsley and truffle crust with potato galette, are typical of the style.
Fixed L/D £££ ALC £££

❀ ❀ LONDON MARRIOTT GROSVENOR SQUARE HOTEL
Grosvenor Square W1A 4AW

☎ 020 7493 1232 📠 020 7491 3201

Popular modern hotel in the heart of Mayfair. If you're after a bargain, try the pre-theatre four course menu for just £12.95 - if you wish you can save dessert and coffee until after the performance. The wine list is comprehensive, with plenty by the glass.
Fixed L £ ALC ££

❀ ❀ ❀ ❀ ❀ LE MERIDIEN PICCADILLY – THE OAK ROOM, MARCO PIERRE WHITE
21 Piccadilly W1V 0BH
☎ 020 7437 0202 📠 020 7427 3574

This premier-division restaurant is run on the drive, ambition and brilliance of one man - Marco Pierre White. The grand-scale room is a fitting setting, with enough gilt, chandeliers, spotlit art, and broad, well-spaced tables to dedicate it as a temple to haute cuisine - only the lovely oak panelling adds warmth. Staff are formal, the tone hushed and discreet. This is complex cooking, standards are impressive, as they might be at the price (though the set-lunch remains a satisfactory bargain), with impact coming through an extraordinary ability to coax the last nuance of flavour out of these, the very best raw materials.
Fixed L £££ ALC £££

❀ ❀ LE MERIDIEN PICCADILLY - LE TERRACE
Le Meridien Piccadilly, 21 Piccadilly W1V 0BH
☎ 0870 400 8400 📠 020 7465 1616

The revamped conservatory-style restaurant is wonderfully bright and airy by day. Overseen by the pneumatically charged, Parisian-based chef Michel Rostang protégé, Pascal Even, interprets Rostang's style in an unashamedly French manner with rich, robust cooking the order of the day.
Fixed L/D £ ALC ££

❀ ❀ MILLENNIUM BRITANNIA MAYFAIR
Grosvenor Square W1A 3AN
☎ 020 7629 9400 📠 020 7629 8168

Well-managed Mayfair hotel that is going from strength to strength. With its well-equipped 24 hour business centre and fitness room, it is perhaps not surprising that the hotel's restaurant, Shogun, offers Japanese fare. Noted dishes are thin crab noodles and sesame-coated prawns, roast duck with teriyaki, and mixed tempura.
Fixed L £ ALC ££

❀ ❀ ❀ MIRABELLE
56 Curzon Street W1Y 8DL
☎ 020 7499 4636 📠 020 7499 5449

Classical 1930s decor is the setting; 'affordable glamour' is the theme. Marco Pierre White scores brilliantly once again. Great boulevardier dishes such as omelette Arnold Bennett and smoked haddock, bubble-and-squeak, beurre blanc sit alongside MPW signatures such as foie gras parfait en gélée with toasted Poilâne bread, and daube of Aberdeen Angus à l'ancienne. The menu is a textbook of British and French classics, all confidently done with great panache and without unnecessary fripperies.
Fixed L £ ALC £££

❀ ❀ MITSUKOSHI
Dorland House 14-20 Lower Regent Street SW1Y 4PH
☎ 020 7930 0317 📠 020 7839 1167

Set in the basement of a Japanese department store, Mitsukoshi offers a number of set-price menus that will deliver the (authentic) goods to the hesitant: an appetiser, then sashimi, tempura, sukiyaki, rice, miso and pickles, and finally fruit, for example. Service is charming and helpful. Prices on a rudimentary wine list soon soar into the stratosphere - drink saké.
Fixed L/D ££ ALC ££

❀ MIYAMA
38 Clarges Street W1Y 7PJ
☎ 020 7499 2443 📠 020 7493 1573

Tucked away, dimunitive Japanese restaurant that offers a good deal for lunch in an area that can be expensive and booked up at that time of day. Expect all the usual characters: miso soup, tempura, sushi, sashimi and teriyaki, and yaki tori.
Fixed L £ ALC ££

❀ ❀ ❀ MORTONS
28 Berkeley Square W1X 5HA
☎ 020 7493 7171 📠 020 7495 3160

Mortons is a private club which has opened its restaurant to the public. It's the chance to see behind hitherto closed doors that adds a dash of spice to the experience. It's a lovely room on the first floor with good views over Berkeley Square, especially if you are fortunate enough to secure a window table. Dishes are described with brevity: salad escabeche, red mullet pepper confit, perhaps, or maize fed chicken, wild mushroom ravioli, which matches Philip Reynolds simple, direct style. The wine list features very little under £20. The clientele are of the sort that used to run the country.
Fixed L £ ALC £££

❀ MULLIGAN'S OF MAYFAIR
13-14 Cork Street W1X 1PF
☎ 020 7409 1370 📠 020 7409 2732

Modern Irish restaurant in a listed building, adorned by portraits of Irish writers. Typical dishes are Strangford Lough oysters, rosemary coated Wicklow lamb, and traditional Irish stew.
Fixed L/D £ ALC ££

❀ ❀ NICO CENTRAL
35 Great Portland Street W1N 5DD
☎ 020 7436 8846 📠 020 7436 3455

With the BBC and Oxford Circus just a block away, it is wise to book for lunch at this smart, well-established restaurant. Sunflower yellow walls (sporting Picasso-style prints), pale-wood flooring and colourful seating create a bright, airy environment in which to enjoy good mainstream French cooking.
Fixed L £ Fixed D ££

❀ ❀ NICOLE'S
158 New Bond Street W1 9PA
☎ 020 7499 8408 📠 020 7409 0381

Nicole's is a fashionable Bond Street watering hole of impeccable taste, set within the Nicole Farhi shop. The restaurant design is as beautifully understated as the clothes, all tan leather upholstery, stainless steel and oak wood floor, with food that is equally classy, offering a light touch that makes even dieting pleasurable.
ALC ££

❀ ❀ NOBU
Metropolitan Hotel 19 Old Park Lane W1Y 4LB
☎ 020 7447 4747 📠 020 7447 4749

Nobu is a fashion statement in itself. The London branch of this ground-breaking New York restaurant is sited on the first-floor of that A-list playground, the starkly minimalist Metropolitan Hotel (whose lobby can, on arrival, present an impenetrable face to the unknown diner who merely wants to eat modern Japanese). The food is astonishing and, without question, some of the most imaginative in town. The quality of the ingredients is impeccably high but such freshness dictates equally sky-high prices. A punchy, modern wine list complements the food exactly.
Fixed L ££ ALC £££

❀ ❀ ❀ L'ODÉON
65 Regent Street W1R 7HH
☎ 020 7287 1400 📠 020 7287 1300

Fabulous views over Regent Street and Piccadilly Circus make this one of the best vantage points in town. L'Odeon has gone through several head chefs since it opened; the current incumbent is Colin Layfield. His menu takes in many modern

Pied à Terre

British ideas with all the usual suspects - confits, risottos, pestos, raviolis, marmalades, lobster oil and truffle dressing - but there are also some more classic leanings.

Fixed L/D £ ALC ££

OPUS 70
The Mayfair Inter-Continental Stratton Street W1A 2AN
☎ 020 7344 7070 ☎ 020 7344 7071
Opus 70 is part of the Mayfair Inter-Continental Hotel, but with its own street entrance. It's a contemporary restaurant providing a thoroughly cosmopolitan setting for dishes from the Far East, America, and Britain.

Fixed L £ ALC ££

PIED À TERRE
34 Charlotte Street W1P 1HJ
☎ 020 7636 1178 ☎ 020 7916 1171
Tom Aikens proves he has the courage of his convictions by presenting braised pig's head with steamed trotter, deep-fried brains and ears and celery purée as one of his most outstanding and challenging dishes. Terrines are prominent among starters with ham hock, sweetbreads, white beans and rosemary vinaigrette enjoyed for its taste and strong visual appeal. Roasting is a favoured treatment of main-course meats and fish: sea bass with red pepper sauce and braised fennel, or lamb fillet with garlic and rocket salad and olive sauce for example. The budget-conscious should stick to the 'suggested wines' on the wine list; those prepared to pay can drink one of France's greatest.

Fixed L £ ALC £££

LA PORTE DES INDES
32 Bryanston Street W1H 7AE
☎ 020 7224 0055 ☎ 020 7224 1144
Stylish Indian on two impressive floors with a 40ft marble waterfall cascading down between carved stone balustrades. At lunch there's a brilliant great value buffet: dishes range from battered aubergine, to 'smoky' tandoori chicken. Not your average curry house.

Fixed L £ ALC ££

PURPLE SAGE
92 Wigmore Street W1H 9DR
☎ 020 7486 1912 ☎ 020 7486 1913
Stylish modern Italian close to Selfridges featuring authentic pizzas from the brick oven, salads, pasta and risottos, including a fine, saffron flavoured shellfish risotto ai profumi di mare. Try too the yogurt sorbet and excellent espresso.

ALC £

RADISSON EDWARDIAN BERKSHIRE HOTEL
Oxford Street W1N 0BY
☎ 020 7629 7474 ☎ 020 7495 1686
Hidden oasis of calm amidst the hustle and bustle of Oxford Street. The hotel's Ascot's Restaurant is smart, wood-panelled and offers distinctly modern British

cooking, with those tell-tale influences from around the world evident in dishes such as chargrilled honey and lemon chicken with coriander and rocket, and pan-fried fillet of beef with smoked bacon, shallots and red wine.

Fixed L/D £ ALC ££

THE RADISSON SAS PORTMAN HOTEL
22 Portman Square W1H 9FL
☎ 020 7208 6137 ☎ 020 7224 4928
Modern international cooking for modern international travellers. There are some interesting ideas. The Portman Corner offers a lunch buffet Monday to Friday, for example, with a supplement if a main course, such as confit of rabbit leg with red onion parcel and herb oil dressing or thyme-scented rump of lamb with spinach and cranberries, is taken from the carte.

Fixed L/D £ ALC ££

RASA W1
6 Dering Street, W1R 9AB
☎ 020 7629 1326 ☎ 020 7491 9540
Bright, friendly Keralan restaurant that is far removed from your average curry house.What is on offer is some of the best Indian vegetarian food in the capital, imaginative, impressive quality, with vibrant flavours through imaginative spicing. This place has hardly drawn breath since it opened - booking is essential.

Fixed L £ ALC £

RITZ HOTEL
150 Piccadilly W1V 9DG
☎ 020 7493 8181 ☎ 020 7493 2687
A legend among great metropolitan hotels and the byword for magnificent style and decor. The Ritz is one of London's most famous landmarks and occupies a prime position on Piccadilly overlooking Green Park. The dining room is a grandiose, sumptuously furnished room where smart and highly efficient staff tend to your every need, offering either an evening carte of international dishes or, by contrast, a lunch menu featuring more traditional items, including grills and roasts from the trolley.

Fixed L ££ ALC £££

R.K. STANLEYS
6 Little Portland Street W1N 5AG
☎ 020 7462 0099 ☎ 020 7462 0088
British bangers are the speciality of this upmarket, child-friendly diner near Oxford Circus - try game, Thai and Caribbean-style varieties plus daily specials such as calves' liver and bacon.

SARTORIA
20 Saville Row W1X 1AE
☎ 020 7534 7000 ☎ 020 7534 7070
Given the Saville Row address, no Conran restaurant could fail to take advantage of the thematic inspiration. It is, however, done stylishly and wittily with 'safari-suit' beige marble floor, 'business-suit' grey

walls, chairs and banquettes, 'shirt-white' table linen. Sophisticated school of River Café cooking includes rabbit risotto with borlotti beans and rosemary, and pan-fried scallops with fresh broad beans, peas and mint.

ALC £

SCOTTS
20 Mount Street W1Y 6HE
☎ 020 7629 5248 ☎ 020 7499 8246
Purple and gold, with the look of a 1930s ocean liner, Scotts sails through a splendid fish and seafood carte in a style that befits its ritzy Mayfair address.

Fixed L £ ALC £££

SOTHEBY'S, THE CAFÉ
34 Bond Street W1A 2AA
☎ 020 7293 5077 ☎ 020 7295 5920
Great little restaurant which spills out into the main corridor of the world-famous auctioneers. Chef Caroline Crumby has been here since the place opened, and there's no doubting her enthusiasm and commitment to organic produce. The daily-changing menu offers a small choice at each course, the style is modern brasserie. Service is swift - as it needs to be during busy lunchtimes - friendly and helpful, and Sotheby's wine department has had a hand in the carefully compiled, short list. Note that The Café is also open for breakfast and afternoon tea.

ALC £

THE SQUARE
6 Bruton Street W1X 7AG
☎ 020 7495 7100 ☎ 020 7495 7150
Philip Howard is one of London's finest, an innovative, inspired chef whose cooking draws an appreciative crowd - The Square is one of the most booked-up restaurants in town. Herb risotto with oysters, salmon, caviar and champagne, roast Bresse pigeon with stuffed Savoy cabbage, crusted brill with leeks, noodles and truffles and tournedos Rossini show the sort of things the kitchen deals in - an understated modern classicism that revels in contrasts of texture and flavour. Service can be stretched at busy times but staff are knowledgeable about food and wine - as they need to be with a list running to around 40 pages (although a page of the sommelier's selection eases choice).

Fixed D £££ ALC £££

STEPHEN BULL RESTAURANT
5-7 Blandford Street W1H 3AA
☎ 020 7486 9696 ☎ 020 7224 0324
Stephen Bull's premier restaurant - the interior has modern but undramatic styling. The daily changing menu has enough variety to make choice difficult. Seared scallops, truffle oil and chives followed by peppered monkfish, fricasse of wild mushrooms, shallot purée and red wine sauce, and a spiced plum crumble tart with mulled red wine ice cream to finish reveal earthy, robust flavours.

Fixed D ££ ALC ££

❀ ❀ TAMARIND
20 Queen Street W1X 7PJ
☎ 020 7629 3561 ☎ 020 7499 5034

The Mayfair address sends the right signals - an up-market Indian restaurant with formal service. Glass-fronted with designer interior, strip-wood floor and arty steel and tan leather chairs, that's Tamarind, and prices do reflect the upscale location. Basically the cooking is Punjabi with the menu offering a mix of the familiar and the unusual. Desserts are simple and include rasmalai and kulfi.
Fixed L/D £ ALC ££

❀ ❀ TECA
54 Brook Mews W1Y 2NY
☎ 020 7495 4774 ☎ 020 7491 3545

A quick glance at the short, sharp menu shows that this is cooking from the modern Italian school: saffron risotto, carpaccio of sea bass on spinach, roasted John Dory in rosemary sauce with chard and cannellini, and chicken breast stuffed with confit of lemon with braised radicchio and sautéed potatoes. Background notes on the wine list make interesting reading, with quality the keynote, not least among the six house wines.
Fixed L £ ALC ££

Tamarind

The Veeraswamy Restaurant

❀ THE VEERASWAMY RESTAURANT
99-101 Regent Street W1R 8RS
☎ 020 7734 1401

Britain's oldest Indian restaurant, dating from 1927, now under same ownership as Chutney Mary with bold modern decor. Food is Southern Indian with some northern 'court' dishes.

❀ THE WASHINGTON MAYFAIR HOTEL
5-7 Curzon Street W1Y 8DT
☎ 020 7499 7000 ☎ 020 7495 6172

Spacious modern restaurant with strong blue colours. Dishes range from battered cod with chips and pea purée to lamb noisette on flageolet beans scented with ginger and rosemary.
Fixed L £ ALC ££

❀ WESTBURY HOTEL
Bond Street W1A 4UH
☎ 020 7629 7755 ☎ 020 7495 1163

Top-drawer hotel restaurant in a prime Bond Street site. The room is light, airy, and relaxing. Luxury items of course, lobster, crab and foie gras - the latter as a terrine with asparagus and leeks - but the kitchen goes into contemporary mode with carpaccio of salmon and tuna with an oriental dressing, and seared duck breast with pak choi, glazed apples and sesame jus. The set-price menus are good value, and the wine list is typical of this style of operation.
Fixed L/D £ ALC ££

❀ ❀ YUMI RESTAURANT
110 George Street W1H 5RL
☎ 020 7935 8320 ☎ 020 7224 0917

One of the nicer Japanese restaurants in London offering the ambience of a neighbourhood restaurant with great atmosphere and staff. There's a sushi bar and some private rooms on the ground floor (given an element of authenticity with their tatami mat floors), and the main restaurant and yet more private dining rooms in the basement. The food is straightforward Japanese.
Fixed D £££ ALC £££

❀ ZEN GARDEN
15-16 Berkeley Street W1X 5AE
☎ 0171 4931381

Sleek, upmarket Chinese restaurant. Dim sum as a lunchtime starter, whole sea bass served with spring onion and ginger, and shallow fried custard buns for dessert show the style.
Fixed L £ ALC £££

Zen Garden

PUBS, INNS & OTHER PLACES

THE ARGYLL ARMS
18 Argyll Street, W1V 1AA
☎ 020 7734 6117
A tavern has been on this site since 1740, but the present building is mid-Victorian and is notable for its stunning floral displays. There's a popular range of sandwiches and the hot food menu is tasty and varied.

THE GLASSBLOWER
42 Glasshouse Street, W1R 5RH
☎ 020 7734 8547
This Irish-managed pub is in the heart of the West End, and is the ideal place for an after-shopping meal or drink.

RED LION
1 Waverton Street, W1X 7FJ
☎ 020 7499 1307
Built in 1752, this is one of Mayfair's most historic pubs. Originally used by 18th-century builders, the clientele is now more likely to be the rich and famous, yet the friendly welcome remains.

BENIHANA
37 Sackville Street, W1
☎ 020 7494 2525
Trendy Japanese restaurant where your meal is cooked in front of you.

BROWN'S HOTEL
Albemarle Street, W1A 4SW
☎ 020 7493 6020
Afternoon tea in a traditional style. No denim.

AUDLEY
41 Mount Street, W1
☎ 020 7499 1843
Victorian pub with plenty of character.

COCK & LION
62 Wigmore Street, W1
☎ 020 7935 8727
Friendly pub serving traditional English fare in upstairs restaurant.

KNIGHTSBRIDGE AND CHELSEA

In Knightsbridge money is visible, but never vulgar. An address on Pont Street Mews is a much-sought after commodity, by those who can afford it anyway, and the corner shop is Harrods.

Brompton Road, the main thoroughfare, is the domain of glamorous women whose job it is to shop and lunch. Harrods, Harvey Nichols and a wide range of haute couture stores are keen to satisfy, and come lunchtime the café and restaurant tables begin to fill up with bulging carrier bags faced with modestly scripted shop and designer names. No parking problems for them, their chauffeurs wait patiently nearby. It's hard to believe that until the 18th century Knightsbridge was a tiny village surrounded by rolling hills. Legend has it that the name comes from the location of a battle between two knights on a bridge over the now-underground River Westbourne.

Just along Brompton Road is museum-land, with the Natural History, Science and Victoria and Albert museums clustered together, perhaps as a timely reminder that there is more to life than shopping. But head south down Sloane Street and along 'the King's Road' and you'll soon be immersed in shopping again, this time Peter Jones, the excellent department store on Sloane Square/King's Road, trendy boutiques and the smartest high-street chains. This was the first street where you could buy a mini skirt in the 1960s. George Best, Mick Jagger and David Bailey were denizens of this area then. A more recent legend tells of how Malcom McLaren and Vivienne Westwood helped put punk on the map, auditioning John Lydon (aka Johnny Rotten) in their shop, Sex, in 1976. In light of punk's virulent anti-monarchism it is apt that King's Road is so named as it was once the private royal route to Hampton Court. Westwood still has a shop here, its backward-running clock a fitting reminder of its location at the World's End.

Chelsea, once known as the 'village of palaces', is at the further end of King's Road, borders the Thames and was once a fishing settlement. Sydney Street, just off King's Road, offers some small, inexpensive and very pleasant restaurants, popular with those who like

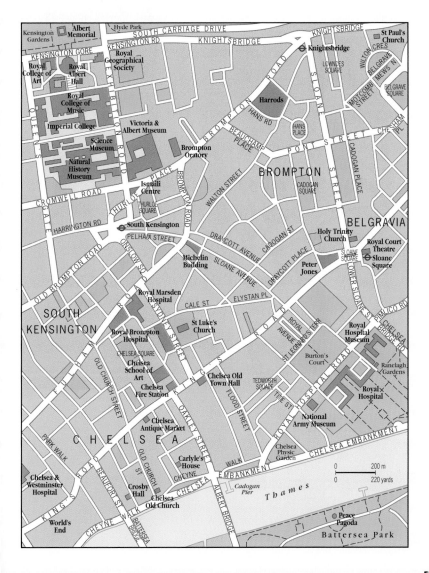

to be seen. Sir Thomas More lived on Cheyne Walk in 1520, and Henry VIII built a residence there, now marked by Cheyne Mews. Oscar Wilde, John Singer Sargent and Augustus John all lived along Tite Street, and Dante Gabrielle Rosseti the pre-Raphaelite, was at home on Cheyne Walk. Today, Chelsea still enjoys its two main attractions - money and art. The recently reopened Royal Court Theatre on Sloane Square has seen the premiers of some of British theatre's most important works, including plays by George Bernard Shaw, and John Osborne's *Look Back In Anger*.

Established in 1676 by the Apothecaries' Company, Chelsea Physic Garden, along Chelsea Embankment, is a delightful location, and was London's first botanical garden. The Chelsea Flower Show takes place every summer in the nearby grounds of the Royal Hospital, which is also home to the Chelsea Pensioners, ex-servicemen who wear their distinctive uniforms at all times. Chelsea is also home to the Territorial Army's HQ at the Duke of York's Barracks, and was the London address of Ian Fleming's spy hero, James Bond.

MUST SEE

Royal Albert Hall

HARRODS
87 Brompton Rd, SW1
☎ 020-7730 1234

Probably the world's most famous shop, Harrod's started out as a small grocer's shop owned by Henry Charles Harrod in 1849. It is now a miniature kingdom whose motto is *'omnia, omnibus, ubique'* - everything, for everyone, everywhere. It now occupies 4 acres. The food halls alone fill seven rooms, and there are over 300 departments and 3,000 staff. The building is illuminated at night, and some 30,000 customers come here everyday. How many of them actually buy anything is another story. One of the few shops with a dress code, it forbids shorts, ripped jeans, vest t-shirts and backpacks. It is currently owned by controversial businessman, Mohamed Al Fayed.

V & A Museum, South Kensington

VICTORIA & ALBERT MUSEUM
Cromwell Rd, SW7
☎ 020-7938 8500
recorded information: 020-7938 8441

The V&A (as it is affectionately known) houses an immense, eclectic collection of 'applied and decorative art', including the largest collection of Indian art outside India, Japanese, Korean and Islamic

galleries, and a huge dress collection. The museum was begun in 1852 by Prince Albert as an attempt to inspire commoners with top-notch design and applied art. It now includes works from all ages and every corner of the globe. The current building was designed by Aston Webb, and the cornerstone ceremony was one of Queen Victoria's last public engagements. There's too much to see in one day (11km of galleries), so take advantage of a guide (either human or leaflet). Temporary shows are always excellent, as are the café and restaurant.

SCIENCE MUSEUM
Exhibition Rd, SW7
☎ 020-7924 4455/4454

The Science Museum's seven floors cover man's achievements in the scientific world, including space travel, flight, telecommunications, medicine, electricity, computing and photography. Good places for children include the Launch Pad, showing how technology works through excellent interactive exhibits; 'Things', intended to peak the curiosity of youngsters; and the Flight Lab, where they can take control in a cockpit. There's an excellent guide to the whole museum, from Amy Johnson's plane, *Gipsy Moth* to Foucault's Pendulum.

NATURAL HISTORY MUSEUM
Cromwell Rd, SW7
☎ 020-7942 5000

The Natural History Museum contains a huge collection of animal and plant specimens ranging from prehistory to the age of global warming. It is also one of those places where old and new attitudes to museum-keeping can be explored, as modern 'user-friendly' exhibits bump up against those unchanged since the mid-19th century. Not only a tourist attraction, the museum is also an important resource for serious researchers. Therefore, what is on display is just the tip of the iceberg. The 150-million-year-old, 26m-long, dinosaur skeleton *Diplodocus carnegii* is the star of the excellent dinosaur exhibition. The 'Creepy Crawlies' exhibition covers insects, spiders and a massive scorpion, while the Hall of Human Biology explains human reproduction and development using models, push-button displays and sound effects. The Whale Gallery beyond, contains a life-size model of a 28m blue whale. The old Geological Museum is now the Earth Galleries and includes a ride through the rotating globe, an earthquake and volcano experience.

SLOANE SQUARE
SW1

A stone's throw from Brompton Road, and the start of King's Road, Sloane Square is synonymous with money and the arts. (Although the term 'Sloane Ranger' is now outdated, it hailed from here in the 1980s.) It is lined with Peter Jones department store, the Royal Court Theatre, and some chic cafés and brasseries. A popular place for lunch after a hard day's shopping.

Natural History Museum

ROYAL ALBERT HALL
Kensington Gore, SW7
☎ 020-7589 3203
box office: 020-7589 8212
Added to the London landscape in 1871as a tribute to Prince Albert, the 8,000-capacity Albert Hall plays host to many cultural and sporting events, from rock concerts to show jumping. It is home to the Royal Philarmonic Orchestra, and one of the best-known classical music festivals in the world, the Henry Wood Promenade Concerts ('the Proms'), takes place here from July to September.

Chelsea Physic Garden

HISTORIC AND ANCIENT SITES

KING'S ROAD
SW3
Chelsea's most famous and prestigious route was a private royal road until 1830. Depending on what you believe, it was a

The Science Museum

short cut to Hampton Court, or a quick way for Charles II to get to Nell Gwynn's house in Fulham. In the 1960s it became the place for fashionable clothing and eating - and it still is. Along the way you'll find Chelsea Antique Market (books, maps and prints), Chelsea Farmer's Market (small foodstalls), Designer's Guild (fabrics) and Osborne & Little (wallpapers and fabrics) as well as countless high street chains and individual boutiques.

CHELSEA ROYAL HOSPITAL
Royal Hospital Rd, SW3
☎ 020-7730 0161
Set up in 1682, this dignified building (designed by Sir Christopher Wren) was modelled on Louis XIVs Hôtel des Invalides in Paris to provide food, accommodation and medical care for aged and injured war veterans. Today it houses about 500 'Chelsea Pensioners' who wear uniform - navy blue for everyday and red for special events. Visitors can see the vaulted chapel, and a statue of the hospital's first patron, Charles II. During May, the Chelsea Flower Show is held here, attended by every keen gardener, including the Queen and plenty of celebrities.

CHEYNE WALK AND TITE STREET
SW3
Pronounced 'chainy', this elegant street is lined with early Georgian houses, including Carlyle's House. No.16 was once the home of Dante Gabriel Rossetti, while George Eliot lived at No.4. Tite Street's houses and studios were once home to

such luminaries as Oscar Wilde (No.34), Whistler (No.96), John Singer Sargent (No.31), Hilaire Belloc (No.104) and Augustus John (No.33). Mark Twain lived around the corner in Tedworth Square.

BONHAMS
Montpelier St, SW7
☎ 020-7393 3900
One of the famous auctioneer houses in the capital. Telephone for details of sales.

MICHELIN HOUSE
81 Fulham Road, SW3
☎ 020-7589 7401
Designed in 1905 for the famous tyre manufacturer, this unusual Art Deco building is now home to a publishing house, The Conran Shop and Bibendum, an exclusive and expensive restaurant and oyster bar.

BROMPTON CEMETERY
Finborough Rd, SW10
The last resting place of many famous people including Emmeline Pankhurst the suffragette, who died in 1928, and Samuel Sotheby's, of the famous auctioneers. The tomb of Frederick Leyland, founder of the National Telephone Company, is well worth seeking out. The cematary is overlooked by Chelsea FC's ground, so don't expect funereal peace on a Saturday.

ROYAL COLLEGE OF MUSIC
Prince Consort Rd, SW7
☎ 020-7589 3643
You can see the finest students of music perform in their own theatre (for free). There's usually a performance of chamber music every lunchtime during term time. Founded in 1882, the Royal College of Music maintains extremely high standards, and has produced some of Britain's greatest musicians.

MUSEUMS

CARLYLE'S HOUSE
24 Cheyne Row, SW3
☎ 020-7352 7087
The home of the renowned historian

Chelsea Pensioners at Chelsea Royal Hospital

Science Museum

Thomas Carlyle between 1834 and his death in 1881, the house remains as it was during his time here. He and his wife Jane (a poet and letter-writer) entertained such luminaries as Dickens, Tennyson and Browning in the first floor drawing room. Carlyle's hat still hangs on the back door, a reminder of when he had to go into the garden for a smoke. A statue of the 'Sage of Chelsea' stands nearby.

NATIONAL ARMY MUSEUM
Royal Hospital Rd, SW3
☎ 020-7730 0717
Through paintings, lifelike models, weapons and uniforms, the museum traces the story of the British soldier from Agincourt (in the 15th century) to Bosnia. You can witness Henry V's archers awaiting their fate at Agincourt and British soldiers scrambling over the top at the Somme. Also on view is the skeleton of Napoleon's horse, Marengo.

CINEMAS

CHELSEA CINEMA
206 King's Rd, SW3
☎ 020-7351 3742
Showing off-beat, stylish films in similar surroundings.

CURZON MINEMA
45 Knightsbridge, SW1
☎ 020-7369 1723
Small independent cinema with plush seats and sophisticated films.

GOETHE INSTITUTE
50 Princes Gate, Exhibition Rd, SW7
☎ 020-7411 3400
It's best if you are German, or at least speak German, as films are in - German.

CINÉ LUMIÈRE
Institut Français, 17 Queensberry Pl, SW7
☎ 020-7838 2146
Current French releases, as well as some of those you missed first time round.

THEATRES

ROYAL COURT
Sloane Sq, SW1
☎ 020-565 5000
The Royal Court stages mainly controversial works by young new talents.

It is the home of the English Stage Company.

MAN IN THE MOON
392 King's Rd, SW3
☎ 020-7351 2876/5701
A fringe theatre in a very popular pub at the bottom end of King's Road. Pleasant surroundings and some good shows.

Chelsea Royal Hospital

PARKS AND GARDENS

CHELSEA PHYSIC GARDEN
66 Royal Hospital Rd, SW3
☎ 020-7352 5646
Begun by the Worshipful Company of Apothecaries in 1673 and continued by physician Sir Hans Sloane when he bought the manor of Chelsea in 1712. This is a rare garden, with herbs and plants as well as rock gardens, and is an important centre for botanical research. The biggest

olive tree (9m) in Britain grows happily here. Retire to the excellent teahouse after viewing the greenery.

RANELAGH GARDENS
Royal Hospital Rd, SW3
Created in the 18th century for London's wealthy citizens, these gardens today provide some welcome tranquillity along the Thames. Often used by the Chelsea pensioners for their constitutionals, it was the setting for a performance by Mozart in the 1740s.

NATURAL HISTORY WILDLIFE GARDEN
Natural History Museum, Cromwell Rd, SW7
☎ 020-938 9123
Part of the museum, this garden covers one acre and plays an important educational role through scientific research of the wildlife habitat. It's also a lovely place to walk around in.

BISHOP'S PARK
Bishop's Park Rd, SW6
Just what you need when you tire of busy Fulham Road and Fulham Palace Road. Inside the riverside park is a small pool and a lovely walk along tree-filled paths.

GREAT FOR KIDS

Children will love going to the museums (the V&A, the Science Museum, the Natural History Museum), as well as the National Army Museum and Harrods

The Man in the Moon Theatre

(see below). And if there's any doubt, there's always McDonalds (49 King's Rd, SW3).

There are loads of Festivals and Events throughout the year in London which children will love. - See Festivals and Events.

Harrods as seen from Brompton High Street

HARRODS
87 Brompton Road, SW1
☎ **020-7730 1234**
Visit Harrods' toy store - you won't be disappointed, although you may be poorer afterwards.

CHELSEA PLAYGROUND
Royal Hospital Grounds, Royal Hospital Rd, SW3
Near to the Chelsea Royal Hospital, this playground has good facilities indoors and outdoors, but unfortunately is only open on Saturdays.

DEALS
Chelsea Harbour, SW10
☎ **020-7795 1001**
Owned by Lord Lichfield (the Queen's cousin) and Viscount Linley (Princess Margaret's son), this is a fun and lively place to bring children to eat. Go on a Sunday to benefit from all the events, which includes face painting and magicians. Burgers and fries with a difference.

HARRODS ICE-CREAM PARLOUR & CRÊPERIE
Harrods, 87 Brompton Rd, SW1
☎ **020-7730 1234**
Sweet and savoury crêpes, washed down with sundaes and milkshakes - the perfect end to a busy day.

DRAGONS
23 Walton St, SW3
☎ **020-7589 3795**
All the gear to kit out your child's life - toys, furniture and clothes, all in a very individual style.

TROTTERS
34 King's Rd, SW3
☎ **020-7259 9620**
Upmarket clothing for babies and children under 10 years.

BOOKS FOR CHILDREN
97 Wandsworth Bridge Rd, SW6
☎ **020-7384 1821**
Packed into two shops and two floors, you'll find every book you could ever want in this delightful shop. The owner is only too pleased to help if you need recommendations.

PLACES OF WORSHIP

HOLY TRINITY BROMPTON
Sloane St, SW1
Many famous people were involved in the construction of 'HTB', as it is commonly known among the Sloane set. The east window is by Sir Edward Burne-Jones, the elaborate interior was inspired by William Morris, and the Italian marbles influenced by Ruskin. It's a very fashionable place to get married.

BROMPTON ORATORY
Thurloe Place, Brompton Rd, SW3
Until Westminster Abbey took on the role, Brompton Oratory was the main Catholic church in London. Every Sunday, its Italianate interior echoes to a sung Latin mass.

CHELSEA OLD CHURCH (ALL SAINTS)
Chelsea Embankment, SW3
The original church was built in 1157, but has been considerably added to since. The south chapel was built by Sir Thomas More, and his wife is buried here. Henry VIII and Jane Seymour (his third wife) were secretly married here before their public ceremony. Inside are the six chained books, a gift from Sir Hans Sloane.

ST LUKE'S CHURCH
Sydney St, SW3
Neo-Gothic in style, St Luke's is well placed for the congregation of King's Road and fashionable Chelsea. Charles Dickens was married to Catherine Hogarth here in 1836.

SPORT AND LEISURE

CHELSEA SPORTS CENTRE
Chelsea Manor St, SW3
☎ **020-7352 6985**
It's essential to look the part at this well-equipped centre, with swimming pool, exercise classes, a gym and sports hall for badminton and the like.

FOOTBALL

CHELSEA FOOTBALL CLUB
Stamford Bridge, Fulham Rd, SW10
☎ **020-7385 5545**
Chelsea's home ground. Matches played on Saturday afternoons in season (September to May). The ground has recently undergone massive

Brompton Oratory

redevelopment, and the new Chelsea Village includes a restaurant, King's Brasserie, and a hotel.

FULHAM FOOTBALL CLUB
Craven Cottage, Stevenage Rd, SW6
☎ **020-7893 8383**
Home ground to FFC, which is well supported by families and individuals who swarm here during home games on Saturdays.

CROQUET

CROQUET ASSOCIATION
Hurlingham Club, Ranelagh Gardens, SW6
☎ **020-7736 3148**
Croquet is the modern form of pell mell, a game that started life in St James's, and gave its name to Pall Mall. Today the

Welcome to Knightsbridge

Hurlingham Club has a fairly posh clientele. The British Open Croquet Championships are held in July.

TENNIS

BISHOP'S PARK
Fulham Palace Rd
Bishop's Park has outdoor tennis courts which are floodlit in the evenings. There's a club (which you don't have to join to play) and lessons can be arranged.

KNIGHTSBRIDGE
SHOPPING

The raison d'être for most people who live around Knightsbridge or those who come to Knightsbridge is shopping. It is the home of some of the most exclusive and expensive shops (apart from Mayfair), and along its streets strut some of the wealthiest women in London.

HARRODS
87 Brompton Rd
☎ 020-7730 1234
Obviously top of the list.

HARVEY NICHOLS
109-125 Knightsbridge, SW3
☎ 020-7235 5000
Designer fashion and foodstuffs, Harvey Nicks is a legend in its own lunchtime, crammed with shopaholics trying to find the latest trend. When you get tired there's a good brasserie on the ground floor. Their window displays are famed for their wit.

PETER JONES
Sloane Sq, SW1
☎ 020-7730 3434
Part of the excellent John Lewis chain, Peter Jones offers clothing, accessories

Stop off at Harvey Nichols on the way to Chelsea

and household goods as well as glass and china and a large haberdashery department. Very popular with the locals as well as tourists.

FASHION

A LA MODE
36 Hans Crescent, SW1
☎ 020-7584 2133
Designer fashions such as Hervé Leger and his contemporaries.

BETTY JACKSON
311 Brompton Rd, SW3
☎ 020-7589 7884
Off-the-peg semi-designer wear incorporating style and comfort.

DOLCE & GABBANA
175 Sloane St, SW1
☎ 020-7235 0335
Wild and frothy designs for those who have everything.

EMPORIO ARMANI
187-191 Brompton Rd, SW3
☎ 020-7823 8818
The slightly cheaper street version of Giorgio Armani's empire, but still offering very high-quality suits and knitwear for men and women.

GUCCI
17-18 Sloane St, SW1
☎ 020-7235 6707
One of fashion's most famous names, specialising in watches, handbags and shirts.

HACKETT
136-138 Sloane St, SW1
☎ 020-7730 3331
High quality tweedy casuals for English gentlemen.

ISSEY MIYAKE
270 Brompton Rd, SW1
☎ 020-7581 3760
The Japanese designer hit London in a big way and is still here, offering fabulous fabrics in all his creations. Pricey and sensuous.

JEAN PAUL GAULTIER
171-175 Draycott Ave, SW3
☎ 020-7584 4648
Gaultier is famous for his French eccentricity, best known in England for his kilts, hosting C4's *Eurotrash* show and dressing pop stars like Björk. Here his designs are slightly tempered, to make them more wearable.

JOSEPH
77 Fulham Rd, SW3
& 26 Sloane Street, SW1
☎ 020-7823 9500
☎ 020-7235 5470
Joseph carries a range of high fashion ranges, as well as its own range of knitwear.

An unusual display on the King's Road

KATHARINE HAMNETT
20 Sloane St, SW3
☎ 020-7823 1002
Very stylish and simple designs from a designer branching out into environmental campaigning.

MAXMARA
32 Sloane St, SW3
☎ 020-7235 7941
This is designer wear on a no-nonsense level. Perfect for work clothing.

PRADA
44 Sloane St, SW3
☎ 020-7235 0008
An absolute must since the supermodels began to wear their clothes and carry their handbags.

WORLD'S END
430 King's Rd, SW3
☎ 020-7352 6551
Vivienne Westwood's second shop. Eccentric and often humorous fashion. Don't set your watch by the clock above the door. It runs backwards.

CAROLINE CHARLES
56 Beauchamp Pl, SW3
☎ 020-7589 5850
A very popular designer collection with attractive, feminine clothing.

HIGH & MIGHTY
81-83 Knightsbridge, SW1
☎ 020-7589 7454
Menswear for those men with unusual measurements - up to 6ft 3in and 60in waistline are catered for.

JANET REGER
2 Beauchamp Pl, SW3
☎ 020-7584 9360
If you want glamorous lingerie, this is the best place to head for.

MANOLO BLAHNIK
49-51 Old Church St, SW3
☎ 020-7352 3863
Very expensive, but very individual shoes.

HOUSEHOLD ACCESSORIES

CONRAN SHOP
Michelin House, 81 Fulham Rd, SW3
☎ 020-7589 7401
Furniture and soft furnishings in wonderful modern designs, as well as kitchenware and accessories for all over the home.

King's Road

Owned by Sir Terence Conran, the creator of Habitat and Heals, this is a well-loved store of those with plenty in their bank accounts.

DESIGNERS GUILD
267-271 & 275-277 King's Rd, SW3
☎ 020-7351 5775
Household accessories such as linen and crockery, all in bright, lively colours.

GARDENS

FULHAM PALACE GARDEN CENTRE
Bishop's Ave, off Fulham Palace Rd, SW6
☎ 020-7736 2640
A delightful find in the midst of Fulham mayhem. Reasonably priced plants, trees and flowers, as well as all the garden statuary and stone you could want.

JEWELLERY

BUTLER & WILSON
189 Fulham Rd, SW3
☎ 0171-352 8255
Modern jewellery covering a wide range from art deco to present day - earrings, rings, costume jewellery.

GIFTS

GENERAL TRADING COMPANY
144 Sloane St, SW7
☎ 020-7730 0411
A fashionable store, and well known for its royal wedding lists.

ROCOCO
321 King's Rd, SW3
☎ 020-7352 5857
A wide range of seriously delicious chocolates for all occasions.

OGGETTI
135 Fulham Rd, SW3
☎ 020-7581 8088
Very stylish gifts for those who have everything else. Executive toys available.

THE TINTIN SHOP
60 Sloane Ave, SW3
☎ 020-7838 0901
Belgian's best-known cultural export is Hergé's irrepressible boy detective. This shop carries every possible item imaginable that pertains to Tintin and his comic colleagues, Snowy, Professor Calculus and Captain Haddock.

Call the AA Hotel Booking Service on 0870 5050505 to book at AA recognised hotels and B&Bs in the UK, or through our internet site: http://www.theaa.co.uk/hotels

Time is reversed at Vivienne Westwood's World's End

WHERE TO STAY
HOTELS
AA RECOMMENDED

★★★★★ ✿ ✿ ✿ ✿ ✿ **THE BERKELEY**
Wilton Place, Knightsbridge SW1X 7RL
(300mtrs along Knightsbridge from Hyde Park Corner)
☎ **020 7235 6000** 🖨 **020 7235 4330**
Considered a bench-mark for the very best in hotel-keeping and service, the Berkeley has an excellent range of bedrooms, some with sizeable balconies. Reception rooms, including the Lutyens Writing Room, are adorned with magnificent flower arrangements, and there are superb leisure facilities. The two restaurants offer a complete contrast of style: modern, influenced by South-East Asia, at Vong (two rosettes), and French cuisine at La Tante Claire (five rosettes), where Pierre Koffmann presides.
168 rooms (28 no smoking) / French & Thai Cuisine / Indoor swimming pool (heated) / Sauna, Solarium, Gym / Lift, Night porter, Air cond / No dogs (ex guide dogs) / No coaches
Price band £££ ⌐

★★★★★ ✿ **CONRAD INTERNATIONAL LONDON**
Chelsea Harbour SW10 0XG
(A4 Earls Court Rd south towards river. Right into Kings Rd left down Lots Rd Chelsea Harbour is in front of you)
☎ **020 7823 3000** 🖨 **020 7351 6525**
This modern hotel is set in a smart development overlooking a small marina at Chelsea Harbour. The superbly equipped private suites come with spacious bathrooms and separate WCs. There is an excellent range of leisure facilities and meeting rooms. The restaurant is informally styled and has a modern menu with 'fusion' influences.
160 rooms (41 family & 62 no smoking) / International Cuisine / Indoor swimming pool (heated) / Sauna, Solarium, Gym, Steam room / Live entertainment / Lift, Night porter, Air conditioning / No coaches
Price band £££ ⌐

Conrad International

★★★★★ ✿ ✿ **HYATT CARLTON TOWER**
Cadogan Place SW1X 9PY
(turn down Sloane St, Cadogan Place is the second turning on the left immediately before Pont St)
☎ **020 7235 1234** 🖨 **020 7235 9129**
In the heart of Knightsbridge, the Hyatt Carlton Tower offers modern bedrooms and bright public areas. Extra facilities are impressive. The ground floor houses the Chinoiserie lounge and Rib Room restaurant with its clubby bar. Modern Italian cooking (Two Rosettes) is on offer in the friendly Grissini restaurant.
220 rooms (61 no smoking) / English & Italian / Indoor swimming pool (heated) / Tennis (hard) / Sauna, Solarium, Gym, Jacuzzi/spa / Beauty treatment / Hair salon / Live entertainment / Lift, Night porter, Air cond / No dogs (ex guide dogs) / No coaches
Price band £££ ⌐

★★★★★ ✿ ✿ ✿ **LANESBOROUGH**
Hyde Park Corner SW1X 7TA
(follow signs to central London and Hyde Park Corner)
☎ **020 7259 5599** 🖨 **020 7259 5606**
Occupying an enviable position on Hyde Park Corner, the Lanesborough offers very high levels of comfort. Twenty-four-hour service from a personal butler ensures that guests are well catered for, and the reception rooms, with their lavish furnishings and magnificent flower arrangements, are delightful. The popular cocktail bar has a wonderful supply of vintage cognac, whiskies and ports, and the conservatory restaurant offers an attractive atmosphere for dining.
95 rooms (24 no smoking) / International Cuisine / Gym, Jacuzzi/spa, Fitness studio / Live entertainment / Lift, Night porter, Air cond / No coaches
Price band £££ ⌐

★★★★★ ✿ ✿ ✿ **MANDARIN ORIENTAL HYDE PARK**
66 Knightsbridge SW1X 7LA
(after passing Harrods, on the righthand side, the hotel is 0.5m on the left opposite Harvey Nichols department store)
☎ **020 7235 2000** 🖨 **020 7235 4552**
Situated between Knightsbridge and Hyde Park, this famous hotel offers a luxurious atmosphere. Marble is used to elegant effect in the reception areas, which include a popular cocktail lounge and the principal restaurant, The Park, where dishes exhibit subtle flavours and combine high quality ingredients. The standard of food, accommodation and service are all excellent.
200 rooms (72 no smoking) / English & European Cuisine / Gym, Fitness centre / Live entertainment / Lift, Night porter, Air cond / No dogs (ex guide dogs) / No coaches
Price band £££ ⌐

Mandarin Oriental

★★★★★⊛ ⊛ ⊛ **SHERATON PARK TOWER**
101 Knightsbridge SW1X 7RN
(close to Knightsbridge Underground Station)
☎ 020 7235 8050 & 7235 3368 Res
🖷 020 7235 3368
This unusual circular hotel offers good standard-sized bedrooms, while the more exclusive rooms enjoy full butler service. Refurbished public areas have a lively atmosphere; the main bar off the lobby has a 'clubby' feel with tasteful polo prints; afternoon tea can be taken in the Rotunda Lounge. Restaurant One-O-One earns Three AA Rosettes, and is overseen by Chef Pascal Proyart, whose cuisine de la mer is excellent.
289 room (all suitable for families & 80 no smoking) / French Cuisine / Health facilities at affiliated club / Live entertainment / Lift, Night porter, Air cond / No dogs (ex guide dogs)
Price band £££ 🍽

★★★★⊛ ⊛ ⊛ **CAPITAL**
Basil St, Knightsbridge SW3 1AT
☎ 020 7589 5171 🖷 020 7225 0011
In the heart of Knightsbridge, this small and exclusive hotel offers individually designed bedrooms featuring hand-made furniture. Public areas are furnished to the same high standard. Dinner in the restaurant is a real treat.
48 rooms / French Cuisine / Lift, Night porter, Air cond / No coaches
Price band £££ 🍽

★★★★⊛ ⊛ **THE CHELSEA**
17 Sloane St, Knightsbridge SW1X 9NU
(from A4, Sloane St is located on the left, just past Harrods. Access to the hotel is also available via Pavilion Road)
☎ 020 7235 4377 🖷 020 7235 3705
This Sloane Street hotel is near Harrods, Harvey Nichols and many designer boutiques. All bedrooms have been refurbished to a high standard with an excellent range of modern facilities. The lounge on the ground floor is popular for coffee and snacks, while the bright and airy restaurant is the setting for some seriously enjoyable food.
222 rooms (70 no smoking) / International Cuisine / Lift, Night porter, Air cond / No dogs / No coaches
Price band £££ 🍽

Sheraton Park Tower

★★★★⊛ **CHELSEA VILLAGE**
Stamford Bridge, Fulham Rd SW6 1HS
☎ 020 7565 1400 🖷 020 7565 1450
This exciting new hotel forms part of the ambitious developments at Chelsea Football Club, and is a bold modern structure just next door to the ground. Bedrooms are well equipped and the range of public areas includes four different styles of eating: modern and global at Kings Brasserie, Irish, seafood, and finally, in the sport-themed Shed Bar, pub food.
160 rooms (64 family & 56 no smoking) / Lift, Night porter, Air cond / No dogs (ex guide dogs)
Price band £££ 🍽

★★★★⊛ ⊛ **GORING**
Beeston Place, Grosvenor Gardens SW1W 0JW
(behind Buckingham Palace, right off Lower Grosvenor Place, just prior to the Royal Mews on the left)
☎ 020 7396 9000 🖷 020 7834 4393
Run by the Goring family since 1910, this hotel is a superb example of British traditional hotel keeping. Bedrooms are beautifully furnished and provide all the modern facilities one would expect from such a highly regarded hotel. Reception rooms include the garden bar and drawing room, both popular for afternoon tea and cocktails. The restaurant menu has a classic repertoire as well as more modern dishes.
75 rooms / English & French Cuisine / Free membership of nearby Health Club / Live entertainment / Lift, Night porter, Air cond / No dogs / No coaches
Price band £££ 🍽

★★★★⊛ ⊛ ⊛ **HALKIN**
Halkin St, Belgravia SW1X 7DJ
☎ 020 7333 1000 🖷 020 7333 1100
The Halkin is one of the more individual of the capital's top hotels combining the best of modern design with attention to detail. The interior has a cool, relaxed atmosphere and bedrooms have state of the art business communications, lighting and air-conditioning control systems. Service is polished and friendly without being intrusive. Stefano Cavallini's modern Italian cooking continues to set high standards.
41 rooms (9 no smoking) / Italian Cuisine / Live entertainment / Lift, Night porter, Air cond / No dogs (ex guide dogs) / No coaches
Price band £££ 🍽

★★★★⊛ **THE LOWNDES**
21 Lowndes St SW1X 9ES
☎ 020 7823 1234 🖷 020 7235 1154
High standards of accommodation and facilities combine with a welcoming atmosphere and excellent service to make the Lowndes hotel a popular choice. Many of the smartly decorated bedrooms and suites have balconies, and in-room dining and 24-hour room service are alternatives to the brasserie. Concierge service and car-parking arrangements are available.
78 rooms (31 no smoking) / International Cuisine / Indoor swimming pool (heated) / Tennis (hard) / Sauna, Gym, Jacuzzi/spa / Lift, Night porter, Air cond / No dogs (ex guide dogs) / No coaches
🍽

★★★★ **THE RUBENS AT THE PALACE**
Buckingham Palace Rd SW1W 0PS
(opposite the Royal Mews)
☎ 020 7834 6600 🖷 020 7233 6037
Overlooking the Royal Mews, behind Buckingham Palace and close to Victoria Station, the Rubens offers bedrooms and public areas that are very comfortable and well appointed. There is a good choice of eating in the two restaurants and also an extensive lounge menu. Room service provides hot dishes throughout the night.
174 rooms (64 no smoking) / English & French Cuisine / Live entertainment / Lift, Night porter, Air cond / No dogs (ex guide dogs)
Price band £££ 🍽

Goring

The Lowndes Hyatt

⭑⭑⭑⭑ THISTLE ROYAL WESTMINSTER

49 Buckingham Palace Rd SW1W 0QT

(opposite the Royal Mews)

☎ 020 7834 1821 📠 020 7931 7542

There is a cosy atmosphere at this discreetly located hotel close to Buckingham Palace and Victoria. One of its strengths is the size of the bedrooms which are spacious by city centre standards. Smartly-dressed staff are friendly and willing to help out. A street-facing brasserie, Le Café, is the setting for informal dining.

134 room (6 family & 67 no smoking) / English & French / Lift, Night porter, Air cond / No dogs (ex guide dogs)

Price band £££ 🍽

The Lowndes Hyatt

⭑⭑⭑⭑ THISTLE VICTORIA

Buckingham Palace Rd, Victoria SW1W 0SJ

(adjacent to Victoria railway station)

☎ 020 7834 9494 📠 020 7630 1978

This Victorian landmark has had a recent facelift to some public areas which has resulted in a clean façade and stunning reception foyer. There is also a lounge, popular for afternoon tea, the quaint Harvard bar and the Clarence restaurant with its friendly team of staff. Bedrooms, which vary in size and outlook, have some attractive features.

366 rooms (35 family & 129 no smoking) / Lift, Night porter / No dogs (ex guide dogs)

🍽

⭑⭑⭑ 🏵 BASIL STREET

Basil St, Knightsbridge SW3 1AH

☎ 020 7581 3311 📠 020 7581 3693

Built in the Edwardian era, the Basil Street Hotel aims to re-create the atmosphere of those days. Day rooms, with their parquet floors, comfortable armchairs and antiques, suggest more a country-house setting than a city hotel. Bedrooms also follow a traditional style of furnishings, but have up-to-date facilities. An enjoyable range of dishes is served in the dining room.

93 rooms (2 family & 6 no smoking) / English & Continental Cuisine / Live entertainment / Lift, Night porter / No coaches

🍽

⭑⭑⭑ PARAGON HOTEL

47 Lillie Rd SW6 1UD

(A4 to central London,0.5m after Hammersmith flyover turn right at traffic lights into North End Rd follow for 0.5m to mini rdbt left into Lillie Rd)

☎ 020 7385 1255 📠 020 7381 0215

This well established hotel is ideally located for the Earls Court Exhibition Centre. There are extensive conference facilities and the bedrooms are modern and well equipped. Two restaurants offer the choice of light meals and pizzas or more formal traditional menus. There is an underground car-park.

501 rooms (96 no smoking) / International Cuisine / Lift, Night porter / No dogs (ex guide dogs)

Price band £££ 🍽

⌂ THE BEAUFORT

33 Beaufort Gardens SW3 1PP

(100yds from Harrods)

☎ 020 7584 5252 📠 020 7589 2834

Harrods is the local neighbourhood store of the Beaufort, a townhouse which stands in a quiet, leafy square only 100 yards or so from the world-famous emporium. The hotel offers guests every comfort and luxury in its well equipped bedrooms - chocolates, flowers, bathrobes, books and videos can all be taken for granted. Service is attentive.

28 rooms (7 family & 6 no smoking) / Lift, Night porter, Air cond / No dogs (ex guide dogs) / No coaches

Price band £££ 🍽

The Beaufort

⌂ CLIVEDEN TOWNHOUSE

26 Cadogan Gardens SW3 2RP

☎ 020 7730 6466 📠 020 7730 0236

As is expected from the Cliveden group, this townhouse bears all the hallmarks of quality and style and is only yards away from Sloane Square. Bedrooms are beautifully furnished and have luxurious appointments. Day rooms consist of two lounges, where refreshments are served, and there is also a sheltered garden. A complimentary executive car chauffeurs guests to the City twice each morning.

35 rooms (9 family & 30 no smoking) / Gym, Beauty treatment. Massage / Lift, Night porter, Air cond / No coaches

Price band £££ 🍽

⌂ **PARKES**

41 Beaufort Gardens, Knightsbridge SW3 1PW

(off Brompton Road, 150yds from Harrods)

☎ **020 7581 9944** ⊕ **020 7581 1999**

Only five minutes from Knightsbridge and the world of fashionable shopping, this charming little townhouse is set in a peaceful square. Its well equipped suites come in a range of sizes, and each has a kitchenette. Breakfast is served in an attractive dining room and there is a small lounge.

33 rooms (16 family) / Lift, Night porter, Air cond / No dogs (ex guide dogs) / No coaches

Price band £££

BED & BREAKFAST
AA RECOMMENDED

♦♦♦♦ **CLAVERLEY HOUSE**

13-14 Beaufort Gardens, Knightsbridge SW3 1PS

(take M4/A4 into London. East on Brompton Rd, Beaufort Gdns is 6th on right after Victoria & Albert Museum)

☎ **020 7589 8541** ⊕ **020 7584 3410**

In a quiet tree-lined cul-de-sac, the Claverley Hotel is only a stroll from Harrods. Bedrooms have bath or shower en suite, and each has an individual style and character. The reading room has comfortable leather Chesterfields, and hot refreshments. A substantial full English breakfast is provided in the elegant dining room.

30 rooms (7 family & 20 no smoking) / No dogs (ex guide dogs) / Lift / No coaches

Price band

♦♦♦♦ **WILLETT HOTEL**

32 Sloane Gardens, Sloane Square SW1W 8DJ

(10mins walk SW of Harrods in Sloane Square opposite tube station)

☎ **020 7824 8415** ⊕ **020 7730 4830**

A beautiful Victorian town house in a tree-lined street off Sloane Square. The hotel has been furnished to a high standard, and all rooms are designed in keeping with the building. A good range of modern facilities is provided. Breakfast is served in the elegant dining room, and room service is available.

19 rooms (4 family) / No dogs (ex guide dogs) / No coaches

Price band £££

♦♦♦ **THE EXECUTIVE HOTEL**

57 Pont St, Knightsbridge SW1X 0BD

(left out of Knightsbridge Tube, past Harrods, left into Beecham Place, Pont St straight ahead, establishment on right)

☎ **020 7581 2424** ⊕ **020 7589 9456**

Enjoying a central location in Knightsbridge, this attractive Victorian terrace house is popular with both business and leisure guests. Bedrooms vary in size, are comfortably appointed and well equipped with modern facilities. Continental breakfast is included in the tariff, but extra is charged for English. Guests also have use of a small lounge complete with honesty bar.

27 rooms (3 family) / Lift

Price band £££

♦♦ **ANNANADALE HOUSE HOTEL**

39 Sloane Gardens, Sloane Square SW1W 8EB

(1 min walk from Sloane Square tube station)

☎ **020 7730 6291 & 7730 505**

⊕ **020 7730 2727**

This attractive red brick building is in a prime location, just a few minutes walk from Sloane Square. Some bedrooms are rather compact. Guests may enjoy the walled garden in the summer months.

15 rooms (4 family) / No dogs / No coaches

Price band ££

RESTAURANTS
AA RECOMMENDED

❀ ❀ ❀ AUBERGINE
11 Park Walk SW10
☎ 020 7352 3449 📠 020 7351 1770
William Drabble is now firmly at home in this small Chelsea restaurant, offering both imagination and luxuries in abundance. However, there is proper thought for techniques which coax brilliant flavours from such prime raw materials. Roasted red mullet with a goats' cheese and basil tortellini reveals an enjoyment of fish cookery and desserts have been extolled to the heavens. The lengthy wine list offers a good, broad selection and plenty of choice by the glass.
Fixed L £ Fixed D £££

Bibendum

❀ ❀ BASIL STREET HOTEL
Basil Street Knightsbridge SW3 1AH
☎ 020 7581 3311 📠 020 7581 3693
Traditional-style restaurant on the first floor of this historic, splendidly old-fashioned hotel. The menu includes home-made soups and pâtés, with main courses such as liver and bacon, and roast cod.
Fixed L £ ALC ££

❀ ❀ ❀ BIBENDUM
Michelin House 81 Fulham Road SW3 6RD
☎ 020 7581 5817 📠 020 7823 7925
It's now over a decade since Sir Terence Conran and his partners converted the Art Deco Michelin building into ground-floor oyster bar and first-floor restaurant. Forget Eurostarring to Paris - this is the place for fried frogs' legs with warm potato purée and black truffles, escargots de Bourgogne and jambon persillé with sauce gribiche. The high spot of dessert is still a huge wedge of chocolate tart: excellent crisp pastry containing a deep filling, with sumptuous pistachio ice cream. The wine list must be one of the best in the land, if pricy, but there are plenty of more approachable bottles too.
Fixed L ££

❀ ❀ BLUEBIRD
350 King's Road SW3 5UU
☎ 020 7559 1000 📠 020 7559 1111
As alive as ever, with the flower shop, street café, kitchen shop and posh supermarket all busy. Overlooking all of this is the vast, hugely popular restaurant, all neutral tones, natural light, soaring Bluebird giant kites overhead, and prompt staff. Sensibly, given the numbers that pass through each day, the kitchen is produce led. Crustacea feature but other must-haves are classics such as sirloin with béarnaise or Chateaubriand (for two) with perfect matchstick fries.
Fixed L/D £ ALC ££

❀ ❀ CADOGAN HOTEL
75 Sloane Street SW1X 9SG
☎ 020 7235 7141 📠 020 7245 0994
A formal Edwardian hotel restaurant with leaden windows, intricate plasterwork and a variety of decorative plates, mirrors and paintings adorning the cream-painted walls. The kitchen works in the modern British style, but with a strong classical base: pan-fried foie gras on a potato galette with a Sancerre and grape butter, for example, but true Brit classics abound as well. The wine list is comprehensive and features a good selection of half-bottles.
Fixed L £ ALC £££

❀ CAMBIO DE TERCIO
163 Old Brompton Road SW5 0LJ
☎ 020 7244 8970 📠 020 7373 8817
Abstracts based on bullfighting themes adorn the walls of this small, bustling Spanish restaurant. An impressive range of sherries and good-value tapas give way to the likes of seafood and chicken paella, suckling pig Segovian-style and beef fillet with port wine.
ALC ££

❀ ❀ ❀ THE CANTEEN
Harbour Yard Chelsea Harbour SW10 0XD
☎ 020 7351 7330 📠 020 7351 6189
This could be Marbella if the sun were shining and the temperature higher. The conservatory-style front section of the Canteen is the best for watching the boats and bustle of Chelsea Harbour's marina. The restaurant's cool, elegant decor of pale yellow and parquet floor forms an impressive backdrop to the smart, accomplished modern British cooking. Skill with puddings shows up in the chef's assiette of perfectly smooth crème caramel, tangy sorbets sitting on tiny meringues, and chocolate mousse on sponge wrapped in a dark and shiny chocolate ribbon.
Fixed L £ ALC ££

❀ ❀ ❀ THE CAPITAL
Basil Street Knightsbridge SW3 1AT
☎ 020 7589 5171 📠 020 7225 0011
Eric Chavot is a skilful chef capable of the sort of great cooking that stays long in the memory. Confidence and clarity are the words that come to mind when describing his cooking. Chilled tomato consommé with red mullet was a study on the themes of hot and cold - the fillet sitting on a circle of warm potato in the centre of the plate, all elements packed with flavour. More striking tastes and textures with a main course of pan-fried brill with

Bluebird

Chutney Mary Restaurant

fèves and petit pois, lightly doused in a frothy mushroom flavoured sauce and a few dots of highly flavoured basil oil. Warm chocolate marbre with coconut sorbet was a skilled version of this increasingly popular gooey dessert cake.
Fixed L £ Fixed D £££ ALC £££

❀ ❀ CARAFFINI
61-63 Lower Sloane Street SW1W 8DH
☎ 020 7259 0235 ☏ 020 7259 0236
Sloane Square's local neighbourhood Italian. Caraffini has lots to commend it: fresh and prettily decked out in pale blues and yellows, flower filled, and stage-managed by Italian waiters in pale-blue shirts who play to the audience; regulars are greeted by name and made much of. The long menu lists mostly trattoria-style dishes, but also includes some simple chargrills. The wine list is reasonably priced.
ALC ££

❀ CHELSEA VILLAGE HOTEL
Stamford Bridge, Fulham Road SW6 1HS
☎ 020 7565 1400 ☏ 020 7565 1450
A must for Chelsea football fans - hard by the stadium! Kings Brasserie has a striking modern look and a menu full of global influences. In other words, dishes range from beef, mushroom and stout pie to seared tuna teriyaki.
ALC ££

❀ ❀ CHEZ MAX
168 Ifield Road SW10 9AF
☎ 020 7835 0874 ☏ 020 7244 0618
Bistro-style atmosphere with attentive, knowledgeable service. The French cooking is both imaginative and good; attention to detail shows in home-marinated olives, baked olive-oil bread and super Charentais butter. Bourgeoise classics include terrine de jambon persillé, blanquette de veau, and pigeon d'Anjou roti aux raisins de Muscat confit et aux morilles, and a tarte au citron was up amongst the greats with its sharp flavour and perfect base.
Fixed L £ Fixed D ££

❀ CHUTNEY MARY RESTAURANT
535 King's Road Chelsea SW10 0SZ
☎ 020 7351 3113/7658 ☏ 020 7351 7694
A stylish Indian evoking the comfortable days of the British Raj. The bright menus take you on a trail-blazing tour of the Indian regions: try a medium-spiced roast duck curry from Kerala, an earthy rogan josh from Kashmir, or a fiery prawn curry from Mangalore.
Fixed L £ ALC ££

❀ THE COLLECTION
264 Brompton Road SW3
☎ 020 7225 1212 ☏ 020 7225 1050
Former fashion warehouse is home to a lively groundfloor bar and mezzanine restaurant. Interesting menus include exotic dishes such as steamed foie gras, pork dumplings with chilli honey dip on the mezzanine; simple noodle and salad dishes on the ground floor.

❀ CONRAD INTERNATIONAL
Chelsea Harbour SW10 0XG
☎ 020 7823 3000 ☏ 020 7351 6525
Mediterranean-style views over the marina set this hotel restaurant apart. Vibrant dishes range from Caesar salad and baked oysters 'Muscovite', to spiced duck with red cabbage, chargrilled lamb with herb and mustard jus and, for pudding, warm raspberry tart.

❀ DAN'S RESTAURANT
119 Sydney Street SW3 6NR
☎ 020 7352 2718 ☏ 020 7352 3265
Something of a place to be seen where the proprietor, the eponymous Dan Whitehead, personally greets his regulars. Look out for the excellent value set lunch menu.

❀ ❀ DAPHNE'S
110-112 Draycott Avenue SW3 3AE
☎ 020 7589 4257 ☏ 020 7581 2232
Chic Chelsea hang-out. The 'designed' interior blends a combination of bare brick and brightly coloured plaster walls with flagstone floors to give a strong Mediterranean look that matches the modern Italian menu. The kitchen delivers soundly prepared grills, roasts, pastas, and risottos, as well as substantial salads that would satisfy more than the loyal clientele of ladies-who-lunch.

❀ ❀ DRONES OF PONT STREET
1 Pont Street SW1X 9EJ
☎ 020 7259 6166 ☏ 020 7259 6177
Decor is cool and chic, as befits any Knightsbridge eatery, with apricot walls and wrought iron chairs. Note pan-Mediterranean cooking, with an emphasis on Italian, and lunch and dinner menus that differ little apart from price. Even if you don't sport the obligatory designer accessories and are without a mobile phone, staff are friendly enough not to make you feel like a hick.

❀ ❀ FIFTH FLOOR RESTAURANT
Harvey Nichols Knightsbridge SW1X 7RJ
☎ 020 7235 5250 ☏ 020 7823 2209
Busy, buzzy restaurant sharing the fifth floor of Harvey Nicks with a food and wine shop, café and sushi bar. Beyond a sizeable bar (bar meals at lunch, snacks at night) the vaulted restaurant offers a fixed-price lunch and slightly longer evening carte. Foodwise the style is mainstream modern without eccentricity.
Fixed L ££

❀ ❀ ❀ FLORIANA
15 Beauchamp Place SW3 1NQ
☎ 020 7838 1500 ☏ 020 7584 1464
Chic, fashionable restaurant attracting more than the Hello! crowd. Fabio Trabocchi is a chef to watch, with a brilliant style of new Italian cooking that is as different from the River Café as that is, in turn, from check-clothed trattorias. His background with the legendary Gualtiero Marchesi shows in the way he daringly takes ingredients and techniques further and further down a complex, modernist path without losing sight of home values. The setting is Chelsea cool; the food makes the flash bulbs pop.
Fixed L £ ALC £££

❀ ❀ FOUNDATION
Harvey Nichols Seville Street Knightsbridge SW1X 7RJ
☎ 020 7201 8000 ☏ 020 7201 8080
Stylish eatery, clamorous bar, located in the basement of Harvey Nichols. A continuous flowing water wall with green and silver lighting running the length of the bar provides a sense of glacial cool in this modern interior, which is simply furnished with plain wood and steel-framed chairs. The overall cooking style is Mediterranean with light lunches (no division indicated between first and main courses). However, the cooking shifts up a gear in the evening.
Fixed L £ ALC ££

❀ ❀ GORING HOTEL

Beeston Place Grosvenor Gardens SW1W 0JW

☎ 020 7396 9000 📠 020 7834 4393

Personally run by the Goring family since 1910, a superb example of the true British tradition of hotel-keeping and hospitality. The Dining Room, with its highly regarded wine list, proffers many old favourites such as grilled Dover sole and lobster Thermidor alongside more contemporary choices. Large carver chairs accommodate the most ample and staff bustle around attending to every whim.

Fixed L ££ ALC £££

❀ ❀ THE HALKIN HOTEL, STEFANO CAVALLINI AT THE HALKIN

Halkin Street Belgravia SW1X 7DJ

☎ 020 7333 1000 📠 020 7333 1100

The dining room of this super-smart hotel is serene and cool, the staff dressed in Armani. This is not just modern Italian cooking, it is 'La Cucina Essenziale', derived from research into ancient Italian culinary traditions but reinterpreted in the light of today's taste and way of life. Stefano Cavallini seeks to replace heavy sauces, fats and cream, with vegetable broth, olive oil and other more suitable elements, and cooking styles are chosen to preserve nutrients and essential flavours. Well, that's what the blurb says, and, remarkably, the actual cooking lives up to the billing. There is a serious wine operation under the guidance of a well-informed and helpful sommelier.

Fixed L ££ ALC £££

❀ ❀ HYATT CARLTON TOWER HOTEL, GRISSINI

Cadogan Place SW1X 9PY

☎ 020 7858 7171 📠 020 7235 9129

Subtly lit, modern and comfortable and done out in natural colours, with a teak floor and lavender banquettes. Conservatory-style windows give views over the gardens of Cadogan Place, and a domed glass roof creates an alfresco atmosphere. The menus might convert sterling to the Euro, but modern Italian is the currency the kitchen deals in, from tuna carpaccio with aged balsamic, olives and Parmesan shavings, to pan-fried duck breast glazed with Vin Santo. You have to ask to see the list of non-Italian wines, but why bother when virtually every Italian region is represented among over 80 bottles?

Fixed L £ ALC ££

❀ ❀ ❀ MANDARIN ORIENTAL HYDE PARK, THE PARK RESTAURANT

66 Knightsbridge SW1X 7LA

☎ 020 7235 2000 📠 020 7235 4552

Grand hotel dining room with high ceilings, chandeliers and formal staff. David Nicholl's has certainly found his feet since moving on from the Ritz, offering simple concepts, clean, fresh, flavours bags of taste, all executed immaculately. Sweet grilled scallops with haricot vert and herb salad, anchovies, piles of ripe tomato concasse with a chiffonade of basil and a few olive pieces, and a plate of signature pot-roast pork: tongue, temple, cheek, all meltingly gelatinous with a piece of brain giving creamy soft velvet notes, with buttered iceberg lettuce, asparagus, and a ravioli of wild mushroom set the pace. Time spent by Nichol's pastry chef in the kitchens of Alain Ducasse shows through in a real tour de force assiette of chocolate dessert. Even after this petits fours still manage to be as good as they ever get.

Fixed L £ ALC ££

❀ ❀ MEMORIES OF CHINA RESTAURANT

67 Ebury Street SW1W 0NZ

☎ 020 7730 7734/4276 📠 020 7730 2992

Comfortable wicker armchairs in the bar area, screens acting as partitions, solicitous and efficient staff are what you'll find at this upmarket Chinese. A number of fixed-price menus are on offer, from a quick executive luncheon to an imperial Mandarin-style banquet, or mix-and-match according to taste from the carte: The wine list is a round-the-world affair. Those who don't want wine could wash it all down with saké (also sold by the quarter- and half-bottle) or Tsingtao beer.

Fixed L/D £ ALC ££

❀ ❀ MILLENNIUM CHELSEA

17 Sloane Street Knightsbridge SW1X 9NU

☎ 020 7235 4377 📠 020 7235 3705

Upscale setting for a cosmo crowd. The blending of Sloane Street prices and European food with an Asian influence is impressive. Kitchen skills are evident and the menu contains some interesting and ambitious ideas along the lines of lobster tail on aubergine moutabel with red wine syrup and capsicum fritter, or supreme of duckling with thyme and wild cranberries. Non-English speaking staff cruise the room.

Fixed L £ ALC £££

❀ ❀ MONKEY'S

1 Cale Street Chelsea Green SW3 3QT

☎ 020 7352 4711

A neighbourhood restaurant of long-standing. Indeed, nothing much has changed since it opened. The combination of the monkey-themed decor and highly attentive service makes this an ideal eating place for both business suits and Chelsea locals, and it succeeds in being 'all things to all people', with reasonable variety and scope to be found within the two set-price menus. There is a reasonable wine list and knowledgeable service.

❀ ❀ OLIVO

21 Eccleston Street SW1W 9LX

☎ 020 7730 2505 📠 020 7824 8190

Striking Italian swathed in Med sand and azure blue tones. Dishes veer towards rustic, displaying a marked Sardinian influence: chargrilled stuffed baby squid with sweet plum tomatoes and basil, say, or lamb casserole with wild fennel and mash.

Fixed L £ ALC ££

❀ ❀ ❀ ❀ RESTAURANT GORDON RAMSAY

66 Royal Hospital Road SW3 4HP

☎ 020 7352 4441 📠 020 7352 3334

It is sometimes hard to separate Ramsay the Chef from Ramsay the Notorious, but perhaps only those with huge talent can get away with such publicity - and no one doubts Ramsay is well endowed with the right stuff. For anyone just tuning in, the old Tante Claire premises have been updated, with panels of opaque glass and cappuccino (how apt!) beige suede seats creating a more spacious, lighter effect. The three-course menu is interspersed by morsels of delicious things: just to keep you going before the dessert, for example, all guests are offered a painter's palette of tiny cornets filled with passion fruit cream, a tiny glass of ice cream and a mini lemon balm brûlée. Coffee and sweetmeats bring the binge to its memorable close. The sommelier has a charmingly unpretentious manner, and although young possesses an encyclopaedic knowledge of his subject.

Fixed L ££ ALC £££

❀ ❀ RHODES IN THE SQUARE

Dolphin Square Chichester Street SW1V 3LX

☎ 0171 7986767 📠 0171 7985685

Everything adds up to a relaxed and comfortable environment, with armchair-type chairs that are great for slouching at Gary Rhodes' Pimlico branch. Lobster omelette Thermidor is now something of a signature dish, with main courses in the shape of loin of pork, perfectly cooked with crackling, sage-sautéed onions, apple

Rhodes in the Square

and mashed potatoes. Jaffa-cake pudding, dense of texture and flavour, comes drizzled with strong chocolate sauce hinting of Grand Marnier.

Fixed L £ ALC £££

❀ ❀ RISTORANTE L'INCONTRO
87 Pimlico Road SW1W 8PH

☎ 020 7730 3663/6327

✆ 020 7730 5062

Lord Linley has been commissioned to update the party room of this ultra-fashionable establishment, and the colour schemes are all set to change. However, the food remains the same. There is a reasonable set lunch, but when the action takes off in the evenings, prices rocket accordingly. The menu has a strong Venetian theme, and the strength lies in flavour rather than presentation. The wine list is predominantly, but not entirely, Italian, and extremely expensive.

Fixed L £ ALC £££

❀ ❀ ❀ ROUSSILLON
16 St Barnabas Street SW1W 8PB

☎ 020 7730 5550 ✆ 020 7824 8617

It is rare to find somewhere so truly original in this age of camp followers and overworked trends. Alexis Gaulthier comes with an impressive pedigree, via Alain Ducasse and Chez Panisse, but is blazing his own path. Menus are strictly seasonal, even the covers depict the appropriate seasonal plants. Ingredients are wonderful - organic Ross chicken, organic Scottish beef, Welsh lamb, Blue Bembridge lobster - and cooked in exciting ways to extract maximum flavour. Gaulthier, however, does not lack a sense of humour: note his spicy, soft-boiled organic Red House Farm egg, with gingerbread fingers and a maple infusion. Boiled egg and soldiers for the chattering classes. Brilliant.

Fixed L/D £ ALC ££

❀ ST QUENTIN BRASSERIE
243 Brompton Road SW3 2EP

☎ 020 7589 8005 ✆ 020 7584 6064

Slick, professional French brasserie with all the expected buzz. Burgundy snails with asparagus, ceps and tarragon in puff pastry, roast monkfish with pancetta, basil and tomato butter sauce, and calves' liver with caramelised shallots, bacon and creamed potatoes have been well reported.

❀ SALLOOS
62-64 Kinnerton Street SW1X 8ER

☎ 020 7235 4444 ✆ 020 7259 5703

Long established family-run Pakistani restaurant in an old mews house. We enjoyed a good chicken shish kebab, and the palak gosht - a mildly spiced dish of lamb and spinach - was excellent.

Fixed L £ ALC ££

❀ SANTINI
29 Ebury Street SW1W 0NZ

☎ 020 7730 4094 ✆ 020 7730 0544

A smart Italian restaurant with a welcoming atmosphere. The cooking emphasises its Venetian roots - try scallops sautéed in wine, butter and olive oil followed by tagliatelle with porcini mushrooms. Finish with an Italian pastry and a great heart-stopping espresso.

Fixed L £ ALC £££

❀ ❀ ❀ 755 FULHAM ROAD
755 Fulham Road SW6 5UU

☎ 020 7371 0755 ✆ 020 7371 0695

Two creamy-coloured floors with two small, narrow rooms, but a menu that is big in scope. Service by smartly uniformed staff is professional and attentive, overseen by Georgina Thompson who manages front of house, whilst husband Alan goes from strength to strength behind the scenes. Strong flavours predominate - roast oxtail with sweet potato and red onion fondue, for example, with fish no exception to the big, bold style. Warm prune and Armagnac beignets filled with ice cream are the test of any kitchen's capabilities - here, they are not to be missed.

Fixed L/D £ ALC ££

❀ ❀ ❀ SHERATON PARK TOWER, RESTAURANT ONE-O-ONE
101 Knightsbridge SW1X 7RN

☎ 020 7290 7101 ✆ 020 7235 6196

Light nautical colours blend in with some colourful food prints and there is a welcome sense of spaciousness. Window tables look down over the heavy traffic and busy shoppers of Knightsbridge. Pascal Proyart's 'cuisine de la mer' fits the setting well and includes scallops and sea bass cooked in half a dozen different ways, especially the latter baked whole in a crust of Brittany rock sea salt (for two). The foundation is French from the Dover sole with sauce dijonnaise to the pan-seared John Dory with forestière potato and beurre piment à l'ail doux. The choice is extensive, an embarrassment of riches perhaps. One of the most intriguing desserts is pear and goats' cheese honey-crusted parcel with ginger ice cream.

Fixed L £ ALC £££

❀ ❀ ❀ ❀ ❀ LA TANTE CLAIRE
Berkeley Hotel Wilton Place Knightsbridge SW1X 7RL

☎ 020 7823 2003 ✆ 020 7823 2001

It could not have been easy for Pierre Koffmann to move from a much-loved Chelsea home to a new location in a corner of The Berkeley Hotel, but any transitional pains have now been smoothed out. One of London's most respected chefs, he has the knack of positively inspiring his staff to welcome and respect all who come to dine chez Koffmann, with the result that the almost

expected holier-than-thou attitude oft found in places of this stature is thankfully missing. On the carte all the Koffmann classics, such as pieds de cochon farcis aux morilles, are reassuringly still in place. Details remain outstanding and include some of the best bread in London. Koffmann still hits the heights and it proves a change of address need mean no loss of excellence.

Fixed L ££ ALC £££

❀ ❀ TURNERS RESTAURANT
87-89 Walton Street SW3 2HP

☎ 020 7584 6711 ✆ 020 7584 4441

Celebrity chef Brian Turner is very much the attentive host in his intimate and welcoming restaurant. A varied choice of around nine main starters, ten main courses and seven desserts provides plenty to choose from. Main courses could involve panaché of monkfish and langoustine tails with a rich and creamy saffron beurre blanc, roast of English lamb in rosemary and herb crust, or calves' kidneys with celeriac timbale and a Pommery cream sauce. To finish, choose white chocolate and raspberry mousse, or apple and almond cake with caramelised apples.

Fixed L £ ALC £££

❀ ❀ VONG
The Berkeley Hotel Wilton Place Knightsbridge SW1X 7RL

☎ 020 7235 1010 ✆ 020 7235 1011

Merging of France and the Orient in the discreet confines of the Berkeley Hotel. Vong is decorated in rich Indonesian hues, reflecting the vivid colours of the oriental spices on display, offset by the use of natural stone, timbers and white orchids. The menu is an inventory of fusion dishes of the sort which all too often excite on paper more than on the palate. Prices, too, might make some blanch. Mostly French, plentiful and well-meaning, staff are under the guidance of a US Vongster from the mother Vong in New York.

Fixed L £ ALC £££

❀ ❀ ZAFFERANO
15 Lowndes Street SW1X 9EY

☎ 020 7235 5800 ✆ 020 7235 1971

The discreet, stylish Belgravia restaurant always plays to a full, cosmopolitan house. Decor is simple with textile wall hangings and some dramatically arranged flowers, but the food is the thing here - Giorgio Locatelli's modern Italian menu still outclasses most of the rest. Dishes that remain in the memory are pork fillet with black cabbage and cannellini beams, flat spaghetti with sweet chilli, garlic and crab, and chargrilled eels with herbs. Ciabatta comes with the now statutory pool of olive oil, but what stands out throughout a meal here is the sheer quality of the ingredients.

Fixed L £ ALC ££

❀ ❀ ❀ ZAIKA

257-259 Fulham Road SW3 6HY

☎ 020 7351 7823 📠 020 7376 4971

Indian restaurant of immense style. The combination of restaurateur Claudio Pulze and Indian chef Vineet Bhatia has hit the ground running. It is hard to pigeon-hole Bhatia's cooking, however, because no other Indian chef in the country cooks as he does. He is ambitious and imaginative, his food based on respect for prime quality ingredients and long-established technique. The menu deliberately stays short to ensure quality and extends well beyond the familiar boundaries of Anglo-Indian food. Bhatia also introduces a welcome lightness of touch, which is the defining characteristic of his skilful team. Desserts try hard, but are perhaps the least successful; tandoori-baked fruits and kulfi are the best bets.

Fixed L £ ALC £

Call the AA Hotel Booking Service on 0870 5050505 to book at AA recognised hotels and B&Bs in the UK, or through our internet site: http://www.theaa.co.uk/hotels

PUBS, INNS & OTHER PLACES

THE ORANGE BREWERY

37-39 Pimlico Rd, SW1W 8NE

☎ 020 7730 5984

Four-storey Victorian pub with its original working gas lamps. Beers and lagers are brewed on site from a full mash brew. Bar grub includes a selection of pies such as beef and beer, and lamb and rosemary. Lots of different sausages too.

THE COOPERS OF FLOOD STREET

87 Flood St, SW3 5TB

☎ 020 7376 3120

Lively and friendly corner pub just off the Kings Road. Offers traditional and modern pub grub. Spacious, rug-floored bar.

THE CROSS KEYS

1 Lawrence St, SW3 5NB

☎ 020 7349 9111

Fine old Chelsea pub dating back to 1765. Just around the corner from Cheyne Walk and the Thames. The unique interior includes a Bohemian-style banqueting room, open-plan glass roofed conservatory, restaurant and first-floor gallery. Mediterranean cooking, and a varied bar menu are on offer.

THE FRONT PAGE

35 Old Church St, SW3 5BS

☎ 020 7352 0648

Backstreet pub nestled between the Thames and Kings Road. Offers a good meal and the chance to catch up with sporting events on a big screen.

THE PHENE ARMS

Phene St, SW3 5NY

☎ 020 7352 3294

In a quiet Chelsea cul-de-sac, this welcoming neighbourhood pub has a charming roof garden for summer alfresco eating. Interesting bar food ranges from chicken ciabatta to Catalan salad and beef fillet with bearnaise.

THE CHELSEA RAM

32 Burnaby St, SW10 0PL

☎ 020 7351 4008

A busy London pub with an emphasis on good food, including fresh fish from Smithfield market. Modern dishes are listed on the daily-changing blackboard menu.

THE SPORTING PAGE

6 Camera Place SW10 0BH

☎ 020 7376 3694

Modern British and European cooking is served here at this smart Chelsea pub. If you like champagne then this is the place for you. It's the largest retail outlet in London for Bollinger Champagne, with all bottle sizes up to jeroboam.

Everything you need ...in just one guide

Indispensable guides developed from the wealth of AA data. Everything you need to plan your visit - in-depth information on accommodation, places to eat and drink and what to see and do.

- Where to stay - B&Bs, hotels, campsites - all AA inspected and quality assessed

- Where to eat - from pubs to top quality restaurants

- Places to visit and days out for the family

- How to entertain the children

- Museums, art galleries, theatres, stately homes, gardens, the big outdoors, historic and ancient sites

- Sports facilities - golf, swimming, leisure centres, sailing, fishing, horse-riding

- Local events, festivals and crafts

- Essential practical information

- Colour photographs throughout

- Easy-to-use

Available from all good bookshops for only £9.99

AA Lifestyle Guides

KENSINGTON, HYDE PARK AND NOTTING HILL

The majestic sweep of Hyde Park separates Kensington and Notting Hill from central London, and both maintain an air of being apart from it. William III first put Kensington on the map when he moved to Kensington Palace in 1689 in the hope that the fresh air of this then-country retreat would help his asthma and bronchitis. New buildings were constructed by his courtiers, and Kensington has retained an aristocratic atmosphere, with streets full of large, fine houses. Kensington Palace sits in Kensington Gardens, west of Hyde Park, and today is home to several members of the royal family, including Princess Margaret and the Duke and Duchess of Kent. Diana, Princess of Wales lived there for a while. West of the palace is Kensington Church Street, with some upmarket shops and restaurants, which leads to Kensington High Street which is more inclined to high-street chain stores. One of the more impressive sights of the area is the Church of St Mary Abbots, which has a 250ft spire, making it London's tallest parish church. Kensington

Market is well worth a visit if you're in the business of getting some second-hand clothes, a haircut or a watch repaired.

Along Kensington High Street is the impressive Commonwealth Institute and Holland Park, which joins Holland Park Avenue and Notting Hill to the north. Holland Park is both an area and a park. The area is very desirably residential, with huge houses complete with nannies or au pairs, and the latest expensive cars. Holland Park itself is crammed with interest, although by London standards it is not a large park. Once the grounds of the all-but-gone Holland House, it now contains an open-air theatre begun by the brave Lady Holland during Cromwell's reign, peacocks and a Japanese garden.

Notting Hill was first established as a residential area in 1870, the last area to succumb to urbanisation. Many of the houses were occupied by the poorly paid West Indian workers who arrived in Britain in the 1950s, and today the Notting Hill Carnival, a festival of West Indian music and culture, is held every August. Hundreds of thousands of funseekers descend on a tiny area around Ladbroke Grove, creating an atmosphere more like Mardi

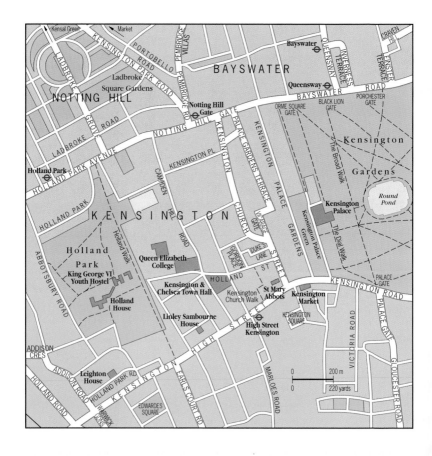

Gras in Brazil than a weekend in West London. Recently the area was the location for a blockbuster movie of the same name, starring Julia Roberts and Hugh Grant. Consequently, the area has seen a marked increase in tourism, but it remains to be seen how long this particular spotlight will shine. Notting Hill Gate itself is not particularly remarkable, but Portobello Road Market is nearby and definitely worth a visit for antiques, knick-knacks and more off-beat items like comics and obscure vinyl. The whole area around Portobello Road is very trendy, with ever-changing fashionable restaurants.

Hyde Park was the first of London's public parks, and is central London's biggest. At one time it was a haven for footpads and criminals, so much so that William III had street lamps put up along Rotten Row, making it the first streetlit street in the country. These days is a lot safer, and the ideal place to walk the dog, do some exercise or boating on the Serpentine, a large lake formed by the damming of the River Westbourne. Those interested in political or religious debate should visit Speaker's Corner, where anyone can get up on a soapbox and harangue the crowd on any subject.

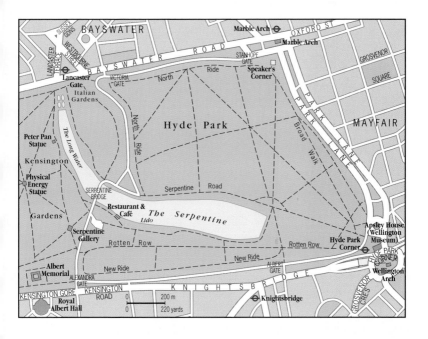

MUST SEE

Kensington Palace

KENSINGTON PALACE
Kensington Gardens, W8
☎ 020-7937 9561
Since the tragic death of Diana, Princess of Wales, who lived here, discussions have been held about making the palace a permanent memorial to her. It is occupied by other members of the royal family, including Princess Margaret, and was first made a royal residence in 1689 by William and Mary. Princess Victoria was born here in 1819, and lived here until she acceded the throne and moved to Buckingham Palace. You can visit the State Apartments (the Privy Chamber; King's Gallery, with works from the royal collection; and the magnificent Cupola Room), and Queen Mary's Gallery. The Court Dress Collection shows the clothing worn by soldiers, diplomats and civil servants during court receptions

KENSINGTON GARDENS
W8
Joined to Hyde Park but separated from it by the Serpentine Bridge, Kensington Gardens is a peaceful area, intended as a calm alternative to the often busy Hyde Park. It has a rich collection of wildlife on the Long Water, including herons and grebes. There's also the 'Sunken Garden' and the Round Pond, where a statue of JM Barrie's character, Peter Pan has been worn smooth by countless children's strokes. The pond is also popular for the sailing of model and remote controlled

boats. The Albert Memorial is on the south side, and has recently been restored. The memorial features a golden Albert holding a catalogue of the 1851 Great Exhibition.

HYDE PARK
SW1
Hyde Park is 1.5 miles long and almost a mile wide. It 1637, it was the first royal park to be opened to the public. The most famous part is Speaker's Corner, near Marble Arch where, on Sundays, soapbox orators harangue the crowds on any subject you can imagine. Rotten Row is a

Police riders in Hyde Park

corruption of route du roi (the king's road), along which monarchs once rode between the West End and Kensington Palace. The Serpentine lake was created in

1730 for Queen Caroline, wife of George II, and the Serpentine Gallery hosts exhibitions of 20th-century art in the summer. Also during the summer, there are softball games, boating on the lake and bandstand music. It's best to avoid the park after dark, for fear of modern footpads.

COMMONWEALTH INSTITUTE
230 Kensington High St, W8
☎ 020-7603 4555
In a typically 1960s building with opaque glass walls and a copper roof, 50 member nations of the Commonweath display their cultures through arts, religion, housing, climate, food and resources. The collection was founded by Queen Victoria in 1893. Most of the exhibits are lively and, although they tend to paint a rather rosy image of Britain's colonial past, they do play a vital educational role.

PORTOBELLO ROAD MARKET
Portobello Rd, W10
A world-famous market offering different interests along its way and on different days. Saturday is antiques, jewellery, paintings and silverware. Monday to Thursday it's fashionable clothes, records,

books, fruit and vegetables, and Friday it's the turn of second-hand junk and just about anything that takes your fancy. Prices are fairly reasonable, although the weekend can be incredibly busy in good weather.

HISTORIC AND ANCIENT SITES

ALBERT MEMORIAL
Kensington Gardens, SW7
At 180 ft high, this flamboyant memorial to Queen Victoria's husband by Sir George Gilbert Scott, is a reminder of the values of the Victorian age. Its corners illustrate the peoples of Asia, America, Europe and Africa, and almost 200 important figures from world history are represented, life-size, in an enormous frieze. Nearly ten

Leighton House

Holland Park House

years of restoration work came to an end when the Queen unveiled the memorial in October 1998.

HYDE PARK BARRACKS
Knightsbridge, SW1
Home of the Household Cavalry, you can see them on their way to Horse Guards' Parade every morning at 10.30am for the Changing of the Guard.

LINLEY SAMBOURNE HOUSE
18 Stafford Terrace, W8
☎ 020-7994 1019
Named after Edward Linley Sambourne, the chief cartoonist for Punch magazine,

The Sunken Garden , Kensington Gardens

who lived here until his death in 1910. The exhibits plunge you into a time capsule, whose furnishings appear unaltered. Sambourne had some distinguished friends, including Alma-Tadema, GF Watts and Millais, whose works adorn the walls.

LEIGHTON HOUSE
12 Holland Park Rd, W14
☎ 020-7602 3316
Lord Frederic Leighton was a painter and sculptor, and President of the Royal Academy. The interior architecture, such as the Arab Hall, bear witness to his fascination with the East, along with a collection of his paintings from his time spent there. A must for fans of the Pre-Raphaelite movement.

BADEN-POWELL HOUSE
Queen's Gate, SW7
☎ 020-7584 7030
Set up in memory of Lord Baden-Powell,

who began the Scout movement in Britain, this museum traces the story of the organisation, and is a pilgrimage destination for Scouts and Guides.

ART GALLERIES

SERPENTINE GALLERY
Kensington Gardens, W2
☎ 020-7402 6075
Housed in a former tea pavilion overlooking Hyde Park, the Serpentine Gallery reopened in 1998. Independently-minded modern art.

SPECIAL PHOTOGRAPHERS COMPANY
21 Kensington Park Rd, W11
☎ 020-7221 3489
Started in the 1980s, this gallery showcases modern photography from British and international photographers.

CINEMAS

GATE CINEMA
87 Notting Hill Gate, W11
☎ 020-7727 4043
Popular for trendy, new films as well as more mainstream ones.

NOTTING HILL CORONET
Notting Hill Gate, W11
☎ 020-7727 6705
An old-fashioned cinema.

ODEON KENSINGTON
Kensington High St, W8
☎ 0870 505 0007
Six screens offering the latest mainstream blockbusters.

UCI WHITELEYS
Whiteleys Shopping Centre, Queensway, W2
☎ 020-7792 3332
Masses of screens and choices, including buckets of popcorn and coke.

THEATRES

THE GATE
The Prince Albert, 11 Pembridge Rd, W11
☎ 020-7229 0706
Started out as a fringe theatre in a pub, and now, still in a pub, with a huge following. Specialises in reviving neglected European plays, using cutting-edge set design.

HOLLAND PARK THEATRE
Holland Park, W8
☎ 020-7602 7856
This open-air theatre is host to the Royal Ballet every summer.

ENTERTAINMENT AND NIGHTLIFE

CUBA
11-13 Kensington High St, W8
☎ 020-7938 4137
A chic nightclub offering the local businessfolk somewhere to let their hair down.

Militaria for sale at Portobello Road Market

NOTTING HILL ARTS CLUB
21 Notting Hill Gate, W11
☎ 020-7460 4459
With luck you might still be able to catch an Outcaste night here. Try Saturday.

SUBTERANIA
12 Acklam Rd, W10
☎ 020-8960 4590
Diverse club nights Fridays and Saturdays. Very picky door policy.

CLEOPATRA TAVERNA
Notting Hill Gate, W11
☎ 020-7935 8509
Traditional Greek entertainment is on offer here, where plate smashing is positively encouraged.

THE TENTH
Royal Garden Hotel, 2 Kensington High St, W8
☎ 020-7937 8000
Dance the night away to a 16-strong violin group playing music from the 1940s at this delightful restaurant on the 10th floor of the Royal Garden Hotel. There are splendid views of Kensington Palace and Gardens and modern British cuisine to complement the dancing.

Notting Hill Gate Underground Station

SHOPPING

DEPARTMENT STORES

BARKER'S OF KENSINGTON
63 Kensington High St, W8
☎ 020-7937 5432
This department store offers clothes for men, women and children, along with household and electrical goods. Now incorporated into Barkers Arcade along fashionable Kensington High Street, it has sealed its reputation as the place to come for quality shopping.

BHS (BRITISH HOME STORES)
Kensington High St, W8
☎ 020-7937 0910
A reasonably priced department store catering to clothing mainly, but also with a very good lighting department and household goods.

The Albert Memorial

FOOD

BOOKS FOR COOKS
4 Blenheim Crescent, W11
☎ 020-7221 1992
Excellent bookshop for cook books, obviously!

& CLARKE'S
122 Kensington Church St, W8
☎ 020-7229 2190
Sally Clarke runs her eponymous restaurant next door to this delightful enclave of breads, truffles and marmalades.

CORNEY & BARROW
194 Kensington Park Rd, W11
☎ 020-7221 5122
An excellent wine shop with a mail order service.

HEALTH AND BEAUTY

CRABTREE & EVELYN
6 Kensington Church St, W8
☎ 020-7937 9335
A superb, but expensive, chain of shops selling bath and shower products, perfumes and other related merchandise. Chic packaging and a very good reputation. There are branches all over the country.

THE GREEN ROOM
21 Earl's Court Rd, W8
☎ 020-7937 6595
A chain of trendy, healthy attitude shops offering many beauty and health treatments and products to go with them. Several branches.

FASHION

Barkers Arcade, on Kensington High Street, has many of the high-street chains such as Kookaï, Esprit, Jigsaw, Benetton etc. Also along Kensington High Street you'll find Marks & Spencer, Hennes, The Gap, Laura Ashley, River Island Clothing Co, etc.

HYPE DF
48-52 Kensington High St, W8
☎ 020-7937 3100
Formerly Hyper Hyper, the latest Kensington fashion emporium offers designer clothes at fairly reasonable prices and in very trendy surroundings.

KENSINGTON MARKET
49 Kensington High St, W8
☎ 020-7938 4343
The opposite of Hype DF, Kensington

Speakers Corner in Hyde Park

Market is for those who love to browse among fashions of yesteryear, as well as those who like to dress in mix-and-(not)-match. Loads of clothes and a slight aroma of moth balls.

HAVE A NICE DAY
45 Pembridge Rd, W11
☎ 020-7727 6306
Club fashion.

KAREN MILLEN
Barkers Arcade, Kensington High St, W8
☎ 020-7938 3758
Very popular among young women executives. You'll find powerful suits in interesting (odd?) cuts and unusual colours. Branches throughout London.

The Serpentine, Hyde Park

A display of flags outside the Commonwealth Institute

THE DISPENSARY
25 Pembridge Rd, W11
☎ 020-7221 9290
Club fashions.

AMAZON
1-3, 7a, 7b, & 19-22 Kensington Church St, W8
☎ 020-7937 4692
This shop with the sprawling address buys up discontinued lines and designer seconds for women and sells them on at a fraction of their original price. Bargain hunter's heaven.

JEWELLERY

DINNY HALL
200 Westbourne Grove, W11
☎ 020-7792 3913
Delicate jewellery at a price.

FRONTIERS
37-39 Pembridge Rd, W11
☎ 020-7727 6132
Antique jewellery.

SHOES

DERBER
380 Kensington High St, W8
☎ 020-7937 1578
Popular and stylish shoes and boots.

PIED À TERRE
Kensington High St, W8
☎ 020-7376 0296
Popular and fashionable shoes for men and women. Branches throughout London

HAIRDRESSERS

ANTENNA
27a Kensington Church St, W8
☎ 020-7938 1866
Less fashionable than it was a few years ago, but still a pretty cool cut. Not cheap.

BLADERUNNERS
158 Notting Hill Gate
☎ 020-7229 2255
Named after the sci-fi film, Bladerunners specialises in hair extensions.

MUSIC

TOWER RECORDS
62-64 Kensington High St, W8
☎ 020-7938 3511
A branch of the excellent music chain - classical, jazz, rock, dance, film soundtracks, or just the latest Number 1.

INTOXICA!
231 Portobello Rd, W11 1LT
☎ 020 7229 8010
Excellent record shop on busy Portobello Road. New and secondhand vinyl, bought, sold and exchanged. Browse among exotica, punk, 60's music and jazz.

ROUGH TRADE RECORDS
130 Talbot Rd, W11 1JA
☎ 020-7229 8541
Probably the best (and most untidy!) indie record shop in London. The base for what was one of Britain's most successful indie labels, it still specialises in everything esoteric, loud and peculiar. No serious music fan should leave London without a visit.

MUSIC & VIDEO EXCHANGE
28 & 30 Pembridge Rd
36 & 38 Notting Hill Gate, W11
☎ 020-7221 1444
Take your old records/CDs for exchange or cash, and pick up some brilliant bargains. Other shops in the chain deal in books, hi-fi's, comics, computers, and clothes.

SPORTS

SNOW & ROCK
188 Kensington High St, W8
☎ 020-7937 0872
All you could possibly want for skiing, mountaineering, orienteering etc.

A bronze rabbit sits at the feet of Peter Pan in Kensington Gardens

London Toy & Model Museum

HOME ACCESSORIES

GRAHAM & GREEN
7 Elgin Crescent, W11
☎ 020-7727 4594
A charming shop stocking gifts and stationery from photo frames to pens.

PARKS AND GARDENS

HOLLAND PARK
W8
A 54-acre green space, Holland Park is filled with formal flower gardens and wilder, woodland areas. The summer ballroom of Holland House (destroyed in World War II) has been converted into a stylish restaurant, the Belvedere. In the summer there is open-air theatre and for children, a great adventure playground.

GREAT FOR KIDS

There are loads of Festivals and Events throughout the year in London which children will love - See Festivals and Events.

LONDON TOY & MODEL MUSEUM
21-23 Craven Hill, W2
☎ 020-7706 8000
Recorded information: 020-7402 5222
Recently expanded, the museum is home to historic toys which will appeal to all ages. 20 galleries with working exhibits covering ships, trains and much more.

HOLLAND PARK
Holland Park Rd and Kensington High St, W8
An enclosure within Holland Park contains peacocks, pheasants, rabbits and squirrels.

STICKY FINGERS
1a Phillimore Gdns, W8
☎ 020-7938 5338
Owned by Rolling Stone Bill Wyman, and names after one of their albums, this is a great restaurant for children. Young diners get given colouring books and balloons along with burgers and fries.

HAAGEN-DAZS ICE-CREAM PARLOUR
88 Queensway, W2
☎ 020-7229 0668
All the flavours, all the toppings for a scrumptious event.

St Mary Abbots Church

NON-STOP PARTY SHOP
214 Kensington High St, W8
☎ 020-7937 7200/7201
Balloons, gifts, jokes, novelties.

CHILDREN'S BOOK CENTRE
237 Kensington High St, W8
☎ 020-7937 7497
Books, videos and CD-ROMs are all available in this long-established shop.

UCI WHITELEYS
Whiteleys Shopping Centre, Queensway, W2
☎ 0171-792 3332
This huge cinema complex offers special deals for children.

PLACES OF WORSHIP

ST MARY ABBOTS CHURCH
Kensington High St, W8
With a fine spire, this delightful church was built on the site of Kensington's original village church.

SPORT AND LEISURE

QUEEN'S ICE SKATING CLUB
17 Queensway, W2
☎ 020-7229 0172
The most central skating rink in London.

HYDE PARK RIDING STABLES
63 Bathurst Mews, W2
☎ 020-7723 2813
A very exclusive riding club who use Hyde Park as their ground.

ROSS NYE'S RIDING STABLES
8 Bathurst Mews, W2
☎ 020-7262 3791
Ride across Hyde Park, or along Rotten Row, and experience London in a completely different way.

SERPENTINE LIDO
Hyde Park, W2
☎ 020-7298 2100
A truly delightful place to swim in summer.

WHERE TO STAY
HOTELS
AA RECOMMENDED

Hogarth Hotel

SW5

★★★★ ✿ SWALLOW INTERNATIONAL
Cromwell Rd SW5 0TH

(on the A4, within minutes of the M4)

☎ 020 7973 1000 📠 020 7244 8194

One of the few London hotels with its own car park. The modern bedrooms, if a little compact, are thoughtfully equipped. In addition to an all-day eating option, there is the more formal Blayneys restaurant where some interesting dishes are offered. The hotel has an indoor leisure facility.

421 rooms (36 family & 76 no smoking) / European Cuisine / Indoor swimming pool (heated) / Sauna, Solarium, Gym, Jacuzzi/spa, Whirlpool spa, Turkish Steamroom / Live entertainment / Lift, Night porter, Air cond / Closed 23–26 Dec 🍴

★★★ ✿ HOGARTH
33 Hogarth Rd, Kensington SW5 0QQ

(turn into Earls Court Rd from Cromwell Rd (A4), take 3rd turning left into Hogarth Rd. Hotel is at the end of the rd on the left)

☎ 020 7370 6831 📠 020 7373 6179

Bedrooms at this purpose-built hotel vary in size but all are well equipped. Top floor rooms benefit from balconies. There is a restaurant/bar, The Terrace, where a range of freshly prepared dishes is available throughout the day, and room service is also available. There are three smart meeting rooms, and the hotel benefits from having its own secure car park for about 20 cars.

85 rooms (12 family & 18 no smoking) / English & French / Lift, Night porter

Price band £££ 🍴

★★ COMFORT INN
22-32 West Cromwell Rd, Kensington SW5 9QJ

☎ 020 7373 3300 📠 020 7835 2040

Convenient for Earl's Court, this cheerful, modern hotel is well suited to business and leisure guests. The bedrooms vary in size, but are smartly kept, with a range of amenities including air-conditioning. The welcoming public areas are bright and comfortable.

125 rooms (6 family & 48 no smoking) / English & Continental Cuisine / Lift, Night porter, Air cond / No dogs (ex guide dogs)

Price band £££ 🍴

⌂ OKI HOTEL
25 Courtfield Gardens, Kensington SW5 0PG

(M4 into London join A4 to Cromwell Rd, turn right at Cromwell Hospital into Knaresborough Pl, hotel is at the end as it becomes Courtfield Gdns)

☎ 020 7565 2222 📠 020 7565 2223

This townhouse in the heart of fashionable Kensington offers accommodation of a very high standard. Rooms are well equipped and comfortable, and there are a bar lounge and a basement dining room where a buffet breakfast is served.

41 rooms / Lift, Night porter / No dogs

Price band £££ 🍴

SW7

★★★★ ✿ BAILEYS HOTEL
140 Gloucester Rd SW7 4QH

(M4, take A4 which turns into Cromwell Road, turn right onto Gloucester Road, hotel on the right opposite tube station)

☎ 020 7373 6000 📠 020 7370 3760

Purpose-built in 1876 and given a new lease of life by its current owners, Baileys has modern bedrooms with useful facilities such as air-conditioning and TV guest-link system. Its own restaurant,

---

Olives, produces enjoyable food in contemporary style. Service is provided by a friendly team of staff.

212 room (80 no smoking) / International Cuisine / Fitness room / Lift, Night porter, Air cond / No dogs (ex guide dogs)

Price band £££ 🍴

★★★★ FORUM
97 Cromwell Rd SW7 4DN

☎ 020 7370 5757 📠 020 7373 1448

(from South Circular onto North Circular at Chiswick Flyover, join A4 Cromwell Rd as far as the Gloucester Rd)

London's tallest hotel has, not surprisingly, panoramic views over London from the majority of its rooms. Bedrooms are smartly decorated and well equipped. Public areas include a business centre, a large shop and several eating options.

910 rooms (36 family & 176 no smoking) / International Cuisine / Fitness room / Live entertainment / Lift, Night porter / No dogs (ex guide dogs) 🍴

★★★★ ✿ THE GLOUCESTER
4-18 Harrington Gardens SW7 4LH

(opposite Gloucester Road underground station)

☎ 020 7373 6030 📠 020 7373 0409

Bedrooms at this smart cosmopolitan hotel are furnished in contemporary styles with marble bathrooms and Air conditioning. Club rooms have the added facility of a dedicated lounge with extra services. There is a wide range of eating options, ranging from informal snacks, to Singaporean cuisine in Bugis, and the showcase Southwest 17, awarded One AA Rosette for its Italian fare.

610 rooms (4 family & 232 no smoking) / English & Continental Cuisine / Lift, Night porter, Air cond 🍴

Forum

Harrington Hall

★★★★ HARRINGTON HALL
5-25 Harrington Gardens SW7 4JW
(head towards Knightsbridge into Gloucester Rd. Take 2nd right into Harrington Gdns hotel on the left)
☎ 020 7396 9696 ⓕ 020 7396 9090
A short walk from the South Kensington museums, this modern, air-conditioned hotel offers well equipped bedrooms, furnished to high quality standards, and well designed reception rooms. The restaurant, where there is sometimes live entertainment, offers a choice of a hot buffet or a traditional full menu.
200 rooms (132 no smoking) / European Cuisine / Sauna, Gym, Leisure centre / Live entertainment / Lift, Night porter, Air cond / No dogs (ex guide dogs)
Price band £££

★★★★ JURYS
109-113 Queensgate, South Kensington SW7 5LR
(from A3218 (Old Bromton Rd), hotel is approx 300 yards on left at junction with Queensgate)
☎ 020 7589 6300 ⓕ 020 7581 1492
This fine hotel offers a traditional Irish welcome. The attractive lobby/bar and library lounge areas are very popular. Kavanagh's bar is lively, while Copplestones restaurant is more sedate. Bedrooms range from stylish fifth-floor cottage rooms with floral fabrics, to smart executive suites.
172 rooms (4 family & 36 no smoking) / European Cuisine / Live entertainment / Lift, Night porter, Air cond / No dogs (ex guide dogs) / Closed 24–27 Dec
Price band £££
See advert on page 239.

★★★★ REMBRANDT
11 Thurloe Place SW7 2RS
(opp Victoria & Albert Museum)
☎ 020 7589 8100 ⓕ 020 7225 3363
The ornate architecture of the Rembrandt connects it stylistically to nearby Harrods. A strength of this plush, comfortable hotel is the leisure centre, designed in a style reminiscent of ancient Rome.
195 rooms (25 family & 28 no smoking) / International Cuisine / Indoor swimming pool (heated) / Sauna, Solarium, Gym, Jacuzzi/spa, Health, fitness & beauty centre / Live entertainment / Lift, Night porter / No dogs (ex guide dogs)
Price band £££

★★★ RADISSON EDWARDIAN VANDERBILT
68/86 Cromwell Rd SW7 5BT
(A4 into central London)
☎ 020 7589 2424 ⓕ 020 7225 2293
Situated on Cromwell Road, convenient for several museums, this terraced Victorian property is popular with both business travellers and tourists. Bedrooms vary in size and decor but all have chintzy fabrics and solid, inlaid-wood furniture.
223 rooms (17 family) / English & French Cuisine / Lift, Night porter / No dogs (ex guide dogs)
Price band £££

W1

★★★★★ HOTEL INTER-CONTINENTAL
1 Hamilton Place, Hyde Park Corner W1V 0QY
(Situated on Hyde Park Corner where junct of Knightsbridge/Park Lane & Piccadilly meet)
☎ 020 7409 3131 ⓕ 020 7493 3476
Situated in a prominent position on Hyde Park Corner, this fine hotel has a very good reputation. Bedrooms vary from inner courtyard rooms to spacious suites. The smart marble foyer houses the Observatory lounge, which provides light meals or afternoon teas, and the Coffee House restaurant provides breakfast and all-day dining, but the jewel in the hotel's crown is Le Soufflé Restaurant, where Peter Kromberg cooks with commendable flair.
458 rooms (240 no smoking) / French, Oriental & International Cuisine / Sauna, Gym, Jacuzzi/spa, Health centre / Live entertainment / Lift, Night porter, Air cond / No dogs (ex guide dogs)
Price band £££

W2

★★★★ ROYAL LANCASTER
Lancaster Ter W2 2TY
(directly above Lancaster Gate Underground Station)
☎ 020 7262 6737 ⓕ 020 7724 3191
Overlooking Hyde Park and Kensington Gardens, the Royal Lancaster's upper storeys also offer fine views across London. There is 24-hour room service and efficient porterage. The choice of eating ranges from the lounge or the Pavement Café, to the smart Park Restaurant or the exotic Nipa Thai.
416 rooms (9 family & 51 no smoking) / International Cuisine / Live entertainment / Lift, Night porter, Air cond / No dogs (ex guide dogs)

★★★★ THISTLE HYDE PARK
90-92 Lancaster Gate W2 3NR
(on Bayswater Rd between Lancaster Gate and Queensway)
☎ 020 7262 2711 ⓕ 020 7262 2147
With all the atmosphere of a country house hotel, the Thistle is situated just steps from Hyde Park and the West End. Bedrooms are quite spacious and the marble bathrooms are an attractive feature. A cosy club-like bar with a glass-canopied extension leads into a smart restaurant where modern dishes are interpreted with aplomb.
54 rooms (10 no smoking) / International Cuisine / Lift, Night porter, Air cond / No dogs (ex guide dogs) / No coaches

Royal Lancaster

★★★ BERJAYA EDEN PARK HOTEL

35-39 Inverness Ter, Bayswater W2 3JS

(From Marble Arch, straight across main rdbt onto Bayswater Rd, turn right into Queensway, the first turn left into Inverness Terrace)

☎ 020 7221 2220 📠 020 7221 2286

This friendly hotel close to Queensway offers attractively furnished and well equipped bedrooms. The restaurant is locally popular, and the comfortable and stylish bar serves complimentary coffee to residents during the afternoon.

75 rooms (8 family) / European Cuisine / Lift, Night porter / No dogs (ex guide dogs)

Price band £££

Central Park

★★★ CENTRAL PARK

Queensborough Ter W2 3SS

☎ 020 7229 2424 📠 020 7229 2904

Central Park is a popular hotel just off the Bayswater Road and close to London's West End. Bedrooms offer all the expected modern comforts, and there are spacious public areas. Garage parking is available.

252 rooms / International Cuisine / Lift, Night porter

★★★ GROSVENOR COURT

27 Devonshire Ter W2 3DP

(from A40 take exit signed Paddington Station, at station turn into Craven Road hotel on right)

☎ 020 7262 2204 📠 020 7402 9351

This centrally located hotel has been recently refurbished to a very high standard and bedrooms are bright, modern and smart. The restaurant offers a short but interesting menu. Staff are friendly and relaxed, and guests may enjoy sitting in the smart lounge.

157 rooms (34 family) / International Cuisine / Lift, Night porter / No dogs (ex guide dogs)

Price band £££

★★★ THE PARK COURT

75 Lancaster Gate, Hyde Park W2 3NN

☎ 020 7402 4272 📠 020 7706 4156

This busy hotel, fashioned from a terrace of 19th-century houses, has well appointed public rooms, extensive conference facilities, a hotel shop, and a spacious lounge and bar. The well equipped bedrooms include a spacious

suite, interconnecting family rooms, and accommodation on the ground floor suitable for guests with disabilities.

390 rooms (25 family & 194 no smoking) / Lift, Night porter

★★★ PLAZA ON HYDE PARK

1-7 Lancaster Gate W2 3LG

(200yds from Lancaster Gate Underground Station)

☎ 020 7262 5022 📠 020 7724 8666

Attractively situated opposite Hyde Park and only a few minutes walk from Marble Arch, this busy hotel is popular with overseas visitors. Its interior is bright and modern in style.

402 rooms (14 family & 100 no smoking) / Mediterranean Cuisine / Lift, Night porter / No dogs (ex guide dogs)

Price band £££

★★★ THISTLE KENSINGTON GARDENS

104 Bayswater Rd W2 3HL

(Corner of Bayswater Rd and Porchester Ter)

☎ 020 7262 4461 📠 020 7706 4560

There are some wonderful views of the city over Hyde Park from this centrally located hotel. Bedrooms have recently been upgraded and offer smart well equipped accommodation. Public areas include an attractive bar and restaurant, and some elegant meeting rooms.

175 rooms (66 no smoking) / International Cuisine / Lift, Night porter, Air cond

★★ DELMERE

130 Sussex Gardens, Hyde Park W2 1UB

☎ 020 7706 3344 📠 020 7262 1863

The welcoming, friendly staff are a big plus at this well-managed hotel. Bedrooms are all well equipped and make the best use of available space. Public rooms include a jazz-themed bar and a particularly comfortable lounge that is provided with books, magazines and newspapers.

38 room (3 family) / Italian & Continental Cuisine / Lift, Night porter / No dogs / No coaches

Price band £££

⚜ THE ABBEY COURT

20 Pembridge Gardens, Kensington W2 4DU

(2 minute walk from Nottinghill Gate Underground station)

☎ 020 7221 7518 📠 020 7792 0858

Situated in Notting Hill and close to Kensington, this elegant five-storey townhouse is in a quiet side road. Rooms are individually decorated and furnished to a high standard and room service offers light snacks. Breakfast is taken in the conservatory.

22 rooms (1 family & 10 no smoking) / Night porter / No dogs (ex guide dogs) / No coaches

⚜ THE DARLINGTON HYDE PARK

111-117 Sussex Gardens W2 2RU

☎ 020 7460 8800 📠 020 7460 8828

Although it doesn't offer the full range of hotel services, this comfortable townhouse provides smart, well maintained rooms with excellent facilities, including good desk space. Breakfast is served in an airy dining room which also offers drinks and snacks in the early evening.

40 rooms (2 family & 5 no smoking) / Lift, Night porter / No dogs (ex guide dogs) / No coaches

Price band £££

⚜ PEMBRIDGE COURT

34 Pembridge Gardens W2 4DX

(off the Bayswater Rd at Notting Hill Gate by underground Station)

☎ 020 7229 9977 📠 020 7727 4982

Just minutes from Portobello Market, this Victorian townhouse provides well

The Darlington Hyde Park

appointed bedrooms with 24-hour room service. In the evenings the restaurant and cellar bar are open.

20 rooms (4 family) / Lift, Night porter, Air cond / No coaches
Price band £££

W8

★★★★★ ❀ ❀ ❀
ROYAL GARDEN HOTEL
2-24 Kensington High St W8 4PT
(next to Kensington Palace)
☎ 020 7937 8000 ✆ 020 7361 1991

In a prestigious location overlooking Kensington Gardens and Hyde Park, this hotel offers the highest standards of customer care. The balcony at Bertie's Bar overlooks the foyer, the Park Terrace is ideal for informal eating, and the contemporary 10th-floor restaurant is the place for Derek Baker's modish cooking. Bedroom accommodation ranges from full suites and split-level park-view rooms to the more compact Trader's rooms.

401 rooms (19 family & 164 no smoking) / International Cuisine / Sauna, Solarium, Gym, Health & fitness centre / Live entertainment / Lift, Night porter, Air cond / No dogs (ex guide dogs)
Price band £££

★★★★ ❀ **COPTHORNE TARA**
Scarsdale Place, Wrights Ln W8 5SR
☎ 020 7937 7211 ✆ 020 7937 7100

This is one of the city's larger hotels, located in a residential area off Kensington High Street. Public areas have a smart atmosphere about them and include the relaxing setting of Café Mozart or Jerome's Restaurant, which has an AA Rosette. Bedrooms are bright and equipped with a useful range of facilities.

831 room (265 no smoking) / International Cuisine / Lift, Night porter, Air cond / No dogs (ex guide dogs)

Royal Garden Hotel

Price band £££

★★★★ **THISTLE KENSINGTON PARK**
16-32 De Vere Gardens, Kensington W8 5AG
☎ 020 7937 8080 ✆ 020 7937 7616

Attractive public areas are a feature of this bright modern hotel which has extensive meeting room facilities. Guests enjoy dining in the all-day coffee shop and the Eaglescarnie bar is particularly friendly and welcoming. Bedrooms vary in size but all are well presented and some are very quiet. There are now some brand new rooms with excellent facilities including air-conditioning.

352 room (14 family & 90 no smoking) / International Cuisine / Lift, Night porter, Air conditioning / No dogs (ex guide dogs)

★★★ **POSTHOUSE KENSINGTON**
Wright's Ln, Kensington W8 5SP
☎ 020 7937 8170 ✆ 020 7937 8289

Positioned close to Kensington High Street, this hotel offers well equipped bedrooms and an extensive range of facilities, including an impressive new leisure club, dedicated conference rooms and several eating outlets, including an all

day conservatory coffee shop and two restaurants. Although some rooms are quite compact, they all offer good facilities.

550 rooms (150 no smoking) / English & Italian cuisine / Indoor swimming pool (heated) / Squash, Sauna, Solarium, Gym, Jacuzzi/spa, Health & Fitness centre with Beauty room / Lift, Night porter

W11

★★★★ ❀ ❀ ❀ **HALCYON**
81 Holland Park W11 3RZ
☎ 020 7727 7288 ✆ 020 7229 8516

Faithfully restored some ten years ago, this elegant hotel is indeed an oasis of calm. Accommodation is amply proportioned and equipped with every comfort. Staff provide attentive and friendly service, and good modern cooking from a seasonally changing menu is served in The Room restaurant.

43 rooms / English & French Cuisine / Lift, Night porter, Air cond / No dogs (ex guide dogs) / No coaches

BED & BREAKFAST
AA RECOMMENDED

Henley House Hotel

SW5

♦♦♦ **HENLEY HOUSE HOTEL**
30 Barkston Gardens, Earls Court SW5 0EN
(turn off A4 Cromwell Rd at junction with A3220, S for 0.4km. Barkstons Gardens on left past underground)
☎ 020 7370 4111 ✆ 020 7370 0026

Close to Earls Court, and overlooking the well maintained garden square of Barkston Gardens, this attractive Victorian house has been thoughtfully furnished with rich decor and soft furnishings. Bedrooms are comfortably appointed and nicely equipped. Public areas include a cosy reception lounge and a breakfast room.

20 rooms (2 family) / No dogs (ex guide dogs) / Lift / No coaches
Price band £££

Five Sumner Place Hotel

♦♦♦ SWISS HOUSE HOTEL

171 Old Brompton Rd, South Kensington
SW5 0AN

(from A4 turn right, at Old Brompton Rd turn left, pass lights, hotel on right)

📞 020 7373 2769 & 7373 9383
📠 020 7373 4983

There is a warm friendly atmosphere at this small well run guest house. Bedrooms are furnished in modern pine and brightly decorated. A choice of continental buffet breakfast is offered and served in the cosy dining room.

16 rooms (7 family & 4 no smoking) / No coaches
Price band ££ 🍽

SW7

♦♦♦♦♦ GALLERY HOTEL

8-10 Queensberry Place, South Kensington
SW7 2EA

(turn off Cromwell Rd opposite Natural History Museum into Queensberry Place in South Kensington)

📞 020 7915 0000 📠 020 7915 4400

This quiet location close to Kensington and Knightsbridge is popular with visitors from far and wide. Bedrooms are individually designed, and some have Air conditioning. Public rooms include the mahogany panelled '4 Cats' lounge-bar. 24-hour room service is available and at breakfast guests have the option of buffet English or continental.

36 rooms / No dogs (ex guide dogs) / Lift
Price band £££ 🍽

♦♦♦♦ FIVE SUMNER PLACE HOTEL

5 Sumner Place, South Kensington SW7 3EE

(300yds from South Kensington underground station)

📞 020 7584 7586 📠 020 7823 9962

All the bedrooms in this elegant Victorian terraced house are individually designed and tastefully decorated. Guests are able to take breakfast among the shrubs and flowers in the bright Victorian-style conservatory, where complimentary newspapers and magazines are available.

13 rooms (4 family & 6 no smoking) / No dogs / Lift / No children under 7 years / No coaches
Price bands £££ 🍽

♦♦♦♦ GAINSBOROUGH HOTEL

7-11 Queensberry Place, South Kensington
SW7 2DL

(off Cromwell Rd, opposite Natural History Museum in South Kensington)

📞 020 7957 0000 📠 020 7957 0001

Located on a quiet street near the Natural History Museum. Bedrooms are individually designed and decorated in fine fabrics, quality furnishings and carefully co-ordinated colours. Guests are offered a choice of breakfast, served in the very attractive dining room. There is a small lounge and 24-hour room service is available.

49 rooms (5 family) / No dogs (ex guide dogs) / Lift
Price band £££ 🍽

♦♦♦ KENSINGTON MANOR HOTEL

8 Emperors Gate SW7 4HH

(from Heathrow A4 towards central London, opposite Forum Hotel, turn left on Grenville Place, then left again. Hotel on right)

📞 020 7370 7516 📠 020 7373 3163

This late Victorian terraced house is located just off the Cromwell Road and within easy walking distance of the museums. The bedrooms vary in size and offer modern, comfortable and well equipped accommodation. A choice of English and continental breakfast is available, and served in the cosy breakfast room.

14 rooms (4 family) / No coaches

W2

♦♦♦♦ MORNINGTON HOTEL

12 Lancaster Gate W2 3LG

(north of Hyde Park, off A40-Bayswater Road)

📞 020 7262 7361 📠 020 7706 1028

A fine Victorian building located in a quiet road close to Lancaster Gate station. The bedrooms continue to be upgraded and provide comfortable, stylish accommodation. There are two lounges and an attractive dining room where a Scandinavian-style breakfast is served.

66 rooms (6 family & 27 no smoking) / Lift / No coaches
Price band £££ 🍽

♦♦♦♦ NORFOLK TOWERS HOTEL

34 Norfolk Place W2 1QW

(close to Paddington Station & St Mary's Hospital)

📞 020 7262 3123 📠 020 7224 8687

This elegant Victorian building is one of the larger bed and breakfast hotels offering comfortable and well equipped accommodation. The public areas include modern and attractive lounge and bar facilities. A choice of breakfast is served in the spacious dining room and Cads café/bar is available for meals until 11.00pm.

85 rooms (3 family) / No dogs (ex guide dogs) / Lift
Price band £££ 🍽

♦♦♦ AVERARD HOTEL

10 Lancaster Gate W2 3LH

(opposite Hyde Park & Kensington Gdns, 2 mins walk from Lancaster Gate tube stn / 10 mins walk from Paddington main line stn)

📞 020 7723 8877 📠 020 7706 0860

The Averard has 60 bedrooms all of which are en suite. The public rooms include a comfortable lounge, a bar area and a superbly appointed restaurant where English or continental style breakfast can be enjoyed.

60 rooms (5 family) / Lift / No coaches / Closed 22-30 Dec
🍽

♦♦♦ BLAKEMORE HOTEL

30 Leinster Gardens W2 3AN

(just off Bayswater Rd. Turn into Leinster Terrace, which leads into Leinster Gardens. Nearest tube stations - Bayswater & Queensway)

📞 020 7262 4591 📠 020 7724 1472

Enjoying a quiet location, this large hotel is just minutes from Hyde Park. The bedrooms are neatly decorated and the executive rooms have been refurbished to a high standard. The spacious public areas include a bar lounge, smart foyer and attractive restaurant which offers a range of popular dishes.

164 rooms / No dogs (ex guide dogs) / Lift
Price band £££ 🍽

Averard Hotel

Byron Hotel

♦ ♦ ♦ BYRON HOTEL
36-38 Queensborough Ter W2 3SH
(just off Bayswater Rd close to Queensway.
From Marble Arch follow signs to Notting
Hill)
☎ 020 7243 0987 **G** 020 7792 1957
This charming terraced house has been
thoughtfully restored to provide
comfortable accommodation, and
maintains a number of its original
features. Bedrooms are compact but have
been tastefully decorated, comfortably
furnished and equipped with modern
facilities. Breakfast is served in the
attractive dining room.
45 rooms (5 family & all no smoking) / No
dogs / Lift
Price band ££ ⬛

♦ ♦ ♦ FLAT 2A
No1 Hyde Park St W2
☎ 020 7402 7491
This smart property is just off the
Bayswater Road, five minutes walk from
Marble Arch and Oxford street. The
accommodation is attractively decorated
and furnished to a high standard, and
benefits from a smart en suite bathroom.
1 room

♦ ♦ ♦ MITRE HOUSE HOTEL
178-184 Sussex Gardens, Hyde Park W2 1TU
(Sussex Gardens is parallel to Bayswater
Road)
☎ 020 7723 8040 **G** 020 7402 0990
A family-run hotel conveniently located for
access to the West End. Bedrooms vary in
size but all are comfortably appointed and
suitably equipped. Guests have use of a
comfortable lounge and bar.
70 rooms (3 family & 10 no smoking) / No
dogs (ex guide dogs) / Lift
Price band ££ ⬛
See advert on inside front cover.

♦ ♦ ♦ NORFOLK PLAZA HOTEL
29/33 Norfolk Square, Paddington W2 1RX
(300 metres from Paddington station)
☎ 020 7723 0792 **G** 020 7224 8770
Located in a quiet residential square, this
hotel has been thoughtfully furnished to
provide comfortable and well equipped

bedrooms, with a number of split level
suites. The public areas include a well
appointed bar and lounge, plus an
attractive restaurant where breakfast is
available.
87 rooms (28 family 5 no smoking) / No
dogs (ex guide dogs) / Lift
Price band £££ ⬛

♦ ♦ ♦ PARK LODGE HOTEL
73 Queensborough Ter, Bayswater W2 3SU
(Queensborough Terrace is just off Bayswater
Rd. Near Kensington Gardens & Hyde Park)
☎ 020 7229 6424 **G** 020 7221 4772
Recently refurbished, well equipped
accommodation is offered at this friendly
bed and breakfast hotel. It is located close
to the Queensway station and offers easy
access to the West End.
29 rooms (2 family & 5 no smoking) / No
dogs (ex guide dogs) / Lift
Price band ££

♦ ♦ KINGSWAY HOTEL
27 Norfolk Square, Hyde Park W2 1RX
(follow sign to Hyde Park/Marble Arch, then
Paddington Station)
☎ 020 7723 7784 & 020 7723 5569
G 020 7723 7317
In a townhouse square close to
Paddington and the Bayswater road side
of Hyde Park, the Kingsway Hotel provides
comfortable, reasonably priced
accommodation. A lift services the six
floors of bedrooms. An enjoyable
breakfast is served in the cosy dining
room.
33 rooms (4 family) / No dogs (ex guide
dogs) / Lift
⬛

♦ ♦ PARKWOOD HOTEL
4 Stanhope Place, Marble Arch W2 2HB
(near Marble Arch tube station)
☎ 020 7402 2241 **G** 020 7402 1574
In a quiet residential street, close to the
attractions of Marble Arch and Oxford
Street, the Parkwood is ideal for budget
conscious shoppers and tourists. Staff are
friendly and breakfast is served in the
intimate downstairs dining room.
14 rooms (4 family & 2 no smoking) / No
dogs / No coaches
Price band ££ ⬛

♦ ♦ RHODES HOTEL
195 Sussex Gardens W2 2RJ
(hotel between Lancaster Gate underground
station and Edgware Rd)
☎ 020 7262 5617 & 020 7262 0537
G 020 7723 4054
A family-run terraced hotel, the Rhodes
offers a comfortable standard of
accommodation in well equipped and
nicely furnished bedrooms. Lounge
facilities are restricted to a small reception
area. Continental breakfast is included in
the tariff and an additional charge is made
for English; both are served in the bright
dining room situated on the lower ground
floor.
18 rooms (5 family) / No dogs
Price band ££ ⬛

W8

♦ ♦ ♦ AMBER
101 Lexham Gardens, Kensington W8 6JN
(A4 Cromwell Rd, turn left before Cromwell
Hospital, then left into Lexham Gardens)
☎ 020 7373 8666 **G** 020 7835 1194
Planters catch the eye outside this
terraced hotel in a residential street just
off Earls Court Road. There is a smart little
lobby and a garden. Nicely appointed
bedrooms do vary in size and outlook but
all are thoughtfully equipped and
comfortable.
40 rooms (2 no smoking) / Lift

♦ ♦ ♦ ATLAS-APOLLO HOTEL
18-30 Lexham Gardens, Kensington W8 5JE
(A4 into London, onto Cromwell Rd, 1st on
left after Cromwell Hospital. Hotel on right)
☎ 020 7835 1155 **G** 020 7370 4853
Originally two separate properties, the
Atlas-Apollo has been created to allow
guests to enjoy the best of the facilities,
and is now a pleasant well run and good
value hotel. Most of the accommodation
has en suite bath or shower, and
upgrading is ongoing. The friendly staff
ensure a warm welcome.
99 rooms (14 family) / No dogs (ex guide
dogs) / Lift / No coaches
Price band £££ ⬛

W14

♦♦♦ ASTON COURT HOTEL

25/27 Matheson Rd, West Kensington
W14 8SN

☎ 020 7602 9954 ☎ 020 7371 1338

Aston Court is a large corner property situated in a mainly residential area. Bedrooms are comfortable, very well equipped and all have the benefit of modern en suite facilities. Public areas include a small comfortable lounge area with a well-stocked bar and a conservatory where tasty English breakfasts are served.
29 rooms (3 family & 14 no smoking) / No dogs (ex guide dogs) / Lift

Aston Court Hotel

♦♦♦ AVONMORE HOTEL

66 Avonmore Rd W14 8RS
(off Hammersmith Road opposite Olympia Exhibition Centre)

☎ 020 7603 4296 & 3121
☎ 020 7603 4035

A small privately owned hotel in a relatively quiet location a few minutes walk from Olympia. Bedrooms, refurbished and attractively decorated, are spacious and well equipped. A choice of breakfast is served in the welcoming dining room, which also has a small bar.
9 rooms (3 family & 2 no smoking) / No dogs
Price band ££ 🖃

Avonmore Hotel

♦♦♦ CENTAUR HOTEL

21 Avonmore Rd W14 8RP
(turn off A4 onto North End Rd, right fork into Mathesow Rd, left into Lisgar Terrace, then into Avonmore Rd at the top)

☎ 020 7602 3857 & 7603 5973
☎ 020 7603 9193

Located very close to Olympia, but in a quiet side street, this small family-run hotel has a warm and friendly atmosphere. The bedrooms and bathrooms, while not large, have been recently re-decorated and are furnished in modern style with attractive soft furnishings. English or continental breakfast is served in the comfortable dining room.
10 rooms (2 family) / No dogs
Price band ££ 🖃

WHERE TO EAT

RESTAURANTS

AA RECOMMENDED

❀ ❀ ABINGDON
54 Abingdon Road W8 6AP
☎ 020 7937 3339 📠 020 7795 6388

A former pub, attractively renovated, with casual, well-informed service from a team said to be a delight to deal with. Coupled with an upbeat modern British menu it all adds up to a seductive, successful formula. Breads are 'just great', side orders are generous, and the short, snappy wine list has nine by the glass.
Fixed L £

❀ ADAMS CAFÉ
77 Askew Road W12 9AH
☎/📠 020 8743 0572

Small North African caf-cum-restaurant run by a friendly team. Expect good value Tunisian and Moroccan dishes. The aromatic tagine dishes are recommended, especially the lamb with prunes, almonds and sultanas.
ALC £

❀ ❀ ALASTAIR LITTLE W11
136a Lancaster Road W11 1QU
☎ 020 7243 2220 📠 020 7792 4504

There's a relaxed, informal feel to this busy 'shop-front' restaurant just off Ladbroke Grove. Simplicity drives the thinking behind Alastair Little's second restaurant, from the straightforward no-frills decor to the Italian-influenced menu that takes in home-made focaccia with rock salt crust and pigeon breast with salsa, broad beans, tomato and plenty of olive oil.
ALC £

❀ ❀ AL SAN VINCENZO
30 Connaught Street W2 2AF
☎ 020 7262 9623

Few restaurants in the Marble Arch area could be counted as proper neighbourhood establishments, but Vincenzo and Elaine Borgonzolo's tiny Al San Vincenzo is just such a place. It's plainly decorated yet with a surprisingly warm and intimate atmosphere. The hand-written menus change regularly and offer decent, rustic, original cooking.
ALC ££

❀ ANGLESEA ARMS
35 Wingate Road W6 0UR
☎ 020 8749 1291 📠 020 8749 1254

Lively London village gastro-pub with great twists including a log-burning spit roaster fired-up outdoors. Arrive early to beat the crowds and try robust, up-to-date cooking.
ALC ££

❀ ASSAGGI
39 Chepstow Place W2 4TS
☎ 020 7792 5501

Italian restaurant with warm Mediterranean decor located over a pub. Assaggi pasta loaf is a cross between ravioli and lasagne, other options could be venison and fish of the day.
ALC ££

❀ ❀ BISTRO 190, FISH RESTAURANT AT 190
190 Queen's Gate SW7 5EU
☎ 020 7581 5666 📠 020 7581 8172

Two very different restaurants under one roof. The immensely popular Bistro 190 on the ground floor of the Gore Hotel: a light, high-ceilinged room with huge windows overlooking Queensgate offering a tremendous laid-back atmosphere, the informality sitting well with the decor and service. To reach Fish at 190 you need to pass through the clamorous bar opposite the bistro 'a great place to people watch', and head downstairs where the atmosphere becomes more discreet, the tone that of a gentleman's club - especially given that the decor is all dark panelled walls with well-spaced tables covered by brilliant white table cloths spotlit from above. The menu is, of course, predominantly fish.
ALC ££

❀ ❀ THE BRACKENBURY
129-131 Brackenbury Road W6 0BQ
☎ 020 8748 0107 📠 020 8741 0905

Small, bustling, neighbourhood restaurant converted from two former shops with a bar at the back and outdoor dining on the pavement in summer. The daily changing menu has a strong Mediterranean bias, offers honest, robust cooking and uses the freshest ingredients. Good espresso coffee and an excellent choice of wines by the glass is complemented by friendly service.
Fixed L £ ALC ££

❀ ❀ CHEZ MOI
1 Addison Avenue W11 4QS
☎ 020 7603 8267 📠 020 7603 3898

A well-loved restaurant, established for over thirty years. The interior, with its deep-red walls and elaborate gilt-framed mirrors couldn't be further from the minimal style that is currently so popular; this is one of the most romantic, intimate restaurants in the capital. Broadly speaking, the cooking is French, but many other influences have, over the years, been incorporated into the repertoire. In addition. the restaurant makes superior

desserts and both the service and the wine list is polished.
Fixed L £ ALC ££

❀ ❀ CHINON RESTAURANT
23 Richmond Way W14 0AS
☎ 020 7602 5968 📠 020 7602 4082

A long, thin room with a patio garden at the back and some tables for fine-weather eating, set in an unremarkable parade of shops. This might be west London, but some of the dishes are straight out of provincial France. But Jonathon Hayes shows a reluctance to be pigeonholed, however, and can turn out a great tempura prawns with lemon and raisin chutney or fried squid with spaghetti as well. Crab ravioli is something of a signature dish: two sheets of the thinnest pasta sandwiching a huge mound of sweet, full-flavoured white crab in a smooth beurre blanc dotted with pesto. Hayes also has a way with fruity puddings, as in passion fruit sorbet with a fruit brûlée, chilled fruit soup, and outstanding lemon tart.
ALC ££

❀ ❀ CIBO
3 Russell Gardens W14 8EZ
☎ 020 7371 2085 📠 020 7602 1371

A bright and cheerful shop-fronted neighbourhood restaurant close to Olympia with much to please in the way of decor: striking paintings of nudes, a 3-D sculpture, crisp white-clothed tables, and a bar which provides the main focal point. Choose from a traditional Italian menu, plus a few specialities, that offers fresh and satisfying cooking.
ALC ££

❀ CLARKE'S
124 Kensington Church Street W8 4BH
☎ 020 7221 9225 📠 020 7229 4564

Lovely, idiosyncratic restaurant that continues to attract the Kensington locals as well as tourists. The ground-floor double-frontage is split in half - Clarke's shop on one side and the restaurant on the other - and in the light, airy basement, the restaurant extends over both. Clarke's upbeat modern lunch menu consists of four starters, three main courses and three desserts - each course one price. In the evening there is a set menu with no choices that changes once a week. There is an impressive wine list which includes many of Californian's best wines. Home-made breads, chocolate truffles, and other delicacies are for sale in the next door shop.

Hilaire

COPTHORNE TARA
Scarsdale Place Wrights Lane W8 5SR
020 7937 7211 **020 7937 7100**
French-style brasserie with a choice of
menus. International favourites include
balti chicken tikka masala, Thai sea bass,
and tagliatelle Don Alfredo with prawns
and mushrooms.
Fixed L/D £ ALC ££

THE COW DINING ROOM
89 Westbourne Park Road W2 5QH
020 7221 0021
The restaurant is set above a busy,
successful pub (which serves quality ales
and wonderfully fresh shell fish - all simply
served). Upstairs, however, Francis Bacon
prints adorn the walls and the atmosphere
is of a private dining room. The daily
changing set-menu (sometimes even
twice daily as they do use only the
freshest ingredients) offers modern British
cooking with a twist; the kitchen
understands how to make the most of a
wide range of ingredients. Service is
charming and efficient.
Fixed D £

DAKOTA
127 Ledbury Road W11 2AQ
020 7792 9191 **020 7792 9090**
Large, airy former pub with log stockade
styling hinting at the cooking's provenance
in America's south-west. Rajas salsa and
guajillo carnita seem a revelation for those
who have rejected TexMex. Pecan-smoked
rabbit, and roasted plums with liquorice
ice cream are a must.
Fixed L £ ALC ££

GREEN OLIVE
5 Warwick Place W9 2PX
020 7289 2469 **020 7289 4178**
Hard by the canals of Little Venice, a
delightful, friendly, busy modern Italian
restaurant. Exposed brick walls and waxed
floorboards contrast with the crisp
damask-clothed tables at which guests
tuck into the likes of Tuscan bean and
vegetable soup, followed perhaps by
grilled swordfish with a warm potato, red
onion and green bean salad in black olive
sauce. Apart from the fizz, the good
selection of wines is exclusively Italian.
Fixed D £

HALCYON HOTEL
81 Holland Park W11 3RZ
020 7727 7288 **020 7229 8516**
Town-house hotel decorated in country-
house mode. Huge floppy sofas in the bar
are a temptation to linger before moving
on to 'The Room', a comfortable restaurant
where contemporary art provides splashes
of colour to white walls and the floors are
of blond wood. This is the scene for some
forward-thinking cooking from a young
chef who is going places. Staff bring a
discreet yet friendly and unstuffy
approach.
Fixed L £ Fixed D £££ ALC £££

HILAIRE
68 Old Brompton Road SW7 3LQ
020 7584 8993 **020 7581 2949**
The shop-fronted restaurant is quite
deceptive. You enter a small, cosy dining
room warmed by lemon colours, but a
visit to the downstairs cloakroom reveals a
small bar and another half-a-dozen tables.
In keeping with the intimacy of the place,
staff go about their business in a friendly,
relaxed unfussy manner, which is just
what is needed. Bryan Webb's hand-
written menu offers around eight choices
at each course with descriptions taking the
direct approach, for example, breast of
duck, potato pancake, cider and apple
sauce. Desserts play it safe with the likes
of a well-made caramelised lemon and
banana tart with caramel ice cream. The
wine list is well balanced, lots of
reasonable prices and good offerings by
the glass.
Fixed L £ ALC ££

THE HOGARTH
33 Hogarth Road Kensington SW5 0QQ
020 7370 6831 **020 7373 6179**
Purpose built hotel off the Earl's Court
Road. The Terrace Bistro and Bar offers all
day service from sandwiches to crispy
chilly squid, Oriental salmon, or ribeye
beef.
Fixed L/D £ ALC £

KENSINGTON PLACE
201/205 Kensington Church Street W8 7LX
020 7727 3184 **020 7229 2025**
Close-packed, high-volume, and refusing
to slow down, Kensington Place is still
crazy after all these years and continues to
pull in the crowds - even on a frosty
winter lunchtime. Buzzing and humming,
it's a fun place and the food is good. The
style is modern with a fresh simplicity the
key note. Desserts range from bread-and-
butter pudding made with quince jam, to
pancakes with orange and Grand Marnier.
Fixed L £ ALC ££

LAUNCESTON PLACE
1a Launceston Place W8 5RL
020 7937 6912 **020 7938 2412**
Few restaurants manage the consistently
high standard of cooking that Launceston
Place achieves. Decorated in pastel
country house shades, it is favoured by
both Kensington shoppers and
enlightened local diners who enjoy the
sound modern British cooking. It is also
notable that the set menu is in no way a
poor relation to the carte. A team of
smart, informed waitresses are skilful and
attentive to detail without displaying the
least servility. A wine list of some ninety
bins offers some real bargains, especially
within the Burgundies.
Fixed L £ ALC ££

LEITH'S RESTAURANT
92 Kensington Park Road W11 2PN
020 7229 4481 **020 7221 1246**
A sense of comfort permeates Leith's and
service is equally accommodating.
Semicircular blue armchairs are arranged
at well-set tables, pale ochre walls are
hung with mirrors and paintings, and
subdued lighting dictates the atmosphere.
Leith's first opened its doors 30 years ago,
but life moves on, and so do menus that
incorporate tartare of sea trout with crispy
Serrano ham, tempura oyster and caviar

crème fraîche. But an element of the security blanket is strong in grilled loin of pork with sweetbread and chicken galette, or pot-roast guinea fowl with morels. Wine lovers will have a high old time with the wine list, while the hard-pressed could opt for a bottle from the house selection.
Fixed L £ Fixed D ££ ALC £££

❀ MANDARIN KITCHEN
14 Queensway W2 3RX
☎ 020 7727 9012/9468 ☎ 020 7727 9468
Spacious and busy modern Chinese restaurant. Fish is a speciality and live lobsters and crabs are a particular feature, served baked or steamed with a variety of sauces.
Fixed L/D £ ALC £

❀ MAS CAFÉ
6-8 All Saints Road W11 1HA
☎/☎ 020 7243 0969
Happening place for an arty clientele with a large bar area and music to enhance the atmosphere. Service is friendly, the cooking accurate, and the food full of flavour.

❀ MILLENNIUM BAILEYS HOTEL
140 Gloucester Road SW7 4QH
☎ 020 7373 6000 ☎ 020 7370 3760
The modern-look Olives sits comfortably alongside 19th-century architectural features. Modern British dishes include roast duck breast with braised cabbage, bacon and cherry sauce.
Fixed D £ ALC £

❀ MILLENNIUM GLOUCESTER
4-18 Harrington Gardens SW7 4LH
☎ 020 7373 6030 ☎ 020 7331 6131
The South West 7 Restaurant, with light-wood panelling, hardwood floors and original artwork, offers an Italian menu with pasta dishes, pizza and a selection of meat and fish.
ALC £

❀ ❀ NOVELLI W8
122 Palace Gardens Terrace W8 4RT
☎ 020 7229 4024 ☎ 020 7243 1826
More bistro than restaurant, with the Novelli signature blue walls and young casual staff. The budget decor is already showing signs of wear and tear but, given the relaxed style, the cooking is good value. A mix of classic French and Mediterranean flavours defines the cooking which carries enough punch to make an impact. Not the most comfortable seating for those over 40, however!
Fixed L £ ALC ££

❀ OFFSHORE
148 Holland Park Avenue W11 4UE
☎ 020 7221 6090 ☎ 020 7313 9700
Bright, glass-fronted restaurant specialising in that particular French-Mauritian seafood Sylvain Ho Wing Cheong is renowned for - French in style with a spicy oriental twist. We heavily endorse the delightfully named 'Picky-Picky' surprise degustation menu.
Fixed L £ ALC ££

❀ ORSINO
119 Portland Road W11 4LN
☎ 020 7221 3299 ☎ 020 7229 9414
Popular Italian eaterie, buzzy atmosphere. Imaginative pizzas, unusual pasta dishes as well as roast John Dory with white beans, tomato and wild garlic, or veal escalopes with asparagus, lemon and butter. Good Italian wine list.
Fixed L £ ALC ££

❀ PHARMACY RESTAURANT
150 Notting Hill Gate W11 3QG
☎ 020 7221 2442 ☎ 020 7243 2345
Trustafarian hang-out designed by Damien Hirst. The ground floor bar is for drinks and snacks, the first-floor restaurant serves mod-Euro dishes such as papardelle with chicken livers and rocket, and chargrilled scallops with leeks and button mushrooms. Weekends are popular.
Fixed L £ ALC ££

❀ THE POPESEYE
108 Blythe Road W14 0HD
☎ 020 7610 4578 ☎ 020 7352 1279
A simple, successful formula prevails here: steaks and nothing but, from grass-eating Aberdeen Angus cattle, fillet, sirloin and popeseye (the Scottish name for rump), all served with great chips by cheerful staff.
Fixed D £ No credit cards

❀ ❀ RAIN
303 Portobello Road W10 5TD
☎ 020 8968 2001
You walk into a heady den with low-lying plump cushions set before a disproportionately large bar before going into the restaurant itself: scratched walls of green and blue, oriental artefacts, organza drapes. It also defines the style as new Asian, or oriental fusion food. Tamarind, wasabi, peanut sauce, Japanese seven spice, lemongrass, oyster sauce, coconut milk and sesame are just some of the seasonings used in the modestly described dishes that deliver more than is promised by the menu. Staff are diligently well-informed to deal with customers' queries, and the wine list is a deliberate attempt to marry grapes with food.
Fixed L £ ALC ££

❀ ❀ THE RED PEPPER
8 Formosa Street W9 1EE
☎ 020 7266 2708 ☎ 020 7266 5522
Lively Italian-style restaurant with a relaxed atmosphere. Freshly-prepared pizzas emerge tantalisingly from the wood-fired brick oven, while more traditional Med dishes include smoked swordfish carpaccio and linguine with new potatoes, green beans and pesto sauce.
ALC £

❀ ❀ ❀ RIVER CAFÉ
Thames Wharf Studios Rainville Road W6 9HA
☎ 020 7381 8824 ☎ 020 7381 6217
Simple modern decor, stainless steel and not a lot of room between tables at this riverside restaurant. Famously dedicated to Italian country cooking with an all-Italian wine list, coarse Tuscan bread arrives with thick, unctuous olive oil and menus are littered with pasta, risotto, bruschetta and salads. Vegetables and herbs play an important part in each dish, and marinades are used to good effect. The favoured cooking vehicles are the chargrill and the wood-fired oven, the former to produce scallops with red chillies, borlotti beans, rocket and red wine vinegar, the latter loin of organic pork stuffed with porcini, thyme, lemon zest and prosciutto fat served with broad beans braised in milk.
ALC £££

❀ ROYAL CHINA
13 Queensway 4QJ
☎ / ☎ 020 7221 2535
Hugely popular Chinese restaurant. Expect an extensive menu of mainly Szechuan and Cantonese dishes, along with a few unexpected specialities. Stewed eggplant with minced pork in spicy black bean sauce in a clay pot and grilled dumplings go down a treat.

❀ ❀ ❀ ROYAL GARDEN HOTEL
2-24 Kensington High Street W8 4PT
☎ 020 7937 8000 ☎ 020 7361 1991
Take the lift from the marble-floored lobby at this tall, modern hotel, get out at the tenth floor and take a table in the contemporary, bright, smart restaurant and gasp at the views over Kensington Gardens and Hyde Park. With its base in the classical repertoire, the kitchen grabs modern ideas, often from the East, and produces zappy dishes of vibrant flavours: seared scallops on sweet-and-sour chicory with sauce vierge, galantine of oriental chicken and tuna with ravigote dressing, and main courses of roasted sea bass with braised leeks and a caramelised onion bhajia, or pan-fried calves' liver with blue cheese gnocchi à l'alsacienne. Puddings end on an upbeat note in the shape of banana soufflé with sweet-and-sour lychee ice cream, or a spot-on bitter redcurrant tart with orange sorbet.
Fixed L £ ALC £££

❀ ❀ ROYAL LANCASTER HOTEL, NIPA THAI
Lancaster Terrace W2 2TY
☎ 020 7262 6737 ☎ 020 7724 3191
Elegant oriental-style dining room and efficient service from some of the friendliest staff in London. There are strong Thai links as The Royal Lancaster is a sister to the Landmark in Bangkok. An all-female team runs the kitchen, with staff in traditional dress out front. The menu is sensibly less extensive than is the norm, and offers a good selection of expected dishes such as curries, salads, and pan-fried dishes. A selection of traditional Thai puddings are offered, but these are an acquired taste.
Fixed L/D ££ ALC ££

❀❀ ROYAL LANCASTER HOTEL, PARK RESTAURANT
Lancaster Terrace W2 2TY
📞 020 7262 6737 📠 020 7724 3191
Some of the best view across Hyde Park and Kensington Gardens can be had from the upper floors of this 18-storey hotel. And considering it is hard against Lancaster Gate Tube station - giving easy access to the rest of the capital - the location couldn't be bettered. Mediterranean in style, The Pavement caters for all-day snacking and grazing, but it's in the smart Park Restaurant that serious cooking takes place, the menu showcasing a sound range of modern British cooking.
Fixed L/D £

❀❀ SNOWS-ON-THE-GREEN
166 Shepherd's Bush Road Hammersmith W6 7PB
📞 020 7603 2142 📠 020 7602 7553
Bright decor bring a hint of the Mediterranean to this double-fronted restaurant. The menu gives more than a nod towards the Med too. Tuscan bean, sausage and cabbage soup with sun-dried tomatoes, for example, with French provincial classics such as a robust coq au vin on a bed of superb mash defining a number of main courses.
Fixed L £ ALC ££

❀ STRATFORDS
7 Stratford Road W8 6RF
📞 020 7937 6388 📠 020 7938 3435
Beach-hut blues and yellows enliven this attractive restaurant and set the tone for the menu's seafood theme. Start perhaps with grilled prawns with a touch of garlic, followed by lightly fried lemon sole served simply with parsley butter.

❀ SUPAN THAI RESTAURANT
4 Fernhead Road W9 3ET
📞 020 8969 9387
Neighbourhood restaurant with a loyal following. Traditionally clad Thai ladies serve a wide range of dishes: stir-fried rice noodles with prawns and black bean sauce, perhaps, or chargrilled marinated chicken with spicy chilli sauce.
ALC £

❀ SWALLOW INTERNATIONAL HOTEL
Cromwell Road SW5 0TH
📞 020 7973 1000 📠 020 7244 8194
One of the few London hotels with its own car park. The hotel's restaurant is hidden away at the back with piano music drifting through from the cocktail bar. Plenty of choice with some traditional, some ambitious dishes: ribeye steaks; baked cod with pancetta.

❀❀ VERONICA'S
3 Hereford Road W2 4AB
📞 020 7229 5079/7229 1452
📠 020 7229 1210
Cheerful neighbourhood restaurant with historical leanings. The kitchen deals exclusively with well-researched old British recipes and the menu gives a potted

history of each one. Around 10 main courses are divided almost equally between meat, fish and vegetarian. Finish with an unusual sweet spinach tart with rosewater.
Fixed L/D £ ALC ££

❀ WILSON'S
236 Blythe Road W14 0HJ
📞 020 7603 7267 📠 020 7602 9018
One of the best kept secrets in Brook Green. A charming, unassuming restaurant du quartier that has been providing satisfying food in a pleasant and relaxed atmosphere for almost two years. With its wheelback chairs, punkas overhead and tartan curtains there's a partly Scottish accent that takes in a kilted proprietor who presides over the service and can, on occasion, be persuaded to play the bagpipes. The main menu, roughly ten choices per course, does not change much, but a short set-price menu has also been introduced. Dishes are straightforward, but not without interest. Desserts are notably good, particularly the raspberry queen of puddings.
ALC £

❀ YAS
7 Hammersmith Road W14 8XJ
📞 020 7603 9148 📠 020 7603 3320
Expect friendly service and simple, freshly cooked food at this Iranian eaterie. Super flat bread comes straight from the tandoor to go with chicken stew with saffron rice, or halibut cooked with herbs, chillis, garlic and tamarind. Plenty of familiar kebabs for the less adventurous.
Fixed D £ ALC £

PUBS, INNS & OTHER PLACES

SW5

THE BLACKBIRD
209 Earl's Court Rd
📞 020 7835 1855
Once the Earl's Court branch of Barclays Bank, The Blackbird is now a pleasant pub with a fine line in pies.

LA DELIZIA
246 Old Brompton Rd, Earls Court, SW5
📞 020 7373 6085
Good pizza place. More branches at Chelsea Manor St, and Chelsea Farmer's Market.

DRAYTON ARMS
153 Old Brompton Road
📞 020 7373 0385
The site of a pub since 1847, The Drayton Arms has live music every Friday and Saturday, and a small theatre on the first floor.

O'NEILLS
326 Earl's Court Rd SW5 9BQ
📞 020 7373 9172
A Victorian brewery-turned-bar established by the eponymous Irishman who worked his way up through the ranks to buy the business. Food with an Irish theme.

THE PRINCE OF TECK
161 Earl's Court Rd
📞 020 7373 3107
Part of the Earl's Court Australian community's support structure.

TUSC
256 Brompton Road
📞 020 7373 9082
Long-established Italian restaurant specialising in smaller dishes with plenty of variety.

SW7

CAFÉ LAZEEZ
93 Old Brompton Rd, SW7 3LD
📞 020 7581 9993
Traditional and modern Indian cooking, close to Christie's auction rooms.

THE CHICAGO RIB SHACK
1 Raphael Street
📞 020 7581 5595
Family friendly and very popular in the evenings. Specialises in barbecued pork, chili, and mud pie.

THE HEREFORD ARMS
127 Gloucester Road
📞 020 7370 4988
Very popular and smart pub with a traditional atmosphere.

PIZZA CHELSEA
93 Pelham St, South Kensington, SW7 2NJ
📞 020 7584 4788
Popular local pizzeria.

TEXAS LONE STAR SALOON
☎ 020 7370 5625
154 Gloucester Road
A busy Tex-Mex restaurant themed around a Western bar, complete with Country and Western music and videos.

W2

THE COW
89 Westbourne Park Rd, W2
☎ 020 7221 0021
Trendy pub owned by Terence Conran's son, Tom. Impressive menu and plenty of oysters.

THE MITRE
24 Craven Terrace
☎ 020 7262 5240
Victorian pub with a no smoking family room and a piano bar.

THE PRINCE BONAPARTE
80 Chepstow Rd W2 5BE
☎ 020 7229 5912
Victorian pub, airy and open plan, offering modern British cooking with Eastern, African and Mediterranean influences.

W6

DEALS
Bradmore House, Queen Caroline St, Hammersmith Broadway, W6 9YD
☎ 020 8563 1001
International cuisine situated inside the Hammersmith Broadway Centre.

THE GATE VEGETARIAN RESTAURANT
51 Queen Caroline St, Hammersmith
☎ 020 8748 6932
Imaginative vegetarian cookery with plenty of variety.

MR WONG WONDERFUL HOUSE
313-317 King St, Hammersmith, W6 9NH
☎ 020 8748 6887
"Wonderful" dim sum!

W8

CAFÉ FLO
127 Kensington Church St, W8 7LP
☎ 020 7727 8142
French brasserie in the same chain as La Coupole in Paris.

COSTA'S FISH RESTAURANT
18 Hillgate St, Notting Hill Gate, W8 7SR
☎ 020 7727 4310
Licensed restaurant behind a takeaway chip shop.

GEALES
2 Farmer St, Notting Hill Gate, W8 7SN
☎ 020 7727 7969
Exellent fish and chip shop. Not just cod and saveloys though. Deep-fried clam and shark turn up on the menu.

MALABAR
27 Uxbridge St, Notting Hill Gate, W8 7TQ
☎ 020 7727 8800
Indian restaurant with Mediterranean decor.

MUFFIN MAN
12 Wrights Lane, off Kensington High St, W8 6TA
☎ 020 7937 6652
A taste of yesteryear at this traditional English teashop.

STICKY FINGERS
1 Phillimore Gardens, off Kensington High St, W8 7QG
☎ 020 7938 5338
Popular diner, packed with Rolling Stones memorabilia.

WINDSOR CASTLE
114 Campden Hill Rd, Kensington, W8 7AR
☎ 020 7727 8491
Traditional English cooking at a 19th-century pub.

W11

BEACH BLANKET BABYLON
45 Ledbury Rd, W11
☎ 020 7229 2907
Crazy decor and trendy crowd.

BUZZ BAR
95 Portobello Rd, W11
☎ 020 7460 4906
Internet access at this cyber-café.

GROUND FLOOR
186 Portobello Rd, W11
☎ 020 7243 801
More of a club than a pub, but you can still get a beer during the day.

MANZARA
24 Pembridge Rd, Notting Hill Gate, W11 3HL
☎ 020 7727 3062
A variety of delicacies with a Turkish or French flavour.

MARKET BAR
240a Portobello Rd, W11
☎ 020 7229 6472
Strange mirrors & weird objects. A Beach Blanket Babylon project.

OSTERIA BASILICO
29 Kensington Pk Rd, W11 2EQ
☎ 020 7727 9372
Italian restaurant with eclectic menu.

Call the AA Hotel Booking Service on 0870 5050505 to book at AA recognised hotels and B&Bs in the UK, or through our internet site: http://www.theaa.co.uk/hotels

AA Hotel Booking Service

The AA Hotel Booking Service - Now you have a free, simple way to reserve a place to stay for a week, weekend, or a one-night stopover.

Do you want to book somewhere in the Lake District that has leisure facilities; a city-centre hotel in Glasgow with parking facilities, or do you need accommodation near Dover which is handy for the Eurotunnel?

The AA Booking Service can take the hassle out of booking the right place for you.

And if you are touring round the UK or Ireland, simply give the AA Hotel Booking Service your list of overnight stops, and from one phone call all your accommodation can be booked for you.

Telephone 0870 5050505

Office hours
Monday-Friday 9am-6pm
Saturday 9am-1pm
Not available Sundays or Bank Holidays

Full listings of AA recognised accommodation available through the Hotel Booking Service can be found and booked at the AA's Internet Site:

http://www.theaa.co.uk/hotels

REGENT'S PARK
AND
BLOOMSBURY

In 1812, Regent Street and Portland Place were designed by John Nash as a sweeping thoroughfare from Carlton House Terrace to Regent's Park, which he also laid out. The idea was to make London a more beautiful city than Paris, and was in part a gesture of triumph after the defeat of Napoleon at the Battle of Waterloo in 1815. Although the project was never completed, it has left the city with a wonderful park and some classical architecture.

Regent's Park dominates the area of Marylebone, and is the venue for softball matches, tennis and boating. It was created as a hunting ground by Henry VIII, but only really came into its own, thanks to George IV (then Prince Regent) who involved John Nash in designing a kind of garden city with villas, circuses, terraces and a pleasure palace. After fifteen years the project ran out of funds, (not even the King has bottomless pockets) but is still a pretty impressive piece of work. It also houses London Zoo, once under threat of closure but now back on track with a new programme of conservation for endangered species.

Regent's Canal forms the northern boundary of the park, and leads to Camden Lock. To the south of the park lies the wide Marylebone Road, incessantly teeming with traffic. Along the road lies Madame Tussaud's, the famous waxworks, the Planetarium, and the Royal Academy of Music. Just behind these you'll come across the Sherlock Holmes Museum on Baker Street. The BBC, at the Regent Street end of Portland Place, is the flagship building for the British Broadcasting Corporation, with a new entertainment feature that allows you to take part in your very own programme.

Heading east from Regent's Park is Bloomsbury, dominated by two major institutions, the British Museum and the University of London. The university's 47 colleges and student halls are scattered around the area. Dillons bookshop, on Gower Street, is the university bookshop and one of the finest in London. The British Museum is one of Britain's top tourist attractions with some six million visitors a year. It's fourteen acres of antiquities are enough to tire the biggest museum fan.

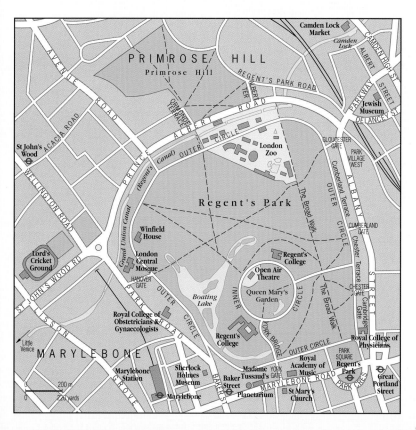

Strolling around the area, you notice its austere architecture with large, white, Georgian houses round grassy squares. Gordon Square was one of the main focuses for the Bloomsbury Group, and was where Virginia Woolf, Vanessa Bell, Lytton Strachey and Bertrand Russell lived during the early 20th century. This group of friends were influential in literature, painting, philosophy and "modern" sexual relations.

Aside from its strong literary connections, Bloomsbury has other buildings of interest such as the Thomas Coram Foundation with paintings contributed to the Foundling's Hospital, and Coram's Fields, an inner-city children's park. Both of these are named for Thomas Coram, a retired sea captain who founded a poor children's hospital in the mid-18th century. At the opposite end of scale is Harley Street, where the most expensive doctors, consultants and dentists have their practices.

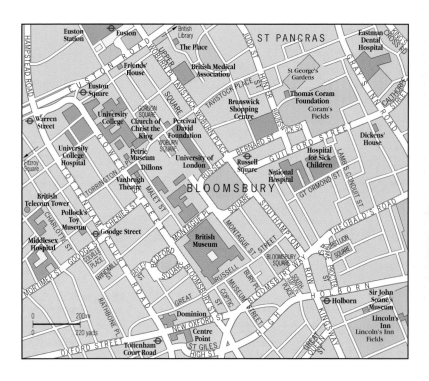

MUST SEE

Central Mosque, Regent's Park

MADAME TUSSAUD'S
Marylebone Rd, NW1
☎ 020-7935 6861
Madame Tussaud learnt the art of waxworks from her uncle in Paris. She brought her work to London in 1802 and became a phenomenal success. Her first exhibit was a series of models of the heads of decapitated French aristocrats. The Chamber of Horrors is particularly popular, and some of the exhibits are original works by Tussaud herself. To be cast in wax and on display here is confirmation of fame. Have your picture taken next to Lenin, Margaret Thatcher or Benny Hill. Book a day ahead to avoid the queues. You can also get a combined ticket with the London Planetarium.

REGENT'S PARK AND PRIMROSE HILL
NW1
Laid out in 1817-28 by John Nash, Regent's Park covers 465 acres. It was once a hunting ground for Henry VIII, and today is a lively place in the summer, with a boating lake, three playgrounds, bandstand music, tennis courts and an Open-Air Theatre. The Outer Circle covers over 2 miles, and Queen Mary's Gardens in the Inner Circle contains a rose garden, planted to honour Queen Mary, wife of George V. Regent's College is now a centre for European studies. The towpath of Regent's Canal (a branch of the Grand

Union Canal) leads round the northern perimeter of the park to London Zoo.

Primrose Hill is 112 acres of open green to the north of Regent's Park. It is a quiet and pleasant place to relax and get away from the activities in the larger park - or to fly a kite. If you feel like a climb, make your way to the top of the park (206ft) and enjoy the splendid views across the capital. Many literary greats have lived in the area, including Sylvia Plath, HG Wells and Friedrich Engels.

BRITISH MUSEUM
Great Russell St, WC1
☎ 020-7636 1555
(recorded information: 020-7580 1788)
Behind the Grecian-style façade is a temple to the arts and achievements of the world's civilisations, with around four million exhibits (there's a good guide). Among them are the Rosetta Stone, the Elgin Marbles (although Greece wants them returned), the treasures of Sutton Hoo, and the 2,000-year-old murdered Lindow Man, found preserved in a peat bog. In the Reading Room, Karl Marx researched and wrote his magnum opus, *Das Kapital.* Now that the British Library has moved (see below), there are plans for a major programme of expansion and

Little Venice

renewal for the year 2000, including a restored Reading Room and Great Court with a vast glass canopy. This is well overdue, since the British Museum was originally designed to cater for just 5% of the number of visitors it receives today.

BRITISH LIBRARY
Euston Rd, WC1
☎ 020-7412 7000
All publishers in the country are obliged by law to send one copy of every book, periodical, newspaper or map they publish to the British Library. Recently moved from its former home in the British Museum (see above), the contravposial Library has been dogged by delays and false starts. It opened in stages throughout 1997, 1998 and 1999. First to open was the Humanities Reading Room, in November 1997 (for readers only). Now, the general public are allowed entrance. On display will be the original manuscripts of Jane Austen, Handel's *Messiah,* two of the four surviving copies of the Magna Carta, and the Lindisfarne Gospels from around AD 698. Although all estimates seem to have been faulty, by now all books should have been moved from the British Museum.

The Planetarium

BROADCASTING HOUSE (BBC)
Portland Place, W1
☎ 020-7580 4468
Built in 1931, the home of the British
Broadcasting Corporation (BBC) echoes
the shape of All Souls' Church. Its 22
studios are located in the core of the
building to avoid noise. The public can
visit the entrance hall, where there is a
bookshop selling BBC publications. (At the
BBC's other studios in Wood Lane, W12,
you can be part of the audience on certain
shows and programmes). The BBC
Experience On Air celebrates more than
75 years of the BBC. You can explore the
history of television from the first black-
and-white images on screen to the latest
CD-ROM interactive technology. Along the
way you can participate in Desert Island
Discs and Mastermind, direct EastEnders,
or hook up with the news on Radio 5 Live.

WALLACE COLLECTION
Hertford House, Manchester Sq, W1
☎ 020-7935 0687
This world-class collection of art, arms and
armour, is housed in an opulent building
with a magnificent white marble staircase.
Put together by the 4th Marquess of
Hertford and his illegitimate son, Sir
Richard Wallace, the collection is rich in
works by Fragonard, Boucher, Watteau and
Poussin, and includes Frans Hals' *The
Laughing Cavalier*, Rembrandt's son, Titus,
Poussin's *Dance to the Music of Time*, and
portraits by Gainsborough, Romney and
Reynolds.

REGENT'S CANAL
Regent's Canal is a branch of the Grand
Union Canal. The areas of Little Venice,
Regent's Park and Camden Lock are very
pretty, with waterside pubs, restaurants
and narrowboats. Narrowboat cruises with
commentaries are run by the London
Waterbus Company (tel: 020-7482 2660).
The Grand Union Canal goes from
Paddington to the Docklands, and
Regent's Canal covers the Regent's Park
and Camden Lock and beyond. It's a great
way to sightsee.

HISTORIC AND ANCIENT SIGHTS

BRITISH TELECOM TOWER
Cleveland St, W1
When it opened in 1965, the Post Office
Tower (as it was then known) was the
tallest building in London (177m or 580ft).
Now overtaken by Canary Wharf and the
NatWest Tower, it is still an impressive
landmark housing a mass of
telecommunications equipment. In 1971,
the Angry Brigade (allegedly) exploded a
bomb in the revolving restaurant at the
top which ended public access. The tower
is rounded to cut down on wind
resistance and make it easier to align the
dozens of aerials that sit atop it. Visits are
by special invitation only.

Regent's Canal

UNIVERSITY OF LONDON UNION (ULU)
Malet St, WC1
☎ 020-7664 2000
The University of London consists of 34
colleges, with a total of around 70,000
students. University College London is
situated here in the heart of literary
Bloomsbury. The Student Union still puts
on plenty of good gigs.

PARK CRESCENT
WC1
Built by John Nash between 1812 and
1818, this was in its time a daring design,
in that it varied wildly from the square
design of before. Nash wanted it to be
circular and to serve as a major entrance
to Regent's Park, but it was only half
finished and is now separated from the
park by busy Marylebone Road.

HARLEY STREET
WC1
Famous for its doctors, dentists,
pyschiatrists and plastic surgeons, Harley
Street still caters for wealthy, private
clients behind impressive, large front
doors. JMW Turner lived at No.64 from
1804 to 1808.

GREAT ORMOND STREET HOSPITAL
Great Ormond St, WC1
The Hospital for Sick Children was set up
in 1851 to reduce the high rate of
mortality among London's children, and
still receives an income from the royalties
of Peter Pan, as stipulated by its author,
JM Barrie. The hospital received further
publicity by being one of the favourite
charities of Diana, Princess of Wales.

MUSEUMS

DICKENS' HOUSE
49 Doughty St, WC1
☎ 020-7405 2127
The novelist Charles Dickens lived here
with his family between 1837 and 1839,
and it was here that he wrote *Nicholas
Nickleby*, *Oliver Twist* and *The Pickwick
Papers*. Quite a feat in just two years. The
chair and desk where he wrote are on
display, as well as first editions of his work.

SHERLOCK HOLMES MUSEUM
239 (although it says 221b) Baker St, NW1
☎ 020-7935 8866
On four floors, this is the fictional home
(221b) of the great detective Sherlock
Holmes, created by Arthur Conan Doyle.
The rooms on view intend to show how
Holmes and Dr Watson lived, including
Holmes' armchair and memorabilia from
different mysteries they solved.

PERCIVAL DAVID FOUNDATION
53 Gordon Sq, WC1
☎ 020-7387 3909
Sir Percival David was an avid collector of
Chinese ceramics, amassing around
17,000 items. The highlights here are two
Yuan dynasty vases, and the 17th-century
Ming vases. The hushed atmosphere
seems to suit the exhibits.

PETRIE MUSEUM OF EGYPTIAN ARCHAEOLOGY
DMS Watson Library, University College
London, Malet St, WC1
☎ 020-7387 7050 (ext 2884)
Bequeathed to University College London

Sherlock Holmes Museum

Charles Dickens' House

by the father of Egyptian archaeology, Sir Flinders Petrie in 1933, the collection here covers Egyptian antiquities, including a linen dress from around 2800 BC and horribly recognisable mummified figures.

MCC MUSEUM
Marylebone Cricket Club, Lord's Cricket Ground, NW8
☎ 020-7432 1033
All cricketing fans will absolutely love this museum. In the Long Room are portraits of the game's best players, and elsewhere are paintings, photographs, bats and the Ashes, cricket's most coveted trophy (actually the remains of a bail from the Test Match series 1882-3 between England and Australia).

RIBA
66 Portland Pl, W1
☎ 020-7307 3699
The Royal Institute of British Architects exhibits work from some of the greatest architects.

SAATCHI COLLECTION
98a Boundary Rd, NW8
☎ 020-7624 8299
Owned by the wealthy advertising success Charles Saatchi, this gallery displays changing exhibitions by modern British designers, artists and sculptors. If an artist's work is shown here, it is almost guaranteed that they will become immensely fashionable.

CINEMAS

ABC BAKER STREET
Baker Street, NW1
☎ 020-7935 9772 (recorded info)
Two screens showing recent releases.

ABC TOTTENHAM COURT ROAD
Tottenham Court Rd, W1
☎ 020-7636 6148 (recorded info)
Three screens showing major releases.

SCREEN ON BAKER STREET
96 Baker St, NW1
☎ 020-7486 0036 (recorded info)
Two screens, showing recent releases.

RENOIR
Brunswick Centre, Brunswick Sq, WC1
☎ 020-7837 8402
Two screens showing arthouse films.

THEATRES AND CONCERT HALLS

WIGMORE HALL
36 Wigmore St, W1
☎ 020-7935 2141
A favourite venue for recitals and chamber music, the Wigmore Hall has superb acoustics. The calm atmosphere makes it a wonderful place for the Sunday morning coffee (or sherry!) concerts. BBC Radio 3 often broadcasts concerts from here.

REGENT'S PARK OPEN-AIR THEATRE
☎ 020-7486 2431/1933
Rather at the mercy of the English weather (performances are cancelled if it is raining), the season runs from May to September. Founded in 1932, it is famous for its Shakespearean productions (June to August) and in particular A Midsummer Night's Dream.

DRILL HALL
16 Chenies St, WC1
☎ 020-7637 8270
A small theatre dedicated to feminist, gay, and politically-aware theatre.

ENTERTAINMENT AND NIGHTLIFE

DOMINION
Tottenham Court Rd, W1
☎ 0870 607 7401
Big names in the music world perform here at this large theatre.

The MCC Museum at Lord's Cricket Ground

THE PLACE
17 Duke's Rd, WC1
☎ 020-7387 0031
Contemporary dance is staged here, and it is the home of the London Contemporary Dance School, who tour the country with their shows, which have been assembled by dancers with the best contemporary dance training. International troupes also perform here.

BLOOMSBURY THEATRE
15 Gordon St, WC1
☎ 020-7388 8822
Part of the University of London, this is the place for contemporary dance.

James Smith & Sons, New Oxford Street

CAMDEN PALACE
1a Camden High St, NW1
☎ 020-7387 0428
A huge nightclub venue with a large dance floor and plenty of top DJs.

SHOPPING

HEAL'S
196 Tottenham Court Rd, W1
☎ 020-7636 1666
A wonderful store with home furnishings and accessories that are understated, colourful and pleasing to the eye.

HABITAT
196 Tottenham Court Rd, WC1
☎ 020-7631 3880
Started by Sir Terence Conran in the 1960s, Habitat has home furnishings and accessories in colourful modern designs.

PURVES & PURVES
80-81 Tottenham Court Rd, W1
☎ 020-7580 8223
Simply designed home furnishings and accessories by British designers.

CONTEMPORARY APPLIED ARTS
2 Percy St, W1
☎ 020-7436 2344
A varied range of crafts and artwork from the latest designers in London.

JAMES SMITH & SONS
53 New Oxford St, WC1
☎ 020-7836 4731
Believe it or not, a whole shop dedicated to walking sticks and umbrellas. A true Bloomsbury-style shopping experience.

PAPERCHASE
213 Tottenham Court Rd, W1
☎ 020-7580 8496
A superb shop for cards, coloured writing paper, desk accessories, pens etc. There are branches throughout London.

CORNELISSEN & SON
105 Great Russell St, WC1
☎ 020-7636 1045
Paints, canvases, brushes, pastels - a fabulous shop for any artist.

GREAT FOR KIDS

There are loads of Festivals and Events throughout the year in London which children will love - See Festivals and Events.
There's a McDonald's at 134 Tottenham Court Rd, a Burger King at 1a Tottenham Court Rd and a Pizza Express at 30 Coptic St.

LONDON ZOO
Regent's Park, NW1
☎ 020-7722 3333
Right in the northern corner of Regent's Park, London Zoo was opened in 1828 and was the first of its kind in the world. By 1993 the zoo was in real financial trouble. Funds were raised through public

The British Museum

donations and a gift from the Kuwaiti government, to save the zoo, and today the emphasis is on conservation, education and breeding of endangered species such as gorillas and Asian lions. You can also see penguins, elephants, rhinos and much more. The Children's Zoo has British farmyard animals which you can pet, as well as some more exotic animals such as llamas and camels.

LONDON PLANETARIUM
Marylebone Rd, NW1
☎ 020-7935 6861
With a recent multi-million pound new look, the Planetarium now takes you even further into the secrets of space travel, stars and planets. The highlight is the cosmic show with speeds you along a simulated 'virtual reality' trip into deepest space. It is made possible by the most advanced Star projector in the world, Digistar 11. A combined ticket with Madame Tussaud's is available.

London Zoo

POLLOCK'S TOY MUSEUM
1 Scala St, W1
☎ 020-7636 3452
Crammed with Benjamin Pollock's recreated theatres as well as toys from as far back as the 18th century. Live theatre shows are held, and the shop sells reproductions of toys from around the world. A brilliant place to bring the children.

REGENT'S PARK, W1
In the summer the boating lake in Regent's Park is very popular with children and their toy boats, mechanised or otherwise. It's also seemingly popular with their fathers. When they get bored, take

them up to Primrose Hill to fly a kite - it's one of the best places in London for it.

CORAM'S FIELDS
93 Guildford St, WC1
☎ 020-7837 6138
This is a 7-acre park connected to the Thomas Coram Foundation. There is a mini city farm and an aviary, as well as a children's nursery.

THE FLOATING BOATER
1 Bishop's Bridge Rd, W2
☎ 020-7724 8740
Take a trip from Little Venice to Regent's Park on one of two charter boats.

JASON'S TRIP
60 Blomfield Rd, Little Venice, W9
☎ 020-7286 3428
Jason's Trip follows the canal from Little Venice to Camden Lock, and also to the London Canal Museum.

PUPPET THEATRE BARGE
Blomfield Rd, Little Venice, W9
☎ 020-7249 6876
Just what it says - a puppet theatre on an old working barge on a pretty backwater of Regent's Canal.

TGI FRIDAY'S
96 Bishops Bridge Rd, W2
☎ 020-7229 8600
Another branch of this all-American children's favourite restaurant, with balloons and a free colouring book.

Lord's Cricket Ground

No.46 Gordon Square was the home of Virginia Woolf, her sister Vanessa Bell and Vanessa's husband Clive Bell. It was here that the circle often met. Among the number of this august group were the writers EM Forster, Roger Fry, and Lytton Strachey, and the painter Duncan Grant. Below are listed a selection of bookshops which continue the literary connections of this famous London area.

DILLONS BOOKSTORE
82 Gower St, WC1
☎ 020-7636 1577
The flagship branch of this nationwide bookstore stocking thousands of books on a wide variety of subjects.

CINEMA BOOKSHOP
13-14 Great Russell St, WC1
☎ 020-7637 0206
Dedicated to film and filmstars, there's a vast collection of books and stills.

PLACES OF WORSHIP

ALL SOULS CHURCH
Langham Pl, W1
Built in 1822, All Souls is a delightful church near to the BBC and created by John Nash. Today it is used for lunchtime and evening concerts.

ST MARY'S CHURCH
Marylebone High St, W1
You can see St Mary's majestic Corinthian portico and circular tower from York Bridge on the south side of Regent's Park, an intention of John Nash, who created the park.

UNIVERSITY CHURCH OF CHRIST THE KING
Gordon Sq, WC1
A huge building with an ornate interior near to the University of London and on pretty Gordon Square. Its intended 300-ft high tower was never built.

ST GEORGE'S BLOOMSBURY
Bloomsbury Way, WC1
This church was built by Hawksmoor and has an elegant spire. The statue is the only one in London of the unpopular king, George I.

SPORT AND LEISURE

LORD'S CRICKET GROUND
St John's Wood Rd, NW8
☎ 020-7289 1611
Lord's is one of the major cricket grounds in the world, and is something of a Mecca for cricket fans. It is the home of Marylebone Cricket Club (MCC) who make all the decisions about the game. National and international matches are played here, and there is a gallery of cricketing memorabilia with guided tours daily (except when a match is on).

REGENT'S PARK GOLF SCHOOL
Regent's Park, NW1
☎ 020-7724 0643
Driving range sessions are available here, as well as all kinds of advice on how to improve your game.

REGENT'S PARK
☎ 020-7486 7905
There are several hard tennis courts in Regent's Park which are open to the public. Also in the park you can play boules, football and softball.

Bloomsbury Square

LITERARY BLOOMSBURY

Bloomsbury is a district of leafy squares, dominated by the University of London and the British Museum, both places of higher education. The area is also associated with a circle of writers known collectively as the 'Bloomsbury Group', because some of their members lived locally.

British Telecom Tower

DAUNT BOOKS
83-84 Marylebone High St, W1
☎ 020-7224 2295
With a gallery running all around the shop, this is the place to come to find that elusive travel guide you've been searching for. They only sell travel guides.

FORBIDDEN PLANET
71 New Oxford St, WC1
☎ 020-7836 4179
The best place in London for science fiction, horror, and film fans to find all their favourite comics, models, magazines, books, and fringe literature.

FRENCH'S THEATRE BOOKSHOP
52 Fitzroy St, W1
☎ 020-7387 9373
The name says it all. A bookshop entirely dedicated to theatre in all its variety.

UNSWORTH, RICE & COE
12 Bloomsbury St, WC1
☎ 020-7436 9836
This bookshop specialises in antiquarian, out-of-print and secondhand books. Well stocked.

WHERE TO STAY
HOTELS
AA RECOMMENDED

Landmark

★★★★ THE MARLBOROUGH -
A RADISSON EDWARDIAN HOTEL
Bloomsbury St WC1B 3QD
(continue past Oxford Street and down New Oxford Street turn into Bloomsbury Street)
☎ 020 7636 5601 ✆ 020 7636 0532
This stylish period hotel offers a wide range of services and a choice of eating options for the international traveller. Bedrooms are smart and individually furnished, and are fully equipped with modern facilities.
173 rooms (3 family & 57 no smoking) / English & French Cuisine / Lift, Night porter
Price band £££ ☞

★★★★★ ❀ ❀ ❀ LANDMARK
222 Marylebone Rd NW1 6JQ
(located on Marylebone Road in front of Marylebone Railway Station)
☎ 020 7631 8000 ✆ 020 7631 8080
At the heart of this magnificent hotel is the Winter Garden, an eight-storey atrium fringed with palm trees, where a pianist plays and afternoon tea is served. Guests can eat in the panelled Cellars, and the main dining room which produces a modern menu.
299 rooms / Mediterranean & Oriental Cuisine / Indoor swimming pool (heated) / Sauna, Gym, Health club / Lift, Night porter, Air cond / No dogs (ex guide dogs)
☞

★★★★ HOTEL RUSSELL
Russell Square WC1B 5BE
☎ 020 7837 6470 ✆ 020 7837 2857
This splendid historic Victorian building has bedrooms which are very traditional in design, and very well equipped. Public areas, which include a choice of restaurants and bars, have real character. Staff are friendly and helpful, and the magnificent ballroom is popular for functions and meetings.
329 rooms (23 no smoking) / Lift, Night porter
☞

★★★★ THE MONTAGUE ON THE
GARDENS
15 Montague St, Bloomsbury WC1B 5BJ
☎ 020 7637 1001 ✆ 020 7637 2516
Off Russell Square and near the British Museum, this is an elegant hotel with stylish, well designed bedrooms and good IT provision. The clubby bar is the ideal venue for cocktails, while meals are served in the Blue Door Bistro.
104 rooms (20 no smoking) / International Cuisine / Sauna, Gym, Jacuzzi/spa / Live entertainment / Lift, Night porter / No dogs (ex guide dogs)
Price band £££ ☞

★★★★ BLOOMS
7 Montague St WC1B 5BP
(off Russell Square)
☎ 020 7323 1717 ✆ 020 7636 6498
Part of an 18th-century terrace, this elegant townhouse offers bedrooms furnished in Regency style. Day rooms consist of a lounge, garden terrace, breakfast room and cocktail bar, all graced with antique pieces, paintings and flowers. The lounge menu is also available as room service, and meals can be delivered from some of the local restaurants.
27 rooms / European Cuisine / Lift, Night porter / No dogs (ex guide dogs) / No coaches
☞

Blooms

The White House

★★★★ ⊛ ⊛ MELIÁ WHITE HOUSE
Albany St NW1
(opposite Gt Portland St Underground and set slightly back from Marylebone & Euston Rd)
☎ 020 7387 1200 ☏ 020 7388 0091
The White House began life in 1936 as an apartment building. Bedrooms on the 'Reserve' floor are the most spacious and have their own dedicated lounge. There are different styles of restaurant, one of which, The Wine Press, can be used for private parties. The café bar has a brasserie-style menu, and there is also a formal dining room.
582 rooms (1 family & 166 no smoking) / International Cuisine / Sauna, Gym / Lift, Night porter /No dogs (ex guide dogs)
Price band £££

★★★ BLOOMSBURY PARK
126 Southampton Row WC1B 5AD
☎ 020 7430 0434 ☏ 020 7242 0665
Located midway along Southampton Row, this hotel caters to all markets. Bedrooms vary in size and shape, with some overlooking the road. Public areas are quite compact; there is a small dining area with an open-air extension and a second bar, Peter's, with direct access off the street.
95 rooms (13 no smoking) / International Cuisine / Lift, Night porter / No dogs (ex guide dogs)

★★★ THE BONNINGTON IN BLOOMSBURY
92 Southampton Row WC1B 4BH
(From M40 Euston Rd opposite Stn turn south into Upper Woburn Place past Russell Sq into Southampton Row Bonnington on left)
☎ 020 7242 2828 ☏ 020 7831 9170
Well placed for the West End, the Bonnington offers traditional standards of service and modern comfort. Bedrooms come in a range of sizes and styles, and some are suitable for families. Waterfalls Restaurant offers a good choice of dishes and as an alternative there is a popular bar with a buffet.
215 rooms (16 family & 85 no smoking) / English & French Cuisine / Lift, Night porter
Price band £££

★★★ POSTHOUSE BLOOMSBURY
Coram St WC1N 1HT
(off Upper Woburn Place near to Russell Square)
☎ 020 7837 1200 ☏ 020 7837 5374
Designed with the business traveller in mind, this large hotel offers a wide range of services and facilities. Newly refurbished rooms are smart, comfortable and well equipped. A new Irish-themed bar has been added, and there is a car park nearby.
284 (29 family & 211 no smoking) / International Cuisine / Lift, Night porter / No dogs (ex guide dogs)
Price band £££

★★★ POSTHOUSE REGENTS PARK
Carburton St, Regents Park W1P 8EE
☎ 020 7388 2300 ☏ 020 7387 2806
This modern hotel with its own car-park is undergoing significant improvements. The smart public areas are modern in design and are air-conditioned. The bedrooms, which have been refurbished, are well designed. There is 24-hour room service and an all-day lounge menu.
326 rooms (184 non smoking) / International Cuisine / Live entertainment / Lift, Night porter / No dogs (ex guide dogs)
Price band £££

★★★ RADISSON EDWARDIAN GRAFTON
130 Tottenham Court Rd W1P 9HP
(central London, along Euston Road, turn into Tottenham Court Road. Past Warren Street Tube)
☎ 020 7388 4131 ☏ 020 7387 7394
Next to Warren Street Tube station, this hotel offers a variety of styles of bedroom, all with modern amenities. Public areas include a smart lounge, a restaurant and a wine bar where food is also available.
324 rooms (8 family & 163 no smoking) / English & French Cuisine / Lift, Night porter / No dogs (ex guide dogs)
Price band £££

★★★ RADISSON EDWARDIAN KENILWORTH
Great Russell St WC1B 3LB
(continue past Oxford Street and down New Oxford Street. Turn into Bloomsbury Street)
☎ 020 7637 3477 ☏ 020 7631 3133
This stylish Edwardian hotel offers a wide range of friendly services and a choice of eating options. Bedrooms are smart and individually furnished, and are fully equipped with modern facilities.
187 rooms (20 no smoking) / English & French Cuisine / Lift, Night porter
Price band £££

★★★ ST GEORGE'S
Langham Place, Regent St W1N 8QS
(Located in Langham Place at the intersection of Regent St and Portland Street)
☎ 020 7580 0111 ☏ 020 7436 7997
Situated inside Henry Wood House, which is shared by the BBC, St George's is quite unique. The reception lobby is on the ground floor, but there are no further public areas until you reach the 15th floor. Here there is a cosy bar area, meeting rooms and a restaurant which makes the most of the views.
86 rooms (8 family & 18 no smoking) / Lift, Night porter

★★★ THISTLE BLOOMSBURY
Bloomsbury Way WC1A 2SD
(Euston Rd underpass into Gower St to Bloomsbury St. At junct with New Oxford St left cont into Bloomsbury Way Hotel on Left after St Georges Church)
☎ 020 7242 5881 ☏ 020 7831 0225
Well situated for theatregoers, this hotel has recently benefited from significant improvement. Bedrooms have been refurbished or refitted and the ground-floor bar and lounge areas have been remodelled. The well-equipped rooms are generally spacious with good quality fabrics and furnishings. Family rooms and suites are available. There is a public car park nearby.
138 rooms (19 family & 42 no smoking) / International Cuisine / Lift, Night porter

BED & BREAKFAST
AA RECOMMENDED

♦♦♦ EURO HOTEL
51-53 Cartwright Gardens, Russell Square
WC1H 9EL
☎ 020 7387 4321 ☏ 020 7383 5044
(M1 junct 1 to Edgware Rd/Marylebone Rd/Euston Rd, right into Judd St, right into Leigh St, over Mardimont St into Cartright Gdns)
This small bed and breakfast hotel in London's stylish Bloomsbury has improved greatly over the years and offers quality accommodation at a reasonable price. Bedrooms are well equipped, and breakfast is served in a wood-floored room which overlooks the gardens outside.
35 rooms (9 family) / No dogs (ex guide dogs)
Price band ££ ➤

♦♦♦ FOUR SEASONS HOTEL
173 Gloucester Place, Regents Park NW1 6DX
(nearest tube station is Baker St, premises close to Regents Park)
☎ 020 7724 3461 & 020 7723 9471
☏ 020 7402 5594
A friendly welcome is assured at this smart and well maintained private hotel in the heart of the West End. The very relaxing bedrooms vary in size, but are appointed in modern style and usefully equipped. Continental breakfast is included in the tariff and room service is offered throughout the day and evening.
16 rooms (2 family & 4 no smoking) / No dogs
➤

♦♦♦ MENTONE HOTEL
54-56 Cartwright Gardens, Bloomsbury
WC1H 9EL
(Between Euston Rd and Russell Square)
☎ 020 7387 3927 & 7388 4671
☏ 020 7388 4671
Situated in the centre of an impressive Georgian terrace near Euston, this friendly hotel is constantly being improved and provides value accommodation. Bedrooms are well equipped and most have the benefit of modern, en suite shower rooms. Comprehensive English breakfasts are served in the basement dining room.
42 rms (14 family) / No dogs / Tennis (hard)
Price band ££ ➤
See advert on page 239.

WHERE TO EAT
RESTAURANTS
AA RECOMMENDED

❀❀ THE ACADEMY
17-21 Gower Street WC1E 6HG
☎ 020 7636 7612 ☏ 020 7636 3442
Converted into a splendid hotel from five Georgian terraced houses and recently substantially refurbished. The restaurant is on the lower ground floor and has a contemporary feel. The menu features a selection of Mediterranean (predominantly Italian) dishes along the lines of goats' cheese tart, various kinds of pasta, lamb with tabouleh, squid with chilli, and chicken with polenta. Music is played on a regular basis.
Fixed L/D £ ALC £

❀❀ THE BIRDCAGE OF FITZROVIA
110 Whitfield Street W1P 5RU
☎ 020 7383 3346
This restaurant is small and decorated with French 18th-century bird cages, eastern ephemera, feathers and a large mirrored glass dragon, the ambience is not unlike a private dining room. The menu is a fusion of many different influences. Sushi with mussel ceviche appears on the same list of first courses as coconut and foie gras soup, and there could also be grilled mackerel with Peruvian mash, Indian risotto with plantain and lotus root, or Birdcage sweetbreads with jasmine-infused polenta.
Fixed L £ ALC ££

❀ IKKYU
67a Tottenham Court Road W1P 9PA
☎ 020 7636 9286
Scruffy, smoky basement restaurant offering a rough and ready but very edible style of Japanese food. Prices are reasonable, service friendly, casual but not very fluent, and the Japanese menu only gives basic English translations. Go with a sense of adventure and you will be well rewarded.
ALC £

❀❀❀ LANDMARK HOTEL,
THE DINING ROOM
222 Marylebone Road NW1 6JQ
☎ 020 7631 8230 ☏ 020 7631 8011
Built in 1899 and now restored to its original style, the Landmark was designed around a glass-roofed atrium. The Dining Room, an impressive room with high moulded ceiling, chandeliers and spectacular flower displays, is the main venue. This is the setting for dishes in the modern European idiom: tortellini of wild mushrooms, truffles and chicken velouté, roast saddle of lamb with caramelised kidneys and sweetbreads in a sauce of tomatoes, olives and basil, then mango and coconut rice pudding. Don't miss out on the petits fours with coffee, either.
Fixed L ££ ALC £££

❀ LEMONIA
89 Regent's Park Road NW1 8UY
☎ 020 7586 7454 ☏ 020 7483 2630
A Mediterranean air at this bustling Greek restaurant - it's a light, airy interior with masses of colourful hanging baskets. From good mezze the menu extends to traditional moussaka, deep-fried baby squid, lamb baked in lemon, spices and herbs, and delicious, honey-soaked baklava.
Fixed L/D £ ALC £

❀❀ ODETTES
130 Regents Park Road NW1 8XL
☎ 020 7586 5486/8766
☏ 020 7586 2575
In the heart of Primrose Hill, this is a feel-good restaurant reflecting the cosmopolitan bustle all around. The upper restaurant is lined with mirrors of all shapes and sizes, ideal for the vain and voyeurs alike. Some dishes are simply classics, peppered fillet of beef with creamed spinach and 'pont-neuf' potatoes fried in duck fat, for example; others take a simple idea and add an unusual element, as in cod with baby squid, coco beans and oven-dried tomatoes, or potted Agen prunes in saffron custard.
Fixed L £ ALC ££

Orerry

⊛ ⊛ ⊛ ORERRY
55-57 Marylebone High Street W1M 3AE
☎ 020 7616 8000 📠 020 7616 8080
The smallest in the Conran gastro-empire which allows for better control and consistency. Clever menus, for instance, are short and to the point. Pressed pork hock and foie gras with green tomato and fennel chutney, epigramme of sole with sauce antiboise, and delicate, a signature bitter chocolate terrine with pistachio sauce are typical examples. A tome of a wine list requires time to study it. There's also a small, cosy, corner bar and for summer evenings, the adjoining food shop's terrace opens up to bar customers. Menus are slightly shorter at lunch.
Fixed L £ ALC £££

⊛ ⊛ VILLANDRY
170 Great Portland Street W1N 5TB
☎ 020 7631 3131 📠 020 7631 3030
Sparsely styled, with simple wooden tables and chairs, the open-plan restaurant fits easily into the rear of one of the most tempting food stores in London. It's a natural partnership - you eat and buy, or buy and eat carefully sourced produce of the highest quality. The menu changes twice daily to reflect market freshness. Typically, organic rib of beef with champ potato cake and wild mushrooms, or grilled fillet of mullet with anchovy rostini, cherry tomatoes and spinach. A changing selection of beers makes an interesting alternative to the short wine list. Note that evening access is via Bolsover Street.
ALC ££

⊛ ⊛ THE WHITE HOUSE HOTEL
Albany Street NW1 3UP
☎ 020 7387 1200
📠 020 7388 0091
The White House was formerly an exclusive block of flats. This eight-storey hotel stands next to Regents Park and is geared mainly to the business executive. The rather formal restaurant offers both a set-menu and a carte, featuring traditional dishes -including the odd flambéed item and a dessert trolley. However there is a good level of consistency from the kitchen. There's a good selection of wines by the glass and the staff are well trained, interested and helpful.
Fixed L/D £ ALC ££

PUBS, INNS & OTHER PLACES

THE CHAPEL
48 Chapel St NW1 5DP
(By A40 Marylebone Rd & Old Marylebone Rd junc. Off Edgware Rr by tube station)
☎ 020 7402 9220
Anglo-Mediterranean food is served at this relaxed establishment, which has stripped floors, old pine tables and chairs, free newspapers and a display of local artists' paintings.

THE ENGINEER
65 Gloucester Av, Primrose Hill NW1 8JH
(Off Regents Pk Rd, on Corner of Princess Rd)
☎ 020 7722 0950
Stylish Primrose Hill pub designed in 1841 by Isambard Kingdom Brunel. Minimalist decor acts as backdrop to modern British cooking based on free-range/organic produce.

MANNA
4 Eskine Rd, Primrose Hill, NW3 3AJ
Stylish vegetarian restaurant with a wide range of organic wines and beers.

THE GLOBE
43/47 Marylebone Rd, Marylebone NW1 5JY
(nr Baker St tube)
☎ 020 7935 6368
Built in 1735, this tall pub was frequented by Charles Dickens and Alfred Lord Tennyson and is a favourite with tourists.

THE LANSDOWNE
90 Gloucester Av, Primrose Hill NW1 8HX
☎ 020 7483 0409
Famous rock stars can often be spotted at this relaxed, traditionally-styled dining pub in secluded Primrose Hill. Constantly changing menu of interesting dishes.

THE QUEENS
49 Regents Park Rd, Primrose Hill NW1
(Nearest tube station - Chalk Farm)
☎ 020 7586 0408
Victorian pub. A wide range of snacks, savouries and blackboard specials is available.

ARISUGAWA
27 Percy Street, W1P 9FF
☎ 020 7636 8913
Formal basement restaurant with Japanese menu.

CHEZ GÉRARD
8 Charlotte Street, W1P
☎ 020 7636 4975
Steak frites done to a turn are a speciality here. Smart and sleek.

HEALS, THE CAFÉ AT HEALS
The Heals Building, 196 Tottenham Ct Rd, W1P 9LD
☎ 020 7636 1666/ext 250
Relaxing in-store café.

MILBURNS RESTAURANT
British Museum, Great Brompton St, Bloomsbury
☎ 020 7580 9212
Self-service café and restaurant. Ideal for relaxing after a hard day's history.

www.theaa.co.uk

Find the "Where to Stay, Where to Eat" pages at www.theaa.co.uk/hotels

Search for...

a town or establishment name, by region or across the whole of Britain & Ireland

Locate your chosen B&B on a road map

Use the contact details or hotlink to get more information or make a booking direct

Booking online is easy with the AA online booking service

www.theaa.co.uk

SOHO AND COVENT GARDEN

In the 1960s and 70s, Soho was a byword for sex clubs and sleaze, a magnet for thrill-seekers and sexual adventurers. The area has since been partly cleaned up, although the clubs and bookshops still operate, and certain streets have a distinctly run-down appearance. Today, however, it is mostly enjoyed for its restaurants and lively atmosphere. Soho is also at the heart of Britain's media industry. Wardour Street is home to offices of most of the major film companies, independant TV producers and theatrical agents. Discarded film cans full of unused stock are a common sight in the local dustbins. Fans of British horror studio Hammer, might like to take a look at No 113, Hammer House.

Old Compton Street offers several cheap eateries, including the famous Pollo Bar, although it does have its share of brothels as well. Frith Street, leading to Soho Square, has been the home of Ronnie Scott's jazz club for almost 40 years, and even though Ronnie is gone, jazz greats and expensive cabarets are still the norm. The French House pub was the headquarters of General de Gaulle during World War II, and the Colony Club (No.41) was attended by the British painters Lucien Freud and Francis Bacon. Today you're more likely to see comedians and writers in and around the area.

Soho is theatreland, with five major theatres on Shaftesbury Avenue alone. Behind Shaftesbury Avenue is London's Chinatown, mostly situated around Gerrard Street. This is

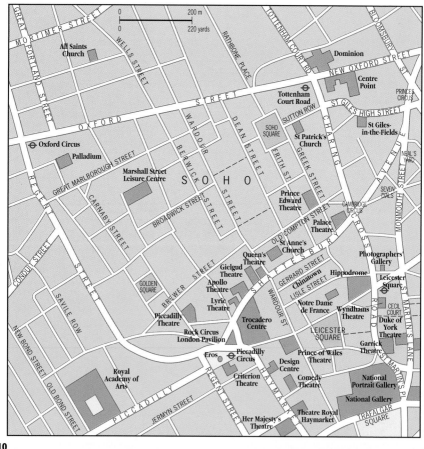

a real must for any visitor, with its pagoda telephone boxes, dim sum eateries and shops full of Hong Kong pop music and manga (comics). There are also plenty of cinemas, with the largest screens and highest prices on Leicester Square. The best collection of bookshops is along Charing Cross Road, and if you head from Leicester Square to Trafalgar Square, you will find a good selection of secondhand and first edition bookshops in Cecil Court.

Following Leicester Square across Charing Cross Road takes you along Long Acre and into Covent Garden. Until 1974, when the wholesale market was moved to Nine Elms in SW8, this was the run-down haunt of vegetable and flower traders, a true vision of Dickensian London. Today, Covent Garden is a traffic-free piazza, with a lively and varied arts and crafts market surrounded by a dazzling variety of gift shops, boutiques, restaurants and cafés. Most days you can also see a wide variety of street performers and buskers, some of whom have gone on to become household names. Around the piazza are many interesting locations: the Royal Opera House, which may or may not be reopened by 2000 after undergoing massive renovations; the London Transport Museum; the Theatre Museum; St Paul's Church and several theatres along Drury Lane. Neal's Yard, towards St Giles Circus, offers a variety of specialist shops including those selling cheese and aromatherapy products. Covent Garden is a bustling and vibrant place at almost any time of day or night, so visitors are advised to beware of pickpockets.

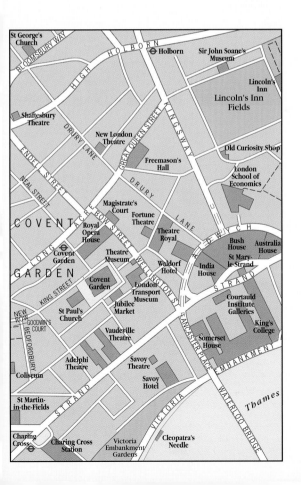

MUST SEE

Chinatown

COVENT GARDEN PIAZZA
WC2

Transformed in 1974 from the old fruit and vegetable market which had stood here for over 300 years, Covent Garden is the heart of central London, with its own community spirit and atmosphere. The name is a corruption of 'Convent Garden', which refers to the garden of St Paul's Abbey that once stood here. Traffic free, it is perfect for strolling around the small shops and stopping off at cafés and restaurants. Entertainers in the form of jugglers, mime artists and comedians are always around, and the market stalls now sell antiques, crafts, jewellery, collectable items and toys (at a price). Along Neal Street are gift shops galore.

LEICESTER SQUARE
WC2

In the middle of this vast cinema-lined square is a statue of, appropriately enough, Charlie Chaplin. The main appeal of the square is the vast, multi-screen cinemas showing all the latest blockbuster releases. These can be very pricey, so it's worth seeing what's on at the indie Prince Charles round the corner in Leicester Place. The Square is also popular as a meeting place due to its access to three major areas of London - Piccadilly Circus, Covent Garden and Trafalgar Square.

SOHO STREETLIFE
W1

The streets forming the once seedy area of Soho have partially cleaned up their act, although you'll still find sex for sale in various forms along Brewer Street and Old Compton Street. In the 16th century it was a hunting ground; apparently named after the ancient hunting cry, 'So-ho!'. During the 18th century it began to earn its name for 'dubious entertainment'. Today it's mostly famous for excellent restaurants of all nationalities, as well as Ronnie Scott's jazz club on Frith Street.

Plenty of famous people have lived in these streets, including Mozart at 20 Frith Street and Karl Marx at 28 Dean Street. This address has long been home to Quo Vadis, one of London's more innovative restaurants. The Groucho Club on Dean Street is a good place for modern star spotting. Wardour Street has long been a centre of the film industry, with offices of Rank and Warner Bros among many others.

St Paul's Church

ST MARTIN-IN-THE-FIELDS CHURCH
Trafalgar Sq, WC2
☎ 020-7930 1862

Founded in the 12th century, the present church dates from 1722. Notable events that have taken place here include the christening of Charles II in 1630, and the burials of Nell Gwynne, Hogarth and Sir Joshua Reynolds. There are free lunchtime concerts that allow you to enjoy this oasis of calm on the edge of bustling Covent Garden. There's also a brass rubbing centre, catacombed restaurant and gallery.

CHINATOWN
Gerrard and Lisle Streets, W1

The cultural and financial centre of the Chinese community in Britain, Chinatown is dedicated to all things Chinese. Even the street signs are in Chinese. There are an amazing choice of restaurants - try Poons, 27 Lisle Street and Wong Kei, 41 Wardour Street (complete with its infamous rude waiters). The annual festivities for the Chinese New Year are held here in late January or early February, and are not recommended for those who are made nervous by loud noises.

HISTORIC AND ANCIENT SITES

ROYAL OPERA HOUSE
Covent Garden, WC2
☎ 020-7212 9458

As well as hosting performances of opera and ballet, the Opera House is home to The Royal Ballet. In July 1997, a major refurbishment programme started, with help from National Lottery funds, and the Opera House re-opened in late 1999. The Royal Ballet is continuing to put on performances around the capital. Famous for exorbitantly expensive seats affordable only by purists and the wealthy.

CHARING CROSS RD, WC2
Best known for its bookshops, Charing Cross Road runs from the Holborn end of Oxford Street to Trafalgar Square and Charing Cross Station. Head for Cecil Court, a small pedestrianised street, for first editions, old prints and secondhand books. Along Charing Cross Road are some of London's best bookshops, including Foyles, one of the biggest bookshops in the world; Silver Moon, a feminist booksellers; and Murder One, which deals in crime, romance and sci-fi.

ART GALLERIES

CONTEMPORARY APPLIED ARTS
43 Earlham St, WC2
☎ 020-7436 2344

A fascinating display of work using a wide variety of materials.

FRITH STREET
60 Frith St, W1
☎ 020-7494 1550

A showcase for national and international contemporary artists, opened in 1989.

PHOTOGRAPHERS' GALLERY
5-8 Great Newport St, WC2
☎ 020-7831 1772

The venue for a varied range of photography, from documentary to abstract. Many of the prints are for sale.

Street Performer in Leicester Square

ZELDA CHEATLE GALLERY
8 Cecil Court, WC2
☎ 020-7836 0506
Photographic gallery specialising in documentary and landscape work by famous names and unknowns.

CINEMAS

ODEON LEICESTER SQUARE
22-24 Leicester Sq, WC2
☎ 020-8315 4212
The biggest cinema in London. All the major blockbusters are on here, usually presented with a glamorous premiere. This is the place to briefly see your favourite stars as they pose for photographs.

ODEON WEST END
Leicester Sq, WC2
☎ 0870 505 0007
Two screens, showing new big releases.

EMPIRE LEICESTER SQUARE
Leicester Sq, WC2
☎ 020-7437 1234
Three screens, showing major releases. Often hosts major premieres.

PRINCE CHARLES
2-7 Leicester Place, WC2
☎ 020-7437 8181
Big releases, classic revivals, foreign films and cult movies. Cheap seats.

ABC SWISS CENTRE
Leicester Sq, WC2
☎ 020-7439 4470
Inside the Swiss Centre, showing new releases.

CURZON SOHO
93-107 Shaftesbury Ave, W1
☎ 020-7734 2255
Plush cinema with one screen.

CURZON PHOENIX
Phoenix Theatre, Charing Cross Rd, WC2
☎ 020-7369 1721
Showing arthouse films.

ODEON MEZZANINE
Leicester Sq, WC2
☎ 0870 505 0007
Five screens, showing recent releases.

WARNER VILLAGE WEST END
Leicester Sq, WC2
☎ 020-7437 4347
A mega nine-screen complex - like a small town.

The newly re-opened Royal Opera House

LUMIÈRE
42 St Martin's Lane, WC2
☎ 020-7836 0691/7379 3014
An art cinema with stunning decor, showing revivals and off-beat films.

THEATRES

FIRST CALL (TICKETING) PLC
73-75 Endell St, WC2H 9AJ
☎ 020-7420 0000 (theatre)
☎ 020-7420 1000 (concert)
Europe's largest ticketing operation. The best place to look for tickets to all of London's major shows and concerts.

THE HALF PRICE TICKET BOOTH
The Clock Tower Building, Leicester Sq
Rather self explanatory name. Half price tickets to major theatres available on day of performance. Only 4 tickets per person and cash only.

DUCHESS
Catherine St, WC2
☎ 020-7494 5075
All kinds of entertainment here - drama, musicals, and comedy. *Don't Dress for Dinner* is the current attraction.

THEATRE ROYAL (DRURY LANE)
Catherine St, WC2
☎ 020-7494 5000
The hit musical *Miss Saigon* has occupied this theatre for many years. The tragic story of doomed love during the Vietnam war is based on Puccini's *Madame Butterfly*.

FORTUNE
Russell St, WC2
☎ 020-7836 2238
The Woman in Black has been frightening audiences at this long-established theatre for many years. Peter Cook and Dudley Moore started out in *Beyond the Fringe* here in the 1960s.

GARRICK
Charing Cross Rd, WC2
☎ 020-7494 5085
Built in 1897, the Garrick stages drama and comedies, and is named after one of 18th-century England's best-loved actors, David Garrick. JB Priestly's *An Inspector Calls* is currently playing.

PHOENIX
Charing Cross Rd, WC2
☎ 020-7369 1721
The hit musical *Blood Brothers* by Willy Russell has been playing here for over a decade.

WYNDHAM'S
Charing Cross Rd, WC2
☎ 020-7369 1736
A long-established and popular theatre.

ALBERY
St Martin's Lane, WC2
☎ 020-7867 1115
Musicals, comedy and drama.

AMBASSADORS
West St, WC2
☎ 020-7836 6111
The original home of *The Mousetrap*. Stages plays in a small and intimate setting.

DUKE OF YORK'S
St Martin's Lane, WC2
☎ 020-7836 5122
Longstanding theatre, once the domain of

George Bernard Shaw and the Ballet Rambert. Puts on major productions.

NEW LONDON
Drury Lane, WC2
☎ 020-7405 0072
Has been staging the hit musical *Cats* for years. In fact, it's London's longest running musical.

SHAFTESBURY
210 Shaftesbury Ave, WC2
☎ 020-7344 4444
The permanent home of the Theatre of Comedy Company. Currently playing *Rent*.

PICCADILLY
Shaftesbury Ave, W1
☎ 020-7439 4805

LONDON COLISEUM
St Martins' Lane, WC2
☎ 020-7632 8300
With an ornate interior, this is London's largest theatre, and home to the English National Opera. Dance, ballet and opera all staged. Plans for major refurbishment are afoot.

LYRIC
Shaftesbury Ave, WC2
☎ 020-7494 5045
Built in 1888, and once host to British acting legend, Sarah Bernhardt and American wit, Tallulah Bankhead.

APOLLO
Shaftesbury Ave, WC2
☎ 020-7494 5070
Presents musicals, comedy and drama.

Covent Garden

GIELGUD
Shaftesbury Ave, WC2
☎ 020-7494 5065
Formerly the Globe Theatre, it is now named after the great British actor, Sir John Gielgud. Stages plays and comedies.

QUEEN'S
Shaftesbury Ave, WC2
☎ 020-7494 5040
Presents drama and other productions.

PALACE
Shaftesbury Ave, WC2
☎ 020-7434 0909
Mostly musical comedies are staged here, although occasional plays pop up. Has been staging *Les Misérables* for many years.

PRINCE EDWARD
Old Compton St, W1
☎ 020-7447 5400
The hit show *Evita* played here and ran for nearly 3,000 performances.

CAMBRIDGE
Earlham St, WC2
☎ 020-7494 5040
Presents musicals and other productions. Currently home to hit musical *Grease*.

ST MARTIN'S THEATRE
West St, W1
☎ 020-7836 1443
Agatha Christie's *The Mousetrap* has been

playing here for half a century, and looks set to continue for another 50.

DONMAR WAREHOUSE
Earlham St, WC2
☎ 020-7369 1732
An off-West End venue, with exciting and sometimes alternative theatre. In 1998 this was the venue for Nicole Kidman's critically-acclaimed performance in *The Blue Room*.

Covent Garden

ENTERTAINMENT AND NIGHTLIFE

Soho is the epitome of nightlife and evening entertainment. (see also Soho Nightlife, later on in this section)

MUSIC

ASTORIA (LA1)
157 Charing Cross Rd, WC2
☎ 020-7434 0403
A great music venue for international rock acts. Like many other large music venues, it was once a theatre. Adventurous booking policy.

THE SOUND REPUBLIC
Swiss Centre, Leicester Sq, W1
☎ 020-7287 1010
Big budget and very new (opened Oct 1998) mid-sized venue concentrating on major pop acts like the Spice Girls, who played here in late '98. MTV often film shows here, so dress your best.

ROADHOUSE
Jubilee Hall, 35 Covent Garden Piazza, WC2
☎ 020-7240 6001
American in decor and dining, concentrating mainly on blues and rock'n'roll.

ROCK GARDEN
Covent Garden Piazza, WC2
☎ 020-7836 4052
Very popular with tourists, for its burger joint as much as the music, which tends towards showcasing new talent in a variety of musical areas. The café area is ideal for people-watching.

AFRICA CENTRE
38 King St, WC2
☎ 020-7836 1973
As might be expected from the name, you'll hear all kinds of African music here.

BUNJIES
27 Litchfield St, WC2
☎ 020-7240 1796
Now a favourite with those producing weird and wonderful sounds, Bunjies was once the local for Bob Dylan.

Theatreland

SHOPPING

FOOD

NEAL'S YARD DAIRY
17 Shorts Gardens, WC2
☎ 020-7379 7646
You can taste any cheese they have here, and there are masses, many of them are matured under the shop.

The Hippodrome

LINA STORES
18 Brewer St, WC2
☎ 020-7437 6482
Excellent Italian deli with olives, fresh pasta and other delights.

SEE WOO
18 Lisle St, WC2
☎ 020-7439 8325
Chinese food, utensils - all you need to beat the takeaways.

NEW LOON MOON
9a Gerrard St, W1
☎ 020 7734 9940
Large Chinese foodshop.

LOON FUNG SUPERMARKET
42-44 Gerrard St, W1
☎ 020-7437 7332
Chinatown's largest and best-stocked supermarket. This is where London's Chinese community does its weekly shop.

PÂTISSERIE VALERIE
44 Old Compton St, W1
☎ 020-7437 3466
A well-established haven for excellent cakes and pastries.

BODY TREATS

CULPEPER HERBALISTS
8 The Market, Covent Garden, WC2
☎ 020-7379 6698
Buy your life-affirming herbal treats here, or have them sent to you by equally life-affirming mail order.

NEAL'S YARD REMEDIES
15 Neal's Yard, WC2
☎ 020-7379 7222
Loads of medicinal remedies and bathroom accessories, all in distinctive bright blue bottles.

PENHALIGON'S
41 Wellington St, WC2
☎ 020-7836 2150
A stylish range of pampering products.

THE BODY SHOP
Covent Garden Piazza, WC2
☎ 020-7836 3543
There's a branch of this hugely successful chain in every corner of London. Stock up on haircare, bath bubbles, skincare and much more.

LUSH
Units 7 & 11, Covent Garden Piazza, WC2
☎ 020-7379 5423
The latest in bathroom accessories - slabs of weird and wonderful soaps to buy by the pound. Try Red Rooster (with cinnamon).

GIFTS AND MISCELLANEOUS

THE MUSEUM STORE
37 The Market, Covent Garden, WC2
☎ 020-7240 5760
Gifts from museums around the world.

ANYTHING LEFT-HANDED
57 Brewer St, W1
☎ 020-7437 3910
Everything for the sinister (left-handed) among us, including corkscrews and scissors.

FASHION

AGNÈS B
35-36 Floral St, WC2
☎ 020-7379 1992
Very popular designer T-shirts and jumpers, in business since 1973. Also make-up.

JONES
13-15 Floral St, WC2
☎ 020-7240 8312/8314
Fashion for men and women. Alexander McQueen is among the designers.

PAUL SMITH
40-4 Floral St, WC2
☎ 020-7379 7133
Started out with very stylish, classic cuts for men, but now also fashion for women and children. One of Britain's most successful designers.

OFFICE
57 Neal St, WC2
☎ 020-7379 1896
Broad range of fashionable footware.

Berwick Street Market

OFFSPRING
60 Neal St, WC2
☎ 020-7497 2463
Sports version of Office (see entry above).

RED OR DEAD
33 Neal Street
☎ 020-7379 7571
1 Thomas Neal's Centre, Earlham St, WC2
☎ 020-7240 5576
Mostly shoes, with a cult following, but now also clothing.

SPACE NK
Thomas Neal's Centre, 41 Earlham St, WC2
☎ 020-7379 7030
Trendy women's clothing, make-up and accessories. Apothecary skincare downstairs.

FRENCH CONNECTION
99-103 Long Acre, WC2
☎ 020-7379 6560
Longstanding fashion chain with trendy changing styles for women.

GAP
30-31 Long Acre, WC2
☎ 020-7379 0779
American college fashion usually with bright colours. Branches all round London and the Home Counties. Include departments for babies and young children.

HOBBS
Unit 17, Covent Garden Piazza, WC2
☎ 020-7836 9168
Very stylish shoes, as well as classics for women.

BASE
55 Monmouth St, WC2
☎ 020-7240 8914
Stocks sizes 16-28 for women.

AGENT PROVOCATEUR
6 Broadwick St, W1
☎ 020-7439 0229
Women's lingerie of a saucy nature. Mail order available.

THE HAT SHOP
58 Neal St, WC2
☎ 020-7836 6718
Absolutely masses of hats to choose from, from baseball caps to Ascot winners.

The folly in Soho Square

SHOES

DR MARTEN DEPARTMENT STORE
1-4 King St, WC2
☎ 020-7497 1460
Home of the world's most famous boot. Everything from black leather to purple velvet - five floors of clothing and shoes.

The Empire, Leicester Square

NATURAL SHOE STORE
21 Neal St, WC2
☎ 020-7836 5254
This shoe shop prides itself on not inflicting any pain on animals or damage to the environment in the production of its shoes.

BOOKS

BLACKWELLS
100 Charing Cross Rd, WC2
☎ 020-7292 5100
With its head office in Oxford, Blackwells Publishers are mainly academic, but their shops have a wide variety of subjects across fiction, general and non-fiction.

BOOKS ETC
120 Charing Cross Rd, WC2
☎ 020-7379 6838
The newest of the successful chains of mega bookstores. Books etc is well stocked with loads of books and there's even a café so you sit awhile and browse.

FOYLES
113-119 Charing Cross Rd, WC2
☎ 020-7437 5660
An immense range of books on every subject. Beware that the paperbacks are stocked according to publisher. Staff are on hand to lend aid to the confused bookbuyer.

MURDER ONE
71-73 Charing Cross Rd, WC2
☎ 020-7734 3485
Devoted to crime, horror, romance and science-fiction books.

SILVER MOON WOMEN'S BOOKSHOP
64-68 Charing Cross Rd, WC2
☎ 020-7836 7906
Self-explanatory name for a feminist bookshop.

EDWARD STANFORD
12-14 Long Acre, WC2
☎ 020-7836 1915
The biggest selection of travel books and maps in London. Mail order is available.

BELL, BOOK & RADMALL
4 Cecil Court, WC2
☎ 020-7240 2161
As is typical of this area, a good selection

Bookshop on Charing Cross Road

of first edition 19th- and 20th-century literature.

SPORTSPAGES
Caxton Walk, 94-96 Charing Cross Rd, WC2
☎ 020-7240 9604
The best sports bookshop in London. Includes sections on football, rugby, martial arts and cricket.

WATERSTONE'S
121-129 Charing Cross Rd, WC2
☎ 020-7434 4291
A vast stock and clear layout make this a very successful chain of bookshops. It was started by Tim Waterstone, once employed by WH Smith.

BERTRAM ROTA
31 Long Acre, WC2
☎ 020-7836 0723
Wide selection of first editions.

MARKETS

BERWICK STREET
43 Neal St, WC2
A noisy and colourful fruit-and-veg market in the heart of Soho

JUBILEE AND APPLE MARKETS
Covent Garden Piazza, WC2
Jubilee Market is mainly for tourists, but gets more interesting on Mondays. Apple Market, which is inside the piazza, has several stallholders offering jewellery, unusual gifts, knitwear and toys - all at quite a price.

GREAT FOR KIDS

LEICESTER SQUARE
If you can't find a film to entertain the children here, then stop looking.

CABARET MECHANICAL THEATRE
33-34 The Market, Covent Garden, WC2
☎ 020-7379 7961
Full of mechanical models made by Sue Jackson, some of which are interactive. A great place for children and adults.

LONDON TRANSPORT MUSEUM
39 Wellington St, WC2
☎ 020-7379 6344
Explore London's historic buses, trams and trains. There are hands-on exhibits and working models - you can drive a bus or tube, and there are lots of organised activities for all age groups. Actors bring to life characters like a 1940s bus conductress or a tunnel miner.

UNICORN ARTS THEATRE
6-7 Great Newport St, WC2
☎ 020-7836 3334
A theatre presenting plays particularly for children. Very popular, with a wide variety of shows, as well as theatre-based activities. Founded in 1948.

ST MARTIN-IN-THE-FIELDS CHURCH
St Martin's Lane, WC2
☎ 020-7930 0089
Children can try their hand at brass rubbing in this famous old church. There are over 100 to try out.

THEATRE MUSEUM
Russell St, WC2
☎ 020-7836 7891
The perfect place to explore behind the scenes not only at the theatre, but also the circus, opera and ballet. There's a

Covent Garden

good guided tour, including make-up demonstrations.

THE LONDON DOLLS' HOUSE COMPANY
29 The Market, Covent Garden, WC2
☎ 020-7240 2288
Everything you could possibly need for your doll's house.

COMIC SHOWCASE
76 Neal St, WC2
☎ 020-7240 3664
American comics, cartoon books, T-shirts and models.

THE BEAD SHOP
21a Tower St, WC2
☎ 020-7240 0931
Zillions of beads to make and decorate anything you fancy.

BENJAMIN POLLOCK'S TOY SHOP
44 Covent Garden Market, WC2
☎ 020-7379 7866
Traditional toy shop selling dolls, model theatres and various other goodies.

THE TINTIN SHOP
43 Floral St, WC2
☎ 020-7836 1131
Go Tintin mad! Belgium's favourite export.

THE KITE STORE
Neal St, WC2
☎ 020-7836 1666
Loads of kites for sale in all different sizes, colours and shapes.

PLACES OF WORSHIP

ST PAUL'S CHURCH
Covent Garden, WC2
Built by Inigo Jones in the 1630s, St Paul's is known as the 'actors' church' because of its proximity to the Theatre Royal and Royal Opera House. There are memorials to Charlie Chaplin, Vivien Leigh and Boris Karloff here.

CROWN COURT CHURCH OF SCOTLAND
Russell St, WC2
Presbyterian church hiding in the heart of London.

NOTRE DAME DE FRANCE
Leicester Place, WC2
A good place to escape the noise of Leicester Square. Built in 1865 for French Roman Catholics. Contains frescos by French artist, Jean Cocteau.

Buskers in Covent Garden

The Swiss Centre, Leicester Square

ST PATRICK'S CHURCH
Princes St, WC2
Near to Soho Square and away from the bustle of Greek Street.

ST GILES-IN-THE-FIELDS, WC2
St Giles High St, WC2
An ornate and popular church, last resting place of the poet, Andrew Marvell.

SPORT AND LEISURE

THE OASIS
32 Endell St, WC2
☎ 020-7831 1804
A complete leisure centre, including a large swimming pool.

PINEAPPLE DANCE CENTRE
7 Langley St, WC2
☎ 020-7836 4004
Begun in the 1980s, this is now an extremely popular venue for dancers and keep-fitters. Various dance classes are on offer including jazz and flamenco. Or relax with a massage.

JUBILEE HALL CLUB COVENT GARDEN
30 The Piazza, WC2
☎ 020-7836 4835
Aerobics, step and a busy gym are all available here.

SOHO NIGHTLIFE

Soho is particularly famous for its pulsating nightlife. Nightclubs are easy to find, as long as your bank manager is in full agreement, and you don't plan to go to work the next day.

STRINGFELLOWS
16 Upper St Martin's Lane, WC2
☎ 020-7240 5534
Exclusive, full of celebrities. A good place of media schmoozing. The owner, Peter Stringfellow is now something of a celebrity himself.

HIPPODROME
Charing Cross Rd, WC2
☎ 020-7437 4311
A longstanding club very popular with tourists and the undiscerning.

LIMELIGHT
136 Shaftesbury Ave, WC2
☎ 020-7434 0572
A legendary club occupying a former church with grand surroundings and prices. Two floors of music.

RONNIE SCOTT'S
47 Frith St, WC2
☎ 020-7439 0747
Most of the jazz greats have played at this legendary venue at some time. Still a good

Ronnie Scott's Jazz Club

venue to spot new rising talent, although it'll cost you. The epitome of the smoky jazz club.

GOSSIPS
69 Dean St, W1
☎ 020-7434 4480
Long-established disco/nightclub with a strong following. Stages a variety of nights including goth, easy listening, fetish and industrial.

THE BORDERLINE
Orange Yard, Manette St, WC2
☎ 020-7734 2095
Excellent and diverse live music. A popular place for big name bands to play secret gigs.

EQUINOX
Leicester Sq, WC2
☎ 020-7437 1446
Massive disco/nightclub with loads of bars.

SALSA
96 Charing Cross Rd, WC2
☎ 020-7379 3277
Always packed out with those eager to learn the latest moves.

ASTORIA (LA1)
157 Charing Cross Rd, WC2
☎ 020-7434 0403
Opposite Centre Point. Famous London concert venue. LA2 is next door, and specialises in indie bands and dancing.

VELVET UNDERGROUND
143 Charing Cross Rd, WC2
☎ 020-7439 4655
A welcoming nightclub in the heart of clubland with masses of velvet to envelop you on the dance floor. Named after Lou Reed's seminal 1960s band.

COMEDY AT SOHO HO
Crown & Two Chairmen, Dean St, W1
☎ 020-437 8192
Comedy acts entertain in this friendly pub.

THE WAG CLUB
35 Wardour St, W1
☎ 020-7437 5534
Famous during the 1980s as the place to be, the Wag continues to pull in the crowds. Regular live music.

BAR RUMBA
36 Shaftesbury Ave, W1
☎ 020-7287 2715
A small venue tucked behind the Pepsi Trocadero Centre, but with plenty of variety in music.

PIZZA EXPRESS
10 Dean St, W1
☎ 020-7437 9595
Although mainly famed for its excellent pizzas, this particular branch also stages live music every night. There's a varied programme from major names to new talent.

WHERE TO STAY

HOTELS

AA RECOMMENDED

Kingsway Hall

★★★★ DRURY LANE MOAT HOUSE

10 Drury Ln WC2B 5RE

(on the corner of Drury Lane & High Holborn, car park access from High Holborn)

☎ 020 7208 9988 ☎ 020 7831 1548

Superbly located for theatre-land, the Moat House offers public areas which include a comfortable lobby lounge, small bar and informal bistro. Rooms vary in size and all are very well maintained. A fitness room, car park and business centre are also available.

163 rooms (95 family & 86 no smoking) / French / Solarium, Gym / Lift, Night porter

Price band £££

★★★★ KINGSWAY HALL

Great Queen Street, Covent Garden, WC2B 5BZ

(from Holborn Underground Station follow Kingsway towards Aldwych. At first lights turn right. Hotel 50mtrs on left)

☎ 020 7309 0909 Fax 020 7309 9696

Situated in Convent Garden, the Kingsway Hall is a smart brand new hotel offering a high standard of accommodation. Air-conditioned bedrooms have been well designed and feature excellent facilities. The range of public areas include a spacious restaurant, lounge bar and a selection of conference rooms.

170 rooms

Price band £££

★★★★ ⊕ RADISSON EDWARDIAN HAMPSHIRE

Leicester Square WC2H 7LH

☎ 020 7839 9399 ☎ 020 7930 8122

This stylish period hotel enjoys a prime location in Leicester Square. Public areas, although not extensive, have been smartly refurbished and ooze style. The restaurant is particularly enjoyable, complemented by Oscar's wine bar. The smart bedrooms are comfortable and include access to the Internet.

124 rooms (20 no smoking) / English & French Cuisine / Lift, Night porter, Air cond

Price band £££

★★★★ ⊕ RADISSON EDWARDIAN MOUNTBATTEN

Monmouth St, Seven Dials, Covent Garden WC2H 9HD

(just off Shaftesbury Av, on the corner of Seven Dials rdbt)

☎ 020 7836 4300 ☎ 020 7240 3540

Situated at Seven Dials, in the heart of theatreland, this hotel is also a popular

choice for business guests. Bedrooms are not over-large, but all have an excellent range of facilities, including Internet access. Public areas include a comfortable cocktail bar and restaurant.

127 rooms (13 no smoking) / English & French Cuisine / Lift, Night porter

Price band £££

★★★ RADISSON EDWARDIAN PASTORIA

3-6 St Martins St WC2H 7HL

☎ 020 7930 8641 ☎ 020 7925 0551

Tucked away in a discreet side street off Leicester Square, this small hotel has smart public areas and an informal restaurant. The bedrooms are tastefully furnished and comfortable, and offer a useful level of room service. Those on the top floor are more spacious and have marble bathrooms.

58 rooms (16 no smoking) / English & American Cuisine / Lift, Night porter / No dogs (ex guide dogs) / No coaches

Price band £££

★★★ THISTLE TRAFALGAR SQUARE

Whitcomb St WC2H 7HG

(Situated 100m from Trafalgar Sq adjacent to the Sainsbury Wing of the National Gallery)

☎ 020 7930 4477 ☎ 020 7925 2149

Tucked away in a side street adjacent to the National Gallery and convenient for many of the West End theatres, this popular hotel offers a sound standard of accommodation. Public areas include a pleasant foyer lounge, a busy traditional pub, and a brasserie which opens out onto the pavement in the warmer months.

108 rooms (36 no smoking) / Modern cuisine / Lift, Night porter / No dogs (ex guide dogs)

WHERE TO EAT
RESTAURANTS
AA RECOMMENDED

L'Escargot – The Picasso Room

⊛ ⊛ ⊛ ALASTAIR LITTLE SOHO
49 Frith Street W1V 5TE
☎ 020 7734 5183 ☏ 020 7792 4504
'Modern, functional' is how this Soho landmark describes itself. It's the cooking that draws the attention, majoring on the quality of ingredients and the utter simplicity of its approach. Staff fit the bill well, casually dressed in jeans, shirts and long aprons and pleasant with it. The short menu changes twice daily, owes a lot to the Mediterranean in general and Italy in particular, and is good value. The terse descriptions - minestrone of broccoli, potatoes and borlotti beans, or truffled breast of chicken with stewed leeks - emphasise the simple technique.
Fixed L/D ££

⊛ ALFRED
245 Shaftesbury Avenue WC2 8EH
☎ 020 7240 2566 ☏ 020 7497 0672
Cheerful eaterie. Expect honest, consistent cooking of uncomplicated dishes from a menu with a distinctly British slant. Nearly two dozen wines come by the glass and there's an exceptional choice of bottled beers.
Fixed L/D £ ALC ££

⊛ AROMA II
118 Shaftesbury Avenue W1V 7DJ
☎ 020 7437 0370/0377
☏ 020 7437 0377
Bright and spacious Chinese offering speciality noodle and dumpling dishes on the light-lunch menu and more unusual Peking and Cantonese specialities in the evening,
ALC £

⊛ ⊛ ATLANTIC BAR AND GRILL
20 Glasshouse Street W1R 5RQ
☎ 020 7734 4888 ☏ 020 7734 3609
This restaurant, located on a back street behind Piccadilly, shares its vast basement with a notable cocktail bar. In the evenings it becomes a bustling, chaotic venue. There are carte, bar, set-lunch and pre-theatre menus. All the dishes change frequently and, in style and influence, come from all over the world.
Fixed L/D £ ALC ££

⊛ CAFÉ DU JARDIN
28 Wellington Street WC2E 7BD
☎ 020 7836 8769 ☏ 020 7836 4123
Popular Theatreland brasserie with a lively roll-call of dishes such as grilled swordfish steak on baby plum tomatoes in a turmeric and basil oil dressing.
Fixed L/D £ ALC ££

⊛ CHRISTOPHER'S
18 Wellington Street WC2E 7DD
☎ 020 7240 4222 ☏ 020 7836 3506
Victorian building on three floors with a stone spiral staircase. All-American menu of bold flavours: Maryland crab cakes with red pepper mayo, and blackened salmon with paprika oil.
ALC ££

⊛ ⊛ L'ESCARGOT - THE GROUND FLOOR RESTAURANT
48 Greek Street W1V 5LQ
☎ 020 7439 7474 ☏ 020 7437 0790
The old lady of Greek Street wears her age well. The Ground Floor makes a strong impression where black banquettes contrast with crisp white linen, colour is injected by a dramatic art collection, notably the works of the Spanish painter Miro. The punchy menu marries modern ideas with classic techniques with dishes such as feuilleté of snails, bacon, button onions, morels and herb purée, and calves' liver with Alsace bacon are in keeping with the brasserie feel. The lengthy wine list is well balanced and offers a good range under £25 (also a fair few over £1,000).
Fixed L/D £ ALC ££

⊛ ⊛ L'ESCARGOT - THE PICASSO ROOM
48 Greek Street W1V 5LQ
☎ 020 7439 7474 ☏ 020 7437 0790
The Picasso Room is the upstairs restaurant at L'Escargot, distinct from its ground floor counterpart by a discreet, intimate setting, and an amazing collection of original Picasso ceramics, prints, drawings. The approach here is more formal, the appointments comfortable and expensive. The kitchen delivers classic French, cooking based on a concise menu du jour with two choices per course, plus a heftier carte.
Fixed L ££ Fixed D £££

⊛ FRENCH HOUSE DINING ROOM
49 Dean Street W1V 5HL
☎ 020 7437 2477 ☏ 020 7287 9109
First-floor dining room over renowned Soho pub. The daily menu offers an imaginative choice of robust fare along the lines of crisp pigs' tails with watercress, and rabbit saddle with beetroot.
ALC £

⊛ ⊛ FUNG SHING
15 Lisle Street WC2H 7BE
☎ 020 7437 1539 ☏ 020 7734 0284
Friendly Cantonese restaurant where approachable staff are willing to advise and recommend dishes. Regarded as one of the best, though not the cheapest, restaurants in Chinatown - a great help when it comes to considering which of the dozens of dishes to order. Will it be whole squid stuffed with seafood, or 'meltingly tender' braised suckling pig subtly spiced with a touch of star anise? The answer is probably to go with as many people as possible, and order as much of the menu as possible.
Fixed D £ ALC £

⊛ ⊛ ⊛ THE IVY
1 West Street Covent Garden WC2H 9NE
☎ 020 7836 4751 ☏ 020 7240 9333
It still remains one of the best addresses in town (as long as you can get in). The original decor has been sympathetically updated; oak-panels, dark green leather banquettes, flattering lighting and modern art on the walls help keep the atmosphere convivial and relaxed. The menu is eclectic and slightly eccentric, one for all comers, which in theory should not work as well as it does in practice. It is divided into many sections from hors d'oeuvre through to coffees and teas. Retro shepherds pie and braised beef in Guinness demand to be eaten with the honeyed parsnips and bubble-and-squeak, but roast mallard with

foie gras, fondant potato and truffled Savoy cabbage goes for the big flavour. However, little can beat the roast poulet des Landes with truffle jus and dauphin potato.

ALC £££

✦ J. SHEEKEY
28-32 St Martin's Court WC2N 4AL
☎ 020 7240 2565 ⓕ 020 7240 8114
Now part of the Ivy and Caprice stable, with a revamp that has updated but kept the individual look of the place. Tables are small and cramped, but the high standard of service soon helps you cease to notice. Star billing still goes to fish and seafood - classics in the repertoire include Morecambe Bay potted shrimps, fish pie, and perfect salmon fishcake with sautéed spinach and sorrel sauce. Strong support comes from a brilliant Caesar salad and a good fettucine with cockles and parsley. The place simply buzzes with life again - it's good to have it back on form.

Fixed L £ ALC £££

✦ LEITH'S SOHO
41 Beak Street W1R 3LE
☎ 020 7287 2057 ⓕ 020 7287 1767
Sleek, modern and crisp - that goes for both interior and food. Saddle of venison, choucroute, liver timbale and caramelised parsnips is a gutsy main course to follow Leith's classic prawn cocktail.

Fixed L/D £ ALC £££

✦ LEXINGTON
45 Lexington Street W1R 3LG
☎ 020 7434 3401 ⓕ 020 7287 2997
Fun restaurant with a live jazz pianist three nights a week. Dishes have a Mediterranean influence, and there is a popular two choice, two course menu at £11.95.

✦✦ LINDSAY HOUSE
21 Romilly Street W1V 5TG
☎ 020 7439 0450 ⓕ 020 7437 7349
You have to ring the bell to be admitted to this Soho house. One of the affable staff opens it promptly and shows you to a table in the ground or first-floor dining room. In an area awash with trend-setters (and trend-followers, come to that), Richard Corrigan is his own man, cooking from the heart in a style rooted in the great British (and Irish) traditions. Shoulder and belly of pork with crubeens and choucroute might feature alongside saddle of rabbit stuffed with black pudding, and pigeon en croûte with Savoy cabbage and wild mushrooms, bold, gutsy-sounding dishes that none the less show restraint in the handling to produce delicate combinations of flavours.

Fixed L £ ALC £££

✦✦ MEZZO
100 Wardour Street W1V 3LE
☎ 020 7314 4000 ⓕ 020 7314 4040
One of the largest restaurants in Europe, divided into an upper level brasserie (Mezzonine) and a more formal restaurant in the basement (Mezzo). On entering, one is immediately struck by the dramatic double height space, and a massive wall of glass that descends through both floors and separates the restaurants from their respective kitchens. In Mezzonine the food comes unerringly quickly from the kitchen, and includes a combination of Mediterranean and Asian dishes. In Mezzo, the array of set menus is overwhelming and the style basically European. Simple, classic grills and crustacea are to be found alongside more complex dishes. The wine list is impressive though safe, and the service is efficient but charmless.

Fixed L £ ALC ££

✦✦ MON PLAISIR
21 Monmouth Street, WC2H 9DD
☎ 020 7836 7243 ⓕ 020 7240 4774
Mon Plaisir has been feeding the capital's Francophiles since the 1940s, and the place hums with people casually tucking into such bistro staples as entrecôte grillée avec allumettes and poulet rôti chasseur. But a new English chef adds another dimension to the repertoire, so there might be confit of quail with a ravioli of pea purée and pearl barley with tarragon vinaigrette, and calves' liver in a lime crust. Staff are all French, and the wine list may as well be: why bother with the handful from the Nouveau Monde when there's French quality to choose from?

Fixed L £ ALC ££

✦✦ NEAL STREET RESTAURANT
26 Neal Street WC2H 9PS
☎ 020 7836 8368 ⓕ 020 7836 2740
The entirely Italian repertoire is still more old-fashioned and more formally presented than in many of the new-wave Italian restaurants. Antonnio Carluccio is famous for his mushrooms, and they feature heavily on the carte. In winter, when truffles are in season, a memorable home-made tagliatelle is served with lashings of white truffle grated in front of the customer. Desserts are excellent. The predominantly Italian wine list, including some special bottles from the Ricasoli Estate, is a treat.

ALC £££

✦✦ NEW WORLD
1 Gerrard Place W1V 7LL
☎ 020 7434 2508 ⓕ 020 7287 3994
Close your eyes, listen and smell and you could be transported to Hong Kong. This is a typically jumbo-size Hong Kong-style restaurant, seating 700 on several floors, and decorated in the traditional 'lucky' colours of red and gold. It's one of the best places in Chinatown for the Sunday dim sum ritual. Other times, choose house specialities such as sesame sautéed chicken with bamboo shoots and carrots, fried squid cake with mincemeat and quick-fried scallops with hot spicy sauce.

Fixed L/D £

✦✦ ORSO RESTAURANT
27 Wellington Street WC2E 7DA
☎ 020 7240 5269 ⓕ 020 7497 2148
A well-kept secret with welcoming atmosphere, informal and jolly. This distinctly Italian old-timer keeps well up to date, offering robust modern cooking based on good quality produce. The informality works well with the cooking style and there's a studied casualness about the place that belies well-timed service. Lots of pre-theatre diners, for example, are handled with exact precision; no missing the curtain call here. Good Italian wine list with half the 70 bins under £20.

Fixed D £ ALC ££

✦✦✦ QUO VADIS
26-29 Dean St W1V 6LL
☎ 020 7437 9585 ⓕ 020 7434 9972
Refurbished, with crisp table linen, hallmarked silver, extra banquette seating and rich brown leather upholstery; all classically smart, despite the MPW masterpieces, such as lizard skeletons on the ceiling and a framed chicken head with solitary egg. Well, at least this challenging chef's debut in the art world provides a talking point. The menu interperses good old-fashioned items with more up-to-date dishes such as a well-composed Caesar salad with fresh anchovies, crisp slivers of pancetta and croûtons, and a salmon and fennel ravioli with Emmenthal glaze, teamed with a tomato sauce.

Fixed L/D £ ALC £££

✦✦ RULES
35 Maiden Lane Covent Garden WC2E 7LB
☎ 020 7836 5314 ⓕ 020 7497 1081
Rules was described by the late Sir John Betjeman as 'unique and irreplaceable, part of literary and theatrical London', and as the century closes, will have been serving its clientele through four centuries. The menu relies on safe English classics like Morecambe Bay potted brown shrimps in spiced lobster butter. The main courses include freshwater and sea fish, prime Aberdeen Angus beef, lamb, and their signature dishes of feathered and furred game. Seasonal birds are provided by the owners' country estate. Thirty seven wines are listed.

Fixed D £ ALC ££

✦✦ THE SUGAR CLUB
21 Warwick Street W1
☎ 020 7437 7776 ⓕ 020 7437 7778
The Sugar Club comes with typical late-nineties metropolitan restaurant décor (pale colours, blond wood) and ultra-cool staff who nevertheless remain approachable and friendly. That the restaurant started life in the mid 1980s in New Zealand gives a clue to the attractive Pacific-rim based fusion menu, perhaps the best of its kind in London at the moment.

ALC ££

⚜ ⚜ TEATRO
93-107 Shaftesbury Avenue W1V 8BT

☎ 020 7494 3040 📠 020 7494 3050

Teatro is a slick, well-run operation that continues to pull in the punters. That the menu is printed in a sans-serif typeface with not a capital letter in sight is testament to the modishness of the kitchen's style. However, the brigade manages to tease all the flavours out of the ingredients, especially in a main course of poulet noir with thyme jus and crisp shallots on Parmesan risotto. Pear tarte Tatin comes with Jersey cream, and breads are good.

Fixed L/D £ ALC £££

⚜ TITANIC
81 Brewer Street W1R 3FH

☎ 020 7437 1912

Blockbuster from Marco Pierre White that's a hit with the punters. Large open foyer, centrepiece bar and a sprawling, noisy dining-room. Easy, witty menu includes fish and chips, and steak hâché à la McDonalds. Open from midnight until 3am for breakfast.

Fixed L £ ALC ££

⚜ VASCO & PIERO'S PAVILION
15 Poland Street W1V 3DE

☎ 020 7437 8774 📠 020 7437 0467

Much-loved by politicians and music types, this charming Soho Italian is as popular as ever. Typical starters from the short carte include carpaccio of tuna, rucola, and tomato, and thinly sliced roast pork with radicchio and Pecorino cheese.

Fixed D £ ALC ££

⚜ ⚜ YMING
35-36 Greek Street W1V 5LN

☎ 020 7734 2721 📠 020 7437 0292

A rather original Chinese restaurant, quite unlike most other Chinese establishments in Soho. The food is described as northern Chinese, but there are many other regional specials to be found on the various menus. Four set menus includes one that's entirely vegetarian, and there's a carte that is an extensive list but includes many home-made additions such as pickles and dumplings. The wine list is well-matched to the menu.

Fixed L/D £ ALC £

PUBS, INNS & OTHER PLACES

CHUEN CHENG KU
17 Wardour St, W1V 3HD

☎ 020 7437 1398

Popular Soho Chinese restaurant. Dim sum are good value.

CRANKS
8 Marshall St, Soho, W1 1LP

☎ 020 7437 9431

Part of a small chain of long-established vegetarian/vegan restaurants.

GOLDEN DRAGON
28-29 Gerrard St, W1

☎ 020 7734 2763

Dim sum palace in the heart of Chinatown.

DRAGON INN
12 Gerrard St, Soho, W1V 7LJ

☎ 020 7494 0870

Popular Chinatown restaurant with a wide range of dim sum.

GOVINDAS
9/10 Soho St, W1V 5DA

☎ 020 7437 4928

Vegetarian/Vegan restaurant owned by the International Krishna Organisation.

HARBOUR CITY
46 Gerrard St, Soho, W1E 7LP

☎ 020 7439 7859

Busy Chinese restaurant spread over three floors.

KETTNERS
29 Romilly St, Soho, W1

☎ 020 7734 6112

Pizza Express' restaurant. (Establishment originally founded by Auguste Kettner, Napoleon III's chef)

MARCHÉ MÖVENPICK
Swiss Centre, Leicester Sq, W1V 7FJ

☎ 020 7494 0498

French, German and Italian, as well as Swiss, food.

PLANET HOLLYWOOD
Unit 75, Trocadero Centre, Coventry St, W1V 7FE

Owned by Arnie, Sly & Bruno - No bookings.

FOOD FOR THOUGHT
31 Neal Street, Covent Garden, WC2H 9PA

☎ 020 7836 9072

Self-service restaurant with varied changing menu.

HONG KONG
6 Lisle St, Leicester Sq, WC2

☎ 020 7287 0324

Large Chinese restaurant with strong Cantonese and Pekinese menus.

LE MISTRAL
Thomas Neal Centre, 16a Shorts Gardens, Covent Garden

☎ 020 7379 8751

Basement wine bar with all-day snack menu.

PRINCE OF WALES
150-151 Drury Ln,
Convent Garden WC2B 5TB

☎ 020 7836 5183

Opened in 1852. Traditional bar food such as steak and mushroom pies or roast pork with apple sauce.

WORLD FOOD CAFÉ
1st Floor, 14 Neal's Yard, Covent Garden, WC2H 9DP

☎ 020 7379 0298

Relaxed vegetarian café

CAMDEN, KING'S CROSS & ISLINGTON

A century or so ago, Camden was little more than a Victorian slum that had grown from a village due to the arrival of the canal in 1816. By 1911 the area had put itself more firmly on the map by getting its own art clique. Over the years the Camden Town group of artists has included Walter Sickert, Lucien Freud (grandson of Sigmund), Frank Auerbach, and Leon Kossoff, and this association with the artistic community has continued to the present day. Modern Camden has a thriving music scene and a mass of craft workshops. The area also has a large Irish immigrant population, which has surely contributed to the area's easy-going flavour. In the 1970s the famous Camden Market shifted from Inverness Street into disused wharfs and warehouses, as the end of the canals signalled the rise of an esoteric market scene. Camden High Street and Chalk Farm Road are the main shopping areas, while the market sits by the lock. The Electric Ballroom, on Camden High Street, was once the area's premier live music venue but is now an eclectic nightclub and day market, leaving the live music to nearby Dingwall's. The Roundhouse, on Chalk Farm Road, was built to house goods-engines in 1847. It's been closed since 1983, although plans are afoot for its future conversion into a studio and theatre complex. It's probably best known for presenting non-conformist art performances in the 1960s and punk in the 1970s. The area remains a hotbed of left-wing and alternative activity, as well as more recently becoming home to some media giants. Compendium Books is the place for anarchist and generally left-field books, while by way of contrast, the nearby TV-AM building is now home to MTV Europe in Britain. All around are media types and bicycle couriers. Camden Town is the place to discover what young London is into, and to spend a few hours sifting through old books, records, or josticks looking for a special gift.

King's Cross is a bit different. A bad reputation has attached itself to the area outside the old Great Northern terminus. Drug addicts and prostitutes have made the place more than a little unsafe at night, but during the day it remains an area of interest. Old St Pancras is just off Pancras Road, and is thought to be London's oldest parish church. It has seen better days, but parts are 11th century. The churchyard was turned into a public garden in 1877 and a few reasonably famous Victorians are buried there. By the old gas works is an unlikely site ideal for kids. The Camley Street Natural Park, is run by London Wildlife Trust and was once a rubbish tip. The recreation of a natural waterland environment is a haven for wildlife. The London Canal Museum nearby is also worth a visit.

The area's most controversial building is undoubtedly the New British Library, which has been dogged by logistical problems and public criticism since its inception. It is a huge structure stocked with just about every book ever published in English. As well as showing

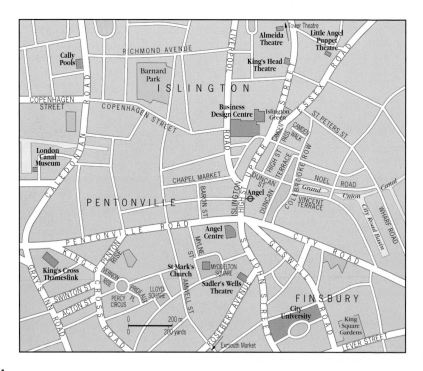

important historic texts, the Library has begun staging temporary exhibitions.
King's Cross Station itself opened in 1850 and was part of the huge railway boom that led
to three major stations occupying this area. Three rival companies built King's Cross, St
Pancras and Euston to corner the market in London arrivals, but with so much railway
overkill its no wonder that half the tracks are idle. St Pancras Station, a masterpiece of neo-
Gothic pomp, has been mainly used for office space since 1935. Euston Station was built
in 1840 but suffered from clumsy reworking. It is still a major terminus. Nearby is the
New St Pancras Church, built around the same time, and modelled on Athenian lines; the
Wellcome Building, home to the offices of the giant medical company; and Salvationist
Publishing Supplies, which has a museum on the Salvation Army.

To the east of King's Cross, Islington has recently gained a reputation as the home of
New Labour. Prime Minister Tony Blair lives here and Chris Smith is the constituency
Labour MP. In the 1970s there was an influx of media professionals, while the 1980s saw
an increase in the yuppie population, due to the borough's proximity to The City. In spite
of all this affluence much of the borough is still poor, and is all but starved of green space,
a very important commodity in central London. Upper Street is the main shopping area
with a thriving antique market on Camden Passage. Independant theatre has a strong base
here, with both the King's Head and the Almeida providing challenging and adventurous
plays and music. Apart from today's champagne socialists, the area has been home to
authors George Orwell and Evelyn Waugh, and playwright Joe Orton, whose defaced
library books are now the pride of Islington Central Library.

MUST SEE

Camden Market

twenty years from drawing board to completion, and although its critics have been many, it's still worth a look.

CAMDEN MARKET
Camden Lock, NW1

A great place to pick up esoteric books, handmade jewellery, second-hand clothes, Eastern knick-knacks, rare records, strange objets d'art and a dazzling array of fashions. Will make you feel young again, or very old depending on your outlook. The market is sprawled all over Camden, including Camden Lock, the Electric Ballroom, The Stables up Chalk Farm Road, and the Victorian Market Hall. Most stalls are open at some point from Wednesday to Sunday.

CANONBURY TOWER
Canonbury Square, N1
(ring Canonbury Academy on 020-7359 6888 to arrange a visit inside the tower)

The tower, which may have Roman foundations, is all that remains of Canonbury House, a Tudor mansion

THE LONDON CANAL MUSEUM
12-13 New Wharf Rd, N1 9RT
☎ 020 7713 0836

The museum covers the development of London's canals (particularly Regent's Canal), canal vessels and trade, and the lifestyle of canal people. Housed in a former ice warehouse and stables, it also illustrates history of the unusual Norwegian ice importation trade, and horse transport. Regular exhibitions and temporary mooring available, so arrivals by boat are possible.

THE JEWISH MUSEUM
Raymond Burton House, 129-131 Albert St, NW1 7NB
☎ 020 7284 1997

An exploration of the religion and history of the Jewish community in both Britain and the world. Housed in an attractive Victorian building in Camden Town, the museum houses a fine collection of rare and beautiful objects with Jewish connections. Guided walks of Jewish London can be arranged.

CAMLEY STREET NATURAL PARK
Camley Street, NW1

Pond, meadow and waterside habitats recreated in an urban setting. Run by the London Wildlife Trust, and transformed from an old rubbish tip.

BUSINESS DESIGN CENTRE
Liverpool Rd, N1
☎ 020-7359 3535

Once home to the 'Aggie' - Royal Agricultural Hall - this was originally a wholesale market for cattle, sheep, pigs and poultry, after the sale of live animals was banned at Smithfield. It was later used for all sorts of events, from gala balls to Cruft's dog show. It now serves as a showcase for the best in British design.

Antiques at Camden Market

THE BRITISH LIBRARY
Euston Rd, NW1
☎ 020 7412 7000

Every publisher in Britain has to send two copies of their publication here, so this is probably the best English library in the world. The current location was over

whose former residents include Oliver Goldsmith and Sir Francis Bacon.

MUSEUMS

THE WELLCOME TRUST BUILDING
183 Euston Rd, NW1
☎ 020-7611 8888

The head offices of this giant pharmacutical company also houses some interesting exhibits. The Science for Life exhibition concentrates on medicine, while Wellcome itself is the subject of a display in the basement.

SALVATIONIST PUBLISHING SUPPLIES
117 Judd St, WC1
☎ 020-7387 1656

This is the headquarters of the Salvation Army's propaganda wing, and has a small museum on the history and activities of William Booth's missionary force and brass band promoter.

St Pancras Station

Canonbury Square, Islington

NATIONAL SOUND ARCHIVE

British Library, 96 Euston Rd, NW1

📞 020-7412 7440

Basically an archive of all kinds of recordings - music, voice, radio, etc. Admittance is free, but it's best to call ahead with your requests.

ART GALLERIES

CRAFTS COUNCIL

44a Pentonville Rd, N1

📞 020-7278 7700

Craft gallery located in a converted Georgian house. Includes exhibits of textiles, woodwork, ceramics, jewellery, furniture and weaving.

ESTORICK COLLECTION OF MODERN ITALIAN ART

39a Canonbury Sq, N1

📞 020-7704 9522

An excellent collection of modern Italian art (obviously!) including Futurists Severini and Boccioni, and other major Italian painters such a Modigliani and surrealist Georgio de Chirico. Also has a good café.

CINEMAS

THE SCREEN ON THE GREEN

83 Upper Street, N1

📞 020 7226 3520

Independant cinema catering to eclectic tastes. A stalwart of indie film.

ODEON CAMDEN TOWN

Parkway, NW1

📞 0870 505 0007

The National Sound Archive

THEATRES

ALMEIDA

Almeida St, N1

📞 020-7359 4404

High quality venue that has come along incredibly in the last ten years or so. It regularly puts on productions with world-famous film actors and actresses, including Kevin Spacey and Cate Blanchett.

Street trading in Camden Passage

KING'S HEAD

115 Upper St, N1

📞 020-7226 1916

London's oldest pub theatre, presenting a mix of musicals, plays, and revues among the burger and chips. Impromptu musical evenings take advantage of the pub's late license.

ETCETERA THEATRE

Oxford Arms, 265 Camden High St, NW1

📞 020-7482 4857

Tiny pub theatre staging two different shows a night.

ENTERTAINMENT AND NIGHTLIFE

Camden is well known for its live music and has plenty of small, sweaty venues where the wise can see the best (and worst) of the international indie, punk and industrial scenes. Recently the semi-regular Camden Crawl, a kind of multi-venued urban festival of indie music, has been very successful.

WKD

18 Kentish Town Rd, NW1

📞 020-7267 1869

Collage of café, bar, club and gallery. DJs start at about 9.30pm.

THE FORUM

9-17 Highgate Rd, NW5

📞 020-7344 0044

North of Camden in Kentish Town, this top concert venue was once the Town & Country Club and puts on a varied mix of live music. Club night is Saturday.

THE CAMDEN PALACE

1a Camden High St, NW1

📞 020-7387 0428

Huge club with big dance floor. Sometimes has live music, but usually dedicates itself to big-time fun and dancing.

THE CROSS

Goods Way Depot, off York Way, N1

📞 020-7837 0828

Monthly weekend parties are very popular at this club located at an old rail depot. Arrive early.

CAMDEN FALCON

234 Royal College St, NW1

📞 020-7485 3834

Busy pub with a small music bar. Plenty of rock and indie newcomers.

Regent's Canal

DUBLIN CASTLE
94 Parkway, NW1
☎ 020-7485 1773
Tiny black-painted music bar with three bands almost every night. Great atmosphere.

HOPE & ANCHOR
207 Upper St, N1
☎ 020-7354 1312
Once a major pub/punk rock venue, this small basement now features indie newcomers.

DINGWALL'S
Middle Yard, Camden Lock, Chalk Farm Rd, NW1
☎ 020-7267 1577
Comfortable venue with a mainly indie booking policy. The big pillars often make it difficult to see the stage.

THE GARAGE
20-22 Highbury Corner, N5
☎ 020-7607 1818
Indie, punk and rock venue with regular clubs upstairs. If you're very brave you could visit the extreme noise club held here once a month.

JAZZ CAFÉ
5 Parkway, NW1
☎ 020-7916 6060
Two-level, intimate venue with an eclectic booking policy and good food available.

THE UNDERWORLD
174 Camden High St, NW1
☎ 020-7482 1932
Located beneath trendy pub the World's End and opposite Camden Town tube station, this neat little venue puts on a lot of well-known indie bands.

UNION CHAPEL
Compton Terrace, N1
☎ 020-7226 1686
Although still a functioning church, the Union Chapel puts on a variety of rock, indie, electronic and folk acts.

COMEDY

COMEDY BREWHOUSE
at The Camden Head, 2 Camden Walk, Camden Passage, N1
☎ 020-7359 0851
Improvisation and stand-up.

Bargain hunting in Camden Passage

JONGLEURS CAMDEN LOCK
Dingwalls, Middle Yard, Camden Lock, Camden High St, NW1
☎ 020-564 2500
Purpose built comedy room forming part of the Dingwalls venue. Late bar and food. Be sure to book in advance.

SHOPPING

COMPENDIUM BOOKS
234 Camden High Street, NW1
☎ 020 7485 8944
A broad collection of broad-minded literature, ranging from surrealism to body art, and from anarchism to 'the Beat Generation'. A must for fans of the esoteric.

RATHBONE BOOKS
76 Haverstock Hill
☎ 020 7267 2848
Specialises in psychoanalytic books.

CAMDEN PASSAGE MARKET
Camden Passage, off Upper St, N1
A wealth of antiques in an indoor arcade. Outdoor stalls, Wednesday and Saturday.

MOLE JAZZ
311 Gray's Inn Rd, WC1
☎ 020-7278 8623
One of England's best jazz shops. CDs and books on the ground floor, and vinyl upstairs.

RHYTHM RECORDS
281 Camden High St, NW1
☎ 020-7267 0123
Great selection of punk, psychedelia, folk, country and rock'n'roll.

GREAT FOR KIDS

THE PLAYHOUSE
The Old Gymnasium, Highbury Grove School, corner of Highbury Grove & Highbury New Park, N5
☎ 020-7704 9424
Playroom with space for up to 70 kids, aged 6 months to 12 years.

LITTLE ANGEL THEATRE
14 Dagmar Passage, off Cross St, N1
☎ 020 7226 1787
The only permanent puppet theatre in London, the Little Angel has been running for nearly 40 years, and can seat up to 110 kids of all ages. The resident company put on a variety of shows (some only suitable for older children), and also welcome puppeteers from around the world.

SPORT AND LEISURE

RACEWAY
Central Warehouse, North London Freight Terminal, York Way, N1
☎ 020-7833 1000
Go-karting track close to King's Cross Station.

WHERE TO STAY
HOTELS
AA RECOMMENDED

★★★★ **HOLIDAY INN**
1 Kings Cross Rd WC1X 9HX
(0.5m from Kings Cross station on the corner of King Cross Rd and Calthorpe St)
☎ 020 7833 3900 🖷 020 7917 6163
Bedrooms at this smart modern hotel come equipped with Air conditioning, fridge and power shower. The lobby leads to a range of attractively furnished public rooms including an intimate cocktail bar and two restaurants, one of which offers Indian cuisine.
405 rooms (163 family & 160 no smoking) / International Cuisine / Indoor swimming pool (heated), Sauna, Solarium, Gym, Jacuzzi/spa / Hair & Beauty salon / Lift, Night porter, Air cond / No dogs (ex guide dogs)
Price band £££ 🖘

★★★ **GREAT NORTHERN**
Kings Cross N1 9AN
(entrance faces side of Kings Cross station)
☎ 020 7837 5454 🖷 020 7278 5270
The Great Northern offers spacious, comfortable accommodation with a good level of facilities. The coffee house is open all day for meals, and there is also a lively bar and a no-smoking lounge. There is 24-hour room service and a laundry service.
82 rooms (16 family & 22 no smoking) / Lift, Night porter / No dogs / No coaches
Price band £££ 🖘

★★★ **JURY'S INN LONDON**
60 Pentonville Rd, Islington N1 9LA
☎ 020 7282 5500 🖷 020 7282 5511
Jury's Inn offers good value rooms, that can easily be adapted to family use, and single guests will be pleased to have the comfort of a double bed. All rooms are air-conditioned. The Angel Tube station is nearby and there are several car parks in the neighbourhood.
229 rooms (116 family & 135 no smoking) / Lift, Night porter, Air cond / No dogs (ex guide dogs) / Closed 24–27 Dec
🖘

★★★ **KENNEDY**
Cardington St NW1 2LP
(A40 to Euston,then A501 to Euston Stn, turn left before Stn into Melton St, then into Cardington St, hotel is on left 200yds from traffic lights)
☎ 020 7387 4400 🖷 020 7387 5122
The Kennedy is a modern hotel close to Euston Station. Both standard and superior rooms are available, the latter being more spacious and having more amenities. Public areas include a lounge bar with satellite TV and all-day snacks, Spires restaurant which has a broad appeal, and a range of smart meeting rooms.
360 rooms (25 family & 67 no smoking) / English & French Cuisine / Lift, Night porter, Air cond / No dogs (ex guide dogs)
🖘

★★★ **THE LONDON RYAN**
Gwynne Place, Kings Cross Rd WC1X 9QN
☎ 020 7278 2480 🖷 020 7837 3776
Conveniently situated for King's Cross and Euston stations, the London Ryan has comfortable, well furnished bedrooms and gives a choice of standard, executive and family rooms. A ground-floor lounge leads to a small bar area and the Casablanca restaurant serves a good range of meals. Extensive room service is also available.
211 rooms (18 family & 89 no smoking) / English & Continental Cuisine / Lift, Night porter / No dogs (ex guide dogs)
🖘

★★★ **THE ROYAL SCOT**
100 Kings Cross Rd WC1X 9DT
☎ 020 7278 2434 🖷 020 7833 0798
Well positioned for both Kings Cross and St Pancras stations, this large, modern hotel is well suited to all visitors. A gradual transformation is under way, which is resulting in some excellent standards of comfort and quality. There are two eating options and a shop.
351 rooms (22 family & 118 no smoking) / English & French Cuisine / Lift, Night porter, Air cond / No dogs (ex guide dogs)
🖘

★★ **HOTEL IBIS EUSTON**
3 Cardington St NW1 2LW
(from Euston station or Eustaon Rd, turn right to Melton St leading to Cardington St)
☎ 020 7388 7777 🖷 020 7388 0001
This busy hotel has the added advantage of a very secure underground car park. Bedrooms are bright, well maintained, and provide good value for this location. The hub of the public areas is the bar/lounge which is open all day for drinks and snacks. There is also an informal restaurant.
300 rooms (150 no smoking) / English & French Cuisine / Lift, Air cond
Price band ££ 🖘

LONDON EUSTON TRAVEL INN CAPITAL
141 Euston Rd NW1 2AU
(situated on the corner of Euston Road (south side) and Duke's Road, between Kings Cross/St Pancras and Euston stations)
☎ 020 7554 3400 🖷 020 7554 3419
220 rooms / No dogs (ex guide dogs)
Price band ££ 🖘

WHERE TO EAT
RESTAURANTS
AA RECOMMENDED

⊛ ⊛ FREDERICK'S RESTAURANT
Camden Passage Islington N1 8EG
☎ 020 7359 2888 📠 020 7359 5173
In its 30 years Frederick's has seen off quite a few of the newer boys, and it's still appreciated for the comfort of the interior, with its mix of the traditional and the innovative, attentive and skilled service. An added bonus is the good-value set lunch and pre-theatre menus of, say, smoked tomato soup with basil oil, and Lancashire hotpot. The full carte is a long affair and wide in scope. Note that children have their own separate set menu on Saturday lunchtimes.
Fixed D £ ALC ££

⊛ ⊛ GRANITA
127 Upper Street Islington N1 1QP
☎ 020 7226 3222 📠 020 7226 4833
Seven years on and Granita is still going strong, its decor simple and stark - bold turquoise walls, tightly packed maple tables and bare floorboards. But when the crowd is in, the noise levels are high and the atmosphere is charged; this is a lively, exciting place to enjoy some great global cooking. The short menu reads like a shopping list of ingredients. That doesn't mean it's all just thrown together, serious thought goes into the creation. A short list of modern wines hits the spot, both in taste and price.
Fixed L £ ALC ££

⊛ ⊛ LOLA'S
359 Upper Street Islington N1 2UD
☎ 020 7359 1932 📠 020 7359 2209
On the first floor of what was a tram shed and convenient for the antique dealers of Islington's celebrated Camden Passage. This is the setting for the sort of cooking Italians would be at home with: tagliatelle with ceps, truffle sauce and rocket salad, or monkfish 'osso buco' with gremolata and olive oil mash, as well as the more modern British slow-cooked pigeon with lightly textured black pudding, braised white beans and spinach. Italy heads up the wine list, where around a dozen bottles are also sold by the glass.
Fixed L £ ALC £

⊛ SAUCE
214 Camden High Street NW1 8QR
☎ 020 7482 0777
Brightly coloured modern diner. Ingredients are 95% organic, and include all day brunch, salads, main plates ranging from veggie burger to braised saffron lamb, and that millennium version of the sandwich - wraps.
ALC £

⊛ ⊛ WHITE ONION
297 Upper Street N1 2TU
☎/📠 020 7359 3533
Part of a steadily growing collection of good-value modern restaurants owned by Bijan Behzadi, the White Onion is, in our opinion, one of the best. Booking is essential. Eric Guignard can cook and he offers a short, punchy menu with strong Mediterranean overtones. The sixty bin wine list offers good quality and covers most of Europe with a few New World.
Fixed L £ ALC £

PUBS, INNS & OTHER PLACES

ALFREDO'S
4-6 Essex Rd, N1
☎ 020 7226 3496
Inexpensive but stylish neighbourhood diner.

MANZE'S
74 Chapel Market, N1
Traditional Cockney grub: jellied eels, pie and mash, fish and chips. Lovely jubbly.

CROWN & GOOSE
100 Arlington Rd, NW1 7HP
☎ 020 7485 2342
Bustling pub with continental feel in the heart of Camden.

THE ENGINEER
65 Gloucester Ave, NW1 8JH
☎ 020 7722 0950
Designed by Isambard Kingdom Brunel in 1841, this pub serves from an imaginative menu, situated near the canal.

THE MANGO ROOM
10 Kentish Town Rd,
Afro-Caribbean food.

THE LANSDOWNE
90 Gloucester Ave, NW1 8HX
☎ 020 7483 0409
This relaxed dining pub is something of a celebrity haunt, and offers a twice-daily changing menu.

THE DUKE OF CAMBRIDGE
30 St Peter's St, N1 8JT
☎ 020 7359 3066
London's first organic food pub, situated in a fine Victorian building. Organic and additive-free meals guaranteed.

THE LORD STANLEY
51 Camden Park Rd, NW1
☎ 020 7428 9488
Gastro-pub on the way to Kentish Town.

THE ALBION
10 Thornhill Rd, N1
☎ 020 7607 7450
A little north of Islington in Barnsbury, this ivy-covered pub has a big back garden and a friendly feel.

HOLBORN, STRAND AND THE SOUTH BANK

Holborn's focal point is Lincoln's Inn Fields, London's largest square. It was laid out in the 17th century but apart from number 59-60 little survives from that time. Lincoln's Inn itself is on the east side of the square and is part of the Inns of Court, the working place of London's barristers. There are three others: Gray's Inn, Middle Temple and Inner Temple. The last two lie within the boundaries of The City. The character of the district is heavily influenced by their medieval, collegiate presence, while the open spaces within them provide tranquillity a stone's throw from some of the busiest London streets. Holborn's main street, also called Holborn, has been a thoroughfare since medieval times, although in those days it transported wool and corn into the City. Dickens lived in a house on the site of what is now the Prudential Assurance building. There he wrote part of *The Pickwick Papers*. Other places of interest for Dickens buffs are the Old Curiosity Shop (after which Dickens named his novel) that lies in Portsmouth Street, and Old Hall, a part of Lincoln's Inn where the author set the court scenes of *Bleak House*. Also around the square is the fascinating Sir John Soane's Museum, where the architect of the Bank of England kept his eclectic art collection. The London School of Economics that played such an important part in the political events of 1968, and the Public Record Office and both nearby.

Heading down Chancery Lane you come to The Strand, originally a bridle path which ran beside the river until the construction of the Victoria Embankment. Its western end is dominated by Charing Cross Station, whose arrival transformed the Strand into the bustling street it is today. The original Charing Cross was in Trafalgar Square where the equestrian statue of Charles I now stands. It was one of the twelve built by 13th-century monarch Edward I to mark the overnight stops of his dead queen Eleanor as she made her way from Nottingham to Westminster. The cross outside the station that bears its name is a Victorian imitation.

The Strand was once one of the most prestigious streets in England, lined with mansions and theatres (the theatres have survived at least). Two fine churches, St Mary-le-Strand and St Clement Danes, serve as a reminder of this former glory, but the area has long had associations with pickpockets and prostitutes, and today its shopfronts and doorways are usually occupied by the homeless trying to keep warm at night. Along The Strand from Charing Cross Station are the Victoria Embankment Gardens, a pleasant cut through from the river, and the Savoy Hotel and Theatre. The Courtauld Institute Galleries at Somerset House have a superb collection of Impressionist paintings, and are next to King's College, one of the London university colleges. Before the college is the grand, sweeping semi-circle of the Aldwych, where Bush House, home to the BBC World Service, sits between the Embassies of Australia and India.

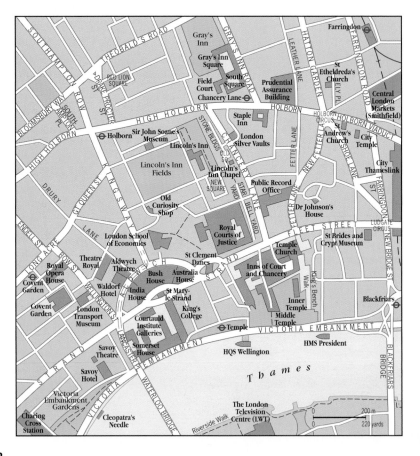

Crossing Waterloo Bridge takes you to the South Bank, the arts complex built of concrete in the 1960s. It includes the Royal Festival Hall, the National Theatre, Queen Elizabeth Hall, Purcell Room, Hayward Gallery, National Film Theatre and Museum of the Moving Image (MOMI). Something for everyone. Also along the South Bank are the now defunct County Hall, a massive building visible from Waterloo Bridge; the Florence Nightingale Museum; Lambeth Palace, home to the Archbishop of Canterbury since 1207; and the Museum of Garden History. The already internationally known Waterloo Station has recently become even more famous due to the new rail terminus which serves the Channel Tunnel. Passengers can now get on a train at Waterloo and get off in Paris or Brussels. Eastwards, towards Rotherhithe and Docklands, is Bankside Power Station, which is being coverted into the new Tate Gallery of Modern Art, and Shakespeare's Globe, the reconstruction of Shakespeare's original theatre.

MUST SEE

Shakespeare's Globe

SHAKESPEARE'S GLOBE
New Globe Walk, Bankside, SE1
☎ 020-7928 6406
Destroyed by fire in 1613, the original Globe Theatre, where many of Shakespeare's plays were performed, has recently been reconstructed. The dream of the late Sam Wanamaker, actor and director, has finally been realised, although not on the original site, which lays beneath a Georgian terrace on Park Street. May to September is the season for The Globe, which had its first performances in 1997. The theatre uses only natural light and has a thatched roof like the original. Unlike the original productions however, women will be acting in these. The Shakespeare's Globe Exhibition tells the story of the reconstruction.
See advert on page 240.

COURTAULD INSTITUTE GALLERIES
Somerset House, Strand, WC2
☎ 020-7848 2526
Apart from the wonderful art now gracing some of its walls, Somerset House has a story of its own. In the 16th century it was the site of a palace occupied by Queen Elizabeth I and other royals. This was demolished to make way for the current building, begun as governmental offices in 1776. It served as home to the Royal Academy of Arts until 1836, when it became the offices of the General Register of Births, Deaths and Marriages. In 1973 it was divided up between a fine art collection and the Inland Revenue. The Courtauld Collection is the largest collection of Impressionist and post-Impressionist paintings in London. Put together by Samuel Courtauld, rayon and nylon magnate, it was donated to London University in 1931. Among the riches are Botticelli's *Holy Trinity with Saint John and Mary Magdalen*, Rubens' *Descent from the Cross*, Manet's *Bar at the Folies-Bergère*, and works by Degas, Renoir and Pissarro, to name but a few. With so much to get round, it is a good idea to buy a plan or take the guided tour.

LAMBETH PALACE
Lambeth Palace Rd, SE1
This is the official residence of the head of the Church of England, the Archbishop of Canterbury. Archbishops have lived here since the 12th century, and the palace has often played a dramatic part in British history. It was here in 1534 that Thomas More refused to sign the Oath of Supremacy (which would make Henry VIII head of the English church), and was carted off to the Tower of London to be beheaded. John Wycliffe, who published The Bible in English, was tried here for heresy in the 14th century.

Guardhouse at Lambeth Palace

MUSEUM OF THE MOVING IMAGE
South Bank, SE1
☎ 020-7928 3535
Built in 1988, MOMI (as it is commonly known) has become one of London's most popular museums, particularly for those interested in film and television, and it's perfect for children. The word 'museum' usually conjures up static exhibits in glass cases - not so here. This museum was one of the first to widely employ visitor participation, for example, you can fly like Superman over London, make your own animations, or be interviewed by Barry Norman, Emma Forbes or Zig and Zag. If anything, MOMI has tended to rest on its laurels a bit, only offering a few changing exhibits. However, for a solid grounding in the history and techniques of film in all its varied forms, this is an excellent place to start.

HISTORIC AND ANCIENT SITES

ROYAL COURTS OF JUSTICE
Strand, WC2
☎ 020-7936 6000
Built in 1874, it is at the Royal Courts that some of the most important civil cases are heard. You can visit the viewing galleries and the Central Hall to see the barristers in action. It was from this imposing Gothic Revival building that the Guildford Four and Birmingham Six walked free.

SAVOY HOTEL
Strand, WC2 0EU
☎ 020-7836 4343
Built in 1889 on the site of the original Savoy Palace, the Savoy Hotel is a byword for luxury and has been a favoured hostelry for many celebrities past and present, including Sarah Bernhardt, Meryl Streep and Placido Domingo. It was from one of the hotel's balconies that Monet painted his famous impressions of Waterloo Bridge. Profits from the Savoy Theatre helped to pay for the building of the hotel. The theatre was built in 1881 as a dedicated stage for the musicals of Gilbert and Sullivan.

OXO TOWER
South Bank, SE1
Visible from Waterloo Bridge, the red, illuminated Oxo Tower has been redeveloped into a successful shopping and restaurant complex. The tower was built when large-scale advertising was not permitted, so the clever gravy people installed three big windows shaped like the letters of their name. When the building was lit from within, they had their giant advert.

OLD CURIOSITY SHOP
13 Portsmouth St, WC2
Although recently closed as a business, this building is alleged to be the home of Little Nell in Charles Dickens' *The Old Curiosity Shop*, which is enough to keep it on the tourist track.

STAPLE INN
High Holborn, WC1

One of London's oldest-surviving timber-framed buildings, Staple Inn was founded in 1378, and served as a training ground for barristers. Its façade survived the Great Fire of London, which reached its limit near Holborn Circus, but suffered damage during the Blitz and had to be reworked.

CHARING CROSS STATION
Strand, WC2

Rebuilt in 1990, this venerable old station brings in thousands of commuters every day, and is one of the busiest in London. Now it has new shopping malls and offices, as well as the famous Charing Cross Hotel.

ALDWYCH WC2

This semi-circle is at the Waterloo Bridge end of the Strand, and is famous for its links with Fleet Street (which leads off it towards the City) and four notable

Staple Inn, High Holborn

inhabited by super-arcade Namco Station, two hotels, a Chinese restaurant, the London Aquarium, and the FA Premier League Hall of Fame.

BANKSIDE POWER STATION
Hopton St, SE1

Opened in 1963 and closed again in 1980,

Hayward Gallery

buildings: Australia House (where eager emigrants can get those sought-after working visas), Bush House (headquarters of the BBC World Service), India House, and the magnificent Waldorf Hotel, where you can still go for afternoon tea and dancing.

WATERLOO BRIDGE

Although now a rather dull structure, Waterloo Bridge is the best spot to get fabulous views of St Paul's Cathedral, the South Bank, and the Houses of Parliament. This view at dusk was the subject of Ray Davies' song *Waterloo Sunset*, recorded by his band The Kinks in 1967. The original structure was built to commemorate Napoleon's victory at the Battle of Waterloo in 1815, but the present bridge was designed by Sir Gilbert Scott in 1937.

COUNTY HALL
York Rd, SE1

Once the headquarters of the GLC (Greater London Council), abolished in 1986 under Margaret Thatcher, County Hall stood empty for several years. There are plans for a Japanese company to transform it into a hotel (it'll be a big one), but at the time of writing it was

the future of Bankside Power Station lay in the balance for years, until it was decided to convert it to house the new Tate Gallery of Modern Art, hopefully opening in 2000. The transfer of all its modern work means that the Millbank Tate Gallery will then be known as the Tate Gallery of British Art.

WATERLOO STATION
SE1

Not a particularly pretty or historic building, Waterloo Station is the first place that most tourists will experience when

they visit London. Its massive concourse is a little shabby and overcrowded, but as an introduction to the bustle of London it can't be bettered. The station has become more famous recently for the stunning glass arch of its international Channel Tunnel platforms. You can reach Paris on the Eurostar train via the tunnel in just 3 hours.

RIVER TRIP

You can take a cruise trip along the Thames from Charing Cross Pier to Greenwich and the Tower of London.
London Tourist Board ☎ 020 7932 2000

MUSEUMS

SIR JOHN SOANE'S MUSEUM
13 Lincoln's Inn Fields, WC2
☎ **020-7405 2107**

This remarkable house (originally three adjoining properties) is among several architectural wonders designed by Sir John Soane (1753-1837) - two others are the Bank of England and the Dulwich Picture Gallery. There are thousands of paintings, sculpture, architectural models and drawings on display all through the house, whose split-level floors and mirrors make an equally fascinating sight. The most famous items are Hogarth's *A Rake's Progress* and the sarcophagus of Seti I, an Egyptian pharaoh. Soane himself is buried in his own, self-designed mausoleum at Old St Pancras Church near King's Cross. Bizarrely, this mausoleum was the inspiration for Britain's traditional red phone box.

Charing Cross Station

IMPERIAL WAR MUSEUM

Lambeth Rd, SE1

☎ 020-7416 5000

This museum concentrates on all aspects of both world wars, and tells the story through the eyes of soldiers, concentration camp victims, RAF pilots, naval personnel and so on. The Blitz Experience and The Trench Experience reconstruct relevant scenes, with sight, sound and smell. Conflicts since 1945 and Secret War are the newest exhibitions, covering more recent military situations such as the Iranian embassy siege in 1980, the activities of MI5 and MI6, and SAS involvement in the Gulf War. The latest additions will be a permanent exhibition on the Holocaust, and a display exploring The Age of Total War. The museum is housed in the old Bethlehem Royal Hospital, better known as Bedlam, which operated from 1815 until 1930.

MUSEUM OF GARDEN HISTORY

St Mary-at-Lambeth, Lambeth Palace Rd, SE1

☎ 020-7261 1891

The former church of St Mary-at-Lambeth

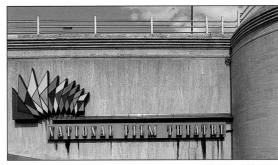

The National Film Theatre

the graveyard is Captain Bligh of the Bounty, who was also a plant hunter.

ST THOMAS' OLD OPERATING THEATRE MUSEUM

9a St Thomas' St, SE1

☎ 020-7955 4791

You can go to the visitor's gallery to see where operations were once carried out with no anaesthetic and little knowledge

Gabriel's Wharf

houses this museum - a must for all garden lovers. It displays botanical paintings and antique gardening tools, and in the churchyard are the plants and flowers that the Tradescants (father and son) brought back from Africa, America and the Mediterranean in the 17th century. John Tradescant was the royal gardener to James I and Charles I, and set up a bizarre, almost Fortean, museum of curiosities in Lambeth in 1629. Buried in

of bacterial infection. Suddenly the NHS doesn't look so bad.

GOLDEN HINDE

St Marie Overie Dock, Cathedral St, SE1

☎ 020-7403 0123

A reconstruction of Sir Francis Drake's trusty ship has recently opened to show visitors what it was like to travel far afield during the 16th century. You'll discover it was not very pleasant. This reconstruction

is a fully functioning craft and has in fact, travelled more seamiles than the original.

MUSEUM OF THE ROYAL COLLEGE OF SURGEONS

35-43 Lincoln's Inn Fields, WC2

☎ 020-7973 2190

Access to this fascinating museum is by appointment only. On display in the Hunterian Museum are anatomical specimens from both humans and animals, including the brain of the man who invented the world's first computer.

ART GALLERIES

HAYWARD GALLERY

Belvedere Rd, South Bank Centre, SE1

☎ 020-7261 0127

Part of the South Bank complex, the Hayward holds temporary exhibitions of contemporary and historical art. Although the gallery opened in the 1960s, it is still one of London's most forward-looking galleries.

BANKSIDE GALLERY

48 Hopton St, SE1

☎ 020-7928 7521

Shows watercolours, prints and engravings by living artists. Home to the Royal Watercolour Society and the Royal Society of Painters/Printmakers.

CINEMAS

NATIONAL FILM THEATRE

South Bank Centre, SE1

☎ 020-7928 3535

Next door to MOMI, the National Film Theatre is one of London's major cinemas, with three screens showing a massive range of restored prints, foreign films, cult classics and children's films, as well as brand new major Hollywood movies. NFT has built a solid reputation as one of England's most important centres of cinematic art. Their adventurous screening policy has led to conflicts with local and national government. The NFT also hosts a multitude of festivals, lectures and personal appearances by major figures in cinema.

Charing Cross Station & Waterloo Bridge

THE BFI LONDON IMAX CINEMA
Waterloo Bullring, South Bank, SE1
☎ 020-7902 1234
A brand new £20 million cinema that will be open every day of the year. The films are shown on the biggest screen in the UK. The IMAX system gives the viewer the impression that they are inside the film, by using a screen so big that the eye cannot see the edge of it. Quite an experience.

THEATRES

ADELPHI
Strand, WC2
☎ 020-7344 0055
Currently showing *Chicago*, a musical about gangster, Al Capone.

ALDWYCH
Aldwych, WC2
☎ 020-7416 6003
An old-fashioned and long-established theatre along the curve of Aldwych. At the time of writing, the current production here was *Whistle Down The Wind*, another Andrew Lloyd Webber production based on a film, this time the 1961 Hayley Mills drama.

ROYAL NATIONAL THEATRE
South Bank Centre, SE1
☎ 020-7452 3000
The National is actually three theatres: the Olivier, the Lyttelton and the Cottesloe, all differing and size and producing a variety of shows - all of very high quality. Trevor Nunn took over as director in October 1997.

OLD VIC
Waterloo Rd, SE1
☎ 020-7928 7616
An old, Victorian theatre, (surprise!) the Old Vic stages drama and musicals. Currently the home of the Peter Hall Company

PLAYHOUSE
Northumberland Ave, WC2
☎ 020-7839 4401
An Edwardian theatre once used as a BBC studio, now staging musicals, drama and comedies.

SAVOY
Strand, WC2
☎ 020-7836 8888
The Savoy is still one of the smartest theatres in town. Attached to the exclusive Savoy Hotel. Originally built in the 19th century to stage the light opera of Gilbert and Sullivan.

STRAND
Aldwych, WC2
☎ 020-7930 8800
The musical *Buddy,* about the life and tragic death of Texan rock'n'roll pioneer Buddy Holly has been running for over a decade at this imposing theatre.

VAUDEVILLE
Strand, WC2
☎ 020-7836 9987
In a listed building, the Vaudeville Theatre stages mostly drama, although it originally ran farce and vaudeville-style entertainment.

YOUNG VIC
66 The Cut, SE1
☎ 020-7928 6363 (recorded info)
An off-West End venue, staging interesting avant-garde plays.

Waterloo Station

ENTERTAINMENT AND NIGHTLIFE

ROYAL FESTIVAL HALL
SE1 ☎ 020-7960 4242 (recorded information)
Within the (rather ugly, concrete) South Bank complex are three venues, all of which stage music and dance events. The venues have recently been rather unimaginatively renamed as RFH 1 (previously the Royal Festival Hall, the largest of the three. Usually staging symphonic works and some popular music), RFH 2 (previously the Queen Elizabeth Hall. Chamber music, small operas) and RFH 3 (previously The Purcell Room. More chamber music and recitals). Phone for details.

CHUCKLE CLUB
London School of Economics, Houghton St, off Aldwych, WC2
☎ 020-7476 1672
A deservedly popular comedy club.

HEAVEN
The Arches, Craven St, WC2
☎ 020-7930 2020
A gay club, and one of London's best clubs, Heaven has been in business for a long time, so it must be doing something right. Lots of bars and dancefloors. Straight clubbers are more likely to attend the monthly parties, which have included Bond villain Goldie's Metalhedz.

MINISTRY OF SOUND
103 Gaunt St, SE1
☎ 020-7378 6528
A well-known name in dance circles, this club is still going strong and offering a great night out. All the big name DJs play here, and the doors often stay open until 9am. The Ministry has its own record label, and a merchandise shop in Covent Garden.

SHOPPING

Along the Strand are several well-known high-street chains for clothes and shoes, as well as a few more unusual shops. Hay's Galleria is a good place for gifts, and there are high-street outlets dotted around Holborn. Below are listed some of the more unusual shops in the area.

Courtauld Gallery

STANLEY GIBBONS INTERNATIONAL
399 Strand, WC2
☎ 020-7836 8444
World famous stampmeister, Stanley Gibbons opened this shop in 1856, and there are some three million stamps for sale.

CHURCH'S
436 The Strand, WC1
☎ 020-7240 3774
Very traditional British (and expensive) shoes for men as worn by many who work in The City. (Charing Cross Station end of the Strand.)

LONDON SILVER VAULTS
Chancery House, 53 Chancery Lane, WC2
☎ 020-7242 3844
An underground maze of shops dealing in a wide range of silverware - antiques, plate and jewellery.

BEATTIES
202 High Holborn, WC2
☎ 020-7405 6285
For model railway lovers, there's everything you could need here. Also stocks all kinds of model kits.

FALKINER FINE PAPERS
76 Southampton Row, WC1
☎ 020-7831 1151
Parchment and hand-made papers for unusual gifts.

THE CHRISTMAS SHOP
27a Hay's Galleria, Tooley St, SE1
☎ 020-7378 1998
An all-year-round supply of festive trimmings and cards.

MARKETS

GABRIEL'S WHARF
56 Upper Ground, SE1
☎ 020-7401 2255 (recorded information)
Beside the Thames on the South Bank, Gabriel's Wharf is a great place to shop for unusual gifts. Basically a village of craft workshops selling jewellery, leather, and crafts as well as restaurants and a bar. Something of an undiscovered London gem.

PARKS AND GARDENS

LINCOLN'S INN FIELDS
A large green area of manicured lawns and statuesque trees, Lincoln's Inn Fields affords some welcome peace and quiet away from busy Chancery Lane.

GREAT FOR KIDS

There are loads of Festivals and Events throughout the year in London that children will love - See Festivals and Events.
There's a McDonald's at 35 Strand, WC2,

NAMCO STATION
County Hall, York Rd, SE1
☎ 020-7967 1066
Housed in the massive and largely empty County Hall, Namco Station is an

interactive games experience. Within are various futuristic wonders as Techno Bowl, Turbo bumper cars, video games and simulators. On a wet and windy day, it may be just the place to take the children.

FA PREMIER LEAGUE HALL OF FAME
County Hall, York Rd, SE1
☎ 020-7928 1800
Another inhabitant of the erstwhile GLC HQ is this fine waxwork tribute to the marvels of British football, whether they be British or not. Along with the models, the hall features a history of the FA, videos, photos and memorabilia.

FLORENCE NIGHTINGALE MUSEUM
St Thomas' Hospital, 2 Lambeth Palace Rd, SE1 ☎ 020-7620 0374
The eponymous heroine of this museum worked tirelessly during the Crimean War to nurse the sick, and was nicknamed 'the Lady of the Lamp' due to her nocturnal ward rounds (the lamp is on display). She set up the first nursing school at St Thomas' Hospital, and the museum recounts her story through photographs, memorabilia and realistic reconstructions.

SHAKESPEARE'S GLOBE EXHIBITION
Bankside, SE1
☎ 020-7902 1500
A special exhibition of the famous recently reconstructed theatre shows craftsmen rebuilding the theatre with the original techniques, as well as telling the story of the original theatre and the work involved in creating it.

Florence Nightingale

VAUXHALL CITY FARM
24 St Oswald's Pl, SE11
☎ 020-7582 4204
A well-equipped city farm with pigs, piglets, ducks, sheep, ponies and donkeys, all very tame and willing to be stroked and talked to.

NATIONAL FILM THEATRE
During the school holidays there are films for children at different times. Phone for details.
☎ 020-7928 3232

SMOLLENSKY'S BALLOON
105 Strand, WC2
☎ 020-7497 2101
A really children-friendly restaurant with burgers and fries and delicious puddings. Loads of entertainment at weekends for the children including puppets, clowns and storytellers.

PLACES OF WORSHIP

ST GEORGE'S RC CATHEDRAL
Lambeth Rd, SE1
Designed in 1840 by Augustus Pugin (also responsible for the Houses of Parliament), St George's was once a centre of Catholic life in London. It was rebuilt in 1953 after war damage.

Temple Church, Inner Temple

Lincoln's Inn

ST ANDREW HOLBORN
Holborn Circus, EC4
Built by Sir Christopher Wren in 1686, although the original church may have dated back to the 10th century, St Andrew's is the largest of Wren's parish churches. Disraeli was baptized here.

ST CLEMENT DANES
Aldwych, WC1
Another of Christopher Wren's churches, St Clement Danes was built in 1680 and bombed in 1941, only to be beautifully restored. It is now dedicated to the Royal Air Force. The building is studded with squadron badges, and books in glass cases list the 120,000 RAF members who have died in conflicts since the force was created. Outside stands the controversial statue of World War II bombing campaign manager, Sir Arthur "Bomber" Harris.

ST MARY-AT-LAMBETH
Lambeth Palace Rd, SE1
Now the Museum of Garden History, this church is adjacent to Lambeth Palace

ST MARY-LE-STRAND
Aldwych, WC1
This tiny 18th-century church is dwarfed by the other large buildings on busy Aldwych, which makes it even more worthy of a visit. Designed by James Gibbs, and built between 1714 and 1717.

TEMPLE CHURCH
Inner Temple Lane, EC4
Along the peace of Inner Temple Lane, you'll find Temple Church, a pretty church built by the mysterious Order of the Knights Templar, the 12th-century

crusaders who invented modern banking. It has a circular nave, known as 'the Round', which is said to have been modelled on the Church of the Holy Sepulchre in Jerusalem.

Middle Temple

SPORT AND LEISURE

ELEPHANT & CASTLE LEISURE CENTRE
22 Elephant & Castle, SE1
☎ 0171-582 5505
A sports hall and well-equipped facilities make this a good sporting venue in a rather run-down area. There are lots of different exercise classes, a swimming pool and squash courts.

LEGAL LONDON

INNS OF COURT
There are four Inns of Court: Gray's Inn,

Lincoln's Inn, Middle Temple and Inner Temple (known collectively as Temple), which are the working place of London's barristers. Meeting the requirements to become a barrister can be tough, and much of the 'testing' is steeped in tradition, such as having to dine 24 times in the halls before being eligible to be called to the Bar.

GRAY'S INN
High Holborn, WC1
One of the four Inns of Court established in the 14th century to provide lodging for lawyers, Gray's Inn suffered greatly during World War II bombing, but has been restored. Some of its most notable features include a statue of Sir Francis Bacon; The Hall, where Shakespeare's *The Comedy of Errors* was first performed in 1594, and the raised terrace, a favourite among studying lawyers during the 17th century.
The Hall is open by appointment only
☎ 020-7405 8164

LINCOLN'S INN
Chancery Lane, WC2
Lincoln's Inn is the proud owner of the best gardens of any of the Inns of Court, Lincoln's Inn Fields, and is well worth visiting. The buildings themselves are also stunning and parts of them date back to the 13th century. This area epitomises all that is eccentric and traditional about London.

TEMPLE
Fleet St, EC1
Temple is made up of Middle Temple and Inner Temple, two of the Inns of Court. Black-gowned barristers can often be seen here on their way to court. The 1880 Temple Bar Memorial marks the boundary between Westminster and the City. Middle Temple Hall has one of the finest hammerbeam roofs in England, as well as a serving table which, it is said, was constructed of wood taken from the Golden Hinde, Sir Francis Drake's famous ship.

Imperial War Museum

WHERE TO STAY
HOTELS
AA RECOMMENDED

SE1

★★★★★ ❀ ❀
LONDON MARRIOTT COUNTY HALL
County Hall SE1 7PB
☎ **020 7928 5200**
This redevelopment of the former Greater London Council HQ takes advantage of views over the river towards the Houses of Parliament. Notable features are the well laid-out bedrooms and first class leisure facilities. The County Restaurant produces food that shows accuracy of execution and hearty flavours.
200 rooms

★★★ **NOVOTEL LONDON WATERLOO**
113 Lambeth Rd SE1 7LS
(opposite Houses of Parliament on the S bank of the river Thames)
☎ **020 7793 1010** 📠 **020 7793 0202**
This modern young hotel, close to Waterloo station, benefits from its own secure car park. Bedrooms are spacious and well equipped with modern facilities including Air conditioning. The open-plan public areas include a garden brasserie, the "Flag and Whistle Pub", a small shop, and leisure facilities.
187 rooms (80 family & 158 no smoking) / International Cuisine / Sauna, Gym, Pool table, Steam room / Lift, Air cond / No coaches
Price band £££ 🍽

⌂ **LONDON COUNTY HALL TRAVEL INN CAPITAL**
Belvedere Rd SE1 7PB
(next to the Royal Festival Hall and South Bank Centre)
☎ **020 7902 1600** 📠 **020 7902 1619**
This modern building offers accommodation in smart, spacious and well equipped bedrooms, all with en suite bathrooms. Refreshments may be taken at the nearby family restaurant. For details about current prices ring 01582 41 43 41.
312 rooms
Price band ££

⌂ **LONDON TOWER BRIDGE TRAVEL INN CAPITAL**
Tower Bridge Rd SE1
☎ **020 7940 3700** 📠 **020 7940 3719**
This modern building offers accommodation in smart, spacious and well equipped bedrooms, all with en suite bathrooms. Refreshments may be taken at the nearby family restaurant. For details about current prices ring 01582 41 43 41.
195 rooms
Price band ££

WC2

★★★★★ ❀ ❀ ❀ **THE SAVOY**
Strand WC2R 0EU
(situated halfway along The Strand between Trafalgar Square and Aldwych)
☎ **020 7836 4343** 📠 **020 7240 6040**
This world-famous hotel continues to retain its position as one of the country's best. In the bedrooms, Art Deco design features have been preserved, and there is a push-button bell system for summoning maid, valet or waiter. The American bar remains a popular watering-hole, the Grill is well attended by the business community, and the River Room is known for the flavours and precision of its menu. Executive chef Anton Edelmann oversees the Savoy's cuisine and earns Three AA Rosettes. Afternoon tea is a highlight for residents and visitors, and Saturday night 'Stomping at the Savoy' is a real treat.
207 rooms (6 family & 48 no smoking) / International Cuisine / Indoor swimming pool (heated) / Sauna, Gym, Tennis at the Vanderbilt Club / Live entertainment / Lift, Night porter / No dogs (ex guide dogs) / No coaches
Price band £££ 🍽

★★★★★ ❀ ❀ **ONE ALDWYCH**
1 Aldwych WC2B 4BZ
☎ **020 7300 1000** 📠 **020 7300 1001**
From its position on the corner of the Aldwych, this hotel enjoys commanding views across Waterloo Bridge and Covent Garden. Once the home of the Morning Post newspaper, the building has been skilfully restored. Accommodation is bright, stylish and fully air-conditioned. The Axis and Indigo restaurants provide quality dining, and the cocktail bar is a popular meeting place.
105 rooms (39 no smoking) / Indoor swimming pool (heated) / Sauna, Gym, Steam room / Lift, Night porter, Air cond / No dogs (ex guide dogs)
Price band £££ 🍽

★★★★★ ❀ ❀ **LE MERIDIEN WALDORF**
Aldwych WC2B 4DD
(from Trafalgar Sq follow road down The Strand signed City. At end of The Strand road becomes Aldwych, Le Meridien Waldorf is situated on left)
☎ **020 7836 2400** 📠 **020 7836 7244**
This historic hotel continues to go from strength to strength. The Palm Court Lounge offers weekend afternoon tea dances and regular jazz evenings. The chandeliered bedrooms have been luxuriously styled and all are air-conditioned. Imaginative cuisine is served in the Palm Court, while the French-styled brasserie is open all day for lighter meals.
292 rooms (154 no smoking) / European Cuisine / Hairdressing salon / Live entertainment / Lift, Night porter / No dogs (ex guide dogs)
Price band £££ 🍽

★★★ **STRAND PALACE**
Strand WC2R 0JJ
☎ **020 7836 8080** 📠 **020 7836 2077**
This busy hotel offers restaurants and bars ranging from a cosy Italian bistro and lively cafe-bar, to the stylish Mask Bar and contemporary 373 The Strand, with its international menu and buffet. Rooms vary in size and style; a supplement buys a room on the smart Club floor, where bedrooms have added luxuries and guests can use an exclusive lounge.
783 rooms (305 no smoking) / International Cuisine / Lift, Night porter / No dogs (ex guide dogs)
🍽

WHERE TO EAT
RESTAURANTS
AA RECOMMENDED

City Rhodes Restaurant

❀ BANK RESTAURANT
1 Kingsway WC2B 6XF
☎ 020 7379 9797 ☎ 020 7379 9014
Always jam-packed with a dynamic atmosphere and fast turnaround. Vibrant 'liberated French' and English cooking offset by ultra-modern design with a great sense of space and American-style cocktail bar. Brilliant for breakfast and weekend brunch too.
Fixed L/D £ ALC ££

❀ LE CAFÉ DU MARCHÉ
Charterhouse Mews Charterhouse Square EC1M 6AH
☎ 020 7608 1609 ☎ 020 7336 7055
Inviting French restaurant in a quiet mews close to the Barbican. Saddle of rabbit wrapped in smoked ham and served with a robust sauce, followed by a fine Bakewell tart, are recommended.
Fixed D £ ALC ££

❀ ❀ ❀ CITY RHODES RESTAURANT
1 New Street Square EC4A 3JB
☎ 020 7583 1313 ☎ 020 7583 1662
Entrance is via a ground floor lobby done up as a sort of shrine to Gary Rhodes, then up a circular staircase into the habitat not of telly Gary or frozen meals Gary, but of Gary the serious chef (although day-to-day cooking is in the capable hands of Michael Bedford). The first-floor room is sleek, well-groomed, and minimalist in style and the cooking is good enough to silence the sceptics. The Rhodes approach is to rework old, and occasionally stodgy sounding classics, by giving them a much lighter touch; roast calves' liver and kidney with sweet red wine carrots and rosemary butter sauce is much lighter than the description implies. Desserts are pure joy - with baked egg custard tart on its way to becoming a new signature dishes.
ALC £££

❀ ❀ CLUB GASCON
57 West Smithfield EC1
☎ 020 7796 0600 ☎ 020 7796 0601
Crowded, clamorous restaurant where reservations well in advance are recommended. Your standard three-course format this is not. Based on south-west France and the Basque region, the menu is divided into sections such as 'la route du sel' (Bayonne ham, spicy Basque pâté, for example), 'les pâturages' (venison cooked on the embers of vine shoots), and, most important, 'les foies gras'. The idea is to order six or seven little dishes to make your own tasting menu. Luckily, waiters are in bountiful supply to explain both the concept and the unfamiliar terms.
Fixed L/D ££ ALC ££

❀ THE EAGLE
159 Farringdon Road EC1R 3AL
☎ 020 7837 1353
Roaringly successful media pub on Farringdon Road known for its huge platefuls of robust Mediterranean-style food, perhaps marinated anchovies with slow-roasted tomatoes on rocket and toasted ciabatta.
No credit cards

❀ ❀ GAUDI RESTAURANTE
63 Clerkenwell Road EC1M 5PT
☎ 020 7608 3220 ☎ 020 7250 1057
Lots of brightly coloured tiles, mirrors, stained glass and much wrought iron give the interior a Gaudi-esque feeling, the staff, professional and friendly, are as Spanish as the menus. Gazpacho sounds familiar enough, but here it's enhanced by cured ham, or steamed lobster. That the kitchen is clearly steeped in the cuisine shows through what are often complex main courses: roast duck leg with deep-fried breast stuffed with foie gras, cinnamon and sesame sauce and wild

mushrooms in a potato nest, for example. The exclusively Spanish wine list has some interesting regional wines and rarer classics, all at reasonable prices.
Fixed L £ ALC £££

❀ ❀ LIVEBAIT
43 The Cut SE1 8LF
☎ 020 7928 7211 ☎ 020 7928 2279
The concept was so successful that Groupe Chez Gerard promptly bought it and opened more branches. The formula is straightforward, the overall atmosphere is that of a chic fishmonger's, and the decor is kept to a minimum. The kitchen uses really fresh fish, and works them in some exotic combinations: a battered tempura squid served on a truffle oil mash with a julienne of mange-tout and lime vinaigrette, for example. The restaurant, and group, have a very good, reasonably priced wine list.

❀ ❀ LONDON MARRIOTT COUNTY HALL
The County Hall SE1 7PB
☎ 020 7928 5200 ☎ 020 7928 5300
A great historic site. The setting is quite special with the erstwhile seat of London government brought back to life as a grand hotel. The restaurant takes what advantage in can of views of the river down towards the Houses of Parliament. Despite the rather formal setting, the kitchen has adopted a brasserie style with punchy flavours to the fore.
Fixed L/D £ ALC ££

❀ ❀ MAISON NOVELLI, NOVELLI EC1
29 Clerkenwell Green EC1R 0DU
☎ 020 7251 6606 ☎ 020 7490 1083
It looks as if it were created on a shoe-string (it was). The kitchen team deliver with the usual Jean-Christophe Novelli flourishes: a meaty, gutsy pressed terrine of rabbit, duck and Toulouse sausage, for example, or roast sea bass, served atop tagliatelli mixed with a robust pesto, oyster froth underlining the sea element. Service is attentive and occasionally smiling. Adjoining is Novelli EC1, a light, airy brasserie with closely packed tables, a lively atmosphere and a generous carte of modern French food.
ALC £££

LE MERIDIEN WALDORF
Aldwych WC2B 4DD

☎ 020 7836 2400 🅕 020 7836 7244

A historic hotel complete with its famous Palm Court Lounge - one of the most romantic settings in town for dinner. The menu revolves around a bistro-style theme and there's also an informal all-day brasserie. A typical meal might take in quail breast in a rose lentil soup with celeriac purée, Mediterranean grouper with coco beans, lemon and pommes Pont-Neuf, and cardamom parfait for dessert. There are regular jazz evenings and the Palm Court afternoon tea dances are a weekend institution.

Fixed L/D ££ ALC £££

MORO
34-36 Exmouth Market EC1R 4QE

☎ 020 7833 8336 🅕 020 7833 9338

Lively, often full-to-bursting restaurant with Spanish-North African-influenced cooking. Bare decor (who notices), brilliant long bar serving tapas, great bread, as well as crab brik with cumin, coriander and harissa, and chargrilled marinated leg of lamb with foul (a white bean dish) and braised chard.

ALC ££

ONE ALDWYCH - AXIS, INDIGO
1 Aldwych WC2B 4BZ

☎ 020 7300 0300 🅕 020 7300 0301

Open all day for breakfast, lunch, afternoon tea and dinner, the light, airy Indigo, part of the magnificent new hotel that once housed the Morning Post newspaper, has built-in viewing entertainment provided by its location on the gallery overlooking the cocktail bar. High-standard brasserie-style cooking brings creamy lobster risotto, duck confit with nicely crisped skin, and raspberry shortcakes. Axis, on the other hand, presents an ambitious kitchen with an up-to-date outlook - fish is a favourite - as well a predilection for taking traditional dishes and giving them a modern spin.

ALC ££-£££

OXO TOWER RESTAURANT
8th Floor Oxo Tower Wharf Barge House Street SE1 9PH

☎ 020 7803 3888 🅕 020 7803 3812

This large, modern, light, airy and fashionable restaurant offers some of the best river views in London, a good-value set menu at lunch and a rather pricier carte in the evenings. Raviolo of sweetcorn with girolles and Parmesan set on a bed of spinach, roast pork with a prune tart and cinnamon jus, and chocolate and black cherry mousse 'en cadeau', sum up the style.

THE PEASANT
24 St John Street EC1 4PH

☎ 020 7336 7726 🅕 020 7251 4476

Ornate corner pub with a traditional feel downstairs and a modern restaurant upstairs. The same rustic Mediterranean menu is offered throughout, so choose your atmosphere.

THE PEOPLE'S PALACE
Royal Festival Hall Belvedere Road SE1 8XX

☎ 020 7928 9999 🅕 020 7928 2355

South Bank mega-eaterie whose major attractions are views over the Thames, the extended opening hours and the facility to pre-order meals. Plus contemporary food with a nod to British tradition in dishes such as haunch of venison with braised red cabbage and mulled wine jus.

Fixed L/D £ ALC ££

QUALITY CHOP HOUSE
94 Farringdon Road EC1 3EA

☎ 020 7837 5093

Mahogany booths and etched mirrors maintain the 19th-century atmosphere of this unfussy, relaxed restaurant. The menu is eclectic: from jellied eels to Beluga caviar, and calves' liver, to eggs, bacon and chips, all tastes and budgets are catered for.

ALC £

RSJ, THE RESTAURANT ON THE SOUTH BANK
13a Coin Street SE1 8YQ

☎ 020 7633 0881 🅕 020 7401 2455

Comfortable restaurant, a short walk from the South Bank Centre. The cooking style has kept up with fashion with fish dishes being particularly good. The menu is supported by a daily changing selection of specials such as guinea fowl and foie gras sausage with petit pois and roast beetroot stuffed with goats' cheese, mushrooms, tofu and crispy carrots. The wine list is justly famous and includes a particularly interesting selection of Loire wines.

ST JOHN
26 St John Street EC1M 4AY

☎ 020 7251 0848 🅕 020 7251 4090

Converted smoke-house with large paper-clad wooden tables. Minimalist menu offers 'nose-to-tail' eating such as tripe, fennel and butter bean soup, pot-roasted Gloucester Old Spot, and cods roe, bacon and spinach.

ALC ££

SAVOY GRILL
Strand WC2R 0EU

☎ 020 7836 4343 🅕 020 7240 6040

Often regarded as the place where men, as opposed to ladies, lunch. Indeed, many view the Savoy Grill as their private club, but it is equally accessible to all who wish to experience a real British institution. The menu is dominated by the regular daily items: Lancashire hotpot on Mondays, roast rib of beef on Thursdays, and so on, but some marginally more interesting dishes are offered on the carte. The service is both professional and solicitous.

Fixed D ££ ALC £££

THE SAVOY, RIVER RESTAURANT
Strand WC2R 0EU

☎ 020 7836 1533 🅕 020 7420 2576

Everyone wants to sit beside the window, so it's a privilege to secure one of the coveted tables. The setting generates a sense of keen anticipation and the atmosphere is relaxed in the best European way, despite the formality of the smoked salmon and dessert trolleys and silver cloches. Luxury ingredients are part of the style and the seasonal menu, matched with wines from the Savoy Cellars, might be centred around roast milk-fed lamb filled with its farce, with new Jersey potatoes baked with onions and melted Parmesan tomatoes.

Fixed L ££ ALC £££

STEPHEN BULL SMITHFIELD
71 St John Street EC1 4AN

☎ 020 7490 1750 🅕 020 7490 3128

Stephen Bull in informal mode - spacious with strong colours, black unadorned tables and wooden floors. The nicely varied menu lists simply described dishes that are built around balance and flavour. Starters such as baby Caesar salad, marinated quail with basil, and roast haggis with potatoes and turnips are typical of the style. Wines are listed by style, and there's a good choice by the glass and half-bottle.

ALC £

Call the AA Hotel Booking Service on 0870 5050505 to book at AA recognised hotels and B&Bs in the UK, or through our internet site: http://www.theaa.co.uk/hotels

PUBS, INNS & OTHER PLACES

THE EAGLE
159 Farringdon Rd EC1R 3AL
☎ 020 7837 1353
Popular pub serving Mediterranean-style food chalked up on a blackboard menu, with lots of grills.

FIRE STATION
150 Waterloo Rd, SE1
☎ 020-7620 2226
Very busy bar with a good restaurant at the back.

BLEEDING HEART
Bleeding Heart Yard, off Greville St, EC1
☎ 020-7242 8238
Busy, informal wine bar. 400 bins available, and a dining area.

STUDIO SIX
Gabriel's Wharf, 56 Upper Ground, SE1
☎ 020-7928 6243
Great outdoor seating, close to the river. Good food and drink selection.

THE PEASANT
240 St John St EC1V 4PH
☎ 020 7336 7726
Converted Victorian pub with original mosaic floor and ceramic mural. In contrast, the upstairs restaurant is of a modern minimalist design. Interesting menu.

PIZZERIA CASTELLO
20 Walworth Rd, SE1 6SP
☎ 020-7703 2556
Busy pizza place near the Elephant and Castle.

CITTIE OF YORKE
22-23 High Holborn WC1V 6BS
☎ 020 7242 7670
Dating from the 17th century, a pub has stood here since 1430. Traditional pub food includes black pudding, or sausage and mash.

JERUSALEM TAVERN
55 Britton St, EC1
☎ 020-7490 4281
Tiny tavern full of media types.

HOLE IN THE WALL
5 Mepham St, SE1
☎ 020 7928 6196
Traditional pub underneath the arches near Waterloo station.

LED
171 Farringdon Rd, EC1
☎ 020-7278 4400
Recently opened bar with big TVs and PlayStations.

NATIONAL FILM THEATRE BAR
South Bank SE1
☎ 020 7928 3535
Serious film-goers can discuss semantics and film theory here over a pint. A nice riverside location.

SMOLENSKY'S ON THE STRAND
105 The Strand, WC2R 0AA
☎ 020-7497 2101
Basement bar and restaurant with live music every night.

Everything you need
...in just one guide

Indispensable guides developed from the wealth of AA data. Everything you need to plan your visit - in-depth information on accommodation, places to eat and drink and what to see and do.

- Where to stay - B&Bs, hotels, campsites - all AA inspected and quality assessed

- Where to eat - from pubs to top quality restaurants

- Places to visit and days out for the family

- How to entertain the children

- Museums, art galleries, theatres, stately homes, gardens, the big outdoors, historic and ancient sites

- Sports facilities - golf, swimming, leisure centres, sailing, fishing, horse-riding

- Local events, festivals and crafts

- Essential practical information

- Colour photographs throughout

- Easy-to-use

Available from all good bookshops for only £9.99

AA Lifestyle Guides

THE CITY

The City is also known as 'the Square Mile', which emphasises how small an area it is compared to the huge impact it has on the nation's (and worldwide) financial affairs. London began here, founded by the Romans, and it has retained its own identity, with its own police force and local authority. Twice it has been destroyed, once by the Great Fire of London in 1666 and then by the Blitz in World War II. The IRA even had a go in 1993. There is so much history and fascination packed into this small area, you'll need several days to get round it all.

Fleet Street is the route to the City from central London. It is but a shadow of its former self since the removal to Docklands of most of the newspaper offices that had scooped their stories here for generations. Today it is still lined with businesses, mostly City financiers, as well as the the Reuters/Press Association headquarters and some shops. To the north of Fleet Street is Dr Johnson's House, a tribute to one of London's literary giants, and further down to the south, tucked away from view is the splendid St Bride's Church, with an interesting crypt museum. Once inside the church it is so peaceful you cannot believe that teeming Fleet Street is just outside. Moving along Ludgate Hill the view of St Paul's Cathedral, Wren's great masterpiece, is magnificent, especially when floodlit at night. Just off Cannon Street are two more of the 50 churches Wren built here, St Stephen Walbrook and St Mary Abchurch. Cannon Street leads to Monument, a memorial to the Great Fire of London, which was the cause of much of the building frenzy that overcame the capital in the 17th and 18th centuries.

Heading north towards Liverpool Street Station you arrive at the money-making heart of The City, with the Bank of England, the Royal Exchange, Lloyd's of London and the NatWest Tower. Nearby is Leadenhall Market, with butchers and fishmongers as well as cafés and pubs, and further north still is Spitalfields Market, with crafts and antiques. The London Wall leads to the Guildhall, where the City's administrative body resides, and the Barbican, the City's controversial and confusing arts centre. The Museum of London at the end of London Wall tells the story of the Roman wall and occupation, while nearby is London's foremost meat market, Smithfield - not for the squeamish.

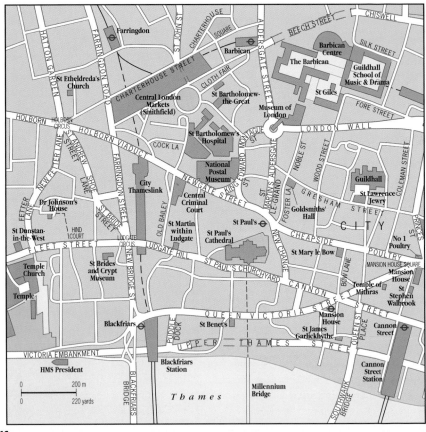

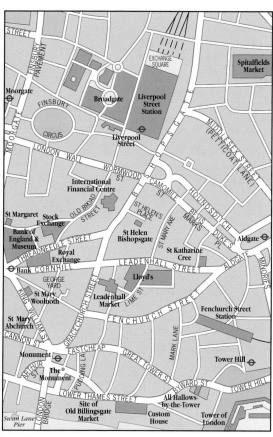

MUST SEE

The Great Fire of London 1666

ST PAUL'S CATHEDRAL

Ludgate Hill, EC4

☎ 020 7246 8348

Ludgate Hill has seen many churches come and go. Wren's building is the fifth. Old St Paul's was a huge Gothic cathedral with a spire of nearly 500 feet, that had been used as a cavalry barracks during Cromwell's Commonwealth. The current St Paul's Cathedral came from the ashes of the Great Fire of London in 1666, and is one of the finest works of Sir Christopher Wren, who was commissioned to build 50 churches in the area. Completed in 1710, it is one of London's greatest landmarks and has withstood the trials of over nearly 300 years, including, miraculously, the Blitzkrieg of the Second World War. In the pavement below the centre of the magnificent dome is a memorial to Wren - *'Si monumentum requiris, circumspice'* ("If you are seeking his memorial, look around you"). The Duke of Wellington's tomb and the sarcophagus of Nelson are in the centre of the crypt. Holman Hunt's religious masterpiece *Light of the World* hangs in the nave. The Whispering Gallery is reached via 259 steps - speak on one side of the round gallery, and a few seconds later your voice will be heard on the other side. Keep going up these steps and you can see one of the best views of central London from the Golden Gallery.

BANK OF ENGLAND

Bartholomew Lane, EC2

☎ 020 7601 5545

The whole area around here is called Bank, after the Bank of England, a magnificent columned building, designed to resemble a fortress, and affectionately known as the "Grand Old Lady of Threadneedle Street". It issues banknotes, sets interest rates and manages the nation's foreign exchange reserves, as well as the national banking system. The only part open to the public is the museum, which includes various bank notes and a diorama of the 1780 attack on the Bank by the Gordon Rioters demanding the repeal of the Catholic Relief Act.

OLD BAILEY

(Central Criminal Court)

Newgate St and Old Bailey, EC4

☎ 020 7248 3277

Built on the site of, and with some of the bricks of, Newgate Prison (famous for its brutality and some really nasty inhabitants), the Old Bailey is where most of Britain's high level trials take place. Among its best known defendants are playwright Oscar Wilde, wife-murderer Dr Crippen, and British fascist and Nazi propagandist William "Lord Haw-Haw" Joyce. The public is admitted to the viewing galleries and the porters on the doors will tell you which trial is likely to be the most 'entertaining'.

MONUMENT

Monument St, EC2

London's commemoration of the Great Fire of London in 1666, Monument is built 202ft from where the fire started in a bakery in Pudding Lane, and is a Doric column 202ft high. The fire that started on a baker's grate claimed 13,000 houses, which were mainly built of wood, 87 churches and 44 livery halls. Bizarrely only 9 fatalities are recorded. Even though the fire destroyed London's plague-carrying brown rats, it came too late to save the 100,000 or so citizens who had perished horribly in the Great Plague of 1665. If you feel like climbing up the 311 steps inside, the view will be a great reward.

DR JOHNSON'S HOUSE

17 Gough Sq, EC4

☎ 020 7353 3745

Dr Samuel Johnson (1709-84) remains one of England's most important scholars. Not only did he work for eight years on the first real dictionary of the English language, he also produced an edition of the works of Shakespeare and *Lives of the Poets*. He lived in this delightful Georgian townhouse from 1748 to 1759, and visitors can look at some of the rooms that he worked in with his team of lexicographers.

MUSEUM OF LONDON

150 London Wall, EC2

☎ 020 7600 3699

This excellent museum is built on the site of a Roman fort and tells the story of the history of London through imaginative reconstructions, with the layers of streets since Roman times effectively revealed. Elsewhere on display are Oliver

The Bank of England

Cromwell's death mask, a 1940s air-raid shelter, and the Lord Mayor's State Coach, made in 1757. Temporary exhibitions are always worth a visit. Phone for details.

HISTORIC AND ANCIENT SITES

LONDON WALL, EC2

The best surviving part of the old London Wall built by the Romans runs alongside the Museum of London. Another slab runs along the northern edge of the road London Wall, you can see it from the pavement. Sadly, London Wall is now lined with uninspiring office buildings.

GUILDHALL

Gresham St, EC2

☎ 020 7606 3030

The Guildhall was built in 1411 by the medieval trade guilds (now the City Livery

Companies) for their meetings and ceremonies. It is the centre of the City's government, from where the City's affairs are run. The Great Hall is a splendid edifice, decorated with coats of arms and banners of the City Livery Companies. The windows record the names of all the Lord Mayors since the 12th century. The legendary giants Gog and Magog guard the West Gallery in the shape of two statues. The Clock Museum displays a collection of over 600 timepieces.

COLLEGE OF ARMS
Queen Victoria St, EC4
☎ 020 7248 2762
It is from here that coats of arms are granted to those deemed worthy. The 17th-century building has been restored and is well worth visiting, although visitors can only enter the Earl Marshall's Court without notice. The official records of English, Welsh and Irish heraldry and genealogy are held here, so you can trace your roots if you want - phone for details.

MANSION HOUSE
Wallbrook, EC4
☎ 020 7626 2500
The official residence of the Lord Mayor of London, Mansion House stands proudly opposite the Bank of England. You can visit several of the state rooms, including the Banqueting Room and Ball Room. Beneath the 'Justice Room' are several cells, one of which was occupied by Emmeline Pankhurst, the suffragette.

ROYAL EXCHANGE
Threadneedle St and Cornhill, EC3
☎ 020 7283 7101
Built in 1844 by Sir William Tite, the Royal Exchange was the first financial trading marketplace in London. It is an impressive building, approached by a broad flight of stairs and Corinthian pillars. Until recently it housed the London International Financial Futures Exchange (LIFFE), where over 20,000 contracts were exchanged

A dragon in The City

Guildhall

every day. Inside are monuments to monarchs and statesmen. The trading has now moved to Cannon Bridge Station (no public access).

BARBICAN CENTRE
Silk St, EC2
☎ 020 7638 8891
Begun in 1956, the centre is on the edge of a huge concrete housing complex,

Rahere's tomb at St Bartholomew's Hospital

which, when completed in 1981, had some charm due to the strategic placement of window boxes and other foliage. Now, however, the buildings are looked dated and dirty. Londoners never stop commenting on its ugliness. It is also a standing joke that although you can get into the complex (especially now that the entrance has been made more obvious), there is a strong chance that you may never get out as it is constructed around a confusing maze of tunnels and staircases! However, for all that, it is one of London's most important arts venues.

ST BARTHOLOMEW'S HOSPITAL
West Smithfield St, EC1
Founded in 1123 by Rahere, Henry I's court jester who nearly died of malaria on his way to Rome, 'Barts' was dissolved in 1537 by Henry VIII, but rescued again in 1544. It was once recorded that 'patients who do not attend church on Sunday will not be fed'. Since then things have relaxed, and the hospital is run by the National Health Trust. There are departments for several specialist areas, and the medical school is part of the

University of London.

BUNHILL FIELDS CEMETERY
between Bunhill Row and City Road
This charming small cemetery sits across the road from John Wesley's House and is one of the major burial grounds for London's Dissenters and non-Conformists. Most of the graves are fenced off, although the park keeper can open gates for those visiting family or doing research. The central paved area contains the graves of poet, artist and visionary William Blake and his wife, a monument to Daniel Defoe, and the tomb of John Bunyan.

MUSEUMS

BANK OF ENGLAND MUSEUM
Bartholomew Lane, EC1
☎ 020 7601 5545
The story of the work of the Bank of England is told here through lively displays that show the bewildering world of the international money markets.

CARTOON ART TRUST
67 Hatton Gardens, EC1
☎ 020 7405 4717
Regular, changing exhibitions devoted to cartoons, with works by artists like Hogarth and Gerald Scarfe on display. Phone for details.

GEFFRYE MUSEUM
Kingsland Rd, E2
☎ 020 7739 9893
In a terrace of handsome brick almshouses, the collection on display here

Nelson's memorial at St Paul's Cathedral

covers furniture and interior design through the ages. A series of rooms traces every major period in English history from Elizabethan times to the 1950s. If you're having trouble deciding on what to do with your own home, this is a great place for ideas. There is a walled herb garden outside and free jazz concerts in summer.

JOHN WESLEY'S HOUSE AND CHAPEL
47 City Rd, EC1
☎ 020 7253 2262
John Wesley was the founder of Methodism (espousing non-conformism and the 'Puritan' work ethic), and lived in this Georgian house until 1791. The house is full of his life including clothes, pens and annotated books, as well as an electric-shock machine which he used to try and dispel bouts of melancholia. Next door is the chapel, visited by Methodists from all over the world. Margaret Thatcher was married here.

ART GALLERIES

WHITECHAPEL ART GALLERY
80-82 Whitechapel High St, E1
☎ 020 7522 7888
☎ 020 7522 7878 (recorded info)
One of the best art galleries in London, the Whitechapel stages temporary exhibitions. 1999 was the gallery's 100th anniversary. 2000 should see a very special edition of the Whitechapel Open which showcases the work of local artists.

ASSOCIATION GALLERY
Association of Photographers,
9 Domingo St, EC1
☎ 020 7739 6669
This gallery concentrates on the commercial world of photography - those pictures taken for advertising and editorial purposes. It also stages temporary photographic exhibitions.

CINEMAS

BARBICAN CENTRE
Silk St, EC2
☎ 020 7638 8891
Two screens, showing the latest Hollywood releases.

THEATRES

BARBICAN CENTRE
Silk St, EC2
☎ 020 7638 8891
Home to the Royal Shakespeare Company and the London Symphony Orchestra, the Barbican is one of London's most important arts venues. The RSC has produced many of England's finest actors and directors, and stages many challenging productions.

NatWest Tower and the Old Stock Exchange

ENTERTAINMENT AND NIGHTLIFE

As the City is an area for business, you'll find it pretty quiet after 6pm, when most of its inhabitants have headed for home (the only residential area here is the Barbican). Pubs and restaurants close around 9pm, and the whole place becomes a ghost town, apart from the odd club, listed below.

BARBICAN CENTRE
Silk St, EC2
☎ 020 7638 8891
Home to the London Symphony Orchestra and the English Chamber Orchestra, the Barbican stages excellent choral and orchestral works.

COMEDY CAFÉ
66 Rivington St, EC2
☎ 020 7739 5706
Devoted to comedy, and an unusual club in these parts.

THE AQUARIUM
256 Old St, EC1
☎ 020 7251 6136
A swimming pool is the main feature of this quirky club.

FABRIC
77a Charterhouse St, EC1
☎ 020 7490 0444
Live music and comedy over five floors.

SMITHFIELDS
334-338 Farringdon St, EC1
☎ 020 7236 8112

MARKETS

BRICK LANE MARKET
E1
This market is at the heart of a large community of Bangladeshis, Pakistanis and Indians. If you like curry, this is where to sample the best. You'll find more or less everything here on market days - from new bicycles to frozen food, with the stalls run by Asian, Cockney and Jewish traders. A slice of East End life.

SMITHFIELD MARKET
Charterhouse St, EC1
Not for the faint-hearted, and certainly not for vegetarians, this is a rough-and-ready, and extremely bloody place - London's main meat market. Since the recent scares about BSE, the market has become even more unpopular with those concerned about the meat trade.

LEADENHALL MARKET
Gracechurch St, EC3
Still with an air of Edwardian and Victorian times, this is a food market where meat, fish and poultry are arranged beautifully on stalls that have operated since 1881.

SPITALFIELDS MARKET
Commercial St, E1
Crafts and antiques are up for grabs during the week, and at weekends it's the turn of organic relishes, spices, herbs, fruit and vegetables. The infamous serial killer 'Jack the Ripper' left his first victim at Spitalfields Market. The eponymous pub nearby has a list of his victims' names.

COLUMBIA ROAD MARKET
E2
Sunday sees a well-stocked flower and plant market set in a road that deals in gardening accessories all week.

GREAT FOR KIDS

There are loads of Festivals and Events throughout the year in London which will love - See Festivals and Events.

HOUSE OF DETENTION
Clerkenwell Close, EC1
☎ 020 7253 9494
Built upon one of London's earliest prison sites, the House of Detention served between 1846 and 1878 as the busiest prison in London. Records of the prisoners have survived and form the basis for the dark, dank, underground exhibition that now tells the story of the prison. You can try out the 'Crime of Your Life', the true

A Victorian fire engine in the Museum of London

NATIONAL MUSEUM OF CHILDHOOD, BETHNAL GREEN
Cambridge Heath Rd, E2
☎ 020 8980 2415 (recorded information)
Not strictly speaking in the City, but in the East End, this is an offshoot of the Victoria & Albert Museum. It houses one of the

The Royal Exchange

story of a prisoner, narrated on tape as you wander around. The museum advertises itself thus: 'Look on and despair all ye who enter here'.

BROADGATE ARENA ICE RINK
Liverpool St and Eldon St, EC2
☎ 020 7505 4068
An open-air ice rink in the middle of the Broadgate complex

BARBICAN CENTRE
☎ 020 7638 8891
Children's films are shown on Saturday afternoons. Phone for details.

largest collection of toys in the world, including dolls' houses, dolls, trains, teddies and puppets. Sadly very few can be handled.

HACKNEY CITY FARM
1a Goldsmiths Row, E2
☎ 020 7729 6381
Actually in the East End of London, not the City, this converted brewery is now home to friendly sheep, chickens, pigs, rabbits and guinea pigs, among others. You can learn gardening, pottery and how to feed animals correctly here.

SPITALFIELDS COMMUNITY FARM
Weaver St, E1
☎ 020 7247 8762
Say hello to goats, hens, horses and ducks at this very friendly farm in an incongruous site on East End wasteland.

STEPNEY STEPPING STONES FARM
Stepney Way and Stepney High St, E1
☎ 020 7790 8204
Some unusual animals are in amongst the pigs hens and rabbits here - chipmunks, ferrets and quails to name but a few. There's also a wildlife area and a well-equipped classroom.

PLACES OF WORSHIP

Sir Christopher Wren built 50 churches in the City area alone around the same time as he designed St Paul's Cathedral. Below is a selection of his, and other architects, church work.

CHRIST CHURCH SPITALFIELDS
Commercial St, E1
One of Nicholas Hawksmoor's most original churches, Christ Church is easily recognised by its octagonal spire. Built in the early 18th century for Huguenot silk-weavers, the church has recently undergone extensive refurbishment.

ST ANDREW-BY-THE-WARDROBE
Queen Victoria St, EC4
The 'Wardrobe' refers to the buliding next door which once housed the king's ceremonial robes. This is one of Wren's churches, completed in 1695 and restored in 1961.

ST BARTHOLOMEW-THE-GREAT
West Smithfield, EC1
This is the oldest church in London, with parts dating to 1123. Hogarth was christened here in 1697, and the founder of St Bartholomew's Hospital is buried here.

ST BOTOLPH ALDGATE
Aldgate High St, EC3
Daniel Defoe was married here in 1683. The original church dated back to the 10th century but was rebuilt in 1744 by George Dance (also responsible for other

Bethnal Green Museum of Childhood, obviously!

Flesh-eating piranha at the London Aquarium

rebuildings of churches in the City). During the restoration the body of a boy was found in one of the vaults. In 1966 it was restored once again.

ST BRIDE'S CHURCH
Fleet St, EC4

St Bride's associations with the press started when Wynkyn de Worde, Caxton's apprentice, brought the first printing press to Fleet Street. He was buried in this church in 1535. Although the press have now moved from Fleet Street, it is still known as the 'Journalists' Church'. Its spire is Wren's tallest (226ft), and was the inspiration for the wedding cake tier that became so popular. If you get a chance to hear the St Bride's Church Choir, you're in for a treat.

ST DUNSTAN-IN-THE-WEST
Fleet St, EC4

An octagonal church built in 1831, there are several notable monuments and icons inside. An early statue of Queen Elizabeth I was moved here from Lud Gate.

ST GILES CRIPPLEGATE
Fore St, EC2

Oliver Cromwell was married here and Milton is buried here. It was originally built in the 12th century, and then restored in 1537 and 1952, after bombing.

ST HELEN BISHOPSGATE
Great St Helen's, EC4

Several 15th-century tomb effigies have been remarkably preserved here, having escaped the Great Fire of London in 1666. Sadly the church did not escape an IRA bomb in 1992.

ST JAMES GARLICKHYTHE
Garlick Hill, EC4

Completed in 1683, this church is particularly noted for its graceful spire, although it was not added until the 18th century.

ST KATHARINE KREE
Leadenhall St, EC4

Built around 1628, this church survived the Great Fire of London in 1666 and is a wonderful example of Gothic vaulting.

ST LAWRENCE JEWRY
Gresham St, EC2

The original church dates to the 12th century, although Wren redid it in 1671, and then after the Second World War it was restored again with replicas of the steeple and original Wren ceiling.

ST MARY ABCHURCH
Abchurch Lane, EC4

The original woodwork is still here in this remarkable Wren church. The carved reredos by Grinling Gibbons was rebuilt in 1948 from the 2,000 pieces it had become under the bombing of the Blitz.

ST MARY-LE-BOW
Cheapside, EC4

Only those born within the sound of the 'Bow Bells' can consider themselves true Cockneys, so this church is of great importance to many Londoners. Wren designed the original church in 1670, and it was restored after bomb damage. The tower and steeple survive from the original, as well as an 11th-century staircase found in the crypt.

ST MARY WOOLNOTH
King William St, EC4

Built in 1716, this is a Nicholas Hawksmoor church (Hawksmoor was Wren's assistant), which houses the police resting place of one John Newton, composer of the hymn *Amazing Grace*.

ST STEPHEN WALBROOK
Walbrook, EC4

This is often considered one of Wren's finest works, after St Paul's, and indeed resembles St Paul's with its large central dome. The Samaritans were founded here in 1953.

TEMPLE OF MITHRAS
Sumitomo Bank, Temple Court,
Queen Victoria St, EC4

The Temple of Mithras was built circa AD 240, and now only this pile of stones is left. Mithras was a Persian god taken up by many Roman soldiers in the 1st century AD. By the time this temple was built the cult was almost equal in size to Christianity, which had yet to gain ascendancy under Constantine. It was discovered in 1954 during building work, and once stood near today's St Stephen Walbrook church (see above). The story of the temple is told in the Museum of London.

BUSINESS LONDON

DAILY EXPRESS BUILDING
121-128 Fleet St, EC4

This unusual building once housed the staff of the national newspaper, the *Daily Express*, and is a fine example of art deco, completed in 1932. In front of it is a vast black glass curtain behind which you can glimpse an art-deco foyer. Currently it stands empty.

NATWEST TOWER
Bishopsgate, EC2

In 1980 this was the tallest building in Britain (660ft) until the Canary Wharf Tower was completed in 1991.

LLOYD'S OF LONDON
Lime St, EC3

Richard Rogers (also responsible for the Beaubourg (or Pompidou) Centre in Paris) designed this extraordinary high-tech building of glass entwined in steel with cranes and gantries. It is most impressive at night when it glows eerily purple and green from concealed spotlights.

NatWest Tower

WHERE TO STAY
HOTELS
AA RECOMMENDED

★★★ THE BARBICAN

Central St, Clerkenwell EC1V 8DS

(From Kings Cross station follow Pentonville Rd Islington. Over junct at Angel into City Rd. 3rd right into Central St, hotel is 150m on the left)

☎ 020 7251 1565 📠 020 7253 1005

Very popular with both tourists and corporate guests, this modern hotel is about a ten minute walk from the Barbican, and the hotel does provide a useful shuttle service. The pleasant bedrooms are well decorated including some smart contemporary executive rooms.

298 rooms (57 family & 30 no smoking) / European Cuisine / Lift, Night porter / No dogs (ex guide dogs)

> **Call the AA Hotel Booking Service on 0870 5050505 to book at AA recognised hotels and B&Bs in the UK, or through our internet site: http://www.theaa.co.uk/hotels**

WHERE TO EAT
RESTAURANTS
AA RECOMMENDED

❀ ❀ ALBA RESTAURANT

107 Whitecross Street EC1 8JD

☎ 020 7588 1798 📠 020-7638 5793

A short walk from the Barbican, this bright, modern restaurant is popular with the local business community. And the modern Italian menu is sensibly short, encouraging some serious cooking on the part of the kitchen. The helpfully annotated wine list is an impressive tour of the best Italian vineyards.

Fixed D £ ALC ££

❀ GLADWINS RESTAURANT

Minster Court Mark Lane EC3R 7AA

☎ 020 7444 0004 📠 020 7444 0001

The basement restaurant has all the current style points: light wood, bright colours. Modern British dishes co-habit with Eastern ones on a menu which avoids fusion confusion. There are global influences certainly, but middle and far-eastern spices are integral, with the odd Caribbean slant to starters and main courses and puddings firmly rooted in Europe.

ALC ££

❀ ❀ ONE LOMBARD STREET, THE BRASSERIE

1 Lombard Street, EC3V 9AA

☎ 020 7929 6611 📠 020 7929 6622

A swanky high-ceilinged restaurant occupying a former banking hall. The Brasserie at One Lombard Street has a neo-classical interior, bare white walls and domed skylights - all of which helps to create a buzzy atmosphere. The pan-European menu is simple and to the point with six or seven choices for each course, including four different caviars, and main courses split according to ingredients: pasta, fish, meat, crustacea. Desserts range from pineapple and mango salad with coconut sorbet to bitter chocolate tart.

ALC ££

❀ SEARCY'S BRASSERIE

Library Floor Barbican Centre Silk Street EC2Y 8DS

☎ 020 7588 3008 📠 020 7382 7247

Modern brasserie in the Barbican Centre that comes into its own when combined with a concert or play. Strong Med influences in carpaccio of scallops with red pepper purée, and cannon of lamb with aubergine and pine kernel caviar.

Fixed L/D £ ALC ££

❀ ❀ TATSUSO RESTAURANT

32 Broadgate Circle EC1M 6BT

☎ 020 7638 5863 📠 020 7638 5864

A pricy Japanese popular with city folk and probably best visited for lunch when the area is in full swing. There's a tepanyaki bar on the entrance floor, where you can watch the chef at work, while downstairs the traditionally-styled restaurant features blond wood, pale colours and silk paintings. The set menus are recommended for simplicity: a typical selection will include sashimi, tempura, Japanese clear soup and toban yaki (sliced beef served in a casserole). All in all, this is a stylish Japanese - but make sure your wallet's stuffed before booking a table.

Fixed L ££ ALC £££

❀ ❀ TWO FOUR TWO

242 Blackfriars Road SE1 9UF

☎ 020 7928 8689 📠 020 7928 4447

Under-the-railway-arches-style wine bar-cum-restaurant near Waterloo Station. Brian Turner (not the TV celeb one) is more or less solo in the kitchen, so his menu is a simple affair - and all the better for it. Fresh, vibrant, seasonal, with the likes of smoked haddock on a warm spinach tart with poached egg, a filled chicken breast with Brie and Jarlsberg with roasted baby leeks and cream, and an absolutely fabulous blueberry and vanilla meringue. Keenly priced, wide-ranging wine list.

Fixed L £

PUBS, INNS & OTHER PLACES

WATERSIDE RESTAURANT
Barbican Centre EC2Y 8DS
☎ 020 7638 4141
Counter-service with helpful staff. Good dessert counter.

VIADUCT TAVERN
126 Newgate St, EC1
☎ 020 7606 8476
19th-century gin palace built opposite what was then the infamous Newgate jail, but is now the Old Bailey.

BIERREX
2-3 Creed Lane, EC4
☎ 020 7329 3188
Tucked away between Carter Lane and Ludgate Hill, not far from St Paul's, this small bar has an American diner feel.

WATER POET
9 Stoney Lane, E1
☎ 020 7626 4994
Busy bar/restaurant.

YE OLDE CHESHIRE CHEESE
Wine Office Court, off Fleet St, EC4
☎ 020 7353 6170
17th-century pub with plenty of nooks and snugs.

HAMILTON HALL
Liverpool Street Station, EC2
☎ 020 7247 3579
Once the ballroom of the Great Eastern Hotel, this chandeliered pub is a favourite with commuters.

YE OLDE COCK TAVERN
22 Fleet St, EC4
☎ 020 7353 8570
Now a favourite among lawyers, Ye Olde Cock was once one TS Eliot's favoured haunts.

DOCKLANDS

To the east of the City lie London's former docklands, covering a vast area the same size as the whole of central London. With the post-war decline in trading, most of the docks fell into disuse, and in the 1980s developers saw the area as an opportunity to create housing and offices. Their plan was to create a whole new area of London with sporting opportunities on the river and quays and high-quality facilities. The transformation has occurred, but at a much slower rate than they predicted, and the area has still to come into its own. The Millennium celebrations will undoubtedly have a great effect on Docklands. The enormous, expensive and contraversial Millennium Dome is located in Greenwich, east of the Isle of Dogs, next to the Blackwall Tunnel. The Meridian Line, which has its home at the Royal Observatory nearby is where the Millennium celebrations started, and cuts through the corner of the Dome.

At the City end of the area are the Tower of London, Tower Bridge, HMS Belfast, St Katharine's Dock and many other well-established London sights. As you venture further east, the picture changes, with Tobacco Dock, a shopping and entertainment complex in need of a boost, the only feature until you reach Canary Wharf on the Isle of Dogs. There are several interesting pubs in the area, however, including the Prospect of Whitby on

Wapping Wall, dating back to Henry VIII and once the local haunt of Samuel Pepys, thieves and smugglers, and Dickens Inn on St Katherine's Way, an artfully converted historic warehouse.

The best way to reach the heart of the Docklands redevelopment, the Isle of Dogs, is by Docklands Light Railway (DLR), which connects to the main London Underground network. The Isle of Dogs is what most people think of as 'Docklands'. It is more of a peninsula than an island, although the South Dock does indeed cut it off from the shore. The South Dock, along with Millwall Docks to the south, West India Dock, Blackwall Basin and Poplar Dock, was built in the 19th century to accommodate the massive trade that Britain had with its Empire and the world. The demise of the docks and the rise of high-priced redevelopment, also known as 'gentrification', has led to something of a chasm between the local East End ex-dock workers and the new business and City-orientated businesses and commuters. A certain amount of discontent surfaced in the late 1980s, which led political groups like Class War to take credit for acts of frustrated violence such as the torching of expensive cars and vandalism of new business premises. The discontent that still rumbles led in 1993 to the election of the openly racist counciller, Derek Beacon

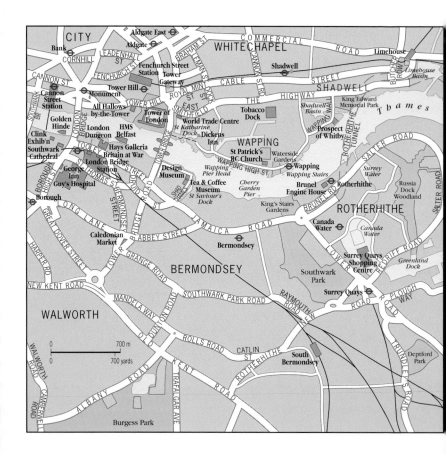

of the British National Party, who had campaigned on housing issues, a severe local problem. Although he was quickly ousted, the area clearly has yet to resolve this class conflict.

Canary Wharf is the main focus of the Docklands redevelopment, the 800ft tower of One Canada Square being the tallest in Britain. It was the first skyscraper to be clad in stainless steel, and can be seen from Kent and Essex. Some national newspapers are now based here, part of the reason perhaps that the building was targeted for a major bomb attack by the IRA in 1996. This bombing led to the closing of the upper floors to the public, although you can still visit the marble atrium. Other attractions in the area, include Billingsgate Fish Market and the Docklands Visitor Centre, with a very good source of maps and other information. Towards the river is the Docklands Sailing Centre, with ample opportunities for waterskiing, jet biking and sailing, and further down the U-shaped 'isle' is Mudchute City Farm. At the tip of the Isle of Dogs is Island Gardens, with excellent views across the river to the Greenwich, which you can reach via a foot tunnel under the river.

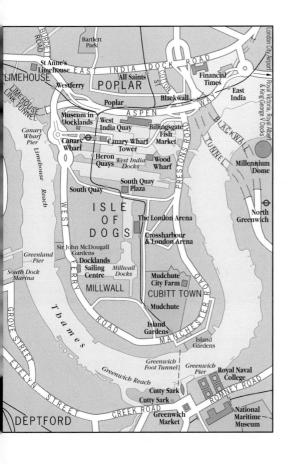

MUST SEE

One Canary Wharf

TOWER OF LONDON
Tower Hill, EC3
☎ 020 7709 0765

One of the most famous sights in all of London, the Tower has served as a palace, prison, mint, observatory and castle, and has borne witness to many of the most important and bloody events of British history. It is always busy with visitors, but is well worth seeing in its entirety. Henry VIII's second and fifth wives Anne Boleyn and Catherine Howard were beheaded here on Tower Green, as well as Sir Thomas More and Sir Walter Ralegh, who was convicted for his suspected involvement in the Gunpowder Plot. William the Conqueror built the original tower to keep an eye on the people of London, and it soon evolved into a large fortress. Most of the Tower that visitors see now was in place by 1307. The Bloody Tower is so called due to the murder here in 1483 of the 'Princes in the Tower', - boy-king Edward V and his brother - whose skeletons were discovered in 1674 during repair work. Sir Walter Ralegh was also imprisoned here. Today the Tower has a less grisly task: to guard the Crown Jewels which are now on display in the Jewel House. To get the most from the tower take a tour conducted by one of the Beefeaters - ex-servicemen who serve as guides and guards.

ST KATHARINE'S DOCK
St Katharine's Way, E1
☎ 020 7481 8350

Originally built in 1824 by Thomas Telford, St Katharine's Dock was the first part of the 1970s Docklands development to open, with a new marina and warehouse conversions for luxury housing. The visiting yachts are worth ogling at, and there are also some historic vessels. The popular Dickens Inn is here, restored from an 18th-century timber-framed brewery. Shoppers can browse around the bizarrely named Thomas More shopping complex.

CANARY WHARF
Isle of Dogs, E14

In 1991, the Canary Wharf Tower (official name One Canada Square) was built to the design of Cesar Pelli. At 800ft it is the tallest building in Europe, and dominates the London skyline (you can't go inside unless you work there). It was built during the recession, and so stood virtually empty for a few years, but it is now filling up with businesses. The whole area around Canary Wharf is gradually developing, and anyone interested in modern architecture should come and take a look.

HMS BELFAST
Morgan's Lane, Tooley St, SE1
☎ 020 7407 6434

A favourite with children and adults alike, you can scramble around the largest and most powerful warship ever built for the Royal Navy. Visit the engine room, mess decks and sick bay, among other places.

TOWER BRIDGE

Although it was built centuries later, the design of the Gothic-style Tower Bridge echoes that of the Tower of London, and is equally well-known as an image of the capital. The two central spans of the drawbridge open up when a tall ship needs to pass through, although this happens less often nowadays. There is a footbridge linking the two towers at the top, which was installed so that pedestrians could cross the Thames here when the bridge was open. To find out when the bridge is likely to be open next
☎ 020 7378 7700.

RIVER TRIP

You can take a cruise boat up and down the river from Tower Pier on Tower Hill, EC3 (tel: 020 7488 0344 or the London Tourist Board 020 7932 2000). Trips from here go to Westminster and Greenwich, with a frequent ferry to HMS Belfast.

HISTORIC AND ANCIENT SITES

It is worth wandering around Wapping High Street, Limehouse and the Isle of Dogs to witness the juxtaposition of the old and the new. Terraced houses occupied by generations of eastenders (the real ones!) are now next door to the luxury converted warehouses occupied by media and film stars, as well as wealthy city business folk. The other important historic buildings around here are several pubs: the Prospect of Whitby at Wapping Wall, once the haunt of Samuel Pepys and artists JMW Turner and Whistler; The Mayflower, from where the Pilgrim Fathers departed for America; and The George.

LONDON BRIDGE CITY
SE1

This newly developed area of converted warehouses (real name Bermondsey) stretches between London and Tower Bridges. It includes the shopping complex of Hay's Galleria. Worth seeing are St Olaf's House, an art-deco building with a

St Katherine's Dock

jazzy façade; Butler's Wharf, a converted warehouse with Terence Conran's excellent restaurant Le Pont de la Tour; and the Design Museum.

TOBACCO DOCK
The Highway, E1
☎ 020 7702 9681

Part of the Docklands redevelopment scheme, this shopping and entertainment area is in need of a boost, and there are plans to do just that. At present there are shops, restaurants and cafés on two floors of a converted tobacco warehouse. The two ships moored here are replicas of the

Development on the Isle of Dogs

original ones which delivered tobacco and wine to London from overseas. Not far from Tobacco Dock is the HQ of Rupert Murdoch's News International, also known as 'Fortress Murdoch' due to its barbed wire-topped fences and paranoid security measures. Not one of London's prettier sites.

BILLINGSGATE FISH MARKET
North Quay, West India Dock, E14
Moved from Lower Thames Street in the City, where it originated, this is a wet and smelly experience - Europe's main fish market.

MUSEUMS

DOCKLANDS MUSEUM
West India Quay
Planned opening Early 2001
This £16 million museum will highlight the history of London's river, port, industry and communities in a Grade I listed warehouse. It will include artefacts paintings, oral testimonies, photographs and archive material from the Museum of London and Port of London's collections.

BRITAIN AT WAR EXPERIENCE
64 Tooley St, SE1
☎ 020 7403 3171
Experience for yourself what life was like in London during the Blitz of World War II. The reconstructions include sight, sound and smell, which can make them rather too realistic sometimes.

DESIGN MUSEUM
Butler's Wharf, off Shad Thames, SE1
☎ 020 7403 6933
Inspired by Sir Terence Conran, the Design Museum concentrates on design through the ages, with temporary exhibitions on a variety of themes. There is also a permanent collection in the Conran Collection Gallery which displays the changing designs of everyday products such as kettles, cars, telephones etc. It's fascinating to see what used to be in every household as recently as the 1970s, and how dated they look next to their newer counterparts. The Blue Print Café next door has a very good reputation.

TOWER BRIDGE EXPERIENCE
Tower Bridge
☎ 020 7403 3761
This museum tells the story of Tower Bridge with exhibits and the Victorian engine rooms with the original steam engines that were used to open the bridge to let the ships through. The museum is housed in the high-level walkway across the top of the towers.

St Katherine's Dock

BRAMAH TEA & COFFEE MUSEUM
Maguire St, SE1
☎ 020 7378 0222
The world's largest teapot is on display here, just one reason to visit. The museum charts the introduction of tea to England in the 17th century to its present status as a national institution. Of course there are loads of different types on sale. In 2000 tea enthusiast Edward Bramah will celebrate 50 years in the tea and coffee business. Expect special exhibitions.

ROYAL ARMOURIES
Tower of London, EC3
☎ 020 7480 6358
This is London's oldest museum and full of ancient exhibits including oriental armour, and armour from Henry VIII and Charles I.

CLINK EXHIBITION
1 Clink St, SE1
☎ 020 7403 6515
A dark and murky past is on display in this exhibition, which recreates a couple of the cells in the Clink Prison, famous for its inmates which included originally heretics, and then local prostitutes, thieves, actors and priests, all of whom lived ribald lives. The Clink was another victim of the anti-Catholic wrath of the 18th-century Gordon riots, and was the prison that gives us the phrase 'in clink'.

ART GALLERIES

CHISENHALE GALLERY
64 Chisenhale Rd, E3
☎ 020 8981 4518
Housed in a converted warehouse (what isn't around here!) this gallery showcases modern and contemporary works.

Tobacco Dock

Tower Bridge

THEATRES

SOUTHWARK PLAYHOUSE
62 Southwark Bridge Rd, SE1
☎ 020 7620 3494
A fringe venue with an interesting repertory.

ENTERTAINMENT AND NIGHTLIFE

THE ARCHES
O'Meara St, off Southwark St, SE1
☎ 020 7207 2980
Underneath the arches near London Bridge station, this is a nightclub with attitude.

SHOPPING

HAY'S GALLERIA
Hay's Wharf, SE1
Part of the development of the old warehouses along the South Bank, Hay's Galleria, just beyond Tower Bridge, is a glass-domed arcade in which shops, wine bars and cafés ply a busy trade. The Thames is right at hand.

MARKETS

BERMONDSEY AND NEW CALEDONIAN MARKET
Bermondsey St and Tower Bridge Rd, SE1
This market is known as the New Caledonian Market and the Bermondsey Antiques Market. It offers antiques and bric-à-brac - haggling is imperative if you don't want to spend an unnecessary fortune.

GREAT FOR KIDS

There are loads of Festivals and Events throughout the year in London which children will love - See Festivals and Events. There's a McDonald's at 8 Tower Hill, EC3 - perfect for after a tiring visit to the Tower.

TOWER HILL PAGEANT
1 Tower Hill Terrace, EC3
☎ 020 7709 0081
Near to the Tower of London, this excellent dark-ride experience is a great way to learn about the life and times of London. You sit in a motorised car and are gently moved through various tableaux of London, with sounds and smells along the

way. After the ride you can look at the fascinating exhibition of over 1,000 Roman and medieval finds discovered by Museum of London archaeologists

Traitor's Gate at the Tower of London

LONDON DUNGEON
28-34 Tooley St, SE1
☎ 020 7403 0606
Beneath the ancient paving stones of Southwark lies a chillingly realistic museum. If your child likes grisly murders and gruesome goings-on, then they'll love it here, where past crimes are reconstructed with horrible realism, right down to the screams. The latest experience is Judgement Day, where you are sentenced and taken in the executioner's barge for your final trip through Traitor's Gate and to the Tower of London to await your fate ... Adults find the whole experience more of a problem! It is not suitable for very young children, or "those of a nervous disposition".

ALL HALLOWS-BY-THE-TOWER
Byward St, EC3
☎ 020 7481 2928
In this splendid church, you can create brass rubbings including knights and animals.

MUDCHUTE PARK AND FARM
Pier St, Isle of Dogs, E14
☎ 020 7515 5901
A working farm since 1977, animals to see and touch here include chickens, pigs, goats, horses, ponies, rabbits, guinea pigs and even a llama. The Mudchute was created by silt dumped after the dredging of Millwall Dock.

LONDON BUBBLE THEATRE COMPANY
3 Elephant Lane, SE16
☎ 020 7237 4434
With their plays aimed at under 11-year-olds, this bubble bounces around London's parks every summer.

PLACES OF WORSHIP

SOUTHWARK CATHEDRAL
Montague Close, SE1
If nothing else, go to hear the beautiful Gothic choir in this charming 19th-century cathedral. The original building dates to 1220, and was known as St Mary Overie (St Mary over the water), but has been

Southwark Cathedral

Design Museum

much remodelled since. The Harvard Chapel was named after John Harvard, founder of the eponymous university in the United States.

ALL HALLOWS-BY-THE-TOWER
Byward St, EC3
It was from here that Samuel Pepys surveyed the terrible devastation of the City after the Great Fire of London in 1666. It is a fine church, with an altarpiece of the Last Supper. There is a brass-rubbing centre for children.

ST ANNE'S LIMEHOUSE
3 Colt St, E14
This Hawksmoor church has the tallest clock tower in the country (only Big Ben is bigger) and it also leans over! Fans of the strange may like to check out Hawksmoor's mysterious Masonic pyramid in the graveyard.

ST GEORGE-IN-THE-EAST
Cannon Rd, E1
☎ 020 7481 1345
Another Nicholas Hawksmoor church, baroque St George's was completely destroyed during World War II, but restored in 1963. Plans are in motion to turn part of the church into rehearsal space for the Guildhall School of Music and Drama.

ST PETER-AD-VINCULA
Tower Hill, EC3
Connected to the Tower of London, this church was much used by prisoners awaiting their grisly fate within the Tower. Many noble and royal people are buried here, including Anne Boleyn, Catherine Howard, Sir Thomas More and Lady Jane Grey, who were beheaded on Tower Green

SPORT AND LEISURE

DOCKLANDS SAILING CENTRE
Kingsbridge, Millwall Dock, E14
☎ 020 7537 2626
Courses here include power-boating, sailing, navigation and boat maintenance, as well as school holiday activities such as dragon-boating, canoeing, sailing and rowing. Plenty to keep everyone busy.

SHADWELL BASIN OUTDOOR ACTIVITY CENTRE
Shadwell Pier, Glamis Rd, E1
☎ 020 7481 4210
Activities here include canoeing, dragon-boating, windsurfing, fishing and sailing.

SURREY DOCKS WATERSPORTS CENTRE
Rope St, Rotherhithe, SE16
☎ 020 7237 5555
Canoeing, raft-racing, sailing and windsurfing for adults and children at this excellent centre which offers full training.

MUDCHUTE PARK AND FARM RIDING SCHOOL
Pier St, Isle of Dogs, E14
☎ 020 7515 5901
An excellent school where children can learn to ride (they have to be over seven), with pony rides for those under seven.

DOCKLANDS LIGHT RAILWAY

The DLR (as it is signposted) is a hi-tech service built in 1987 to serve the newly regenerated Docklands area. It runs on raised tracks between Bank or Tower Gateway (next to Tower Hill tube) to Island Gardens on the Isle of Dogs, taking in Shadwell, Limehouse and Canary Wharf on the way. From these red, white and blue trains there are excellent views of the huge stretches of water that form the Docklands, giving a good impression of the whole area. From Island Gardens you can take the pedestrian tunnel under the Thames to reach Greenwich. The newly extended Jubilee Line also has stations in the area, including Canada Water and Bermondsey.

Docklands Light Railway

WHERE TO STAY
HOTELS
AA RECOMMENDED

E1

★★★★⚘ **THISTLE TOWER**
St Katherine's Way E1 9LD
(adjacent to Tower Bridge on North side of River Thames)
☎ 020 7481 2575 ℱ 020 7488 4106
This busy hotel has wonderful views - even the docks to the rear are attractively landscaped. Many of the bedrooms are very sumptuous, but few can match the opulence of the suites which come with full butler service. The Princes Room provides carefully crafted dishes served by a professional and friendly team of staff.
800 rooms (478 no smoking) / International Cuisine / Gym / Live entertainment / Lift, Night porter, Air cond
⬦

E14

⌂ **TRAVELODGE**
Coriander Av, East India Dock Rd E14 2AA
(fronts A13 at East India Dock Road)
☎ 020 7531 9705
This modern building offers accommodation in smart, spacious and well equipped bedrooms, all with en-suite bathrooms. Refreshments may be taken at the nearby family restaurant.
132 rooms

Call the AA Hotel Booking Service on
**0870 5050505 to book at AA recognised
hotels and B&Bs in the UK,**
or through our internet site:
http://www.theaa.co.uk/hotels

WHERE TO EAT
RESTAURANTS
AA RECOMMENDED

⚘ **APPRENTICE RESTAURANT**
Cardamon Building 31 Shad Thames SE1 2YR
☎ 020 7234 0254 ℱ 020 7403 2638
The eating outlet of the Butler's Wharf Chef School, with the upbeat modern cooking and service provided by students. A meal here can, at times, exceed the restaurant's rating. Both prices and decor are modest.
Fixed L/D £ ALC £

⚘ **BENGAL CLIPPER**
Butlers Wharf SE1 2YE
☎ 020 7357 9001 ℱ 020 7357 9002
Spacious, modern Indian set in the old cardamom warehouse at Butlers Wharf. The menu's strength are its Bengali and Goan dishes: try golda chingri pardanashin' - giant prawns served in the shell of a baby coconut.
Fixed L £ ALC ££

⚘ **BLUE PRINT CAFÉ**
The Design Museum Shad Thames Street SE1 2YD
☎ 020 7378 7031 ℱ 020 7357 8810
Conran bistro/brasserie on the first floor of the Design Museum. Short ambitious menu belts out tagliatelle with asparagus, roast cod with saffron potatoes, and raspberry shortcake.
ALC ££

⚘⚘ **THE BIG CHEF**
Second Floor Cabot Place East Canary Wharf E14 4QT
☎ 020 7513 0513 ℱ 020 7513 0557
The Big Chef takes pride of place at the top of an escalator, lording it above floors of shops and offices in Canary Wharf; it's all rather reminiscent of a swish US shopping mall, especially when you note that it shares the top floor with a number of other 'eateries', which are mainly of the large chain variety. The main menu is predominantly French, frequently employing terms like 'ravigote' and 'beurre maitre d'hôtel', and the cooking is good, well-presented and looks pretty on the plate. The wine list is reasonably priced and not dominated by Grand Crus, as one might expect; the staff are predominantly French.

Bengal Clipper

⊛ ⊛ BUTLERS WHARF CHOP HOUSE
The Butlers Wharf Building 36e Shad Thames
SE1 2YE

☎ 020 7403 3403 📠 020 7403 3414

Part of Sir Terence Conran's "Gastrodome'
at Butlers Wharf, within sight of Tower
Bridge. The restaurant is divided into a bar,
which serves simple dishes, a restaurant,
and a terrace which is only used in fine
weather. The menu pays homage to the
'best' of British cooking. First-class
ingredients are used in a variety of
straightforward dishes: Dorset crab
mayonnaise, fish and chips, and steak-
and-kidney pudding, and roast rump of
lamb, served more adventurously with a
beetroot mash and mint cream. The wine
list is supplemented by good beers.
Fixed L £ ALC ££

⊛ CANTINA DEL PONTE
The Butlers Wharf Building 36c Shad Thames
SE1 2YE

☎ 020 7403 5403 📠 020 7403 0267

Less pricy, informal Conran Gastrodome
eaterie with a riverside location and an
Italian-inspired menu offering pizza, pasta
or risotto, as well as roast rump of lamb,
grilled tuna, and pannacotta with
raspberries and grappa. Portions on the
whole are generous.
Fixed L £ ALC ££

⊛ FISH!
Cathedral Street Borough Market SE1 9AL

☎ 020 7836 3236

It's a posh fish bowl squeezed between
Southwark Cathedral and old Borough
Market, with trains rumbling overhead into
London Bridge station. Fast-paced set-up.
Eat sea bass, halibut, swordfish, brilliant
chips, or some great British traditions like
potted shrimps, and bread-and-butter
pudding.
ALC ££

⊛ THE HOTHOUSE
78-80 Wapping Lane E1 9NF

☎ 020 7488 4797 📠 020 7488 9500

Warehouse conversion bar/restaurant near
Tower Bridge. The menu has a classic
French base but incorporates mainstream
modern British and North African
influences in say, fish soup provençale or
lamb fillet on hot tabouleh couscous.

⊛ ⊛ LE PONT DE LA TOUR
The Butlers Wharf Building 36d Shad Thames
SE1 2NQ

☎ 020 7403 8403 📠 020 7403 0267

Impeccably stylish restaurant,with a high-
flying atmosphere, the cooking is steeped
in the classical mould, deft in touch and
confident in execution. The menu reads
like a dream: whole roast buttered lobster
with herbs; grilled veal chop with a sauté

of ceps, roast shallot and Armagnac purée.
The wine list rises to the occasion with a
long and interesting list, ably supported by
knowledgeable staff.
ALC £££

⊛ THE THAI GARDEN
249 Globe Road E2 0JD

☎ 020 8981 5748

Close to the heart of Bethnal Green, a
simple vegetarian and fish Thai eaterie
that offers good-value set menus and a
keenly priced carte. Expect deep-fried
curried seafood, pomfret fish topped with
chilli sauce, and Thai aubergines and
mixed vegetable curry with coconut cream.
Fixed L/D £ ALC ££

⊛ THE THISTLE TOWER
St Katharine's Way E1 9LD

☎ 020 7481 2575 📠 020 7488 4106

Elegant riverside hotel restaurant blessed
with wonderful views. A contemporary
menu with imaginatively crafted dishes
includes roasted cannon of lamb with
grain mustard polenta, and warm plum
tart with elderflower sorbet.
ALC £££

PUBS, INNS & OTHER PLACES

BARLEY MOW
Narrow St, E14

☎ 020 7265 8931

Nice location fronting onto the Thames at
a bend in the river.

GRAPES
76 Narrow St, E14

☎ 020 7987 4396

18th-century riverside pub, mentioned in
Dickens' *Our Mutual Friend.*

TOWN OF RAMSGATE
Wapping High St, E1

☎ 020 7488 2685

Small medieval pub with a grisly past.
Connections include Captain Blood,
Hanging Judge Jeffries, and Bligh and
Christian of Mutiny on the Bounty fame

HENRY ADDINGTON
20-28 MacKenzie Walk, E14

☎ 020 7512 9022

Named after the early 19th-century British
prime minister who sanctioned the
original Canary Wharf.

PROSPECT OF WHITBY
57 Wapping Wall, E1

☎ 020 7481 1095

16th-century pub, once a Samuel Pepys
haunt.

lifestyle guides for the new
Millennium

- New Quality Standards & Diamond Classification for 2000
- Over 3000 places to stay, annually assessed for quality
- New AA food assessments and AA Best British Breakfast Award

AA
Bed & Breakfast 2000

England, Scotland

AA
Best Pubs & Inns 2000

Over 1
England

- Over 1600 Pubs & Inns selected for food & atmosphere
- The best traditional recipes for fish pie and steak and ale pie
- Pubs with good fish and seafood highlighted

AA
The Restaurant Guide 2000

The best 1800 restaurants in England, Scotland, Wales & Ireland

- Over 1800 of Britain's best restaurants
- All restaurants have AA Rosette Awards
- AA Restaurant of the Year and other Awards

AA
The Hotel Guide 2000

Royal Mail

4000 Hotels in England, Scotland, Wales & Ireland

- New Quality Standards
- Quality Percentage Score makes hotel choice easy
- AA Rosette Awards highlight fine food

DULWICH AND GREENWICH

For most, Greenwich conjures up images of royalty and ships. Henry VIII and his daughters Mary I and Elizabeth I were born here, and it was here that Elizabeth signed the order for the execution of Mary Queen of Scots. Henry VIII loved the palace here, but William and Mary preferred Kensington and converted the palace into the Royal Naval Hospital, which in 1873 became the Royal Naval College that we see today.

Notwithstanding the new stations on the extended Jubilee Line, the best way to arrive in Greenwich is by boat (trips are available from Westminster, Charing Cross and the Tower of London), although views of the Royal Naval College and the National Maritime Museum are best from Island Gardens across the river on the tip of the Isle of Dogs. The first sight is the magnificent Cutty Sark, in dry dock since 1954, and next to it Sir Francis Chichester's Gipsy Moth IV. Inland behind the National Maritime Museum is Greenwich Park which contains the Old Royal Observatory and Flamsteed House.

Greenwich is currently undergoing a resurgence partly due to the presence of the Meridian Line at the Royal Observatory, which was the starting point for the Millennium celebrations. The other major attraction in Greenwich is undoubtedly the Millennium Dome which generated as much controversy over its price (£700 million was a conservative estimate) and contents, as it did interest in tourists planning to visit it. The area will surely benefit from the attention paid to it during the early 21st century, although it remains to be seen how much attention there will actually be.

Historically, Greenwich has been regarded as one of London's most attractive areas. Daniel Defoe dubbed it "the most delightful spot of ground in Great Britain." Apart from the tourist sights the town itself was laid out in the 1820s by John Nash which was fine for the horse and cart but is not so suitable for the density of traffic that crams into the area. Greenwich Market is a bustling and noisy affair, which specialises in antiques, crafts, fashion, second-hand books and a massive variety of paraphenalia.

Dulwich is Greenwich's quieter and more suburban neighbour, although not without historic interest. Dulwich Picture Gallery is England's oldest public gallery and will reopen in 2000 after a £9 million refurbishment. Dulwich Old College dates from 1619, the original school for the poor (now Dulwich College) founded by Edward Alleyn. Dulwich Park is especially colourful in May, and there are some good tennis courts. Along London Road, east of the park, is the Horniman Museum, full of odd and interesting artefacts collected by tea magnate Frederick Horniman. Fans of the prehistoric lizard world may like to wander around Crystal Palace Park in search of the 30-odd life-size dinosaur models that menace the area around the Lower Lake.

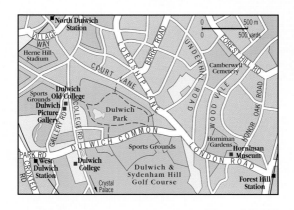

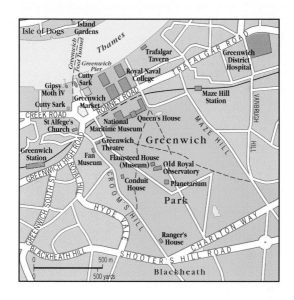

CUTTY SARK
King William Walk, Greenwich, SE10
☎ 020 8858 3445

Once the fastest tea clipper in the world, the magnificent Cutty Sark beat the world record for sailing between London and China (107 days). Built in 1869, she is now in dry dock at Greenwich, and visitors can clamber all over the ship, see how the sailors used to live, and where they slept and ate (and feel lucky that you don't have to!). There's a good collection of naval relics and figureheads inside.

NATIONAL MARITIME MUSEUM
Romney Rd, Greenwich, SE10
☎ 020 8858 4422

This is the main attraction in Greenwich, and occupies several buildings in Greenwich Park. It tells the story of the sea and the Royal Navy through ships (scale models and life-size models), paintings (portraits of famous explorers and navigators), and an interactive gallery, All Hands, which lets you experience what it was like to be at sea through the ages.

The Millennium Dome

THAMES BARRIER VISITOR CENTRE
Unity Way, SE18
☎ 020 8854 1373

In 1928 fourteen people drowned in flooding in central London, and in 1953 the number rose to 300. The Thames Flood Barrier was built in 1984 to prevent further disasters. Each of its gates weighs 3,000 tonnes and is 50ft high, constituting the world's biggest moveable flood barrier.

Thames Barrier

The Nelson Gallery explores the career of one of Britain's greatest naval commanders, and includes the blood-soaked uniform he was wearing when fatally wounded. In the next two years eleven new galleries are planned. Also within the National Maritime Museum are the Queen's House (see below) and the Royal Observatory.

The Visitor Centre explains the workings of the barrier and why it was built. Phone for details of the monthly raising of the gates.

HISTORIC AND ANCIENT SITES

OLD ROYAL OBSERVATORY
Romney Rd, Greenwich SE10
☎ 020 8858 4422

An annexe of the National Maritime Museum, and a focal point for the Millennium celebrations, the observatory is high on the hill in Greenwich Park. Established by Charles II in 1675 as a base for the Astronomer Royal, John Flamsteed, it's job was to set the standards of measurement for time, distance, latitude and longitude. In 1884 the famous Meridian Line was created to mark zero longitude, and it is from here that Greenwich Mean Time is measured, the standard by which time is set all round the world. You can stand astride the Greenwich Meridian, which marks the dividing line between the eastern and western hemispheres.

DULWICH OLD COLLEGE
Gallery Rd, Dulwich, SE23

This was the original school founded in 1619 by Edward Alleyn, and now serves as offices. The school buildings have moved up the road (see below).

DULWICH COLLEGE
College Rd, Dulwich SE23
☎ 020 8693 3601

The famous boys' school is housed in Renaissance-style buildings by Charles Barry, son of the architect jointly responsible for the Houses of Parliament.

THE MILLENNIUM DOME
Greenwich Peninsula

On a site near the river, London's £750 million project to celebrate the Millennium is an incredible sight. A vast hub-cap shaped structure, twice the size of Wembley Stadium, tall enough to accommodate Nelson's Column, the Dome contains 14 themed zones all sponsored by major companies. The zones include Faith, Talk, Mind, Rest, Home Planet, Body and Learning. The whole venture seemed doomed to cause massive controversy from its inception, so its probably for the best that this massive display will only be open for one year, or so it seems. What will happen to the Dome then is still under discussion.

SKYSCAPE
Greenwich Peninsula

Alongside the Dome stands this futuristic entertainment venue with two 2,500 seat cinemas which can be converted into a live performance venue. There will also be

Royal Naval College

Meridian telescope at the Observatory

a foyer with views of the Dome and the river. Events here will be seperately ticketed to the Dome. Live entertainment and performances will also take place in selected areas throughout the day, both within the Dome and in the Piazza.

MUSEUMS

HORNIMAN MUSEUM
London Rd, Dulwich, SE23
☎ 020 8699 1872
Inside this eccentric art-nouveau building is Frederick J Horniman's equally eccentric collection. A traveller in his business, tea imports, Horniman just gathered together anything that took his fancy, and now they are on display here: stuffed animals, masks, puppets, musical instruments (which you can play) and fossils. Children will love it. A large permanent exhibition of African art opened in 1999.

FAN MUSEUM
12 Crooms Hill, Greenwich, SE10
☎ 020 8858 7879
Set in a lovely house on the western edge of Greenwich Park, this is the only museum given over specifically to fans in the world. The fans are displayed in themes that include fan production, fan materials, the fan and the Empire, and the fan as a political tool á la *Dangerous Liasons*.

FLAMSTEED HOUSE
Greenwich Park, SE10
Built in 1675 by Christopher Wren, Flamsteed House looks just as it did when John Flamsteed, the first Royal

Astronomer, lived here with his wife. Early time-measuring instruments and telescopes are displayed, and the large ball on top of one of the towers still drops down its mast at 1pm every day, which allows passing ships to set their chronometers accurately.

VINTAGE WIRELESS MUSEUM
☎ 020 8670 3667
This extraordinary collection is housed at a private address, and visitors must phone for an appointment. The owner will take you on his enthusiastic tour of 1,000 items including radios, TVs and telephones.

CRYSTAL PALACE MUSEUM
Anerley Hill, SE19
☎ 020 8676 0700
Housed in the engineering school where

John Logie Baird invented the televison, this museum is devoted to the story of the Crystal Palace, a massive glass and steel structure built to house the 1851 Great Exhibition. Included are archive photographs and other exhibits.

ART GALLERIES

DULWICH PICTURE GALLERY
Gallery Rd, Dulwich, SE23
☎ 020 8693 8000 (recorded information)
The collection at this superb gallery was donated by Sir Francis Bourgeois in 1811. It covers over 300 masterpieces including Rembrandt's portrait of *Jacob III de Gheyn* and Van Dyck's *Madonna and Child*, as well as major works by Rubens, Gainsborough and Raphael. A new extension housing the Sackler Centre for Arts Education will be opening in May 2000

Cutty Sark

THEATRES

GREENWICH THEATRE
Crooms Hill, Greenwich, SE10
☎ 020 8858 7755
Stages a variety of shows including new works, revivals and classics, often with famous names.

ENTERTAINMENT AND NIGHTLIFE

UP THE CREEK
302 Creek Rd, Greenwich, SE10
☎ 020 8858 4581
Smoky, loud and very funny comedy club. Has some top comedians, but you'll need stamina.

Horniman Museum Gardens

Flamsteed House

SHOPPING

Greenwich and Dulwich both have high streets with the usual high-street chains, but if you want something different try Greenwich Market (see below).

MARKETS

The best place for shopping in these parts is undoubtedly Greenwich Market (although it is only open at the weekend), where the variety of goods on offer is complemented by the lovely surroundings.

GREENWICH VILLAGE AND MARKET

College Approach, Greenwich, SE10

This covered market has secondhand clothes, gifts, CDs, jewellery and some excellent crafts, many made locally. One of the most scenic and pleasant markets in London.

PARKS AND GARDENS

CRYSTAL PALACE PARK

Crystal Palace, SE20

Just to the south of Dulwich is where the magnificent Crystal Palace once stood. First built in Hyde Park to house the Great Exhibition, (the Victorian Millennium Dome, if you will) it was moved, piece by piece, to this site and rebuilt in 1851, and in 1854 became home to a huge amusement park. In 1936 it burnt to the ground and today all that remains is the boating lake (complete with life-size models of dinosaurs). Today there is also a mini fair, mini steam train and pony rides, as well as a maze. Athletic events and pop and orchestral concerts take place in summer.

DULWICH PARK

SE21

Best in May, when the azaleas and rhododendrons are in full bloom, Dulwich Park is a delightful open space with a boating lake, children's playground, tennis courts, putting green, aviary and café. It was once the favourite garden of Queen Mary, wife of George V, and today is popular with families who come to fly their kites.

GREENWICH PARK

Charlton Way, SE10

Henry VIII liked Greenwich Palace the best, and spent a lot of time in its 200 acres of hunting. In 1616 the palace was turned into the Queen's House and Royal Naval College. Today the park gives superb panoramic views of London from Greenwich Hill and houses several important buildings including Flamsteed House and the Royal Observatory. In summer brass bands perform, and there are children's playgrounds and tennis courts. The London Marathon starts from here in spring.

BROCKWELL PARK

Dulwich Rd, SE24

In 1892 this once private park, home of glassmaker John Blades, was opened to the public. There are extensive views from the hill and occasional fun fairs. There is also a children's paddling pool and tennis and netball courts. Brockwell is the venue each year for the Gay Rights Festival, and was often the venue for rallies, protests and festivals in the 1980s. On November 5, 'Bonfire Night', there is a fabulous fireworks display.

NUNHEAD CEMETERY

Linden Grove, SE15

The Friends of Nunhead Cemetery have kept this an important wildlife sanctuary, although very few burials now take place here. There is a wide variety of breeding grounds which attract birds, foxes, bats and squirrels, and visitors can go on an organised tour.

GREAT FOR KIDS

There are loads of Festivals and Events throughout the year in London which children will love - See Festivals and Events.

HORNIMAN GARDENS

Forest Hill, SE23

A small zoo with goats, rabbits and other tame animals can be found in these gardens.

PLACES OF WORSHIP

ST ALFEGE GREENWICH

Greenwich High Rd, SE10

This is the parish church of Greenwich, and stands on the site where St Alfege, the Archbishop of Canterbury, was killed by invading Danes in 1012. Nicholas Hawksmoor designed the church in 1714, and it was later restored in 1941.

Display of maritime memorabilia

WHERE TO STAY
HOTELS
AA RECOMMENDED

★★★ BARDON LODGE
15-17 Stratheden Rd SE3 7TH
☎ 020 8853 4051 📠 020 8858 7387
On the edge of the pretty village of
Blackheath, this is a friendly hotel, popular
for small conferences during the week and
equally in demand by weekend visitors to
Greenwich. The Vanbrugh Hotel across the
road is under the same ownership and
offers budget accommodation.
*32 rooms (4 family) / English &
Continental Cuisine / Night porter
Price band £££* 📇

★★ CLARENDON
8-16 Montpelier Row, Blackheath SE3 0RW
*(A2, turn off at Blackheath junct, hotel on left
just before village overlooking Blackheath &
Greenwich Royal Park)*
☎ 020 8318 4321 📠 020 8318 4378
This imposing Georgian building stands on

Call the AA Hotel Booking Service on
0870 5050505 to book at AA recognised
hotels and B&Bs in the UK,
or through our internet site:
http://www.theaa.co.uk/hotels

the edge of the Royal Hundred of
Blackheath with commanding views over
open countryside. Bedrooms are neat and
well equipped. Function and meeting
rooms are available. The Chart Bar is an
attractive feature of the hotel.
*193 rooms (37 family & 22 no smoking) /
English, French & Italian Cuisine / Pool
table / Live entertainment / Lift, Night
porter
Price band ££* 📇

Clarendon

★★ HOTEL IBIS
30 Stockwell St SE10 9JN
☎ 020 8305 1177 📠 020 8858 7139
This modern hotel is located in the heart
of Greenwich. Public areas are restricted to
a bar serving limited snacks and soft
drinks. The restaurant is operated by a
high profile brasserie company which also
provides a full choice self-service
breakfast.
*82 rooms (22 no smoking) / Lift
Price band ££* 📇

BED & BREAKFAST
AA RECOMMENDED

♦♦♦♦ BEDKNOBS
58 Glengarry Rd, East Dulwich SE22 8QD
*(just N of Dulwich Village, opposite Dulwich
Hospital in E Dulwich Grove)*
☎ 020 8299 2004 📠 020 8693 5611
Located in a residential road within easy
walking distance of the railway station,
this Victorian terraced house provides

Melrose House Hotel

homely accommodation. Breakfast is
taken at one table in the attractive dining
room, from a menu which includes many
healthy options.
*3 rooms (1 family) / No dogs / No coaches
Price band £* 📇

♦♦♦ MELROSE HOUSE HOTEL
89 Lennard Rd SE20 7LY
*(corner of Courtenay Road/Lennard Road
between Penge High St and Sydenham
High St)*
☎ 020 8776 8884 📠 020 8776 8480
Proprietor Frances Roberts offers a warm
welcome at this attractive Victorian house.
Bedrooms are individual in style,
comfortably furnished and feature extra
touches such as tissues, books and luxury
toiletries. Breakfast is served at a
communal table, a spacious conservatory
overlooks the pretty garden.
*3 rooms (1 family) / No dogs (ex guide
dogs) / No coaches / Pool table / Closed
24-26 Dec*

♦♦♦ VANBRUGH HOTEL
St Johns Park, Blackheath SE3 7TD
☎ 020 8858 7000 📠 020 8858 7387
Just one mile from Greenwich, this small
hotel is ideal for those seeking budget
accommodation close to the Millennium
celebrations. Bedrooms are furnished and

equipped to a high standard. In addition to a comfy lounge area there is a small rear garden, and guests are served a simple continental breakfast in the dining room.

30 rooms (3 family)
Price band £ £

◆ ◆ THE PILOT INN
68 Riverway, Greenwich SE10 0BE
(follow signs for Greenwich Yacht Club)
☎ 020 8858 5910 ⓕ 020 8293 0371
There is a friendly atmosphere at this popular inn situated close to the river and

right next to the Millennium Dome. The bedrooms, which are located in an adjacent annexe, are furnished in a modern style, with bright decor and colourful soft furnishings. Sound British meals are offered, plus a generous breakfast.

7 rooms (1 family) / No dogs
Price band £

◆ ◆ WESTON HOUSE HOTEL
8 Eltham Green, Eltham SE9 5LB
(hotel at junct of A205/A210. Left at Kidbrooke BR Station, at 1st traffic lights turn left, hotel opposite McDonalds)
☎ 020 8850 5191 ⓕ 020 8850 0030
An early Victorian villa located in the conservation area of Greenwich. It offers a friendly welcome and modestly furnished, well equipped bedrooms. A choice of breakfast is served in the brightly decorated dining room.

9 rooms (1 family) / No dogs
Price band £

WHERE TO EAT
RESTAURANTS
AA RECOMMENDED

✿✿ BABUR BRASSERIE
119 Brockley Rise Forest Hill SE23 1JP
☎ **020 8291 2400/4881** 📠 **020 8291 4881**
A life-size model tiger leaps out from above the doorway at this renowned Indian just off the South Circular. The menu of around a dozen main dishes is serious, far removed from the standard curry house formula, and the emphasis is on regional dishes. The cooking is also notable for freshness and distinct spicing.
ALC £

✿✿ CHAPTER TWO
43-45 Montpelier Vale
Blackheath Village SE3 0TJ
☎ **020 8333 2666** 📠 **020 8355 8399**
Restaurant chic rules with pale wood, firm use of colour, and abstracts on the wall while the menu brings us bang up-to-date with a range of traditional ideas and dishes given a modern spin. Grilled tuna, caramelised onions and sauce vierge makes a brilliant start to the meal; main courses could include a stunning grilled smoked haddock with superb curried saffron risotto and baby spinach - a kedgeree for our times. Desserts are typically well thought out. Try the baked chocolate cheesecake with plum compote.
Fixed L/D £ ALC £

✿ LAWN
1 Lawn Terrace Blackheath SE3 9LJ
☎ **020 8379 0724** 📠 **020 8379 9014**
Formerly One Lawn Terrace, a contemporary first-floor restaurant now owned by the Bank group. Dishes in the Bank style include Parmesan risotto and wild rocket, and duck confit with wok vegetables and plum sauce.
Fixed L/D £ ALC £££

Thailand

✿✿ LAICRAM THAI
1 Blackheath Grove Blackheath SE3
☎ **020 8852 4710**
Good cooking, with a restrained chilli quotient, from a menu that's sensibly not over-long. Starters are all freshly cooked - minced pork dumplings in garlic and soya sauce, for example - and roast duck curry is a speciality of the house. Desserts shed a new light on a part of the menu usually best avoided - try the mango mousse or mini-selection of sticky rice, coconut milk pudding and sweet baked cake, all wrapped in vine leaves, and be prepared to be won over.

✿ THAILAND
15 Lewisham Way SE14 6PP
☎ **020 8691 4040**
Informal Thai restaurant on a small scale - just like eating in someone's home. Chicken curry with coconut may be standard in all Thai restaurants, but this one is the sweetest, roundest of them all, fragrant with sweet basil, lemongrass, galangal and kaffir lime leaves.

Babur Brasserie

PUBS, INNS & OTHER PLACES

THE CROWN AND GREYHOUND
73 Dulwich Village
☎ **020 8693 2466**
Victorian village pub with four bars. Popular on Saturdays for wedding receptions.

CUTTY SARK
Ballast Quay, SE10
☎ **020 8858 3146**
Named after the Victorian tea and wool clipper docked nearby, this lovely riverside pub is one of the best in the area.

TRAFALGAR TAVERN
5 Park Row, SE10
☎ **020 8858 2437**
Good riverside location, mentioned in Dickens' *Our Mutual Friend*.

HAMPSTEAD

Hampstead is probably best known for its 800-acre Heath and the village-like feel of the place. It has also had strong connections to writers and artists for centuries, and remains home to those in the media who seek some measure of rural peace, while still maintaining proximity to the centre of their trade. In the 18th century Hampstead enjoyed a brief vogue as a fashionable spa, but bad building conditions and sloping ground prevented the Victorian expansion of the area, which explains its continuing Georgian charm. The area's reputation as a literary centre was cemented in the 19th century, and although no organised group, such as the Bloomsbury or Camden Town Groups emerged, Hampstead has been the home to an incredible range of celebrities. Among this illustrious number are William Blake, Ian Fleming (who named the villain of the James Bond novel *Goldfinger* after the Hungarian architect who built a nearby modernist house that Fleming disapproved of), George Orwell, Keats, Boy George, Agatha Christie and Sid Vicious. The current MP is Glenda Jackson, erstwhile star of stage and screen.

The Heath is a massive sprawl of grass, trees, lanes and ponds, that features a wide range of environments including green pastures, landscaped parkland and dense woodland. A Sunday stroll across it is the ideal therapy for any who are tired of the bustle of London.

The line of ponds that run down the eastern edge of the Heath still retain their traditional names and functions. These include the Model Boating Pond, Kenwood Ladies' Bathing Pond, Bird Sanctuary Pond, and Highgate Men's Bathing Pond.

Part of the Heath is known as Parliament Hill and not without good reason. Roundhead cannon were stationed here to defend the capital from Royalist attack during the Civil War, yet this is not the only connection. A Saxon parliament is thought to have met here, Gunpowder Plotters are said to have gathered here in anticipation of the destruction of the House, and elections to Parliament were held here in the 17th century. The hill is nowadays more popular with kite-fliers, and the sight of all those kites in the air at the weekend is only equalled by the excellent view of London the hill provides.

Kenwood House is one of the Heath's most interesting sights, modelled by Robert Adams in the 17th century for one of Britain's least popular people, Earl of Mansfield, Attorney-General and Lord Chief Justice. The Earl had sent over a hundred people to be hung and nearly 500 to be transported. The Gordon rioters attempted to sack Kenwood House but were tempted into drunkeness by the landlord of the nearby Spaniards Inn. The house is now home to the Iveagh Bequest, a fine collection of 17th and 18th-century art including work by Franz Hals, Vermeer and Joshua Reynolds.

The village of Hampstead is a rare feast for the historically inclined and literary-minded visitor, rewarding the curious not only with a mass of detail and colour, but also an excellent place to take a walk, not to mention fly a kite.

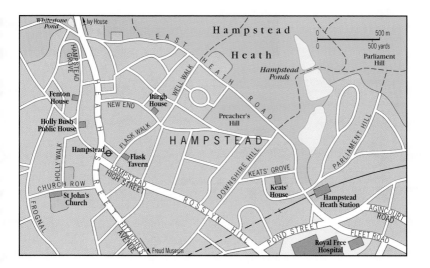

MUST SEE

Fenton House

promoter of psychoanalysis, after he fled Nazi persecution in the late 1930s. (Freud's works were among those destroyed in the infamous book-burning ceremonies.) From summer 1938 to September 1939, when he died, the willing recipient of a lethal dose of morphine, administered by his doctor, Freud battled with cancer here. On show at this small museum are rooms where he worked, his large collection of erotic antiquities and the Freud archive. The house was also home to Freud's daughter, Anna, who was an important child psychoanalyst.

HAMPSTEAD HEATH

Easily the best thing about Hampstead, this huge expanse of varied landscapes offers the perfect escape for those who are 'tired of London'. Sometimes known as north London's 'green lung', the Heath was the target of Sir Thomas Maryon Wilson, who was Lord of the Manor during much of the 19th century. During his reign he put forward fifteen bills in Parliament calling for the development of the area. He failed and in 1871, the year of his death, the part of the Heath that he owned was given to the nation. It now measures some 800 acres and belongs to the Corporation of London. The Heath has three rivers, 28 ponds and a running track.

CHURCH ROW

Off the southern end of Heath St, NW3
This beautiful street is Hampstead at its most village-like. The Row leads down to the charming church of St John at Hampstead where John Constable and his wife are buried. Nearby lies Hugh Gaitskell, Labour Party leader from 1955 to 1963. More luminaries including Laszlo Biro, inventor of the ballpoint pen, Marie Lloyd, music hall star, and Joseph Lister, pioneer of antiseptic surgery are buried in the nearby Hampstead Cemetary.

KENWOOD HOUSE

Hampstead Lane, NW3
☎ 020 8348 1286
Built for hanging judge the Earl of Mansfield, in the 1760s, Kenwood House was left to the nation in 1927. The Iveagh Bequest, left by the Earl of Iveagh, head of the Guinness family, includes many Old Masters including Rembrandt, Gainsborough and Joshua Reynolds.

HIGHGATE CEMETERY

Swain's Lane, N6
☎ 020 7340 1834
Probably best known as the last resting place of *Das Kapital* author, Karl Marx, Highgate Cemetary is an overgrown wilderness of tombs, statuary and headstones. Part of its higgledy-piggledy nature is due to bombing suffered during the war. Much of the cemetary can only be visited on one of the excellent guided tours.

MUSEUMS

FENTON HOUSE

Hampstead Grove, NW3
☎ 020 7435 3471
One of Hampstead's biggest and oldest houses, Fenton House was built in the late 17th century, and houses an odd

Highgate Cemetery

combination of collections. The Benton Fletcher collection of early keyboard instruments, a range of pottery poodles, Chinese snuffboxes and 9th-century Oriental porcelain.

FREUD MUSEUM

20 Maresfield Gardens, NW3
☎ 020 7435 2002/5167
Home to Sigmund Freud, the creator and

KEATS' HOUSE

Wentworth Place, Keats Grove, NW3
☎ 020 7435 2062
Poet John Keats lived and wrote some of his most famous poems here from 1818 to 1820. A plum tree in the garden marks the spot where he sat and wrote *Ode to a Nightingale*. The museum contains the usual books and letters, along with the bed where he first discovered his consumption. Love of his life, Fanny Brawne, lived next door and her house is part of the museum.

Keat's House

Kenwood House

GREAT FOR KIDS

HAMPSTEAD SCIENTIFIC SOCIETY OBSERVATORY
Lower Terrace, NW3
☎ 020 8346 1056
At this evening attraction, (open weeknights from 8-10pm, clear skies permitting) visitors can look through a variety of telescopes at the planets and stars.

HIGHGATE WOOD
Muswell Hill Rd, N6
☎ 020 8444 6129
Great for kids, this large wood has a playground, trails and a nature hut.

Waterlow Park

GALLERIES

CAMDEN ARTS CENTRE
Arkwright Rd, corner of Finchley Rd, NW3
☎ 020 7435 2643
Borough of Camden community arts centre, with three gallery spaces, regular contemporary and historical exhibitions and talks by artists.

SHOPPING

DAVID & CHARLES WAINWRIGHT
28 Rosslyn Hill, NW3
☎ 020 7431 5900
A wide selection of goods from the Pacific.

SKATE ATTACK
95 Highgate Rd, NW5
☎ 020 7267 6961
Everything and anything to do with skates.

ENTERTAINMENT AND NIGHTLIFE

HAMPSTEAD COMEDY CLUB
The Washington, England's Lane, NW3
☎ 020 7207 7256
Comic turns every Saturday night.

KENWOOD LAKESIDE CONCERTS
Kenwood House, Hampstead Lane, NW3
☎ 020 7973 3427
Popular classical concerts in some lovely scenery, from July to September. Often involves fireworks.

LAUDERDALE HOUSE
Waterlow Park, Highgate Hill, N6
☎ 020 8348 8716
More popular classical music in some lovely scenery. London-based musicians in a small stately home.

THEATRES

HAMPSTEAD THEATRE
Avenue Rd, NW3
☎ 020 7722 9301
Strange looking theatre with a good reputation for exciting contemporary productions.

NEW END THEATRE
27 New End, NW3
☎ 020 7794 0022
Small theatre staging risqué but not too shocking productions.

PENTAMETERS
Three Horseshoes Pub, 28 Heath Rd, NW3
☎ 020 7435 3648
Eccentric venue staging a wide range of productions.

CENTRAL SCHOOL OF SPEECH AND DRAMA
64 Eton Ave, NW3
☎ 020 7722 8183
One of London's best drama schools, 'Central' pushes its students hard and stages some ten productions a term. Some are open to the public, and some are free. No guarantee of quality can be offered however. Remember, these are not yet professionals.

CINEMAS

SCREEN ON THE HILL
203 Haverstock Hill, NW3
☎ 020 7435 3366
Arthouse cinema.

EVERYMAN CINEMA
Hollybush Vale, NW3
☎ 0845 606 2345
Recently reopened repertory cinema.

SPORT & LEISURE

SWISS COTTAGE SPORTS CENTRE
Winchester Rd, NW3
☎ 020 7413 6490
Gym, two indoor pools, table tennis, squash, football, the works.

HAMPSTEAD HEATH PONDS
Hampstead Heath, NW3
☎ 020 7485 4491
Unusual outdoor swimming ponds.

PARLIAMENT HILL LIDO
Hampstead Heath, Gordon House Rd, NW5
☎ 0171-485 3873

WHERE TO STAY

HOTELS

AA RECOMMENDED

W3 HAMPSTEAD AND SWISS COTTAGE

★★★★ LONDON MARRIOTT HOTEL REGENTS PARK
128 King Henry's Rd NW3 3ST
(at the junct of Adelaide Rd and King Henry's Rd. Approximately 200yds off Finchley Rd, A41)
☎ 020 7722 7711 📠 020 7586 5822
Situated at Swiss Cottage, this large, modern hotel boasts a very good standard of accommodation. The spacious bedrooms all have large beds and excellent facilities; executive rooms have the benefit of a dedicated club lounge. Smart public areas include an open plan marbled lobby and bar-lounge.

Additionally, there is indoor leisure, free parking and a shop.
303 rooms (157 family & 102 no smoking) / International Cuisine / Indoor swimming pool (heated) / Sauna, Solarium, Gym, Hair & Beauty salon / Live entertainment / Lift, Night porter, Air cond / No dogs (ex guide dogs)
Price band £££

★★★ FORTE POSTHOUSE HAMPSTEAD
215 Haverstock Hill NW3 4RB
(take A41 to Swiss Cottage, just before this junction take feeder road left into Buckland Cres onto Belsize Av left into Haverstock Hill)
☎ 020 7794 8121 📠 020 7435 5586
Suitable for business and leisure travellers, this bright hotel provides modern accommodation in well equipped bedrooms. A recent refurbishment has completed two floors of smart 'Millennium' rooms. The Traders bar and restaurant is open for lunch and dinner.
140 rooms (170 no smoking) / Lift, Night porter

BED & BREAKFAST

AA RECOMMENDED

♦♦♦♦ SANDRINGHAM HOTEL
3 Holford Rd, Hampstead NW3 1AD
(from Hampstead Tube Station turn right into Heath St, take 4th street on right, then 1st left into Holford Rd)
☎ 020 7435 1569 📠 020 7431 5932
This impressive Victorian House is located in a quiet residential street just a short walk from Hampstead village. There is a comfortable lounge with flame fire and honesty bar, and the breakfast room overlooks a pretty walled garden. Bedrooms vary in size but all have TV, telephone and thoughtful extras such as mineral water and a decanter of sherry. Breakfast is not to be missed, with choices such as French toast, eggs Benedict and smoked salmon and scrambled eggs in addition to the traditional grill.
17 rooms (2 family & all no smoking) / No dogs (ex guide dogs) / No children under 8 years / No coaches

♦♦♦ THE LANGORF HOTEL
20 Frognal, Hampstead NW3 6AG
(approx 3m N of Oxford St and 3m S of M1, just off A41 Finchley Rd)
☎ 020 7794 4483 📠 020 7435 9055
This elegant Edwardian building has been thoughtfully and tastefully furnished and decorated throughout. Bedrooms are comfortably appointed with colourful decor, extras include 24 hour room

service, telephones and hairdryers. There is a small cosy reception lounge and an attractive dining room, where snacks and drinks are available all day. The continental breakfast buffet has plenty for all to choose from.
31 rooms (4 family) / No dogs / Lift / No coaches
Price band £££

♦♦♦ SWISS COTTAGE HOTEL
4 Adamson Rd, Swiss Cottage NW3 3HP
☎ 020 7722 2281 📠 020 7483 4588
This attractive hotel is in a peaceful residential area a short distance from the bustle of the Finchley Road, and five minutes from Regent's Park. Accommodation is comfortable and well equipped; a range of light snacks is served in the elegant public rooms throughout the day.
54 rooms (5 family) / No dogs (ex guide dogs) / Lift

♦♦♦ LA GAFFE
107-111 Heath St NW3 6SS
(at top end of Heath St, 200yds from Hampstead Underground)
☎ 020 7435 4941 & 435 8965
📠 020 7794 7592
A warm Italian welcome is assured at this friendly family-run guest house. Bedrooms are compact and modestly furnished but

La Gaffe

well equipped, and the colourful soft furnishings add to the comfort of the rooms. A popular Italian restaurant is available to guests.
18 rooms (1 family & all no smoking) / No dogs (ex guide dogs) / No coaches
Price band £££

NW6 KILBURN

♦ ♦ ♦ DAWSON HOUSE HOTEL
72 Canfield Gardens NW6 3ED

☎ 020 7624 0079 & 7624 6525

📠 020 7644 6321

This small hotel is situated in a quiet residential area in South Hampstead, offering easy access to the centre of London. The accommodation is comfortable and well equipped, with modern en suite facilities. There is a guest lounge and an attractive rear garden.

15 rooms (2 family) / No dogs / No children under 5yrs / No coaches

NW11 GOLDERS GREEN

♦ ♦ ♦ CENTRAL HOTEL
35 Hoop Ln, Golders Green NW11 8BS

(M11/M40 to A406 E, turn right at Finchley Rd onto A598, hotel near 1st traffic lights)

☎ 020 8458 5636 📠 020 8455 4792

This privately owned and run commercial hotel is located off the Finchley Road with good access to the North Circular. Bedrooms are bright, fresh and well equipped with modern en suite facilities. Breakfast is served in the dining room located in the main building.

26 rooms / No dogs
Price band £,£ 💳

Anchor Hotel

♦ ♦ ANCHOR HOTEL
10 West Heath Dr, Golders Green NW11 7QH

(North Circular A406 onto A598 Finchley Rd. At tube turn left then 1st right)

☎ 020 8458 8764 📠 020 8455 3204

Privately owned and run, this popular guest house has comfortably appointed and suitably equipped bedrooms. It is located close to Golders Green tube station (on the Northern line) and the town centre.

11 rooms (3 family) / No dogs (ex guide dogs) / No coaches
Price band £,£ 💳

WHERE TO EAT
RESTAURANTS
AA RECOMMENDED

⚜ ⚜ BYRON'S RESTAURANT
3a Downshire Hill Hampstead NW3 1NR
🕾/🕿 020 7435 3544

Informal restaurant in a quiet side street off Hampstead High Street. Around eight starters and main courses see the likes of first-class saffron and chilli risotto with prawns, then well-timed pan-fried calves' liver on wilted spinach with rich sage-flavoured gravy, The wine list is fairly short but interesting, with some less common French bottles.

Fixed L £ ALC £

⚜ ⚜ CUCINA
45a South End Road NW3 2QB
🕾 020 7435 7814 🕿 020 7435 7815

The spacious colourful room is enhanced by lots of different artwork, and offset by a sharp, snappy menu that nods towards the Sugar Club in style. Thus one can expect Pacific rim dishes along the lines of

hot-and-sour tiger prawn laksa with coconut and lime gremolata, and chargrilled mahi mahi with Cajun-spiced sweetcorn and pepper 'succotash'. However, the more classic twice-baked goats' cheese soufflé, and chargrilled rib of beef with frites sit just as happily on the menu. The one side of A4 that represents the wine list is punchy, modern and to the point with prices, on the whole, below the £20 mark.

Fixed L/D £ ALC £

⚜ GLOBE
100 Avenue Road Swiss Cottage NW3 3HF
🕾 020 7722 7200 🕿 020 7722 2772

Eclectic modern cooking in a lively atmosphere. An abundance of glass and bright blue and yellow decor will cheer up any dull day. Enthusiastic and friendly staff.

Fixed L £ ALC £

⚜ ⚜ QUINCY'S RESTAURANT
675 Finchley Road NW2 2JP
🕾 020 7794 8499

The sort of cosy, informal little restaurant all neighbourhoods should have. Monthly changing menu with daily soup and fish dishes, a short choice, but it is all thoughtfully constructed, with cooking that is judicious and well-tempered. Dishes are concisely described - seared chicken with chickpea salsa, soy and chilli, for example - and vegetarian choice is well balanced Dinner only, but it's a bonus to find somewhere so good open on Sunday night.

Fixed D £ £

PUBS, INNS & OTHER PLACES

THE HOLLYBUSH
22 Holly Mount, NW3
🕾 020 7435 2892

Quiet unspoilt pub not far from Hampstead tube.

THE FLASK
14 Flask Walk, NW3
🕾 020 7435 4580

Atmospheric old pub with original Victorian panelling, conservatory and garden. A favourite haunt of comedians and artists. Good, home-cooked food.

JACK STRAW'S CASTLE
North End Way, NW3
🕾 020 7435 8885

Not the home of the New Labour cabinet minister, but a pub named after a leader of the Peasants' Revolt, who was executed outside.

FREEMASONS ARMS
32 Downshire Hill, NW3 1NT
🕾 020 7433 6811

Overlooking Hampstead Heath, the Freemasons Arms has the largest pub garden in central London. The Pell Mell pitch is part of the original 19th-century buildings.

BAR ROOM BAR
48 Rosslyn Hill, NW3
🕾 020 7 435 0808

Converted pub with an oyster bar.

SPANIARDS INN
Spaniards Rd, NW3 7JJ
🕾 020 8731 6571

A popular 16th-century pub with a checkered past. It has been a toll-house and the home of a Spanish ambassador. Visitors have included Dick Turpin, Keats, Byron and Dickens. The huge garden includes an aviary.

LOUIS PATISSERIE
32 Heath Rd, NW3
🕾 020 7435 9908

European-style tearoom

MARINE ICES
8 Haverstock Hill, NW3
🕾 020 7485 3132

Old-fashioned Italian ice cream parlour. Italian restaurant next door.

WHERE TO STAY
HOTELS
AA RECOMMENDED

HEATHROW

★★★★ THE EXCELSIOR
Bath Rd UB7 0DU
(adj M4 spur at junc with A4)
☎ 020 8759 6611 📠 020 8759 3421
Heathrow's largest hotel offers its international clientele a wide range of eating and drinking options, including an Irish-themed pub, a fish restaurant and a carvery, as well as an all-day cafe. There is a choice of room styles, with the Crown Club offering more comfortable rooms.
830 rooms (55 family & 390 no smoking) / Indoor swimming pool (heated) / Sauna, Solarium, Gym, Jacuzzi/spa / Lift, Night porter, Air cond

★★★★ FORTE CREST HEATHROW
Sipson Rd, Langley SL3 8PT
(M4 junct4, keep left, take first left into Holloway Lane, left at mini rdbt then immediately left through hotel gates)
☎ 020 8759 2323 📠 020 8897 8659
This large, modern hotel, well situated for both the airport and M4/M25 motorways, has services and amenities designed for the international traveller. Bedrooms are smart and comfortable, there is a wide choice of restaurant and refreshment facilities and good modern conference and meeting rooms.
610 rooms (284 family & 359 no smoking) / English, Italian & Chinese Cuisine / Lift, Night porter / No dogs (ex guide dogs)

★★★★ HEATHROW MARRIOTT
Ditton Rd, Langley SL3 8PT
(from junct 5 of M4/A4, follow 'Langley' signs and turn left at traffic lights into Ditton Road)
☎ 01753 544244 📠 01753 540272
This large busy hotel, just off the M4, manages successfully to juggle the demands of international travellers without losing the personal touch that makes all guests feel welcome. A wide range of services is offered, plus a choice of eating options and an indoor leisure centre. Bedrooms are comfortable and well equipped.
380 rooms (149 family & 231 no smoking) / Mediterranean Cuisine / Indoor swimming pool (heated) / Tennis (hard) / Sauna, Solarium, Gym, Beautician / Live entertainment / Lift, Night porter, Air cond / No dogs (ex guide dogs)
Price band £££

★★★★✿ HOLIDAY INN CROWNE PLAZA
Stockley Rd UB7 9NA
(leave M4 junct 4 follow signs to Uxbridge on A408, hotel entrance approx 400yds on left)
☎ 01895 445555 📠 01895 445122
Close to Heathrow and the motorways, this modern hotel offers a particularly good range of facilities for the international traveller, as well as service and accommodation of a high quality. There is a choice of bars serving food, and a modern French restaurant. Conference facilities are versatile, and there is a 24-hour leisure complex as well as golfing. Air-conditioning, mini bars and 24-hour room service are standard in all bedrooms, from the 'executive' style through to the 'superiors' and luxurious 'club' rooms.
458 rooms (220 family & 187 no smoking) / European Cuisine / Indoor swimming pool (heated) / Golf, Sauna, Solarium, Gym, Jacuzzi/spa, Beauty therapy room / Helipad / Lift, Night porter, Air cond

★★★★ LONDON HEATHROW MARRIOTT HOTEL
Bath Rd
☎ 020 8990 1100 📠 020 8990 1110
This brand new hotel has all the hallmarks expected of a modern airport hotel. There is a spacious atrium with several eating and drinking options leading from it. Secure car parking, meeting rooms and very good leisure facilities, all in very good condition, make this a well-rounded establishment. Spacious bedrooms are very well sound-proofed and equipped with a useful range of amenities.
390 rooms (20 family & 20 no smoking) / International Cuisine / Indoor swimming pool (heated) / Sauna, Solarium, Gym, Jacuzzi/spa / Lift, Night porter, Air cond
Price band £££

★★★★ RAMADA
Bath Rd TW6 2AQ
(leave M4 junct4 follow spur road towards airport, take 2nd turning left & follow road to rdbt take 2nd exit. This road leads to hotel)
☎ 020 8897 6363 📠 020 8897 1113
This busy hotel, formerly one of the Ramada group, offers views of one of Heathrow's main runways. There are well equipped, up-to-the-minute conference facilities, and the Icarus bar is a popular meeting place.
650 rooms (140 no smoking) / International Cuisine / Sauna, Solarium, Gym / Live entertainment / Lift, Night porter, Air cond / No dogs (ex guide dogs)

★★★ FORTE POSTHOUSE HEATHROW AIRPORT
118 Bath Rd UB3 5AJ
(leave M4 junct 4, take spur road to Heathrow Airport, 1st left off towards A4, on to A4 Bath Road, through 3 traffic lights, hotel on left)
☎ 0870 400 9040 📠 020 8564 9265
Well positioned for both the business and leisure traveller, this bright hotel provides accommodation equipped to up-to-date modern standards, especially Posthouse's new Millennium rooms.
186 rooms (100 no smoking) / International Cuisine / Lift, Night porter, Air cond / No dogs (ex guide dogs)
Price band £££

★★★ THE HEATHROW PARK
Bath Rd, Longford UB7 0EQ
☎ 020 8759 2400 📠 020 8759 5278
This quiet hotel offers extensive and sizeable meeting facilities, two dining choices, shop and business centre. Three styles of bedroom are available, some of which have more facilities than others. The first-floor restaurant and bar have good views of the airport's western runway. Free use of a nearby health centre is provided.
310 rooms (55 family & 140 no smoking) / Continental Cuisine / Night porter, Air cond

★★★ MASTER ROBERT
Great West Rd TW5 0BD
☎ 020 8570 6261 📠 020 8569 4016
The Master Robert is conveniently located three-and-a-half miles from Heathrow on the A4 towards London. The well equipped bedrooms are modern in style having been recently refurbished and are set in motel-style buildings behind the main hotel premises. Public areas include a residents bar lounge, a restaurant and a popular bistro.
94 rooms (8 family & 33 no smoking) / English & Continental Cuisine / Night porter / No dogs (ex guide dogs)
Price band £££

★★★ NOVOTEL
Junction 4 M4, Cherry Ln UB7 9HB
(leave M4 junct 4 follow signs for Uxbridge(A408), take 2nd exit off traffic island into Cherry Ln signed West Drayton. Hotel on left)
☎ 01895 431431 📠 01895 431221
With convenient access to the M4 and M25 motorways, the Novotel offers comfortable and well equipped accommodation for business and leisure guests alike. The rooms have been upgraded to the new company standard. Overlooked by bedrooms above, the huge

indoor atrium is bright and airy, offering spacious public areas, with a cocktail bar, indoor swimming pool and fitness centre. The keen and enthusiastic team of staff are on hand to assist at all times.

178 rooms (29 family & 112 no smoking) / International Cuisine / Indoor swimming pool (heated) / Gym / Lift, Night porter
Price band £££ 🗲

★★HOTEL IBIS
112/114 Bath Rd UB3 5AL
☎ 020 8759 4888 📠 020 8564 7894
This busy hotel provides good levels of comfort for the budget conscious business and leisure user. Modern and well maintained facilities are provided in the bedrooms and on the ground floor there is a well run buffet style restaurant as well as a bar where snacks are available throughout most of the day and night. A regular shuttle service is available to and from the airport.

354 rooms (134 no smoking) / International Cuisine / Lift, Night porter
Price band ££ 🗲

⌂ TRAVEL INN
362 Uxbridge Rd UB4 0HF
(from M4 junct 3 follow A312 north, straight across next rdbt onto dual carriageway, at A4020 junc turn left, Travel Inn is 100yds on the right)
☎ 020 8573 7479 📠 020 8569 1204
This modern building offers accommodation in smart, spacious and well equipped bedrooms, all with en-suite bathrooms. Refreshments may be taken at the nearby family restaurant.
40 rooms
Price band £

GATWICK

★★★★ COPTHORNE EFFINGHAM PARK
West Park Rd, RH10 3EU
(from M25 jct 10, take A264 towards East Grinstead, straight over rdbt, at 2nd rdbt L along B2028. Hotel on R)
☎ 01342 714994 📠 01342 716039
This peacefully located hotel is set in 40 acres of grounds, and offers a wide range of leisure facilities. The main restaurant is an open-plan, Mediterranean-themed brasserie, and snacks are also available in the leisure club bar.

122 rooms (6 family & 36 no smoking) / English & Mediterranean cuisine / Indoor swimming pool (heated) / Golf (9) / Tennis (hard) / Sauna, Solarium, Gym / Croquet lawn / Dance studio / Lift, Night porter / No dogs (ex guide dogs)
Price band £££ 🗲

★★★★ 🏵 🏵 COPTHORNE LONDON GATWICK
Copthorne Way, RH10 3PG
(on A264, 2m E of A264/B2036 rdbt)
☎ 01342 714971 📠 01342 717375
Set in 100 acres of wooded, landscaped gardens containing jogging track, a putting green and a petanque pit. The hotel itself is built around a 16th-century farmhouse and has comfortable bedrooms divided into three categories. In addition to the brasserie there is a more formal restaurant, the Lion D'Or, where a wide-ranging menu is served.

227 rooms (10 family & 98 no smoking) / English & Continental cuisine / Indoor swimming pool (heated) / Tennis (hard), Squash, Solarium, Gym / Live entertainment / Lift, Night Porter
Price band £££ 🗲

★★★★ LE MERIDIAN LONDON GATWICK
North Terminal, RH6 0PH
(M23 jct 9, follow dual carriageway to 2nd rdbt, hotel large white building straight ahead)
☎ 0870 4008494 📠 01293 567739
This modern hotel, just minutes from the terminals, has smart rooms with a wide range of facilities. A new executive club floor has recently opened, with its own lounge and extra services. Visitors have a range of eating options, including a brasserie, a French-style café and an Oriental restaurant. The north terminal is reached via a covered walkway.

494 rooms (36 family & 228 no smoking) / European & Oriental cuisine / Indoor swimming pool (heated) / Sauna, Solarium, Gym / Lift, Night porter, Air cond
Price band £££ 🗲

★★★ POSTHOUSE GATWICK AIRPORT
Povey Cross Rd, RH6 0BA
(from M23 jct 9 follow signs for Gatwick, then Reigate. Hotel on L after 3rd rdbt)
☎ 01293 771621 📠 01293 771054
Suitable for both the business and leisure traveller, this bright hotel provides modern accommodation in well-equipped bedrooms with en suite bathrooms.
210 rooms (19 family & 105 no smoking) / International cuisine / Lift, Night porter 🗲

★★★ STANHILL COURT
Stanhill Rd, Charlwood RH6 0EP
(N of Charlwood towards Newdigate)
☎ 01293 862166 📠 01293 862773
Set in 35 acres of grounds, this baronial-style hotel has retained many of its original Victorian features, such as stained-glass panels. Many rooms have four-poster beds, all are individually decorated and well equipped. There is a cosy lounge, enclosed conservatory patio bar and wood-panelled restaurant.

12 rooms (3 family & 2 no smoking) / International cuisine / Tennis (hard) / Fishing / Croquet / Night porter / No dogs (ex guide dogs) / No coaches 🗲

★★★ THISTLE GATWICK
Brighton Rd, RH6 8PH
(2m N of Gatwick, on A23. At Shell petrol station, L into Horley Row, then immediately R)
☎ 01293 786992 📠 01293 820625
A hotel of two parts, one side consists of the original inn, parts of which date back to the 16th century, while the main part houses meeting rooms, a restaurant with cocktail bar, and comfortable bedrooms. Like most hotels in the area, the Thistle provides a shuttle service to Gatwick.

78 rooms (2 family & 55 no smoking) / International cuisine / Outdoor swimming pool / Night porter 🗲

★★ 🏵 LANGSHOTT MANOR
Langshott Ln, RH6 9LN
(from A23 take Ladbroke Rd, turn off the Chequers rdbt to Langshott, after 0.75 miles, entrance to hotel is on R)
☎ 01293 786680 📠 01293 783905
This small Elizabethan manor house is set in beautiful gardens. The cosy day rooms include a morning room/bar and a gallery sitting room. Bedrooms combine modern comforts with individuality. Dinner is served in the beamed dining room.

15 rooms (all no smoking) / European cuisine / Croquet lawn / Night porter / No dogs (ex guide dogs) / No coaches

⌂ TRAVEL INN
North Terminal, Longbridge Way RH6 0NX
(from M23 head for North Terminal, at rdbt take 3rd exit, hotel on R)
☎ 01293 568158 📠 01293 568278
This modern building offers accommodation in smart, spacious and well equipped bedrooms, all with en suite bathrooms. Refreshments may be taken at the nearby family restaurant.
121 rooms
Price band £

⌂ TRAVELODGE
Church Rd, Lowfield Heath, RH11 0PQ
(1 mile S of Gatwick, off A23 jct 10 M23)
☎ 01293 533441 📠 01293 535369
This modern building offers accommodation in smart, spacious and well equipped bedrooms, all with en suite bathrooms. Refreshments may be taken at the nearby family restaurant.
126 rooms
Price band ££

BED & BREAKFAST

AA RECOMMENDED

HEATHROW

♦ ♦ ♦ ♦ THE COTTAGE
150-152 High St, Cranford TW5 9PD
(leave M4 junct 3 onto A312 to traffic lights & turn left. Continue and turn left after 1st pub on left)
☎ 020 8897 1815 📠 020 8897 3117
This hotel is so peacefully situated, tucked away in a cul de sac behind the Jolly Gardener Pub on the High Street, that it could be miles from Heathrow, but is in fact only 10 minutes away. Nearby attractions include Windsor and Hampton Court. Accommodation provides a high level of comfort.
11 rooms (2 family & all no smoking) / No dogs

♦ ♦ ♦ ♦ HARMONDSWORTH HALL
Summerhouse Ln, Harmondsworth Village UB7 0BG
☎ 020 8759 1824 & 0385 236597
📠 020 8897 6385
Tucked away in the old part of Harmondsworth and close to two village pubs this guest house is ideal for those who are visiting the area or catching flights from Heathrow. Bedrooms are individual and vary in size, with the larger ones being extremely spacious. All are equipped with hairdryers and remote control televisions.
9 rooms (3 family & 4 no smoking) / No coaches

♦ ♦ ♦ LONGFORD
550 Bath Rd, Longford UB7 0EE
(approx 1.5m from M25 junct 14)
☎ 01753 682969 📠 01753 794189
Situated on the edge of the village of Longford, this guest house is conveniently located for Heathrow Airport and the motorway network. The building, which dates from the 17th century, retains some of its original period features including timber-framed walls. Downstairs there is a comfortably furnished residents' lounge and a breakfast room.
5 rooms (all no smoking) / No dogs / No children under 10 years / No coaches
Price band £

♦ ♦ CIVIC
87/89 Lampton Rd TW3 4DP
☎ 020 8572 5107 📠 020 8814 0203
Popular with holidaymakers using nearby Heathrow Airport, this guest house, with off-street parking, is close to the centre of Hounslow and a few minutes' walk to the Metro. Rooms continue to be modernised and updated, many now have en suite showers, and all have satellite TV. Breakfast is served in the spacious dining room.
15 rooms (8 family & 3 no smoking) / No dogs (ex guide dogs)
Price band ££

♦ ♦ SHALIMAR HOTEL
Staines Rd TW3 3JJ
(exit M4 junct 3, to Hounslow, at rdbt turn left, at next rdbt bear right, at 3rd traffic lights turn right, next lights turn left)
☎ 020 8577 7070 & 8572 281 & (free) 0500 238239
📠 020 8569 6789
This centrally located hotel, handy for Heathrow Airport, offers simply decorated, well equipped bedrooms. A number of new luxury rooms have recently been completed. There is an attractive open-plan restaurant, bar and lounge overlooking the garden.
39 rooms (5 family & 2 no smoking) / No dogs (ex guide dogs)
Price band £

♦ SKYLARK
297 Bath Rd TW3 3DB
(100yds from Hounslow tube station)
☎ 020 8577 8455 📠 020 8577 8741
Situated near Heathrow Airport and Hounslow station, this guest house continues to be updated and improved. Some of the bedrooms are small but are adequately furnished in modern style.
18 rooms (3 family & 2 no smoking) / No dogs
Price band ££

Shalimar Hotel

GATWICK

♦ ♦ ♦ ♦ BARNWOOD HOTEL
Balcombe Rd, Pound Hill RH10 7RU
☎ 01293 425800 📠 01293 425808
The Barnwood has all the facilities and services expected of a modern hotel. Public areas are well furnished and decorated, and the restaurant offers an interesting menu with a range of Indonesian as well as more traditional British dishes.
35 rooms (3 family & all no smoking) / No dogs (ex guide dogs)
Price band ££

♦ ♦ ♦ ♦ GAINSBOROUGH LODGE
39 Massetts Rd, RH6 7DT
(2 miles NE of Gatwick, next to the A23)
☎ 01293 783982 📠 01293 785365
Accommodation is split between the main Edwardian lodge and the next door bungalow, which is reserved for non-smokers. Day rooms include a TV lounge and a conservatory breakfast room where the friendly owners offer a particularly wide choice of breakfast dishes, including vegetarian specialities.
18 rooms (5 family) / No dogs

♦ ♦ ♦ ♦ THE LAWN
30 Massetts Rd RH6 7DE
(exit M23 Jct 9, follow signs to A23 Redhill, at rdbt by garage take 3rd exit, Massetts Rd 200 yards on R)
☎ 01293 775751 📠 01293 821803
This fine detached Victorian house offers en suite and no smoking bedrooms. The rooms are brightly decorated and equipped with many thoughtful extras. A choice is offered at breakfast. Guests may leave their cars here for a fee while on holiday.
7 rooms (3 family & all no smoking) / No coaches
Price band ££

♦♦♦♦ ROSEMEAD
19 Church Rd, RH6 7EY
(M23 Jct 9, follow A23 Redhill signs thru 3 rdbts, Church Rd is 4th on R)

☎ 01293 784965 ✆ 01293 430547

Guests can expect a warm welcome at this non-smoking Edwardian guest house. Bedrooms are brightly decorated and include portable fans and beverage facilities. Breakfast is taken in the smart dining room and secure parking is available for guests who want to leave their cars behind when they go abroad.
6 rooms (2 family & all no smoking) / No coaches

♦♦♦♦ TRUMBLES
Stan Hill RH6 0EP

☎ 01293 862925

Set in a peaceful countryside location, this charming guest house offers comfortable and well equipped bedrooms. An indoor koi pond provides the focus of public areas that include an attractive lounge and spacious conservatory where breakfast is served. Complimentary transfer to the airport is available.
6 rooms (1 family & all no smoking) No coaches

♦♦♦♦ VULCAN LODGE
27 Massetts Rd, RH6 7DQ
(exit M23 at J9, take R exit at 4th rdbt, Massetts Rd 2nd on R, premises 0.25miles on R)

☎ 01293 771522 ✆ 01293 786206

Guests are warmly welcomed to this charming, non-smoking guest house. Bedrooms are all individually decorated,

well equipped and feature many thoughtful extras. There is a comfortable lounge, and breakfast is served in a delightful dining room.
4 rooms (1 family & all no smoking) / No dogs (ex guide dogs) / No coaches
Price band £ 🍴

♦♦♦♦ WAYSIDE MANOR FARM
Norwood Hill, RH6 0ET
(M25 Jct 8, S on A217 thru Reigate follow Gatwick signs. 2 miles S of Reigate R into Ironsbottom, 2nd R Collendean Lane, up to X-rds Norwood Hill)

☎ 01293 862692 ✆ 01293 863417

Ten minutes from Gatwick in a rural location, this charming Edwardian farmhouse has spacious bedrooms with many extras. Breakfast is taken at a large table in the elegant dining room. Dinner is not available but there is a good country pub nearby. Overseas visitors or guests without a car can be collected from Gatwick for a nominal charge.
3 rooms (all no smoking) / No dogs / no coaches
Price band £

♦♦♦ CORNER HOUSE HOTEL
72 Massetts Rd, RH6 7ED
(M23 Jct9, over 1st rdbt, 4th exit on 2nd rdbt to Crowley/Redhill A23, 3rd exit at next rdbt 2nd turning on R, Massetts Rd 1st on L)

Corner House offers free transport to and from Gatwick 24 hours a day. There is also reduced rate, long-term parking on site. Bedrooms are well equipped, and some are in a separate building across the road. A full bar is available and the restaurant offers an excellent selection.
25 rooms (6 family & all no smoking)
Price band £ 🍴

♦♦♦ LITTLE FOXES
Charlwood Rd, Ifield Wood RH11 0JY
(M23 Jct10, Crawley Avenue and straight over 2 rdbts, at 3rd turn R into Ifield Ave, house 1 mile on L)

☎ 01293 529206 ✆ 01293 551434

Located in a rural setting Little Foxes offers comfortable accommodation and a relaxing atmosphere. Bedrooms are brightly decorated and furnished with modern pine. Guests are offered a choice at breakfast and an honesty bar is available.
10 rooms (3 family & 4 no smoking) / No dogs (ex guide dogs) / No coaches
Price band £ 🍴

♦♦♦ PRINSTEAD
Oldfield Rd, RH6 7EP
(M23 Jct 9, follow signs for airport. At rdbt take A23 and continue to Texaco garage, take 1st R into Woodyard Ave)

☎ 01293 785233 ✆ 01293 820624

This spacious Victorian guest house is located in a quiet road. Rooms are divided between the main house and an adjoining building and are all neatly decorated and furnished. Courtesy transport to Gatwick can be arranged.
8 rooms (All no smoking) / No dogs (ex guide dogs) / No coaches
Price band £ 🍴

WHERE TO EAT
RESTAURANTS
AA RECOMMENDED

⊛ CROWNE PLAZA LONDON – HEATHROW
Stockley Road UB7 9NA

☎ 01895 445555 ✆ 01895 445122

Smart restaurant from the Simply Nico chain serving modern British food (seared tuna, with lime and chilli, and rump of lamb with Tatin provençale) and a fairly serious choice of wines.

⊛⊛ COPTHORNE, COPTHORNE LONDON GATWICK
Copthorne Way RH10 3PG

☎ 01342 714971 ✆ 01342 717375

The average airport hotel is unlikely to boast the 100 acres of gardens and woodlands that belong to this much extended 16th-century farmhouse. The glass-partitioned Lion d'Or restaurant is traditional in style with exposed beams, cosy corners and crisp linen. Poached trout fillet with butter, lemon and caper sauce, and strawberry charlotte are typical menu examples. Espresso is served Turkish style in a glass beaker - be warned, it's a potent brew.
Fixed L £ ALC ££

Call the AA Hotel Booking Service on 0870 5050505 to book at AA recognised hotels and B&Bs in the UK, or through our internet site: http://www.theaa.co.uk/hotels

WHERE TO STAY
HOTELS
AA RECOMMENDED

Mount View

E4 CHINGFORD

♦♦♦ RIDGEWAY HOTEL

115/117 The Ridgeway, North Chingford E4 6QU

☎ 020 8529 1964

A friendly and informal hotel, the Ridgeway is family run and offers spacious and comfortable, well equipped bedrooms, all en suite. There is a combined restaurant, reception and bar and the menu has some Greek specialities.

20 rooms
Price band £££ 🍽

E6 EAST HAM

⌂ TRAVEL INN

1 Woolwich Manor Way, Beckton E6 4NT

(from A13 take A117, Woolwich Manor Way, towards City Airport, hotel on left after first rdbt)

☎ 020 7511 3853 ☎ 020 7511 4214

This modern building offers accommodation in smart, spacious and well equipped bedrooms, all en suite. Refreshments may be taken at the nearby family restaurant.

40 rooms
Price band £

E11 LEYTONSTONE

♦♦♦♦♦ LAKESIDE

51 Snaresbrook Rd, Wanstead E11 1PQ

(0.5m from end of M11 close to Snaresbrook Underground Station)

☎ 020 8989 6100

Overlooking a lake and within walking distance of an underground station, the house has many original features and is comfortably furnished. The spacious bedrooms are well equipped with modern facilities. A generous breakfast is served in the elegant lounge/dining room overlooking an attractive garden, weather permitting afternoon tea can be served on the patio.

3 rooms (all no smoking) / No dogs / No children under 12 years / No coaches

E18 SOUTH WOODFORD

♦♦♦ GROVE HILL HOTEL

38 Grove Hill, South Woodford E18 2JG

(off A11 London Rd, close to South Woodford tube station. Grove Hotel is off A11 just beyond The George pub)

☎ 020 8989 3344 & 8530 5286
☎ 020 8530 5286

A privately owned commercial hotel located in a quiet residential area. Bedrooms vary in size, and are modestly furnished and decorated. Breakfast is served in the nicely appointed dining

room and guests are offered a choice of English or continental.

21 rooms (2 family)
Price band £ 🍽

N4 FINSBURY PARK

♦♦♦♦♦ MOUNT VIEW

31 Mount View Rd N4 4SS

(A406, A1 to Highgate tube station, left into Shepherds Hill, end of road turn right, through Crouch End, left fork by bank)

☎ 020 8340 9222 ☎ 020 8342 8494

Situated in a quiet area of Crouch End, with its village-like atmosphere, this elegant Victorian house is tastefully decorated. Each bedroom has an original fireplace and a stripped wood floor with oriental rugs. The open plan dining room and kitchen look on to a pretty garden. Breakfasts are hearty and feature vegetarian options if desired. French and Dutch are spoken.

3 rooms (all no smoking) / No coaches
Price band £££ 🍽

N8 HORNSEY

♦♦♦ WHITE LODGE HOTEL

1 Church Ln, Hornsey N8 7BU

(A406 follow sign to Bounds Green, Hornsey High Rd and Church Lane)

☎ 020 8348 9765 ☎ 020 8340 7851

There's a warm and friendly atmosphere at this family run guest house. The bedrooms are neatly furnished and well decorated. There is a small comfortable lounge and a continental breakfast is served in the cosy dining room.

16 rooms (5 family & 4 no smoking) / No dogs (ex guide dogs) / No coaches
🍽

♦♦ ABER HOTEL

89 Crouch Hill N8 9EG

(Hotel 350yds S of A1201/A103 junction)

☎ 020 8340 2847 ☎ 020 8340 2847

The Aber Hotel provides comfortable, well maintained accommodation. There is a small lounge for the guest use and a choice of breakfast is offered. On street parking is available outside and the property is convenient to both bus and train routes into the centre of town.

9 rooms (4 family & all no smoking) / No dogs / No coaches
Price band £ 🍽

N10 MUSWELL HILL

★★★ RAGLAN HALL

8-12 Queens Ave, Muswell Hill N10 3NR

(North Circ B550 for Muswell Hill. At roundabout take last exit to Queens Avenue. Hotel is 75yds on the right.)

☎ 020 8883 9836 ☎ 020 8883 5002

Service and hospitality are hallmarks at Raglan Hall, which has an attractive frontage on the tree-lined Queens Avenue in Muswell Hill. Bedrooms vary in size but all are well equipped. Public areas centre on a relaxing bar and meals are carefully prepared.

46 rooms (8 family & 6 no smoking) / Mediterranean Cuisine / Night porter / No dogs (ex guide dogs)
Price band £££ 🍽

♦ ♦ ♦ GROSVENOR
18 Grosvenor Rd, Muswell Hill N10 2DS
(A406 & follow signs for Muswell Hill/Friern Barnet. Right onto Colney Hatch Lane (B550). Take 5th turn on left to top & bear left)
☎ 020 8883 0487 ⓕ 020 8374 9518
Situated in a residential street in the heart of Muswell Hill, this property offers accommodation that is bright and well presented, with smart modern facilities. Families are welcome. Breakfast is served by a pretty bay window overlooking the garden. Tennis can be arranged nearby.
2 rooms (all no smoking) / No dogs / No children under 10 years / No coaches
Price band £

Grosvenor

NW2 BRENT CROSS, CRICKLEWOOD

♦ ♦ ♦ THE GARTH HOTEL
64-76 Hendon Way, Cricklewood NW2 2NL
(on A41, 4.5m from Oxford Street. 1.5m from M1)
☎ 020 8455 4742 & 8209 1511
ⓕ 020 8455 4742
Located to the north, in easy reach of the M1 and the West End, this family-run hotel continues to improve with the upgrading of the bar and lounge areas. The bright bedrooms are suitably furnished and equipped. An evening meal is available, served in the attractive Tivoli restaurant. Continental breakfast is included in the tariff, an additional charge is made for cooked breakfast.
53 rooms (9 family & 25 no smoking) / No dogs (ex guide dogs)

♦ ♦ ♦ VICTORIAN LONDON
89 Somerton Rd NW2 1RU
☎ 020 8830 6589 ⓕ 020 8830 7589
A semi-detached house located in a residential avenue close to major transport links. It is decorated in Victorian style, especially evident in the hall which is filled with ornaments and memorabilia. The compact bedrooms are well equipped, have free standing shower cabinets and heavy drapes.
3 rooms (all no smoking) / No dogs / No children under 4 years

NW4 HENDON

♦ ♦ ♦ PEACEHAVEN HOTEL
94 Audley Rd, Hendon Central NW4 3HB
(turn off A41 at Hendon Central, turn right into Vivian Ave then 5th left into Audley Rd)
☎ 020 8202 9758 & 020 8202 1225
ⓕ 020 8202 9758
Located in a quiet residential area, Peacehaven is within easy walking distance of Hendon Central tube station and has convenient parking in the street. Privately owned and run, it has a warm atmosphere and offers modern accommodation with comfortable, well equipped bedrooms.
13 rooms / No dogs (ex guide dogs)
Price band ££

NW7 MILL HILL

⌂ WELCOME LODGE
Welcome Break Service Area, London Gateway, M1, Mill Hill NW7 3HB
(on M1, between junct 2 & 3 - northbound. Accessible from southbound carriageway)
☎ 020 8906 0611 ⓕ 020 8906 3654
This modern building offers accommodation in smart, spacious and well equipped bedrooms, suitable for families and businessmen, and all with en suite bathrooms. Refreshments may be taken at the nearby family restaurant.
101 rooms
Price band ££

SE9 ELTHAM

♦ ♦ ♦ YARDLEY COURT
18 Court Rd, Eltham SE9 5PZ
(leave M25 junct 3 onto A20 to London, turn right at traffic lights at Court Rd, Mottingham 0.5m on left)
☎ 020 8850 1850 ⓕ 020 8488 0421
Ideally located on the town edge, one mile from the A20 and within walking distance of the station with its fast links to London, this Victorian detached villa offers value accommodation with modern facilities. Bedrooms are of a good size and are well equipped. Tasty English breakfasts are taken in the modern dining room which overlooks the pretty rear garden.
9 rooms (1 family & 3 no smoking) / No coaches

SE19 NORWOOD

♦ ♦ ♦ CRYSTAL PALACE TOWER HOTEL
114 Church Rd, Crystal Palace SE19 2UB
(hotel on A212 at Crystal Palace)
☎ 020 8653 0176 ⓕ 020 8653 5167
Situated close to the National Sports Centre, this Victorian villa has been carefully renovated to provide simply appointed, well-equipped accommodation with friendly and attentive service. Tasty English breakfasts are taken in the cosy dining room and other public areas retain many original features including moulded cornices and carved doors. The large car park is an additional advantage.
9 rooms (4 family) / No coaches
Price band ££

⌂ TRAVELODGE
200 York Rd, Battersea SW11 3SA
(from Wandsworth Bridge southern rdbt, take York Road A3205 towards Battersea. Travelodge 0.5m on left)
☎ 020 7228 5508
This modern building offers accommodation in smart, spacious and well equipped bedrooms, all with en suite bathrooms. Refreshments may be taken at the nearby family restaurant.
80 rooms
Price band ££

SW4 CLAPHAM

★ ★ ★ THE WINDMILL ON THE COMMON
Southside, Clapham Common SW4 9DE
☎ 020 8673 4578 ⓕ 020 8675 1486
A traditional 18th-century pub forms the nucleus of this comfortable hotel which has been skilfully extended to provide modern bedroom accommodation. There are three large bars, a bistro counter, a small lounge and a separate wood-panelled restaurant.
29 rooms (15 no smoking) / European Cuisine / Night porter
Price band £££

⌂ LONDON PUTNEY BRIDGE TRAVEL INN CAPITAL
3 Putney Bridge Approach SW6 3JD
☎ 020 7471 8300 ⓕ 020 7471 8315
This modern building offers accommodation in smart, spacious and well equipped bedrooms, all with en-suite bathrooms. Refreshments may be taken at the nearby family restaurant.
Price band ££

SW15 PUTNEY

❀ PHOENIX BAR & GRILL
162 Pentlow St, Putney SW15 1LY
☎ 020 8780 3131 ⓕ 020 8780 1114
Enjoy a quiet lunch at this large, white fronted building on the western fringe of Putney. The front terrace opens up the room in summer. Service is pleasant and cheerful, and the menu is simple yet modern, hinting at confident technique and bold flavours.

SW19 WIMBLEDON

★★★★⊛ ⊛ CANNIZARO HOUSE

West Side, Wimbledon Common SW19 4UE

(approaching from A3 follow A219 signed Wimbledon into Parkside and past old fountain sharp right then 2nd on right)

☎ 020 8879 1464 📠 020 8879 7338

This familiar Wimbledon landmark is a haven of peace and quiet close to London. The bedrooms, furnished and decorated in country-house style, look out on the original park, particularly lovely in spring when daffodils, then bluebells and azaleas are at their best. Reception rooms are richly decorated and endowed with oils, murals and massive fireplaces. The restaurant and private dining rooms serve a high standard of cuisine, and in summer, cocktails on the terrace make an elegant prelude to a meal.

45 rooms (6 no smoking) / Lift, Night porter / No dogs (ex guide dogs) / No coaches / No children under 8 years

♦♦♦ KINGS LODGE HOTEL

5 Kings Rd, Wimbledon SW19 8PL

☎ 020 8545 0191 📠 020 8545 0381

Well appointed accommodation is available at this small privately-owned hotel within walking distance of Wimbledon station. Bedrooms vary in size and are furnished to meet the needs of both the commercial and tourist visitor. Evening meals (available by arrangement) and breakfast are served in the attractive dining room.

7 rooms (4 family) / No dogs (ex guide dogs) / No coaches

♦♦♦ WORCESTER HOUSE

38 Alwyne Rd, Wimbledon SW19 7AE

(turn off A3, to Worple Rd & follow to end, turn left & 2nd right to Alwyne Rd)

☎ 020 8946 1300 📠 020 8946 9120

Now under the guidance of enthusiastic, friendly new owners who are gradually refurbishing the property. The location is quiet and excellent for walking into

Wimbledon centre. Bedrooms are all en suite and well equipped.

9 room (2 family)

Price band ££

♦♦ TROCHEE HOTEL

21 Malcolm Rd, Wimbledon SW19 4AS

(turn off A3 to Worple Rd, and before road ends turn left into Malcolm Rd)

☎ 020 8946 1579 & 3924

📠 020 8785 4058

This friendly hotel, located in a quiet residential area, is in easy walking distance of the shops and Wimbledon station. Bedrooms are sensibly equipped, and some are in a separate building.

17 rooms (2 family) / No dogs (ex guide dogs)

♦♦ WIMBLEDON HOTEL

78 Worple Rd, Wimbledon SW19 4HZ

(M25, A3, Merton exit)

☎ 020 8946 9265 & 8946 1581

📠 020 8946 9265

Situated within walking distance of centre and transport links, this double fronted Victorian house has been converted into well equipped accommodation. Bedrooms are simply appointed and most have the benefit of en suite facilities. English breakfasts are taken in the bright modern dining room and a small television lounge is available for guests use.

14 rooms (6 family) / No dogs

Price band ££

W6 HAMMERSMITH

★★★ NOVOTEL

Hammersmith Int. Centre, 1 Shortlands W6 8DR

(turn off A4 onto Hammersmith Broadway, then follow signs for City Centre, take first left and hotel is on the left)

☎ 020 8741 1555 📠 020 8741 2120

This large purpose-built hotel, situated close to Hammersmith Underground Station, is easily accessible from the M4 and Heathrow Airport, and has the advantage of its own secure car park. Practical, spacious bedrooms are well equipped with a wide range of modern facilities which include Air conditioning. The open-plan public areas include a brasserie, a choice of bars including the Frog and Bulldog Pub, a useful shop and a range of conference and function rooms.

629 rooms (184 family & 415 no smoking) / International Cuisine / Live entertainment / Lift, Air cond

★★★ VENCOURT

255 King St, Hammersmith W6 9LU

(from Central London-A4 to Hammersmith then follow A315 towards Chiswick)

☎ 020 8563 8855 📠 020 8563 9988

This modern hotel is close to the centre of Hammersmith where there is good public transport. Rooms have the expected modern comforts and most have good views over London, especially on the upper of the 12 storeys. The open-plan public areas include a lounge bar, where

Phoenix Bar & Grill

Vencourt

snacks are served all day, and a small restaurant for more substantial meals.
120 rooms (25 family & 18 no smoking) / English & French Cuisine / Lift
Price band £££

Premier West Hotel

♦♦♦ PREMIER WEST HOTEL
28-34 Glenthorne Rd, Hammersmith W6 0LS
(A4 for central London(Hammersmith exit), 2nd exit at Broadway rdbt into King St, 2nd right to end, into Glenthorne St-hotel on left)
☎ 020 8748 6181 📠 020 8748 2195
Closed 24 Dec-2 Jan
This popular hotel continues to upgrade, caters well for both commercial and tourist clientele, and is close to Hammersmith station for easy access to the West End. The comfortably furnished bedrooms vary in size and have many modern amenities. A short carte menu is offered at dinner plus a good choice of breakfast, served in the attractive restaurant.
26 rooms (5 family) / No dogs (ex guide dogs)
Price band ££

WHERE TO EAT
RESTAURANTS
AA RECOMMENDED

N3 FINCHLEY

⊛ RANI
7 Long Lane Finchley N3 2PR
☎/🖷 020 8349 4386
Renowned Indian vegetarian, comfortably furnished and adorned with photos of rural India. Gujerati dishes, samosas and parathas, are enhanced by excellent home-made chutneys and exceptional breads. Pleasant service.
Fixed D £ ALC £

N8 HORNSEY

⊛ ⊛ LES ASSOCIÉS
172 Park Road N8 8JT
☎ 020 8348 8944
Set back from the main road, this little neighbourhood restaurant has a terrace at the front; within walls are strewn with big paintings and charcoal drawings. The hand-written carte is in French and supplemented by daily specials. The service is directed by the charming patron.
Fixed L £ ALC ££

N16 STOKE NEWINGTON

⊛ THE FOX REFORMED
176 Stoke Newington Church Street N16 0JL
☎/🖷 020 7254 5975
Wine bar at the heart of community life, with its own reading circle, backgammon club, and tutored wine tastings. Wholesome cooking is offered from regular and specials menus.

⊛ RASA
55 Stoke Newington Church Street N16 0AR
☎ 020 7249 0344 🖷 020 7249 8748
Pass the shrine to Krishna and take a seat at one of the metal-framed chairs in the bright and cheerful surroundings. This is the original Rasa, dedicated to the vegetarian cuisine of Kerala, and plenty of friendly, helpful staff, plus an informative menu describing the backgrounds of the dishes and how they are normally served in their homeland, make the experience rewarding. Clear flavours and subtle combinations of herbs and spices are the kitchen's stock in trade.
Fixed L/D £ ALC £

N19 HIGHGATE

⊛ THE RAJ VOGUE
34 Highgate Hill N19 5NL
☎ 020 7272 9091 🖷 020 7281 1485
The most traditional of Indian restaurants, comfortable with red plush chairs. The menu offers favourite dishes from every region of the sub-continent, including tandoori specialities.

NW6 SWISS COTTAGE

⊛ ⊛ SINGAPORE GARDEN
83/83a Fairfax Road NW6 4DY
☎ 020 7328 5314 🖷 020 7624 0656
Cream walls, plain wood floors, with tables laid with wipeable paper squares, paper napkins and fresh carnations add up to unremarkable decor. There is a long menu which is primarily Chinese, with a section of Singapore and Malaysian dishes; it is from these two latter areas that the cooking is of particular note.
Fixed L/D £ ALC £

NW10 WILLESDEN

⊛ ⊛ SABRAS
Willesden High Road NW10 2RX
☎ 020 8459 0340
Charming old timer with twenty-five years under its belt. The atmosphere at this family-run restaurant is comfortable, with upholstered chairs, and functional Formica-topped tables. The menu is entirely vegetarian, covering mumbai specialities from Bombay, south Indian pancakes, north Indian dal-subji dishes, and some offerings from the owners home province, Gujarati. The restaurant does offer some wines and beers, but it is well worth trying their excellent lassi or the freshly-pressed apple and carrot juice.
No credit cards

SW8 BATTERSEA

⊛ ⊛ THE STEPPING STONE
123 Queenstown Road SW8 3RH
☎ 020 7622 0555 🖷 020 7622 4230
The urban rustic menu changes daily and the cooking is modern and straightforward. Trelough duck breast with Puy lentils and braised chicory with orange, or roast halibut with mussels, saffron mash, leeks and crème fraîche are typical offerings. Weekday 'Early Bird' dinners (tables vacated by 8.45) are particularly good value.
Fixed L/D £ ALC £

SW11 BATTERSEA

⊛ ⊛ BUCHAN'S
62-64 Battersea Bridge Road SW11 3AG
☎ 020 7228 0888 🖷 020 7924 1718
Modern British cooking with a heavy accent on Scottish that is popular with the locals. Neeps tatties, a wee dram, Scotch broth and Angus fillet feature beside pan-fried guinea fowl laid over a potato, prune and pear compote with ribbons of vegetables, and roast fillet of monk fish set on a slice of Jerusalem artichoke with a lime tomato and parsley nut butter. Four desserts are offered with a selection of British cheeses.
Fixed L £ ALC £

⊛ ⊛ RANSOME'S DOCK
35-37 Parkgate Road Battersea SW11 4NP
☎ 020 7223 1611 🖷 020 7924 2614
This small restaurant is stylish and the kitchen keen on sourcing first-class ingredients (some of the meats being identified, such as Shorthorn beef, Tyrolean bacon and Trelough duck). The cooking has a strong modern European feel. The range of dishes takes in penne with Fontina and Parmesan cheeses, and Dutch calves' liver, and filo turnovers with spinach, and Feta cheese. There is a very good wine list, a popular weekend brunch menu, and the service is friendly and courteous.
Fixed L £ ALC ££

SW12 BALHAM

⊛ BOMBAY BICYCLE CLUB
95 Nightingale Lane SW12 8NX
☎ 020 8673 6217 🖷 020 8673 9100
Bentwood chairs, flowers, palms by the large windows and murals on the walls are the setting for Indian fare of crispy vegetable samosas, cod curry, gosht kata masala (curried lamb with cardamom), Bombay mushrooms and top-drawer naan. Finish with ice cream.
ALC ££

Buchan's

WHERE TO STAY & WHERE TO EAT

SW13 BARNES

❀ ❀ ❀ RIVA RESTAURANT
169 Church Road Barnes SW13 9HR
☎/☎ 020 8748 0434
Simple, understated decor is offset by big mirrors and cathedral-sized arrangements of flowers. Tables, however, are small and close, yet the spot-on service - no fuss, no intrusion, no rush - is a major plus. A short menu features northern Italian cooking, but the food comes with a difference - at its base is a good use of fresh herbs and excellent quality primary ingredients, at the heart a perfect understanding of flavour and texture contrasts. The all-Italian wine list offers about thirty bins with prices ranging from £9.50 to £40.
ALC ££

Sonny's Restaurant

❀ ❀ SONNY'S RESTAURANT
94 Church Road Barnes SW13 0DQ
☎ 020 8748 0393 ☎ 020 8748 2698
Restaurant, café and small delicatessen rolled into one. There might be dishes such as grilled monkfish with a risotto of lemon and ginger and coriander essence, or black pasta with pan-fried calamari and scallops, and pig's trotters with grain mustard dressing and Jerusalem artichoke crisps. The set two-course lunch is so popular that service can become stretched. The two-page wine list is helpfully annotated, with a decent choice by the glass.
Fixed L £ ALC £

SW14 EAST SHEEN

❀ CROWTHERS RESTAURANT
481 Upper Richmond Road West East Sheen SW14 7PU
☎/☎ 020 8876 6372
Neighbourhood restaurant noted for attentive service and modern Anglo-French cooking. The kitchen makes good use of fresh produce. Begin with grilled aubergine with tomato, Feta and pesto and follow, perhaps, with herb-crusted lamb with rosemary jus.
Fixed D £

❀ ❀ REDMOND'S
170 Upper Richmond Road West SW14 8AW
☎ 020 8878 1922 ☎ 020 8878 1133
Redmond's is a quiet lunch-time venue (with the exception of Sunday lunch), but comes alive at night when the menu is marginally more expensive. It's a bright open setting with plain walls adorned with zany, colourful avant-garde paintings. Redmond Hayward's evolving menu reads like many these days: modern English with the odd nod towards somewhere else, perhaps Japan and the Maghreb. The wine list is very helpfully annotated and written for enjoyment with a special section for halves, magnums and dessert.
Fixed D £

SW15 PUTNEY

❀ THE COOK HOUSE
56 Lower Richmond Road Putney SW15 1JT
☎ 020 8785 2300
Minimalist restaurant with a terracotta floor and the menu written on glass over the open-plan kitchen, with options like fish stew, pot-roasted rabbit, and rib-eye of Angus beef. Unlicensed.
ALC £

❀ ❀ PUTNEY BRIDGE
The Embankment SW15 1LB
☎ 020 8780 1811 ☎ 020 8780 1211
Award-winning, strikingly modern building beside the Thames. A long glass frontage in the upstairs restaurant gives wide views over the water; downstairs is the bar. Menus are based squarely on France with the rest of Europe getting a look in too. Crab remoulade, ravioli of duck confit with mushrooms, and pithiviers of snails with two sauces could be starter choices, with main courses split equally between fish and meat. The long wine list, strongest in France, has a fair range by the glass.
Fixed L £ ALC £££

SW17 WANDSWORTH,TOOTING

❀ ❀ ❀ CHEZ BRUCE
2 Bellevue Road Wandsworth Common SW17 7EG
☎ 020 8672 0114 ☎ 020 8767 6648
Upscale modern restaurant with service to match. Putty-coloured walls, fresh flowers, modern lighting, white-clothed tables with serious glasses (wines by the glass feature quite well, as do half-bottles), and staff who make guests feel at home, all help to produce a good atmosphere chez Bruce Poole. He describes his style as 'mainly classical French with 30 per cent of whatever we feel like': Mozzarella and pimento crostini with balsamico and pesto, or osso buco with risotto milanese falling into the latter category, plaice goujons with tartare sauce and steamed red mullet with a bourride sauce and provençale tart in the former. Rhubarb compote with rhubarb sorbet is a popular pudding, and orange and almond cake hits the button but takes off with its additional smooth, perfectly balanced lemon-yogurt ice cream.
Fixed D ££

❀ KASTOORI
188 Upper Tooting Road SW17 7EJ
☎/☎ 020 8767 7027
Bright, spacious 'pure vegetarian' Indian. The menu is laden with strong Gujerati and Indo-African influences. Various thalis are a good introduction to the style, but if you can't decide, try one of the Thanki 'family specials'.
ALC £

SW19 WIMBLEDON

❀ ❀ CANNIZARO HOUSE
West Side Wimbledon Common SW19 4UE
☎ 020 8879 1464 ☎ 020 8879 7338
Well-loved historical landmark that is a haven of peace and quiet. The staff are dedicated to the task of making guests feel well looked after, and a driver is even available at times to assist in short journeys. Classical French cuisine is given a modern interpretation. Seared scallops of foie gras are served upon an apple and potato rösti with Calvados scented jus, and braised shin of veal with root vegetables is enhanced by a rich braising liquor with a sage and asparagus soufflé.
Fixed L £ ALC £££

W4 CHISWICK

❀ THE CHISWICK
131-133 Chiswick High Road W4
☎ 020 8994 6887 ☎ 020 8994 5504
Popular neighbourhood restaurant with bare wooden tables and casual Mediterranean bistro-style setting. Menu choices include onion and rosemary soup, whole devilled quail with tortilla, and a good traditional roast beef with Yorkshire pudding for Sunday lunch.

W5 EALING

❀ MOMO
14 Queens Parade W5 3HU
☎ 020 8997 0206/0306
☎ 020 8997 0206
Tiny, unpretentious neighbourhood restaurant serving Ealing's large Japanese community. There are few of the usual hallmarks, although tempura, teriyaki and sushi make appearances, the interest lies in the more unusual dishes on offer. Very friendly staff.
Fixed L £ ALC ££

Call the AA Hotel Booking Service on
0870 5050505 to book at AA recognised
hotels and B&Bs in the UK,
or through our internet site:
http://www.theaa.co.uk/hotels

PUBS, INNS & OTHER PLACES

N16 STOKE NEWINGTON

MAGPIE & STUMP
132 Stoke Newington Church St, N16
☎ 020 7254 0959
Good pub on a busy street. Pub grub downstairs, restaurant meals upstairs.

NW10 WILLESDEN

WILLIAM IV BAR & RESTAURANT
786 Harrow Rd, NW10 5JX
☎ 020 8969 5944
Modern and antique furniture fills this tastefully refurbished pub with three bars, a restaurant and popular heated garden. The innovative British menu is well worth a look

SW11 BATTERSEA

THE CASTLE
115 Battersea High St, SW11 3JR
☎ 020 7228 8181
Ivy-covered pub tucked away in 'Battersea Village', with rugs and rustic furnishings on bare boards, open fires, an enclosed patio garden, and decent weekly-changing menus.

DUKE OF CAMBRIDGE
228 Battersea Bridge Rd, SW11 3AA
☎ 020 7223 5662
Stylishly modernised pub offering an interesting range of traditional dishes with a modern twist.

SW19 WIMBLEDON

FOX & GRAPES
Camp Rd, SW19
☎ 020 8946 5599
Great summer pub right on the edge of Wimbledon Common.

W5 EALING

THE WHEATSHEAF
41 Haven Ln, W5 2HZ
☎ 020 8997 5240
Large Victorian pub with rustic appearance inside. Wooden floors, panelled walls, beams from an old barn, and real fires in winter.

W6 HAMMERSMITH

ANGLESEA ARMS
35 Wingate Rd, W6 0UR
☎ 020 8749 1291
Traditional corner pub, with a Georgian façade, basic decor, real fires and a relaxed, smoky atmosphere, that positively bustles with eager diners.

THE DOVE
19 Upper Mall, W6
☎ 020 8748 5405
Tiny unspoilt pub around 300 years old. A small rear terrace overlooks the Thames.

BLACK LION
2 South Black Lion Lane, W6
☎ 020 8748 7056
Set back from the river, this friendly pub has an indoor skittle alley.

EXCURSIONS

OUT OF TOWN

Within easy reach of London there are numerous stately homes, historic towns and some delightful countryside, all of which are well worth exploring. Many of the stately homes are run by the National Trust, who preserve and maintain the homes for the public to visit. The British Travel Centre on Lower Regent Street have guide books, leaflets and advice on where and when to go and there are local tourist information offices at the destinations.

AUDLEY END HOUSE AND GARDENS
Audley End, Saffron Walden, Essex
☎ 01799 522399

A splendid Jacobean country mansion, Audley End was built in 1603, by Thomas Howard, Earl of Suffolk, to entertain King James I. What you see today is only a third of the original building - and it's still huge. The treasures within are equally impressive - Jacobean carved wooden screens, paintings (including Canaletto's famous masterpiece *Venice*) and exquisite furniture. Once you've tired of the awe-inspiring house, there are 40 hectares (100 acres) of grounds in which to stroll. Landscaped by Capability Brown in 1762, the best vantage point is at the top of the hill behind the house. From there you can

Hatfield House

see the grounds laid out with ornamental buildings and bridges. Next to the Stables Yard is the garden centre and farm shop with fresh fruit, vegetables and plants for sale. (43 miles north east)

HATFIELD HOUSE
Hatfield, Hertfordshire
☎ 01707 262823

Hatfield was built in 1611 for Robert Cecil, Earl of Salisbury, and is still the home of the Cecil family. Within are famous portraits, rare tapestries, furniture and memorabilia from Queen Elizabeth I's reign. She lived in the Tudor Old Royal Palace, and learned here that she had become Queen of England in 1558. Inside are all kinds of interesting designs - the curved gates at the foot of the stairs were there to stop the dogs getting upstairs. In the library is the warrant ordering the execution of Mary Queen of Scots (Elizabeth's elder sister). There are wooded grounds and lakes as well as a 15th-century garden. (25 miles north)

KNEBWORTH HOUSE AND GARDENS
Knebworth, Hertfordshire
☎ 01438 812661

Knebworth House is well hidden as you approach along the long drive, and is well worth the wait - it is a Gothic fantasy with turrets, domes and gargoyles making up an extraordinary façade. It is the home of the Lytton family (and has been since 1490), and as such has seen many changes over the centuries. The house today displays a variety of styles and designs from the Jacobean Banqueting Hall to simple Edwardian elegance. Legend has it that Queen Elizabeth I stayed here for a night in 1588, so naturally she has a room named after her! The formal gardens house a herb garden and circular flowerbeds created by Jekyll. There's an Adventure Playground with Fort Knebworth, Astroglide and other popular rides, a deer park, and a narrow-gauge railway. Knebworth has also been the venue for occasional open-air rock concerts, such as the heavy metal extravaganza Monsters of Rock. (phone for details). (30 miles north)

WOBURN ABBEY
Woburn, Bedfordshire
☎ 01525 290666

The treasures on view inside this 18th-century abbey are impressive and historically important. The original Cistercian settlement was founded in 1145, on which the present abbey stands. It is partly occupied by Lord Tavistock and his family. Inside is the Armada Portrait of Elizabeth I as well as works by Van Dyck, Reynolds, Gainsborough, Holbein and Canaletto. There is a collection of Meissen and Japanese porcelain as well as some Wedgwood caneware from the 19th century. The highlight of the porcelain is the Sèvres dinner service presented by Louis XV in 1763. Several state rooms can also be visited, including the Yellow Drawing Room, Queen Victoria's Bedroom, the State Dining Room and the Canaletto Room. The abbey is set in a 3,000-acre park, part of which has been converted into a safari park (phone above number for details). (44 miles north west)

HAMPTON COURT PALACE
East Molesey, Surrey, KT8 9AU
☎ 020-8781 9500 & 8781 9501

Hampton Court Palace was built in 1514 by Cardinal Wolsey as a gift for Henry VIII, with whom he was trying to curry favour after he had refused to annul the king's marriage to Catherine of Aragon. It didn't work. Henry not only took the palace, but everything else the Cardinal owned and then imprisoned in the Tower of London. The Palace was the place of Edward I's birth, has gardens designed by Elizabeth I, and was rebuilt by Christopher Wren on the orders of William and Mary. Queen Victoria finally opened it to the public in 1838. The interior is sumptuous and full of rich decoration and furniture (there are timed tickets during summer). Or you can explore the vast grounds which include the famous Maze, laid out in 1714 and still puzzling most who enter. (10 miles south west)

Knebworth House and Gardens

Hampton Court Palace

RICHMOND
Surrey: Tourist Information Centre, Old Town Hall, Whittaker Avenue
☎ 020-8940 9125

To the west of London, Richmond is a very attractive, riverside town with chic shopping, good restaurants, little alleys and the 2,500-acre Richmond Park. In summer, during the Richmond Festival, plays are performed at the lovely Orange Tree theatre/pub. In Old Palace Yard is the gatehouse of Richmond Palace, which was mostly destroyed by the Parliamentarians after the execution of Charles I. You'll find antiques along the alleys leading down to the river, and Ham House along the Thames, a bold, Jacobean building dating from 1610. Inside are paintings by Lely, Reynolds and Constable, as well as exquisite furnishings and woodwork. Richmond Park is a wonderful escape from the busy town, where red and fallow deer wander freely among man-made ponds. The Isabella Plantation is spectacular in late spring when the azaleas and rhododendrons are in full bloom. (5 miles west) In a (slightly) more contemporary vein, Richmond was the home of those rock stars with stamina, The Rolling Stones.

ROYAL BOTANIC GARDENS AT KEW
Kew Road, Kew, Middlesex
☎ 020-8940 1171

The Royal Botanic Gardens has an unrivalled collection of plants housed in spectacular glasshouses and tranquil gardens. Even during the gloomy winter there are bright, tropical plants in the glasshouses, while spring and summer are the best times to visit, when the whole gardens are ablaze with colour and scent. The gardens began with George III's mother, Princess Augusta in 1759. The 19th-century botanist, Sir Joseph Banks, and head gardener, William Aiton were largely rsponsible for laying the foundations of this great collection. Of particular interest is the Palm House, opened in 1848, and the Princess of Wales Conservatory (named after Diana, Princess of Wales), opened in 1987. The most

Richmond

famous part is probably the Chinese Pagoda, which is 163 feet high. Guided tours are available. (5 miles west)

PUBLIC RECORD OFFICE MUSEUM
Ruskin Ave, Kew, TW9 4DU
☎ 020-8876 3444

The Public Record Office houses one of the finest, most complete archives in Europe, comprising the records of the central government and law courts from the Norman Conquest to the present day. Contains some documents of great historic importance, including Domesday Book. Planned opening Spring 2000.

WINDSOR CASTLE
Windsor, Berkshire
☎ 01753 831118

Windsor Castle was badly damaged by fire in 1992, during which the State Apartments and St George's Chapel (the burial place of Henry VIII) were almost completely destroyed. After painstaking work, they reopened in 1997 with a new look mirroring their former glory. It is the largest castle in England and still used by the royal family, so opening times are complicated. Don't miss Queen Mary's Dolls' House, built over 3 years by over a thousand craftsmen. (20 miles west)

LEGOLAND WINDSOR
Windsor Park, Berkshire
☎ 0990 040 404

This amazing park is built entirely from Lego and is divided into different themed zones. In Miniland are miniature versions of major European buildings, like the Eiffel Tower and the Leaning Tower of Pisa. There's also a Duplo Gardens for younger children and for older ones the Legoland Driving School and Wild Woods. (20 miles west)

THORPE PARK
Staines Road, Chertsey, Surrey
☎ 01932 569393

Thorpe Park offers 500 acres of family fun, and over 100 attractions are included in the admission price. Among the rides are No Way Out - the world's first "blackwards" ride, Loggers Leap - the highest log flume ride in the UK, Depth Charge water slide, Thunder River, Tea Cup ride, and the Canada Creek Railway. There are also a farm and plenty of other shows and attractions. There is free transport around the park by land train or water bus. (21 miles south west)

Windsor Castle

SISSINGHURST CASTLE GARDENS
Sissinghurst, nr Cranbrook, Kent
☎ **01580 715330**
Here Vita Sackville-West and her husband,
Harold Nicholson, created a garden of
exquisite colour and fragrance to
complement their transformation of a
ruined 16th-century mansion. The gardens
are informal, including themed areas such
as the white garden and the herb garden.
It is usually busy at summer weekends

HEVER CASTLE
Edenbridge, Kent
☎ **01732 865224**
This magnificent, 13th-century castle was
once the home of the ill-fated Anne
Boleyn, second wife of Henry VIII. It is said
that he courted her here, only to have her
beheaded three years later. The castle was
restored by American millionaire William
Waldorf Astor, and today the grounds
include an Italianate garden, a vast lake,
rose garden and maze. Inside are
furnished rooms from the 13th century as
well as many fine portraits. (25 miles
south east)

CHARTWELL
Westerham, Kent
☎ **01732 866368**
The home of Winston Churchill and his
family, Chartwell is well worth visiting. The
atmosphere in the house is reminiscent of
a family time, and was restored as such at

Bluebell Railway

discovered in England. Inside are full size
skeletons of a man, baby, dog and goose,
as well as pottery and ceramics from
excavations. Included in the admission fee
is an audio tour which tells you the story
of the villa.

BLUEBELL RAILWAY
Sheffield Park Station, nr Uckfield,
East Sussex
☎ **01825 723777, 722370 & 722008**
Opened in 1960, and the first of the
disused steam passenger lines to be
restored to working order, the Bluebell
Railway runs along a 5-mile stretch
through rolling Sussex Weald countryside
from Sheffield Park to Horsted Keynes. The
whole experience transports you to the

Leeds Castle

the wishes of Lady Churchill, who wanted
the public to see the house at a time
when they were happiest there. There is
an exhibition of Churchill's professional
accomplishments, as well as his private
side as a family man. He built several of
the walls in the gardens, apparently
relishing the simplicity of the work (note
that they're not very straight!). Also in the
grounds is a stunning rose garden and
Churchill's studio, full of paintings which
he never estimated.

LULLINGSTONE ROMAN VILLA
Lullingstone Lane, Eynsford, Kent
☎ **01322 863467**
The impressive remains of a Roman villa,
Lullingstone has extensive Roman mosaics
and original foundation walls. It is also the
proud possessor of a chi-rho, the fish
symbol of Christianity, one of the first

BRIGHTON
East Sussex: Tourist Information Centre, 10
Bartholomew Square
☎ **01273 323755**
Brighton has come a long way in recent
years. Originally popular with the Prince
Regent (later George IV) in the early 19th
century, who began its status as a
fashionable resort, it then went into
decline during the early 20th century, and
has recently been given facelifts and a
new lease of life. The Royal Pavilion is a
spectacular, if bizarre, blend of Indian,
Chinese, Russian and Gothic styles, built
for the eccentric Prince Regent in 1823.
The Palace Pier offers modern-day, English
seaside entertainment such as slot
machines, funfair rides and fake tattoos.
(The original pier, West Pier, has been
allocated National Lottery funds for repair
and restoration.) The Lanes, a warren of
backstreet alleys, house antiques, jewellery
and clothes shops. The Sussex Toy and
Model Museum, near to station, has
traditional toys and railways. The town
also enjoys a vibrant nightlife. (56 miles
south)

LEEDS CASTLE
Maidstone, Kent
☎ **01622 765400**
Leeds Castle can truly live up to its name
as 'the loveliest castle in the world'. Built
on two small islands in a lake, the castle
was built by the Normans nearly 900 years
ago. It has a fascinating history which
includes being listed in the Domesday
Book, serving as a royal residence to six of
England's queens, as a playground and
palace to Henry VIII and as a private
home. Inside is a magnificent collection of
medieval furnishings, paintings, tapestries,
treasures - and dog collars! The grounds
include an aviary, the Culpeper Garden
(with herbs, roses, lavender and lupins,
among others), a maze, and wood garden.
(40 miles east)

age of steam, from the late-Victorian-style
restoration of Sheffield Park Station,
complete with vintage enamel
advertisements and old-style signals to the
historic coaches, restored with minute
attention to detail. There's also a museum
packed with relics telling the story of the
line and the people who originally worked
on it. Visit in spring and see the splendid
sight that gave the railway its name -
carpets of bluebells either side of the line.
(46 miles south)
*(Please be aware that there is no parking
available at Kingscote Station. Telephone for
more information)*

WHERE TO STAY
HOTELS
AA RECOMMENDED

Berkshire

WINDSOR

★★★★ OAKLEY COURT
Windsor Rd, Water Oakley SL4 5UR
(leave M4 junct 6, head for Windsor, then right onto A308 Maidenhead. Pass racecourse & hotel is 2.5m on right)
☎ 01753 609988 📠 01628 637011
Originally built in 1859, this splendid and much extended Victorian Gothic mansion is enviably situated in extensive grounds leading down to the Thames. Stylish public rooms are comfortable and there are a number of useful conference suites including a converted boathouse. Only a handful of bedrooms are in the main house with the majority located in adjoining wings. All rooms are spacious, beautifully furnished and many enjoy river views. The Oakleaf restaurant offers guests an interesting range of carefully prepared dishes and during summer, alfresco dining is available. The hotel is also equipped with a smart leisure club, and boating trips can be easily arranged.
115 rooms (45 no smoking) / English & French Cuisine / Indoor swimming pool (heated) / Golf 9, Fishing, Snooker / Sauna, Solarium, Gym, Croquet lawn, Jacuzzi/spa, Boating / Live entertainment / Night porter / No dogs (ex guide dogs)
Price band £££

★★★ THE CASTLE
High St SL4 1LJ
(M4 junct 6/M25 junct 15-follow signs to Windsor town centre and castle. Hotel located at the top of hill by the castle opposite the Guildhall)
☎ 01753 851011 📠 01753 830244
Situated in the shadow of Windsor Castle, this hotel is popular with tourists, but also offers strong conference and banqueting services. Bedrooms in the older main building have been tastefully modernised and are traditionally furnished in keeping with the style of the property, while the mews boasts splendid executive rooms, all very well equipped. The elegant restaurant serves innovative British cooking, and there is also a less formal café offering a bistro and snack service. The lounge is an attractive venue for afternoon tea and there is a small open-plan bar.
111 rooms (26 family & 32 no smoking) / English & Continental Cuisine / Lift, Night porter
Price band £££

Royal Adelaide

★★★ ROYAL ADELAIDE
46 Kings Rd SL4 2AG
☎ 01753 863916 📠 01753 830682
An elegant Georgian property sporting a fully refurbished interior which overlooks the Long Walk running from Windsor Castle to Virginia Water. Public areas include a bar/reception lounge and an informal restaurant serving à la carte and table d'hôte menus. Bedrooms are tastefully decorated and furnished.
39 rooms (1 family) / English & French cuisine / Night porter

★★★ YE HARTE & GARTER
High St SL4 1PH
(in town centre opposite front entrance to Windsor Castle)
☎ 01753 863426 📠 01753 830527
Located in the heart of Windsor, close to the Castle, which can be seen from many of the bedrooms, this inn is an extended and modernised Victorian building. There is a choice of bars serving a range of informal meals, and there is also a separate restaurant with a full menu.
42 rooms (4 family) / International Cuisine / Live entertainment / Lift, Night porter / No dogs (ex guide dogs)
Price band £££

★★ AURORA GARDEN
Bolton Av SL4 3JF
(take junct 6 M4 onto the A332 for Windsor. At first rdbt, second exit towards Staines. At third rdbt third exit for 500yds. Hotel is on right)
☎ 01753 868686 📠 01753 831394
A naturally welcoming and friendly atmosphere characterizes this privately run hotel. Located in a quiet residential neighbourhood, close to Windsor park and half a mile or so from town. The landscaped water gardens and patio are enjoyed by guests throughout the year. The restaurant, which overlooks the

garden, provides a wide choice of cuisine at dinner. Breakfast is a hearty affair, the cold buffet is particularly good. Bedrooms offer many extras including cable TV.
19 rooms (7 family) / English & French Cuisine
Price band £££

♦♦♦ MELROSE HOUSE
53 Frances Rd SL4 3AQ
(M4 Junct 6 signposted Windsor, follow signs for Staines, left into Frances Rd, 3rd rdbt from M4)
☎ 01753 865328 📠 01753 865328
Recent improvements have been made to this elegant Victorian house, located in a peaceful residential area within walking distance of the town. Bedrooms vary in size, are brightly decorated and well equipped. Guests are offered a choice at breakfast, which is served in the spacious breakfast room. The house benefits from plenty of off street parking.
9 rooms (2 family & 3 no smoking)
Price band ££

♦♦♦ NETHERTON HOTEL
96 St Leonards Rd SL4 3DA
☎ 01753 855508 📠 01753 621267
An attractive Edwardian villa with bright fresh bedrooms, all featuring co-ordinating fabrics and modern facilities. There is a small lounge and a light and airy breakfast room. Dedicated facilities for disabled guests are also available. Off street parking is provided at the rear of the property.
11 rooms (5 family) / No dogs

♦♦ CLARENCE HOTEL
9 Clarence Rd SL4 5AE
(from M4 junct 6 follow dual carrriageway to Windsor, turn left at 1st rdbt into Clarence Rd)
☎ 01753 864436 📠 01753 857060
A Grade II listed Victorian Townhouse in the heart of Windsor with easy access to shops and local attractions. While space in some rooms is limited, accommodation is well maintained and offers excellent value

for money. Decorative murals found in many rooms are an unusual and thoughtful touch. Added facilities include a lounge with well stocked bar and steam room. Breakfast is served in the restaurant overlooking attractive gardens.

20 rooms (6 family)
Price band ££

Buckinghamshire

MILTON KEYNES

★★★ COURTYARD BY MARRIOTT MILTON KEYNES

London Rd, Newport Pagnell MK16 0JA
(0.5m from junct 14 of M1 on the A509)
☎ 01908 613688 📠 01908 617335

Very conveniently positioned for the M1 motorway, yet in a quiet spot, this popular hotel is designed around a handsome three-story Georgian House and a pretty courtyard. The Coach House offers bright, inviting public rooms, including a range of conference rooms; a small gym is an added bonus. Bedrooms are smartly decorated and offer good facilities, particularly to the business guest.

49 rooms (1 family & 26 no smoking) / International Cuisine / Night porter / No dogs (ex guide dogs)

★★★ FORTE POSTHOUSE MILTON KEYNES

500 Saxon Gate West MK9 2HQ
(M1 junct 14 over 7 roundabouts right at 8th hotel on left)
☎ 01908 667722 📠 01908 674714

This large modern hotel is situated in the city centre, and offers opulent public areas, with glass-sided lifts overlooking the lounges and restaurants. Bedrooms are comfortably appointed and include several designed for women.

150 rooms (79 no smoking) / International Cuisine / Indoor swimming pool (heated) Sauna, Solarium, Gym, Health & fitness centre / Live entertainment / Lift, Night porter

★★ DIFFERENT DRUMMER

94 High St, Stony Stratford MK11 1AH
☎ 01908 564733 📠 01908 260646

This attractive townhouse hotel on historic Stony Stratford's High Street offers a warm welcome to its guests. The smart Italian restaurant, Al Tamborista, is a popular dining spot and enjoys a good local reputation. Bedrooms are generally spacious, whilst the hotel lounge incorporates a bar and is particularly comfortable.

12 rooms (2 family) / English & Italian Cuisine / No dogs (ex guide dogs) / No coaches

Essex

SAFFRON WALDEN

◆◆◆◆ ROWLEY HILL LODGE

Little Walden CB10 1UZ
(1.25m N of town centre on B1052. On left of road - establishment has three tall chimneys)
☎ 01799 525975 📠 01799 516622

Guests can expect a friendly welcome at this small, country guest house. Dating back to 1830 and originally a lodge it has been carefully modernised. Both bedrooms are nicely decorated, comfortably furnished, equipped with a good range of useful extras and have delightful views. Breakfasts are served around the large wooden table in the dining room.

2 rooms (all no smoking) / No dogs (ex guide dogs) / No coaches
Price band £

◆◆◆ CRICKETER'S ARMS

Rickling Green and Quendon CB11 3YG
(exit B1383 at Quendon, premises 300yds on left opposite cricket green)
☎ 01799 543210 📠 01799 543512

Very much a traditional inn, full of historical charm and character, the Cricketers Arms is popular with local diners and residents alike. A mellow red brick building, it sits beside the village green, and enjoys a welcoming and informal atmosphere. Most of the attractively decorated accommodation is housed in a modern extension.

10 rooms (2 family)
Price band ££

Greater London

HAMPTON COURT

★★★★ THE CARLTON MITRE

Hampton Court Rd KT8 9BN
(from M3 junct1 follow signs to Sunbury & Hampton Court Palace, continue until Hampton Court Palace rdbt, turn right & The Mitre is on the right)
☎ 020 8979 9988 📠 020 8979 9777

The hotel dates back in parts to 1665 and was originally lodging for courtiers who could not be accommodated at Hampton Court Palace opposite. Located on the Thames with riverside terrace, restaurant and brasserie all commanding good views. Bedrooms are generally spacious with good facilities, some also with views. Parking is limited.

36 rooms (2 family & 16 no smoking) / International Cuisine / Jacuzzi/spa / live entertainment / Lift, Night porter, Air cond
Price band £££

★★★ LIONGATE

Hampton Court Rd KT8 9DD
(from London approach via A3 and A308. From SW leave M3 at junct 1 and follow A308)
☎ 0500 636943 (Central Res)
📠 01773 880321

Opposite the Lion Gate entrance to Hampton Court and by the entrance to Bushy Park (which some of the bedrooms overlook), this hotel has well equipped bedrooms, either in the main house or in a small mews across the road. There is a bar and a separate restaurant.

29 rooms / English & Continental Cuisine / Night porter / No coaches
Price band £££

Greater London

HARROW

★★★ CUMBERLAND

1 St Johns Rd HA1 2EF
☎ 020 8863 4111 📠 020 8861 5668

This popular hotel stands in the town centre and caters for both the business

Cumberland Hotel

and leisure markets. The bedrooms, which are modern and well equipped, are divided between the main house and two other nearby buildings. There is a quiet lounge area, and a restaurant serving a wide choice of food.

84 rooms (6 family & 51 no smoking) / International Cuisine / Sauna, Gym, Small Fitness Room / Night porter / No dogs (ex guide dogs)

★★★ QUALITY HARROW HOTEL
Roxborough Bridge, 12-22 Pinner Rd HA1 4HZ
(at junct of A404/A312)
☎ 020 8427 3435 📠 020 8861 1370
This privately owned hotel is housed in a number of interlinked houses dating from the early 20th century. Bedrooms are well equipped and smartly furnished, and the five courtyard rooms are particularly peaceful. Public areas include a smart conservatory restaurant.
76 rooms (2 family & 28 no smoking) / International Cuisine / Night porter
Price band £££

★★★ NORTHWICK PARK
2-12 Northwick Park Rd HA1 2NT
(off A4006)
☎ 0500 636943 (Central Res)
📠 01773 880321
Convenient for access to central London, and sheltered from the main road, this long, low building offers a variety of styles of comfortable bedrooms, some being designated as 'superior'. There is a modern bar and restaurant, and a large function room.
75 rooms (3 family & 30 no smoking) / Night porter
Price band £££

★★ LINDAL
2 Hindes Rd HA1 1SJ
(off A409, opposite Tesco Superstore)
☎ 020 8863 3164 📠 020 8427 5435
This family-run establishment provides easy access to Harrow shopping centre and offers attractively furnished, modern bedrooms. Day rooms consist of a combined bar-lounge, a breakfast room and a dining area.
19 rooms (3 family & 5 no smoking) / Night porter / No dogs (ex guide dogs)
Price band ££

♦♦♦ HINDES HOTEL
8 Hindes Rd HA1 1SJ
(15 min from M1 on A409)
☎ 020 8427 7468 📠 020 8424 0673
This established property continues to improve and offers bright well-appointed accommodation. Bedrooms are smart and well equipped, half are en suite. The lounge is most comfortable and the breakfast room light and airy. Plenty of parking is available.
14 rooms (2 family) / No dogs (ex guide dogs)
Price band £

Greater London

ILFORD

⌂ TRAVEL INN
Redbridge Ln East IG4 5BG
(at bottom of M11 (signed London East/A12 Chelmsford) follow A12 Chelmsford signs, Travel Inn on left at bottom of slip road)
☎ 020 8550 7909 📠 020 8550 6214
This modern building offers accommodation in smart, spacious and well equipped bedrooms, all with en suite bathrooms. Refreshments may be taken at the nearby family restaurant.
43 rooms
Price band ££

⌂ TRAVELODGE
Beehive Ln, Gants Hill IG4 5DR
☎ 020 8550 4248 📠 020 8550 4248
This modern building offers accommodation in smart, spacious and well equipped bedrooms, all with en suite bathrooms. Refreshments may be taken at the nearby family restaurant.
32 rooms
Price band ££

♦♦♦ WOODVILLE
10-12 Argyle Rd IG1 3BQ
(exit M25 onto M11, then A406 exit at Ilford junct, past Ilford station take 2nd left, from Cranbrook Rd into Beal Rd, then 2nd left into Argyle Rd)
☎ 020 8478 3779 📠 020 8478 6282
Located in a mainly residential road within easy walking distance of the railway station. Woodville is a conversion of three former large terraced houses and offers comfortable well equipped bedrooms, many of which have modern en suite facilities.
16 rooms (5 family) / No dogs (ex guide dogs)
Price band £

♦♦ CRANBROOK HOTEL
22-24 Coventry Rd IG1 4QR
(exit A406 E onto A118, at top turn onto A123, second turning on right, at Ilford Station turn left, second right)
☎ 020 8554 6544 & 4765
📠 020 8518 1463
Offering a relaxed atmosphere, this long-established hotel is situated close to the town centre and Gants Hill underground

station. Public areas include a bar-lounge and a beamed dining room where a three-course fixed-price dinner menu is offered Monday to Thursday.
30 rooms (5 family)

♦♦ PARK HOTEL
327 Cranbrook Rd IG1 4UE
(on A123 just south of junct with A12, Gantshill Rbt)
☎ 020 8554 9616 & 020 8554 7187
📠 020 8518 2700
The Gallardo family's guest house is opposite Valentines Park, and convenient for the town centre. Bedrooms are simply furnished but suitably equipped, ongoing refurbishment is gradually bringing attractive results. Evening meals are available by arrangement and there is a cosy lounge.
20 rooms (3 family)
Price band ££

Greater London

PINNER

♦♦♦ TUDOR LODGE HOTEL
50 Field End Rd, Eastcote HA5 2QN
(turn off A40 at Swakeleys rdbt to Ickenham, A466 to Eastcote. Or turn off A40 at A312 towards Harrow, then left at Northot Stn to Eastcote)
☎ 020 8429 0585 & 020 8866 6027
📠 020 8429 0117
A friendly little hotel with a family atmosphere provided by long serving staff. There are 11 golf courses within five miles and Heathrow is 20 minutes away. Bedrooms, varying in size and style, are well equipped, those with kitchenettes are popular for families. A good choice of budget accommodation.
26 rooms (18 family & 10 no smoking) / No dogs (ex guide dogs)
Price band ££

Greater London

RICHMOND UPON THAMES

★★★★ RICHMOND GATE
Richmond Hill TW10 6RP
(from Richmond head to the top of Richmond hill and the hotel on left opposite the Star & Garter home at Richmond gate exit)
☎ 020 8940 0061 📠 020 8332 0354
A Georgian country house offering high

Woodville

standards of hospitality and service. Stylish bedrooms equipped to a very high standard include luxury doubles and suites, smaller garden wing rooms and several four-posters; best rooms are in the main house. Dining options are the informal Victorian conservatory bistro and candlelit Gates on the Park Restaurant. Cedars health and leisure club has a fitness room, swimming pool, jacuzzi, sauna, steam room and snack bar.

66 rooms (2 family & 11 no smoking) / International Cuisine / Indoor swimming pool (heated) / Sauna, Solarium, Gym, Jacuzzi/spa, Health & beauty suite / Live entertainment / Night porter / No dogs (ex guide dogs)
Price band *£££*

★★★ RICHMOND HILL
Richmond Hill TW10 6RW
(located at the top of Richmond Hill on B321)
☎ 020 8940 2247 & 940 5466
🖷 020 8940 5424

An imposing Georgian Manor house built in 1726 on Richmond Hill, nearby are views of the Thames and open parkland. Rooms come in a variety of sizes and styles. The restaurant offers a fixed price menu and an impressive array of dishes on its carte. The stylish, well designed health club with large pool is shared with sister hotel the Richmond Gate.

138 rooms (9 family & 48 no smoking) / English & French Cuisine / Indoor swimming pool (heated) / Sauna, Solarium, Gym, Jacuzzi/spa, Health & beauty suite / Live entertainment / Lift, Night porter
Price band *£££*

Tudor Lodge Hotel

♦♦♦ HOBART HALL HOTEL
43-47 Petersham Rd TW10 6UL
(on A307, 200yds from Richmond Bridge)
☎ 020 8940 0435 🖷 020 8332 2996

Built around 1690, this pleasant historic hotel is located on the fringe of the town by the bridge. Many of the spacious bedrooms have views of the river and all offer a good range of modern facilities. The hotel benefits from a comfortably furnished lounge and attractive breakfast room - its walls painted with murals - where a good choice of breakfasts is

served. There is also a fine meeting room, overlooking the river, which can accommodate up to 60 people.
19 rooms (4 family & all no smoking) / No dogs
Price band *££*

Greater London

RUISLIP

★★★ BARN HOTEL
West End Rd HA4 6JB
(take A4180 (Polish War Memorial) exit off the A40 to Ruislip, 2m to hotel entrance off a mini rdbt before Ruislip Underground Station)
☎ 01895 636057 🖷 01895 638379

A skilfully extended hotel, parts of which date from 1628. Rooms in the oldest part have four-poster beds and have kept their old beams and uneven floors, while those in the extension are modern in character. There is a pleasant restaurant and a timber-clad bar.
57 rooms (3 family & 3 no smoking) / International Cuisine / Night porter
Price band *£££*

Hertfordshire

HATFIELD

★★★ HATFIELD OAK
Roehyde Way AL10 9AF
(M25 junct 23 take A1(M) northbound to junct 2, at rdbt take exit left, hotel in 0.5m on right)
☎ 01707 275701 🖷 01707 266033

This is a modern hotel with a strong business market, located within minutes of the A1(M). Rooms are well equipped including features such as trouser press and modem access. Executive rooms are more spacious. There is 24 hour room service and guests have a choice of dining in the bar/brasserie or main restaurant.
76 rooms (14 family & 39 no smoking) / Night porter
Price band *£££*

⌂ TRAVEL INN
Lemsford Rd AL10 0DA
(from A1(M) junct 4 follow A1001 towards Hatfield, Travel Inn on top of Hatfield Tunnel)
☎ 01707 268990 🖷 01707 268293

This modern building offers accommodation in smart, spacious and well equipped bedrooms, all with en suite bathrooms. Refreshments may be taken at the nearby family restaurant.
40 rooms
Price band *££*

Hertfordshire

STEVENAGE

★★★ NOVOTEL
Knebworth Park SG1 2AX
(off junct 7 of A1(M), at entrance to Knebworth park)
☎ 01438 742299 🖷 01438 723872)

Pleasantly located in a Green Belt site, this modern red-brick building is only moments from the A1(M), which makes it a popular meeting and conference venue. All the large bedrooms are well appointed for both business guests and families.
100 rooms (20 family & 75 no smoking) / International Cuisine / Outdoor swimming pool (heated) / Lift
Price band *£££*

★★★ CROMWELL
High St, Old Town SG1 3AZ
(leave A1(M1) junct8. Follow signs for town centre, over 2 rdbts. Join one-way system. Turn off into Old Town. Hotel is on the left after mini rdbt)
☎ 01438 779954 🖷 01438 742169

Easily accessible from the nearby A1(M), this High Street hotel has retained much of its historic charm, and offers many useful facilities for business and leisure guests alike. The attractive bedrooms are well equipped, and some are more modern in style than others. Amongst the range of public areas, there are two bars and large meeting rooms.
57 rooms (4 family & 14 no smoking) / Night porter
Price band *£££*

★★★ FORTE POSTHOUSE STEVENAGE
Old London Rd, Broadwater SG2 8DS
(off B1970)
☎ 01438 365444 🖷 01438 741308

Suitable for both the business and leisure traveller, this hotel provides spacious accommodation in well equipped bedrooms. There is some character to the older part of the building which contains the bar and restaurant.
54 rooms (27 no smoking) / International Cuisine / Night porter

★★★ HERTFORDPARK
Danestrete SG1 1EJ
(in town centre adjacent to BHS & Westgate Multi-Store)
☎ 01438 779955 🖷 01438 741880

In the heart of Stevenage, surrounded by shops, this purpose-built hotel is popular with business guests. Spacious, well equipped bedrooms offer peace and quiet. The bar and restaurant are located on the first floor, and are both popular. The coffee shop is an ideal meeting place; conference and meeting facilities are available. A nearby multi-storey offers free car parking.

98 rooms (42 no smoking) / International Cuisine / Lift, Night porter
Price band ££

⌂ TRAVEL INN
Corey's Mill Ln SG1 4AA
(close to A1(M) at intersection of the A602 Hitchin Rd & Corey's Mill Lane)
☎ 01438 351318 📠 01438 721609
This modern building offers accommodation in smart, spacious and well equipped bedrooms, all with en suite bathrooms. Refreshments may be taken at the nearby family restaurant.
40 (rooms)
Price band £

Kent

CRANBROOK

★★ KENNEL HOLT
Goudhurst Rd TN17 2PT
(between Goudhurst and Cranbrook on A262)
☎ 01580 712032 📠 01580 715495
This Elizabethan manor house is a charming retreat with immaculately kept five-acre gardens. The relaxing public rooms are full of original features. Individually-styled bedrooms, some including four-poster beds, are comfortable and furnished in keeping with the style of the property.
10 rooms / European Cuisine / Croquet lawn, Putting green / No dogs / No coaches
Price band £££

♦♦♦♦ FOLLY HILL COTTAGE
Friezley Ln, Hocker Edge TN17 2LL
(turn off A21 onto A262, through Goudhurst, past Kennel Holt Hotel sign on right, take 2nd left, Cottage on left at end of lane)
☎ 01580 714299 📠 01580 714299
Built in the 19th century, this pretty farm cottage can be found at the end of a winding lane in a wonderfully peaceful part of the Kent countryside. The accommodation is modern and very well presented, each has its own private bathroom and lots of thoughtful extra touches. Guests have use of a small lounge adjoining the bedrooms. Both rooms overlook the pretty garden and outdoor pool as well as the fields beyond. Breakfast is served around a communal table in the sunny dining room.
2 rooms / No dogs / No children under 10 years / No coaches / Outdoor swimming pool
Price band £

♦♦♦♦ THE OAST
Hallwood Farm TN17 2SP
(A229 from Cranbrook 1m. Past Duke of Kent pub on left. Farm turning 400yds on right)
☎ 01580 712416 📠 01580 712416
Converted from a 17th-century building originally used for drying hops, the Oast is situated on the edge of the village of Cranbrook. The building forms part of a 200 acre arable and sheep farm. Both rooms are tastefully decorated in keeping with the style of the building, retaining many of the original beams. Rooms are equipped with a host of thoughtful extras and benefit from modern en suite facilities. A traditional farmhouse breakfast is served in the comfortable dining room.
2 rooms / No dogs (ex guide dogs) / No children under 10 years /230 acres, fruit, sheep
Price band ££

Kent

MAIDSTONE

★★★★ MARRIOTT TUDOR PARK HOTEL & COUNTRY CLUB
Ashford Rd, Bearsted ME14 4NQ
(leave M20 at junct 8 Lenham. At rdbt turn right and head to Bearsted and Maidstone. Hotel is situated 1m on the left hand side)
☎ 01622 734334 📠 01622 735360
This fine country hotel offers an excellent venue for both business and leisure users. The superb facilities and good levels of comfort in the bedrooms are part of a successful formula which also includes friendly and helpful staff. The main restaurant, Fairviews, offers uncomplicated dishes which are generally well executed; guests also have the option of the more relaxed environment of the Long Weekend brasserie. Make time to enjoy the excellent range of leisure options, be it golf, a workout, swim or a visit to the beauty salon.
118 rooms (47 family & 65 no smoking) / Continental Cuisine / Indoor swimming pool (heated) / Golf 18, Tennis (hard) / Sauna, Solarium, Gym, Putting green, Jacuzzi/spa, Driving range, Beauty salon, Steam room / Live entertainment / Lift, Night porter / No dogs (ex guide dogs)
Price band £££

★★★ RUSSELL
136 Boxley Rd ME14 2AE
☎ 01622 692221 📠 01622 762084
This attractive Victorian house is set in two acres of grounds on the edge of Maidstone, only minutes from the major routes. Bedrooms continually upgraded, have modern en suite facilities including remote control colour TV and hairdryer. The attractive restaurant offers good home-cooked food and has a strong local following. The hotel is a popular venue for wedding receptions and meetings.
42 rooms (5 family) / French Cuisine / Jacuzzi/spa / Night porter / No dogs (ex guide dogs)

★★★ LARKFIELD PRIORY
London Rd, Larkfield ME20 6HJ
(M20 junct 4 take A228 to W Malling at 1st rdbt take 2nd exit signposted to Maidstone (A20), after 1m hotel on left)
☎ 01732 846858 📠 01732 846786
Dating from 1890, this hotel has been extended and upgraded to provide levels of comfort demanded by today's business travellers. Accommodation is being steadily refurbished and the new rooms are bright and smart. The restaurant boasts a conservatory annex, and the bar lounge is a pleasant alternative for lighter meals and snacks.
52 rooms (24 no smoking) / International Cuisine / Night porter
Price band ££

★★ GRANGE MOOR
St Michael's Rd ME16 8BS
(off A26, Tonbridge Road. Church on lft, turn left hotel on right)
☎ 01622 677623 📠 01622 678246
A friendly, family-run hotel, just off the A26. Bedrooms, some in a nearby building, are well equipped and modern in style, though some have four-poster beds. The popular bar serves a good range of bar meals, there is a small lounge and several dining and function rooms.
47 rooms (6 family) / English & French Cuisine / Night porter
Price band ££

⌂ ROADCHEF LODGE
ME17 1SS
(M20 junct 8)
☎ 01622 631100 📠 01622 739535
This modern building offers accommodation in smart, spacious and well equipped bedrooms, all with en suite bathrooms. Refreshments may be taken at the nearby family restaurant.
58 rooms
Price band ££

⌂ TRAVEL INN
London Rd ME16 0HG
(leave M20 junct 5 take London Rd and head towards Maidstone. Half a mile from junct 5)
☎ 01622 752515 📠 01622 672469
This modern building offers accommodation in smart, spacious and well equipped bedrooms, all with en suite bathrooms. Refreshments may be taken at the nearby family restaurant.
40 rooms
Price band ££

♦♦♦♦ CONWAY HOUSE
12 Conway Rd ME16 0HD
(exit M20 junct 5, left onto A20, at traffic lights/crossroads (with BP petrol station) right into Conway Rd)
☎ 01622 688287 📠 01622 662589
Bedrooms are individually furnished in modern style and brightly decorated with attractive co-ordinating soft furnishings. A choice of breakfast is served in the pleasant dining room, guests share a large table.
3 rooms (1 family & 1 no smoking) / No coaches
Price band £

♦♦♦ GROVE HOUSE
Grove Green Rd, Weavering St ME14 5JT
(M20 junct 7 follow signs to TV studios, right at rndbt, then left into Grovewood Dr, 2nd left past Tesco & left again into Grove Green Rd)
☎ 01622 738441
Situated in a quiet residential area close to the TV studios, this impressive modern house offers homely accommodation for the business or leisure traveller. Bedrooms are equipped with lots of little extras to make your stay more comfortable.
3 rooms / No dogs / No children under 10 years / No coaches
Price band £

♦♦♦ WILLINGTON COURT
Willington St ME15 8JW
(1.5m E of Maidstone, at junct of A20 Asford Rd & Willington St)
☎ 01622 738885 ☎ 01622 631790
Not far from the town centre, this Grade II listed building has been thoughtfully decorated and furnished to complement the character of the building. Bedrooms are of a good size and comfortably furnished and well equipped with many useful extras. A choice of breakfast is served in the oak-beamed dining room which has an inglenook fireplace. There are two small cosy lounges.
8 rooms (all no smoking) / No dogs (ex guide dogs) / No children under 13 years / No coaches
Price band £

♦♦♦ ROCK HOUSE HOTEL
102 Tonbridge Rd ME16 8SL
(on A26, 0.5m from town centre)
☎ 01622 751616 ☎ 01622 756119
Close to the town centre, this family run hotel has a friendly atmosphere. Brightly decorated bedrooms offer sound standards of comfort.
14 rooms (4 family & 4 no smoking) / No dogs (ex guide dogs)
Price band £ £

Kent
WESTERHAM

★★★ KINGS ARMS
Market Square TN16 1AN
(from junct 6 of M25 follow signs to Westerham on A25, enter Westerham and hotel is on right hand side in middle of town)
☎ 01959 562990 ☎ 01959 561240
This attractive Georgian hotel is located in the centre of the town and is steadily improving. The bedrooms, all named after past Kings of England, are well proportioned and individually decorated to retain their character. The public areas include the Conservatory Restaurant with its imaginative menu, a comfortable lounge and the popular downstairs Jail House Sports Cafe and bar. The hotel also has its own secure car park.
17 rooms (3 no smoking) / English & French Cuisine

⌂ ROADCHEF LODGE
Clacket Lane TN16 2ER
(between junct 5 & 6 on M25 westbound)
☎ 01959 565789 ☎ 01959 561311
This modern building offers accommodation in smart, spacious and well equipped bedrooms, all with en suite bathrooms. Refreshments may be taken at the nearby family restaurant.
58 rooms
Price band £ £

Surrey
CHERTSEY

★★★ THE CROWN
7 London St KT16 8AP
(adjacent to Old Town Hall)
☎ 01932 564657 ☎ 01932 570839
The Crown offers a range of well proportioned and good quality bedrooms along with public bar, garden bar and conservatory, and an attractive traditional style restaurant. Home-cooked food offers a number of tempting dishes both in the restaurant and the bar. Other facilities include a popular function suite.
30 rooms (4 family & 13 no smoking) / Night porter
Price band £ £

East Sussex
UCKFIELD

★★★★ BUXTED PARK COUNTRY HOUSE HOTEL
Buxted TN22 4AY
(on A272. Turn off the A22, A26, or A267 on to the A27 towards Heathfield then Buxted)
☎ 01825 732711 ☎ 01825 732770
A Georgian mansion set in 300 acres of beautiful Sussex countryside, Buxted Park retains a grand country house atmosphere in its extensive day rooms. A gilt coat-of-arms above the fireplace in the elegant chandeliered drawing room is one of many original features. Bedrooms, mostly in the Garden Wing, (a 20th-century addition) are stylishly decorated and well appointed. The original Victorian orangery is the stylish setting for some good cooking from an interesting menu.
44 rooms (10 family) / Outdoor swimming pool (heated) / Snooker / Sauna, Solarium, Gym, Croquet lawn, Putting green, Jacuzzi/spa, Beauty salon / Night porter / No dogs (ex guide dogs)

★★★ HORSTED PLACE SPORTING ESTATE & HOTEL
Little Horsted TN22 5TS
(2m S on A26 towards Lewes)
☎ 01825 750581 ☎ 01825 750459
One of Britain's finest examples of Gothic revivalist architecture, Horsted Place is surrounded by its own estate which includes a golf club. Inside there are many fine architectural features, including a splendid Pugin staircase. Bedrooms are notably spacious and well appointed, many are suites.
17 rooms (5 family) / English & French Cuisine / Indoor swimming pool (heated) / Golf, Tennis (hard), Croquet lawn / Live entertainment / Lift, Night porter / No dogs (ex guide dogs)
Price band £ £ £

♦♦♦♦ HOOKE HALL
250 High St TN22 1EN
(N end of Uckfield High St)
☎ 01825 761578 ☎ 01825 768025
Lovingly restored by the owners, this Queen Anne town house features pleasant day rooms full of antique furniture, fine paintings and ornaments, creating a wonderful country house feel. The bedrooms have been individually decorated in great style. Breakfast (charged as an extra) is taken in the elegant setting of the restaurant, which serves Italian dishes at other times.
10 rooms / No dogs / No children under 10 years / No coaches
Price band £ £

♦♦♦♦ SOUTH PADDOCK
Maresfield Park TN22 2HA
(in centre of Maresfield village, enter the park under the lodge opp the church & The Chequers Hotel, cross 5 speed bumps, South Paddock is on left)
☎ 01825 762335
Set in over three acres of immaculate grounds, this elegant country house offers spacious, tastefully decorated bedrooms. Comfortable lounges have open fires and tasty English breakfasts (with a range of home made preserves) are taken in the dining room at one family table.
3 rooms (all no smoking) / No dogs (ex guide dogs) / No children under 10 years / No coaches / Croquet
Price band £

♦♦♦ HIGHLANDS
Framfield TN22 5SA
(turn off A22 to Uckfield, follow signs to B2102. Just before Framfield turn left at Hammonds Green into lane signed Buxted, house 500yds on right)
☎ 01825 890788 ☎ 01825 890803
Highlands is situated in its own gardens near the village of Framfield. Parts of the house are over 400 years old. The two spacious bedrooms are in the original house and offer comfort with good extra facilities. Meals are substantial and can be enjoyed in the dining room, which features antique furniture. There is also a guest lounge with plenty of reading matter.
2 rooms / No dogs (ex guide dogs) / No coaches / Fishing
Price band £

WHERE TO EAT

RESTAURANTS

AA RECOMMENDED

KENT

❀ ❀ ❀ CHAPTER ONE

Locksbottom Farnborough Common BR6 8NF

☎ 01689 854848 ❸ 01689 858439

This distinctive Tudor-style building with a large car park (exactly what's needed given its out-of-town setting and popularity) has been a restaurant since 1937, and a recent makeover provides the current clean and stylish look. The bar-brasserie is worth recognition in its own right - expect chicken Caesar salad, and grilled salmon with warm potato salad, French beans and black olives - but it's the restaurant that earns the place its rosettes. Eastern influences might surface in a main course of oriental salmon with basil couscous, but the repertoire also extends to chump of pork with braised pig's cheek sauce and caramelised apple mash, and praiseworthy fillet of cod on seafood risotto - clams, mussels and squid - spiked with saffron broth.

Fixed L £ ALC ££

MIDDLESEX

❀ FRIENDS RESTAURANT

11 High Street Pinner HA5 5PJ

☎/❸ 020 8866 0286

Tudor building with oak beams and open fireplaces in a semi-rural location. Dishes might include hot vichyssoise with Welsh rarebit, and pan-fried pollock fillet with a crab crust.

Fixed L/D £ ALC ££

Friends Restaurant

❀ ❀ MIMS

63 East Barnet Road EN4 8RN

☎/❸ 020 8449 2974

A black-painted etched-glass-fronted restaurant next to a filling station and a newsagent's. The daily-changing menus are hand-written, the cooking techniques are simple - grilling, pan-frying, steaming and roasting - show skill, jazzed up with intelligent combinations, garnishings and flavoured oils. Breads are made in-house and served with flavoured butters of perhaps tomato and garlic, and a short wine list manages to pack in quite a lot of interest.

Fixed L/D £

❀ ❀ MONSIEUR MAX

133 High Street Hampton Hill TW12 1NJ

☎ 020 8979 5546 ❸ 020 8979 3747

French bourgeois food is served by predominantly French staff, all knowledgeable and quietly efficient. Terrines, ballotines, duck confit, salad lyonnaise, coq au vin, and choucroute are amongst dishes that gladden the heart of Francophiles. Bread arrives as you sit down, then rillettes of pork and duck, haricots verts, pear chutney and toasted pain Poilâne, followed by roasted lemon sole with girolles, braised Puy lentils, grilled pancetta and champagne sauce.

Fixed L/D £

SURREY

❀ ❀ AYUDHYA THAI RESTAURANT

14 Kingston Hill KT2 7NH

☎/❸ 020 8549 5984/8546 5878

Teak-panelled restaurant, very atmospheric with wood carving, artefacts, a small temple shrine and many (Thai) royal portraits. The menu is a large affair, but is lifted above the average by authentic, quality ingredients and clarity of flavours. Tried and tested starters include chicken marinated in screwpine leaves, and minced pork with coriander, garlic and soy sauce, wrapped in a thin pancake and deep-fried. Good spicing and coconut creaminess Is properly balanced in a classic green chicken curry.

ALC £

❀ ❀ COULSDON MANOR

Coulsdon Court Road Croydon CR5 2LL

☎ 020 8668 0414 ❸ 020 8668 3118

First courses set the tone for upmarket, country house cooking - terrine of morel mushroom and truffle with sherry and caramelised shallot dressing, for example. Well-honed kitchen skills and industry are demonstrated in a typical main course of charred and steamed supreme of salmon placed onto lobster mash with a beetroot jus and carrot spaghetti, and in labour-intensive desserts such as baked Alaska filled by a liquid cranberry centre with a clementine coulis.

Fixed L £ ALC ££

❀ ❀ MCCLEMENTS' RESTAURANT

2 Whitton Road Twickenham

☎ 020 8744 9598

Small, local restaurant near Twickenham Station, with candles and fresh flowers on the table. The menu is short and the wine list reasonably priced, with a few wine 'greats' at somewhat prohibitive prices at the back. Dishes include roast monkfish and scallops with saffron and vegetable jus, and a splendid assiette of desserts: lemon mousse, crème brûlée, chocolate tart, raspberry sorbet, praline parfait and coconut ice cream on apple tart - an impressive performance given the restricted size of the kitchen.

AA

www.theaa.co.uk

Find the "Where to Stay, Where to Eat" pages at www.theaa.co.uk/hotels

Search for...

a town or establishment name, by region or across the whole of Britain & Ireland

Where to stay, Where to eat

in East Anglia

Search for:

⦿ This region
○ Whole Site

Book Now

Locate on map

Select region
Select priority

♦♦♦♦♦
Lavenham Priory
Water Street
LAVENHAM
Sudbury
England
CO10 9RW

Telephone: 01787 247404
Facsimile: 01787 248472
Email: tim.pitt@btinternet.com
Website: www.btinternet.com/~laupriory

Lavenham Priory, Lave

Locate

Locate your chosen B&B on a road map

Use the contact details or hotlink to get more information or make a booking direct

Book Now

Booking online is easy with the AA online booking service

AFTERNOON TEA – A GREAT BRITISH INSTITUTION

Not just a fixture on a tourist itinerary, but an ultimate treat for many Brits. It's an excuse to dress up and check out places that might otherwise be inaccessible (nearly all the hotels listed here adhere to a jacket and tie code), and it's an agreeable way to spend the afternoon.

BROWN'S HOTEL
33-34 Albemarle Street W1

📞 020 7518 4108

Tea in the Drawing Room is one of the cosiest experiences London has to offer; rather like travelling back in time to an English country house of the Edwardian era. Enjoy a magnificent old-fashioned Victoria sponge cake and remember that the whole tea will leave you wishing you hadn't made arrangements for dinner. Tea served daily 3-6pm. Essential to book.

THE DORCHESTER
54 Park Lane W1

📞 020 7629 8888

The Promenade, where tea is served, is seriously luxurious. Deep, comfortable armchairs and thick carpets create a soothing atmosphere, staff glide carrying trays of this and that, a piano plays in the background. Tea brings some of the best pâtisserie in London. Tea served daily 3-6pm. Essential to book.

MERIDIEN WALDORF
Aldwych WC2

📞 020 7836 2400

A larger, more dramatic Palm Court than at the Ritz. It's like stepping back to the 30s, especially if you go to the tea dance held every Saturday and Sunday; rather like being in an Agatha Christie novel. No formal dress code, but it's worth making the effort. Tea served Mon-Fri 3-5.30pm. Tea dance Sat 2.30-5.30pm, Sun 4-6.30pm

THE RITZ
Piccadilly W1

📞 020 7493 8181

The Palm Court is surprisingly small but makes up for it with opulent Louis XVI decor. It is probably the most touristy afternoon tea in town, as well as the most expensive, yet it remains, nevertheless, a great experience. Booking for either of the two afternoon sittings is required one month in advance during the week, three months at weekends. Tea served daily at 3.30pm & 5pm

THE SAVOY
The Strand WC2

📞 020 7836 4343

Tea is served in the stately Thames Foyer. To the sound of a piano, an astonishing array of miniature food is served: tiny sandwiches, scones with jam and cream, delicate cakes and pastries. Tea served daily 3-5.30pm.

LEGENDARY LONDON

An Exploration of the City's Ancient Myths and Mysteries

by Jennifer Westwood

Above: Lud and his sons, outside St Dunstan's Church, Fleet Street. Around the time of Julius Caesar, Lud became king, fortified London, and renamed it 'Kaer-Lud'. After he died, his body was burnt near Ludgate, then the principal gate into the city. The original Lud (possibly the Celtic god Lludd or Nudd) was a god of healing and water-divinity, and regarded as the city's protective deity. These statues date from the 16th century.

Legendary London

London, like Babylon and Rome, is one of the great cities of the imagination. Legends claim it is immeasurably ancient, the guardian of the nation's "luck", a place of mystery and magic. Many go back at least to 1136 and Geoffrey of Monmouth's *History of Britain*, part-invention, part-tradition, shot through with Celtic myth.

Gogmagog

Legend dates the founding of London to before 1000 BC. After the Fall of Troy, Brutus, great-grandson of the Trojan hero Aeneas, came with his men to the island of Albion, then inhabited only by giants. Brutus parcelled it out among his followers and named it Britain. One day, the giants attacked them. The Trojans killed all but one, Gogmagog, who was made to wrestle with Corineus, Duke of Cornwall. Corineus hurled Gogmagog off a cliff to his death on the rocks, at a place known afterwards as "Gogmagog's Leap". "Gogmagog" is the biblical Gog and Magog rolled into one. By Tudor times, "Gogmagog's Leap" was located at Plymouth Hoe, where from the 15th to the 17th century was a turf-cut figure called "the gogmagog". At Totnes is the "Brutus Stone", in the 16th century held to mark the spot where Brutus first landed. The legend, adapted to fit London, now said that when Brutus founded Troynovant ("New Troy" = London), he made Gogmagog the porter of his palace (the Guildhall).

There Gogmagog stands to this day, one of two Guildhall giants who have existed in different forms for centuries. Sometimes they took part in processions: "Gogmagog the Albion" and "Corineus the Briton" saluted

Queen Elizabeth I from the Temple Bar as she passed through the City on the day before her coronation. Earlier giants were destroyed in the Great Fire of London; eaten by rats and mice; and destroyed in the Blitz. They were variously called Gogmagog and Corineus,

Above: Magog/Corineus.

Samson and Hercules, Gog and Magog. But their costumes have scarcely changed: Gog/Gogmagog is armed with a morningstar, Magog/Corineus wears the Tudors' idea of Trojan dress.

Sabrina

The ruins of subterranean structures of Roman cities - hypercausts, mithraea (temples of Mithras), drains - fascinated later generations, giving rise to tales of secret passages, labyrinths and caves. Perhaps it was the London Mithraeum, re-discovered in 1954, that inspired the legend of Sabrina. Brutus's son and heir Locrine had a cave dug under Troynovant in which to hide his mistress, Estrildis, from his wife, Gwendolen, and her powerful father, Duke Corineus. Estrildis lived there in hiding for seven years, and bore Locrine a daughter, Sabrina.

When Corineus died, Locrine put Gwendolen aside and made Estrildis his queen. But Gwendolen raised an army and he was killed in battle. She assumed rule of the kingdom, discovered the cave, and had Estrildis and her daughter drowned in the river since then called Sabrina (Severn). Echoing through this tale are hints of sacrifice to rivers. "Old Father Thames" is a figure of speech to us, but to the Celts river-names could signify vengeful deities who had to be appeased.

The Talking Head

Hidden under Troynovant, too, was its *palladium* or protective talisman. A 14th-century Welsh story tells how Bran, a gigantic king of Britain, dying after defeat in battle in Ireland, commanded his last seven followers to cut off his head and take it to "the White Hill" in London. They were to bury it there facing France. On their journey, which lasted nearly a hundred years, Bran's head talked to them the same as ever. Finally they reached London and buried the head in "the White Hill", and while there it kept the land safe from invasion. However, adds a later tradition, King Arthur dug up the head, being too proud to let anyone defend Britain but himself.

"The White Hill", probably Tower Hill, may have been special to the Celts: Brutus the founding-father was also buried there. The keeping of the head as a talisman uncannily recalls the Celtic practice of keeping heads as trophies, placing human skulls round the portals of shrines, and carving great stone heads such as still exist in Britain and Ireland. Perhaps these, too, were tribal guardians. And perhaps, though the custom of keeping ravens on Tower Hill is said to have been introduced by King Charles II, it is no coincidence that they, too, are said to protect the country from invasion. Or that in the 16th century Englishmen believed it was unlucky to kill a raven, because it might be a reincarnation of Arthur.

The Stone of Brutus

Sometimes also alleged to be a palladium is the limestone boulder known as London Stone. In the Middle Ages, it was a landmark - mentioned for example, in the *White Book of London*, compiled in 1419 by John Carpenter and Richard Whittington (the Dick Whittington of legend). It originally stood on the south side of the street known as Candlewright, Candlewick and eventually Cannon Street. Later, it was built into the wall of St Swithin's Church. Unlike the church, it survived both the Blitz and post-war development, and is now set into a wall on the north side of Cannon Street, next to St Swithin's Lane.

But what is it? One 18th-century Welsh visitor thought it might have been part of a "Druidical circle"; subsequently others suggested a Bronze Age fetish or Celtic "stone of inauguration", like the Stone of Scone. They referred to Shakespeare's *Henry VI*, in which the rebel Jack Cade, on entering London in 1450, struck the stone declaring himself lord of the city (more likely, this was connected with the custom of beating the bounds.) Yet others said it was a foundation stone, the "stone of Brutus", brought from Troy and laid on the altar of the Temple of Diana (there was a persistent idea that a temple to Diana once occupied the site of St Paul's Cathedral).

In the 19th century "an old saying" was reported that "so long as the stone of Brutus is safe, so long shall London flourish". This seems to be bogus. Though from the 16th century on we are told that Londoners' revered the stone, the evidence speaks of abuse and neglect. Twice moved in the 18th century as a nuisance, it came close to total destruction and only survived because of antiquarian interest.

The 16th-century topographer William Camden thought it was a Roman milliary or milestone, from which distances were

Above: Gog/Gogmagog

measured; Sir Christopher Wren, who had seen its foundations, guessed it was part of an elaborate monument connected with a larger building complex. He was right: excavations mainly 1964-5 between Upper Thames Street and Cannon Street revealed this complex, probably the Roman Governor's Palace.

London Bridge is Broken Down

The first London Bridge, 55 metres downstream from its present site, was probably built by the Romans in the year of their invasion (AD 43). For the Celts, this first bridging of the Thames at the risk of offending its god must have been momentous. Some say this accounts for the bridge's role in London's later traditions.

Above: The Temple of Mithras, discovered in 1954.

The mysterious singing game "London Bridge Is Broken Down" is first mentioned in 1659. Whatever it is built with, the bridge cannot be made to stand, until a watchman is set to guard it. The Opies in their *Oxford Dictionary of Nursery Rhymes* suggest that the watchman's original role was to thwart supernatural opposition to the bridge. Traditions of human sacrifice are connected

Above: This bust of Mithras can be seen at the Museum of London. The cult of Mithras was a warrior creed popular among Roman legionaries who spread it throughout the Empire, going underground when Christianity became the state religion. Mithras is connected with the cult of Sol Invictus (the Unconquerable Sun) and astrology, especially Taurus and Scorpio. The cult's teachings depicted Mithras as a saviour offering rebirth into eternal life, thus making him a direct threat to the spread of Christian beliefs.

with many bridges. Even London Bridge was once said to have had its stones bespattered with the blood of children. Perhaps such traditions are less about appeasing gods, than giving a bridge a ghostly guardian.

Many mythologies contain a bridge to the Otherworld. It has been argued that the Celts saw London Bridge this way. Certainly it is a place where the extraordinary happens. Bretons told of a man discovering a wonderful cure for blindness on London Bridge; Norsemen of a cripple healed by following directions received there. A Welshman who met a wizard on the bridge was led by him to a treasure-cave in Wales where Arthur lay sleeping. "The Pedlar of Swaffham" dreamed he would hear "joyful news" on the bridge and there learned of a crock of gold buried in his own garden.

The Land of Cockayne
Late in its history, London was identified with Cockayne, the topsy-turvey world of medieval tales, where roast pigs run along streets paved with pastry. In Cockayne no one need work and the living is easy. The name may be connected with Latin *coquere*, "to cook", and one Victorian scholar argued that Cockayne was based on Celtic rumours of public kitchens in Roman London.

Old French *trouver cocaigne*, "to find Cockayne", meant "to meet with good fortune". And that is the secret of London. This is the magical heart of Britain, a Land of Heart's Desire where wishes *are* horses that beggars may ride, and everyone's ship comes in, and peasants can be kings. New Troy, Cockayne or London, it is a dazzling city where the streets are paved with gold and simply standing on bridges can make your fortune.

STATUES & MONUMENTS

LONDON IS FULL OF STONE AND BRONZE TRIBUTES
TO THE FAMOUS AND LEGENDARY. HERE IS A SHORT
LIST OF SOME OF THE MOST INTERESTING AND BEST
KNOWN.

ELIZABETH NIGHTINGALE, WESTMINSTER ABBEY.
(The Abbey has hundreds of statues and monuments. If you're at all interested in this sort of thing, expect to spend all day here.)
Mrs Nightingale's main claim to fame is this elaborate monument which depicts her unfortunate death. She was struck by lightning, which is shown as Death in the shape of a hooded skeleton emerging from a black cavern to hurl a killing lance at her, while her horror-stricken husband tries vainly to deflect it. The monument was created by Francis Roubiliac, and was a subject of fascination for the young William Blake.

Above: Prospero and Ariel at BBC Broadcasting House

WILLIAM BLAKE, WESTMINSTER ABBEY.
Blake was a truly unique individual. Not only was he an accomplished painter and engraver who discovered a new form of etching that revolutionised the art, he also wrote some of the most memorable poetry in the English language. His best known works are the poems *'Tyger! Tyger! Burning Bright'*, and *'Jerusalem'*, and a painting of God called *'Ancient of Days'*.

SIR ISAAC NEWTON, WESTMINSTER ABBEY.
Designed by William Kent and sculpted by Michael Rysbrack, this monument shows the great physicist reclining against a pile of books, while on the sarcophagus cherubs play with scientific instruments.

Below: Sir Joseph Bazalgette, Sewage Engineer.

SIR JOSEPH BAZALGETTE CB
ENGINEER OF THE LONDON MAIN DRAINAGE SYSTEM
AND OF THIS EMBANKMENT

SIR WINSTON CHURCHILL, PARLIAMENT SQUARE
Cast by Ivor Roberts-Jones in 1973, Britain's wartime leader is shown at his most indomitable gazing towards Big Ben and Westminster Bridge.

JAN CHRISTIAAN SMUTS, PARLIAMENT SQUARE
South African general, statesman and prime minister. Apart from fighting the Germans in World War 1, he was instrumental in the founding of the League of Nations.

NELSON MANDELA, SOUTH BANK.
The leader of the ANC was imprisoned for his actions against South Africa's racial policy of apartheid. He was later released and became leader of South Africa when apartheid was dismantled. This bust was erected while he was still in prison in the 1980s.

Above: Madonna with child, All-Saint's Church.

PROSPERO & ARIEL, BBC BROADCASTING HOUSE, PORTLAND PLACE.
Eric Gill created this stylized, art deco sculpture of two characters from Shakespeare's *The Tempest*, to adorn the BBC's HQ in 1932. The use of Ariel to represent broadcasting is an intentional pun.

SIR JOSEPH BAZALGETTE, EMBANKMENT.
A little known but important figure, is this Victorian engineer, who designed the London main drainage system, and the Embankment itself.

MADONNA WITH CHILD, ALL SAINT'S CHURCH, MARGARET STREET.
The most common statue in Europe (apart from the Crucifixion) is undoubtedly the Madonna with Child. London has hundreds, and this one is particularly ornate.

Below: T.E.Lawrence, St Paul's Cathedral

Above: Not John Dee, but Michelangelo at the Royal Academy.

MICHELANGELO AND RAPHAEL, ROYAL ACADEMY.
These two giants of the Renaissance are commemorated by alcoved statues on the outside of the Royal Academy at Burlington House, Piccadilly. There's also a statue of Sir Joshua Reynolds outside. Reynolds was a prolific artist and the first president of the Academy when it was opened in the 1760s.

JOHN BUNYAN, BUNHILL FIELDS.
Bunyan was the author of Christian novel *The Pilgrim's Progress*, and *Grace Abounding*. He spent 12 years in prison in Bedford for heresy.

LAWRENCE OF ARABIA

LAWRENCE OF ARABIA, ST PAUL'S CATHEDRAL.

Like Westminster Abbey, St Paul's is crammed with memorials to the famous. A visit to both of these churches would overload even the most avid statuary fan. T. E. Lawrence was a controversial figure. A thoughtful adventurer who spent time as a junior archaeologist, an army intelligence agent, an Arab rebel against the Turks, and a delegate to the 1918 Peace Conference. He attempted to escape his own fame by joining the RAF under an assumed name, and wrote a fine autobiography called *The Seven Pillars of Wisdom*.

CHARLES I, TRAFALGAR SQUARE.

A romantic story attends Hubert le Sueur's equestrian statue of the tragic king. It shows Charles as if he was six feet tall, although he actually only stood 5ft 4in. During the Commonwealth it was hidden by the royal brazier, John Rivett, who pretended he had melted it down and ostentatiously sold candlesticks, spoons, thimbles and other objects supposedly made from the metal. When the Stuart dynasty was restored in 1660, he triumphantly produced the statue unharmed and it was later put in its present position. The king looks down Whitehall to the spot where he was executed in 1649, and since the 1890s a wreath has been laid at the statue every year on the anniversary, January 30th.

EROS, PICCADILLY CIRCUS

Although this is one of the world's best-known statues, many visitors may not realise that it was erected in the 1890s originally as a memorial fountain to the seventh Earl of Shaftesbury, a celebrated philanthropist. It represents the Angel of Christian Charity, although to be fair, it resembles Eros more than anything else. The sculptor, Sir Alfred Gilbert, explained the figure represented 'the blindfolded Love sending forth indiscriminately, yet with purpose, his missile of kindness.' The base of the fountain is carved with a prodigious riot of fishes, crabs, lobsters and molluscs. Quite what these have to do with Christian Charity seems unclear.

Below: The Albert Memorial, Hyde Park

Above: William Blake, Westminster Abbey.

THE ALBERT MEMORIAL, HYDE PARK

This incredible memorial was designed by George Gilbert Scott, who was then knighted by a mourning Queen Victoria. The statue of Albert was sculpted by John Foley and shows the prince seated in a shrine beneath an elaborate Gothic spire, 175ft high and inlaid with mosaics and enamels. Albert is perusing the catalogue of the Great Exhibition of 1851, which had been one his favourite causes. He is supported by a host of improving intellectual and moral abstractions - ranging from Chemistry to Prudence - represented in statues by some of the Victorian era's leading sculptors. A white marble frieze shows over 160 lifesize figures of notable artists, musicians and authors. The four angles deal with Agriculture, Manufacture, Commerce and Engineering, while further down are four more allegorical groups showing the continents of Europe, Asia, Africa and America. Clearly, this monument is as much a tribute to the mindset of the Victorian ruling classes as it is to Victoria's husband. An astounding structure.

BOUDICA (AKA BOADICEA, BOUDICCA, OR BOUDIGA), WESTMINSTER BRIDGE

Although Boudica was a first century leader who fought the Romans, her legend is relatively modern. She only really got under way as a national heroine with the publication of William Cowper's poem *'Boadicea'* in 1762. Because of the coincidence of names, (Boudica is roughly the equivalent to 'Victoria' in old Celtic) and the fact that she was a strong queen like Victoria herself, she became a useful symbol for empire builders, and the Victorians romanticized her, whitewashing her recorded atrocities (she is believed to have killed some 70,000 occupants of Londinium). It is a young, militaristic Victoria as much as the Celtic queen who is commemorated on the Victoria Embankment, near Big Ben, in this bronze group of Boudica and her daughters in a chariot, made by Thomas Thorneycroft in the 1850s and unveiled in 1902.

Above: John Bunyan's tomb in Bunhill Fields.

FLORENCE NIGHTINGALE, WATERLOO PLACE, LOWER REGENT STREET.

A more recent, and rather less problematic heroine is commemorated in this 9ft tall statue by A.G.Walker. In 1915 it was added to the Guards Monument, which had been erected in 1859 in honour of the 22,000 guardsmen who died in the Crimean War, with the figures of

Above: Charles II in Trafalgar Square

soldiers cast from captured Russian guns. Reliefs on the plinth of her statue show Miss Nightingale in various scenes from the Crimea. She is balanced on the other side of the memorial by Sidney Herbert, the Secretary of War who was her principal ally in the fight for effective nursing under combat conditions.

EMMELINE PANKHURST, VICTORIA TOWER GARDENS.

Standing next to the building that symbolises her struggle, the Houses of Parliament, this statue shows the suffragette leader holding a lorgnette (glasses on a stick for those who don't know). The government recoiled from putting the statue in Downing Street, as was originally suggested, but the figure was duly unveiled in 1930 by the Prime Minister Stanley Baldwin.

THE MONUMENT, FISH STREET HILL, NEAR PUDDING LANE

The Monument is 202 feet high, and stands 202 feet from the bakery in Pudding Lane where the Great Fire of London began in 1666. Inside, 311 black marble steps can be climbed for a marvellous view over the Thames from the upper gallery. The column was designed by Sir Christoper Wren and is crowned by a gilded copper urn of flames. On the pedestal a relief shows a gloomy City of London among the burning ruins, but King Charles in Roman attire is ordering Science and Architecture to the rescue, while a new city rises behind, Peace and Plenty flying overhead. In 1681 anti-Catholic hysteria prompted an inscription blaming papists for the fire to be added. This was obliterated in James II's time, reintroduced in William III's and finally erased in 1831.

GEORGE WASHINGTON, OUTSIDE THE NATIONAL GALLERY, TRAFALGAR SQUARE.

The first American President stands here, not far from James II in Roman costume. Other presidents include Roosevelt and Eisenhower in Grosvenor Square, near the American Embassy, Roosevelt chatting with Churchill on a park bench in New Bond Street, and John F Kennedy in Marylebone Road.

MAHATMA GANDHI, TAVISTOCK SQUARE.

Something of a shrine to the Indian leader, this statue depicts Gandhi sitting cross-legged at prayer. A bust of Jawaharlal Nehru, first prime minister of India, stands in Montreal Place, off the Aldwych.

EVENTS AND FESTIVALS

Above: The Royal Albert Hall, venue for the Henry Wood Promenade Concerts, better known as 'The Proms.'

London plays host to a vast number of annual festivals and events, from colourful pageants and ceremonies to some more eccentric events such as pancake tossing. It is best to contact the London Tourist Board (020 7932 2000) to check dates of events for 2000-1 and for contact telephone numbers.

DAILY EVENTS

CEREMONY OF THE KEYS
HM Tower of London, EC3
'Halt! Who comes there?' 'The keys.' 'Whose keys?' 'Queen Elizabeth II's keys.' 'Pass the keys. All's well.' The routine of locking up the Tower of London between the Sentry and the Chief Yeoman Warder has taken place every night for the past 700 years.

CHANGING THE GUARD
Buckingham Palace, Horse Guards and St James's Palace, SW1
The best of the ceremonies is at Buckingham Palace at 11.30am daily during summer, 11.30am alternate days during winter. The new guard and its regimental band lines up at Wellington Barracks from 10.45am, then march to the palace for the changing of the sentries. It's a colourful display.

JANUARY

LONDON INTERNATIONAL BOAT SHOW
Earls Court, SW5.

WEST LONDON ANTIQUES & FINE ART FAIR
Kensington Town Hall, W8.

DAILY TELEGRAPH TRAVEL & SPORTS SHOW
Olympia 2, W14.

ROAD RACING & SUPERBIKE SHOW
Alexandra Palace, N22.

FEBRUARY

CHINESE NEW YEAR CELEBRATIONS
Soho, W1.
2000 is the Year of the Dragon.

FINE ART & ANTIQUES FAIR
Olympia, W14.

MARCH

NATIONAL WEDDING SHOW
Olympia, W14.

SAILBOAT AND WINDSURF SHOW
Alexandra Palace, N22.

DAILY MAIL IDEAL HOME EXHIBITION
Earls Court, SW5.

CHELSEA ANTIQUES FAIR
Chelsea Old Hall, SW3.

HEAD OF THE RIVER RACE
Mortlake to Putney.

LONDON CLASSIC MOTOR SHOW
Alexandra Palace, N22.

LONDON INTERNATIONAL BOOK FAIR
Olympia, W14.

BRITISH ANTIQUE DEALERS ASSOCIATION FAIR
Duke of York's HQ, SW3.

OXFORD & CAMBRIDGE BOAT RACE
Putney to Mortlake, River Thames.

APRIL

CHELSEA ART FAIR
Chelsea Old Town hall, SW3.

FLORA LONDON MARATHON
From Greenwich, SE10 to The Mall, SW1.

LONDON HARNESS HORSE PARADE
Battersea Park, SW11.

MAY

ROYAL WINDSOR HORSE SHOW
Home Park, Windsor.

RUGBY: TETLEYS BITTER CUP FINAL
Twickenham, Middx.

LONDON DOLLSHOUSE FESTIVAL
Kensington Town Hall, W8.

FA CHALLENGE CUP FINAL
Wembley Stadium, Wembley.

CHELSEA FLOWER SHOW
Royal Hospital, SW3.

ROYAL ACADEMY SUMMER EXHIBITION
Royal Academy of Arts, W1.

JUNE

BIGGIN HILL INTERNATIONAL AIR FAIR
Biggin Hill Airfield, Kent.

BEATING THE RETREAT: MASSED BANDS OF THE HOUSEHOLD DIVISION
Horse Guards Parade, SW1.

FINE ART & ANTIQUES FAIR
Olympia, W14

DERBY DAY
Epsom, Surrey.

TROOPING THE COLOUR
Horse Guards Parade, SW1.

GROSVENOR HOUSE ART & ANTIQUES FAIR
Grosvenor House, W1.

COVENT GARDEN FLOWER FESTIVAL
Covent Garden Piazza, WC2.

ROYAL ASCOT
Ascot Racecourse, Berks.

MIDDLESEX SHOW
Middlesex Showground, Middx.

WIMBLEDON LAWN TENNIS CHAMPIONSHIPS
All England Club, SW9.

Above: Wimbledon

INTERNATIONAL HENLEY ROYAL REGATTA
Henley-on-Thames, Oxfordshire.

GREENWICH AND DOCKLANDS INTERNATIONAL FESTIVAL
Various venues in Greenwich.

JULY

HAMPTON COURT PALACE FLOWER SHOW
Hampton Court Palace, Surrey.

THE ROYAL MILITARY TATTOO
Horse Guards Parade, SW1.

BBC HENRY WOOD PROMENADE CONCERTS
Royal Albert Hall, SW7.

FARNBOROUGH INTL EXHIBITION AND FLYING DISPLAY
Farnborough Airfield, Hants.

AUGUST

KENSINGTON ANTIQUES FAIR & CONTEMPORARY ART FAIR
Kensington Town Hall, W8.

NOTTING HILL CARNIVAL
Ladbroke Grove, W10.

SEPTEMBER

CHELSEA ANTIQUES FAIR
Chelsea Old Town hall, SW3.

GREAT RIVER RACE
River Thames.

HORSE OF THE YEAR SHOW
Wembley Arena, Wembley.

OCTOBER

INTERNATIONAL FESTIVAL OF FINE WINE AND FOOD
Olympia, W14.

TRAFALGAR DAY PARADE
Trafalgar Square, WC2.

NOVEMBER

LONDON TO BRIGHTON VETERAN CAR RUN
Hyde Park, W2.

LORD MAYOR'S SHOW
through the streets of the City of London.

REMEMBRANCE DAY SERVICE AND PARADE
Cenotaph, Whitehall, SW1.

WORLD TRAVEL MARKET
Earls Court, SW5. Trade only.

NATIONAL HONEY SHOW
Kensington Town Hall, W8.

ROYAL SMITHFIELD SHOW
Earls Court, SW1.

Above: Henley Regatta

SPECIAL MILLENNIUM EVENTS & FESTIVALS

The year 2000 looks like being a very important one for special events and exhibitions. Here we present a list of major exhibitions and so on that are taking place in London during 2000 only.

FAST FOWARD>>REWIND<<LONDONER'S FUTURE TRANSPORT 1900-2026 AD (UNTIL JUL 2000)
London Transport Museum, WC2
Exhibition looking at 20th century transport, and speculating on future trends into the 21st century.
www.ltmuseum.co.uk

MEDICINE AND HUMANITY: THE KING'S COLLEGE LONDON DEBATES (JAN-NOV 2000)
Southwark Cathedral, SE1
Lectures followed by Q&A sessions.

JUDAICA 2000 (MAR-SEP 2000)
Jewish Museum, Camden NW1
Exhibition marking the new millennium and featuring outstanding examples of contemporary Jewish ceremonial art made by British craftsmen and women.
www.jewmusm.ort.org

LAMBETH PALACE MILLENNIUM OPENING (APR-NOV 2000)
Lambeth Palace, SE1
Home to the Archbishop of Canterbury, Lambeth Palace will be opening to the public, offering guided tours and an exhibition.

PHARMACY PAST, PHARMACY FUTURE (APR-DEC 2000)
Museum of the Royal Pharmaceutical Society of Great Britain, SE1
2000 years of medicine explored, along with a speculative peek into future medical discoveries.

ROYAL ARMOURIES MILLENNIUM EXHIBITION (APR-DEC 2000)
Tower of London, Tower Hill, EC3
An exhibition illustrating the history of the Tower of London, including specially commissioned artworks and a copy of the Domesday Book.

ART NOUVEAU 1890-1914 (APR-JUL 2000)
Victoria & Albert Museum SW7
Major exhibition of art and design from the turn of the (last) century. Compares 19th century *fin-de-siecle* with 20th century *fin-de-siecle*.

TREASURE OF THE TWENTIETH CENTURY (MAY-JUL 2000)
Goldsmiths Hall, Foster Lane, EC2
A unique opportunity to see silver, jewellery and art medals from the Goldsmith' Company's 20th century collection, on view to the public for the first time.

MUSEUMS AND GALLERIES MONTH 2000 (MAY-JUN 2000)
Various venues SE10
The Heritage Lottery Fund has given £350,000 to museums and galleries around the country to access funding for special events and activities. Highlights include exhibitions, welcome days, artists, designers, and craftspeople working with others to explore the ways that objects and art from the past can inspire the future.
www.may2000.org.uk

FESTIVAL DREAM 2000: SIGMUND FREUD & THE INTERPRETATION OF DREAMS (MAY-JUN 2000)
Various venues
A cultural season about the role of dreams in art and culture, 100 years after Freud's publication of his interpretation of dreams.
www.austria.org.uk/aci

WORLD OF JEWISH MUSIC 2000 (JUN-JUL 2000)
Various venues
This year's London International Jewish Music Festival features more than 50 events including opera, concerts, recitals, dance, film, theatre and so on.
www.jmht.org

CLOSE ENCOUNTERS - NEW ART FROM OLD (JUN-SEP 2000)
National Gallery, Trafalgar Square, WC2
Works by major contemporary artists inspired by paintings in the Gallery's collection.

FEET FIRST 2000 (JUN-JUL 2000)
Various venues
Multicultural, participatory dance event including a programme of world dance styles. Five week workshop programme, ending with an outdoor summer dance party in Finsbury Park, N7.
www.artsworldwide.org.uk

YOUTH FESTIVAL (JUN-JUL 2000)
Various venues in Newham
A borough-wide celebration of the creativity and optimism of Newham's young people.

EAT, DRINK & BE MERRY: THE BRITISH AT TABLE 1600-2000 (JUN-SEP 2000)
Kenwood House, Hampstead NW3
Touring exhibition exploring the evolution of British taste in food, drink and table presentation from the reign of Elizabeth I to Elizabeth II.

GREENWICH AND DOCKLANDS INTERNATIONAL FESTIVAL (JUN-JUL 2000)
Various venues in Greenwich
Multi-arts festival with a wide range of events, some ticketed and some free, both inside and outside.

TIMELY GUESS: PHARMACEUTICAL PLANTS AT THE MILLENNIUM (JUL-SEP 2000)
Chelsea Physic Garden, SW3
Exhibition of work by photographer in residence, Sue Smell, of plants used in pharmaceuticals alongside portraits of people treated by them.
www.cpgarden.demon.co.uk

CREATING SPARKS (SEP 2000)
Various venues in South Kensington SW7
Science and arts festival involving talks, shows, debates, workshops, exhibitions and conferences, organised by the British Association for the Advancement of Science.
www.britassoc.org.uk

TELLING TIME (OCT 2000-JAN 2001)
National Gallery, Trafalgar Sq, WC2
Gallery-wide event focusing on the relationship between time and painting. Includes major works from the Gallery's collection and loans of important works from abroad.

BRAND NEW (OCT 2000-JAN 2001)
Victoria & Albert Museum, SW7
Exploration of the diversity of international commercial design, reflecting the rise of global consumerism.

YEAR OF THE ARTIST (ALL YEAR 2000)
2000 has been designated the Year of the Artist by the Arts Council, which will be organising a wide range of exhibitions, events and debates.

COMMEMORATIVE BLUE PLAQUES

Since 1866, blue (and sometimes brown) plaques have been used to mark houses and other buildings associated with famous people or events. The idea of placing the plaques on buildings was devised by William Ewart and the first was placed on the birthplace of Lord Byron in Holles Street. Today there are hundreds of them all over London commemorating artists, composers, scientists, politicians, writers and many others. Until recently the tradition was that the person commemorated must have been dead for over 20 years and born over 100 years ago, but recently the mould was broken when Jimi Hendrix was commemorated. Although he died in 1970, he was only 27 at the time.

Here is a small selection of those remembered:

Jane Austen (1775-1817), author of *Sense and Sensibility* and *Pride and Predjudice* stayed at the site of 23 Hans Place, SW1

Lord Robert Baden-Powell, (1857-1941) Founder of the Scout Movement, lived at 9 Hyde Park Gate, SW7

John Logie Baird (1888-1946), television pioneer, lived at 3 Crescent Wood Road, Sydenham, SE26

Bela Bartók, (1881-1945), Hungarian composer of ballet and opera. His works included *Duke Bluebeard's Castle* and *The Wooden Prince,* as well as numerous concerto and chamber music. 7 Sydney Place, SW7

Sir Max Beerbohm (1872-1956), Caricaturist and writer. 57 Palace Gardens Terrace, W8

Hilaire Belloc (1870-1953), poet, essayist, historian and MP, lived at 104 Cheyne Walk, SW3

Arnold Bennett (1867-1931), Novelist, creator of the *Clayhanger* books. 75 Cadogan Square, SW1

E.F. Benson (1867-1940), writer. Creator of the *Mapp and Lucia* books. 25 Brompton Square, SW3

William Bligh (1754-1817), commander of HMS Bounty and famous mutineer, lived at 100 Lambeth Road, SE1

Andrew Bonar Law (1858-1923), Prime Minister (1922-23). 24 Onslow Gardens, SW7

Elizabeth Barrett Browning (1806-61), Poet and wife of Robert Browning, lived at 99 Gloucester Place, W1

Isambard Kingdom Brunel (1806-59), the famous civil engineer, builder of iron bridges, ships and railways, lived at 98 Cheyne Walk, SW3

Canaletto (1697-1768), Italian painter, lived at 41 Beak Street, W1

Charlie Chaplin (1889-1977), comic film actor and director, lived at 287 Kennington Road, SE11

Gilbert Keith Chesterton (1874-1936), Poet, novelist and critic. Creator of *Father Brown,* clerical detective. 11 Warwick Gardens, W14

Frédéric Chopin (1810-49), Polish composer and musician, gave his first London concert at 99 Eaton Place, SW1

Sir Winston Churchill (1874-1965), British Prime Minister 1940-45, 1951-55 , lived at 34 Eccleston Square, SW1

Sir Henry Cole (1808-1882), Campaigner and educator. First Director of the Victoria and Albert Museum. 33 Thurloe Square, SW7

Dame Ivy Compton-Burnett (1884-1969), Novelist. Author of *Brothers and Sisters* and *Mother and Son.* 5 Braemar Mansions, Cornwall Gardens, SW7

Sir Arthur Conan Doyle (1859-1930), creator of world-famous detective, Sherlock Holmes, lived at 12 Tennison Road, SE25

Sir Stafford Cripps, (1899-1952). Labour statesman, member of the Attlee government. 32 Elm Park Gardens, SW10

Charles Darwin (1809-82), pioneer of evolution theory, author of *On the Origin of Species by Means of Natural Selection,* lived on the site of 110 Gower Street, WC1, which is now part of University College

Charles Dickens (1812-70), social campaigner and author of many classic novels including *Oliver Twist, The Pickwick Papers* and *Nicholas Nickleby* lived at 48 Doughty Street, WC1 (the house is now open to the public) Commemorated on the £10 note.

Sir Edward Elgar (1857-1934), composer of *The Enigma Variations* and Master of the King's Musick, now commemorated on the £20 note, lived at 51 Avonmore Road, W14

George Eliot, (1819-1880), Pseudonym of Mary Ann Evans, novelist, whose works included *The Mill on the Floss, Middlemarch* and *Silas Marner.* 4 Cheyne Walk, SW3

T.S. Eliot, (1888-1965) Poet, author of *The Wasteland,* and *The Hollow Men.* 3 Kensington Court Gardens, W8.

Friedrick Engels (1820-95), Socialist philosopher, novelist, and co-author, with Karl Marx, of *The Communist Manifesto,* lived at 121 Regent's Park Road, NW1

Sir Alexander Fleming, (1881-1955) Discoverer of penicillin. 20a Danvers Street, SW3

Ford Madox Ford (1873-1939), Novelist, critic and collaborator with Joseph Conrad. 80 Campden Hill Road, W8

Sigmund Freud (1856-1939), the founder of psychoanalysis, lived at 20 Maresfield Gardens, NW3 (the house is open to the public)

Mrs Elizabeth Cleghorn Gaskell (1810-1865), Novelist. Author of *Wives and Daughters* and *Cranford.* 93 Cheyne Walk, SW10

David Lloyd George (1863-1945), Liberal statesman and Prime Minister (1916-22), lived at 3 Routh Road, SW18

Kenneth Grahame, (1859-1932) Author of *Wind in the Willows.* 16 Phillimore Place, W8

Nell Gwynne (c.1650-87), actress, orange girl and mistress of Charles II, lived at 79 Pall Mall, SW1

Radclyffe Hall, (1880-1943) Novelist and poet. Author of *The Well of Loneliness.* 37 Holland Street, W8.

Joseph Aloysius Hansom, (1803-1882) Architect, editor and inventor of the Hansom cab. 27 Sumner Place, SW7

John Fitzgerald Kennedy (1917-63), President of the United States, lived at 14 Prince's Gate, SW7 from 1961-3

Henry James, (1843-1916) American writer. *Author of Portrait of a Lady, The Bostonians,* and *The Ambassadors.* 34 De Vere Gardens, W8

Mohammed Ali Jinnah, (1876-1948) Founder of Pakistan. 35 Russell Road, W14

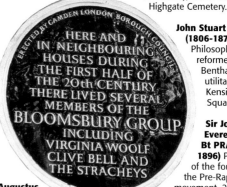

Augustus John, (1878-1961) Artist who painted portraits of Dylan Thomas, George Bernard Shaw and Thomas Hardy. 28 Mallord Street, SW3

Dr Samuel Johnson, (1709-1784), Author and lexicographer. Creator of the seminal *Dictionary of the English Language.* Hind Court, EC4

James Joyce, (1882-1941) Irish author of *Ulysses, Finnegan's Wake,* and *Portrait of the Artist as a Young Man.* 28 Campden Grove, W8

Charles Kingsley, (1819-1875) Writer. Author of children's classic, *The Water Babies.* 56 Old Church Street, SW3

Lillie Langtry, (1852-1929) Actress known as *The Jersey Lily.* Mistress of the Prince of Wales, later Edward VII. Cadogan Hotel, 22 Pont Street, SW1

Percy Wyndham Lewis, (1882-1957) Painter from the Vorticist school of British Futurism. 61 Palace Gardens Terrace, W8

Jenny Lind, (1820-1887) Singer, known as *The Swedish Nightingale.* Became professor of music at the Royal College of Music. 189 Old Brompton Road, SW7

Stephane Mallarme, (1842-1898) Symbolist poet, 6 Brompton Square, SW3.

Karl Marx (1818-83), communist and political author, lived at 28 Dean Street, W1 (now Leoni's Quo Vadis restaurant), and is buried in Highgate Cemetery.

John Stuart Mill (1806-1873), Philosopher, social reformer and Benthamite utilitarian. 18 Kensington Square, W8

Sir John Everett Millais, Bt PRA (1829-1896) Painter. One of the founders of the Pre-Raphaelite movement. 2 Palace Gate, W8

A.A. Milne (1882-1956) Author of the classic *Winnie the Pooh.* 13 Mallord Street, SW3

Piet Mondrian (1872-1944), Dutch modern painter who specialised in rectilinear abstracts, one of the founders of the *De Stijl* movement. Lived at 60 Parkhill Road, NW3

Wolfgang Amadeus Mozart (1756-91), Austrian child genius, composer and musician, composed his first symphony at 180 Ebury Street, SW1

Jawaharlal Nehru, (1889-1964) First Prime Minister of India. 60 Elgin Crescent, W11

Lord Horatio Nelson (1758-1805), British naval hero, immortalised by the statue in Trafalgar Square, lived at 103 New Bond Street, W1

Florence Nightingale (1820-1910), nursing pioneer, known as 'the Lady with the Lamp', during the Crimean War, lived and died in a house on the site of 10 South Street, W1

George Orwell (1903-50), Novelist and essayist. Author of *1984, Animal Farm* and *Down and Out in Paris and London.*

Sylvia Pankhurst, (1882-1960) Women's rights campaigner and pacifist. 120 Cheyne Walk, SW10

Mervyn Peake, (1911-1968) Author and Artist. Creator of the *Gormenghast* trilogy. 1 Drayton Gardens, SW10

Lucien Pissarro (1863-1944), painter, printer, type designer and engraver, son of Camille Pissarro, lived at 27 Stamford Brook Road, W6

Dame Marie Rambert, (1888-1982) Founder of Ballet Rambert. 19 Campden Hill Gardens, W8

Dante Gabriel Rosetti, (1828-1882) Poet and pre-Raphaelite painter. 16 Cheyne Walk, SW3

Siegfried Sassoon, (1886-1967) Writer. Author of anti-war classic, *Counterattack.* 23 Campden Hill Square, W8

Captain Robert Falcon Scott (1868-1912), Antarctic explorer, lived at 56 Oakley Street, SW3, from where he departed on his last tragic exploration.

George Bernard Shaw (1856-1950), Irish dramatist, socialist and essayist, lived at 29 Fitzroy Square, W1. Among his plays were *Major Barbara, Man and Superman,* and *Pygmalion,* better known in its film version *My Fair Lady.*

Jean Sibelius, (1865-1957) Finnish Composer. 15 Gloucester Walk, W8

LYTTON STRACHEY 1880-1932 Critic and Biographer lived here

Tobias Smollet, (1721-1771) Author of *The Adventures of Roderick Random* and *Humphry Clinker.* 16 Lawrence Street, SW3 (In which Chelsea China was manufactured 1745-1784)

Bram Stoker, (1847-1912) Irish author of *Dracula, Lair of the White Worm* and *The Lady of the Shroud.* 18 St. Leonards Terrace, SW3

Dr SAMUEL JOHNSON AUTHOR. LIVED HERE. B·1709. D·1784.

Lytton Strachey (1880-1932) Biographer and member of the Bloomsbury Group. Author *Eminent Victorians, Queen Victoria* and *Elizabeth and Essex.* 51 Gordon Square, Bloomsbury

Algernon Charles Swinburne, (1837-1909) Poet. 16 Cheyne Walk, SW3

Dame Ellen Terry, (1847-1928) Actress and theatre manager. One of the finest Shakespearean actresses of the 19th century. 22 Barkston Gardens, SW5

William Makepeace Thackeray, (1811-1863), Novelist, author of *Vanity Fair.* 2 Palace Green, W8 & 16 Young Street, W8

Mark Twain (1835-1910), American writer famous for his stories of Huckleberry Finn and Tom Sawyer, lived at 23 Tedworth Square, SW3

Vincent van Gogh (1853-90), Dutch painter, lived at 87 Hackford Road, SW9

Chaim Weizmann, (1874-1952) Zionist and first President of Israel. 67 Addison Road, W14

Dick Whittington (c.1358-1423), English merchant, four times Lord Mayor of London and star of countless pantos, lived at a house on the site of 20 College Hill, EC4

James Abbot McNeil Whistler, (1834-1903), Painter and etcher. 96 Cheyne Walk, SW10

William Wilberforce, (1759-1833) Opponent of slavery. 44 Cadogan Place, SW1

Oscar Wilde (1854-1900), poet, dramatist and sparkling wit, lived at 34 Tite Street, SW3. Included among his works are *The Picture of Dorian Gray, Lady Windemere's Fan* and *The Importance of Being Ernest.*

Sir Christopher Wren (1632-1723), one of Britain's greatest architects, lived at 49 Bankside, SE1, during the building of St Paul's Cathedral, which he designed.

Everything you need
...in just one guide

Indispensable guides developed from the wealth of AA data. Everything you need to plan your visit - in-depth information on accommodation, places to eat and drink and what to see and do.

- Where to stay - B&Bs, hotels, campsites - all AA inspected and quality assessed

- Where to eat - from pubs to top quality restaurants

- Places to visit and days out for the family

- How to entertain the children

- Museums, art galleries, theatres, stately homes, gardens, the big outdoors, historic and ancient sites

- Sports facilities - golf, swimming, leisure centres, sailing, fishing, horse-riding

- Local events, festivals and crafts

- Essential practical information

- Colour photographs throughout

- Easy-to-use

Available from all good bookshops for only £9.99

AA Lifestyle Guides

THE BEST FISH AND CHIPS IN TOWN

FORGET MODERN BRITISH COOKING, AND THE REST OF THE FOOD REVOLUTION, HERE ARE FOUR EXPERT CHIPPIES FRYING UP REAL FOOD.

FISH CENTRAL
151 King's Square Central Street EC1
☎ 0171 253 4970
Regarded by many as the best fish and chip shop in the capital, offering more than the basic take away. In the restaurant there are all manner of fishy delights listed, from sea bass to sole. Booking recommended.
Open Mon-Sat 11am-2.30pm & 4.45-10.30pm

NORTH SEA FISH RESTAURANT
7-8 Leigh Street WC1
☎ 0171 3875892
A popular cab-drivers pit stop. They usually take over the back while the rest of us sit in the front room amongst the pink velvet upholstery and stuffed fish. Portions are gigantic, the fish very fresh. Booking recommended for dinner. Take away service.
Mon-Sat noon-2.30pm, 5.30-10.30pm

ROCK AND SOLE PLAICE
47 Endell Street WC2
☎ 0171 8363785
Opened in 1871, this claims to be the oldest surviving chip shop in London. The Covent Garden location draws an eager pre-theatre crowd to the restaurant where booking is recommended for dinner. Take away service.
Daily 11.30am-10pm, 9pm Sun

SEASHELL
49-51 Lisson Grove NW1
☎ 0171 7238703
Perhaps the most famous of all London's chippies - certainly the most popular with tourists. Success has seen some slippage in quality and queues are common as bookings are not taken for parties of less than six.
Mon-Sat noon-10.30pm, Sun noon-3pm

FASCINATING FACTS

DID YOU KNOW?

Above: The starting point of The Great Fire of London.

London receives over 23 million visitors a year, and its bus and underground network carry 5 million passengers every day.

The Black Death in 1348 killed nearly half the population of the city.

Houndsditch is so called because Londoners used to throw their dead animals into the boundary ditch.

The Poll Tax Riot of 1990 was in part, a continuation of protests from 1381, when Jack Straw and Wat Tyler led thousands of commoners in the Peasant's Revolt against the Poll Tax of the day. Riots in London led to the death of the Archbishop of Canterbury, the destruction of the Savoy Palace and the fatal stabbing of Tyler by the Lord Mayor, William Walworth.

During the reign of Catholic Queen Mary, (1553-8) 300 Protestants were burnt at the stake at Smithfield. This earnt her the nickname 'Bloody Mary'.

The plague of 1665 killed 100,000 people, and ignorance about the cause of the epidemic (fleas carried by rats) led to the Lord Mayor's order that all cats and dogs should be killed. The slaughter left 40,000 dogs and 200,000 cats dead.

The Great Fire of London in 1666 raged for three days, destroyed 87 churches and more than 13,000 houses. The cause was an untended baker's oven.

In 1858, the windows of the Houses of Parliament had to be draped with sheets soaked in chloride of lime to keep the 'great stink' of the sewers at bay.

Charles I wore two shirts to his execution so that he would not shiver in the cold and give the impression that he was afraid

Below: Guglielmo Marconi contemplates the radio contraption that will make him a household name.

(Above): The Imperial War Museum, previously Bedlam.

- Elizabeth Nightingale, buried in Westminster Abbey, died in 1731 of a miscarriage, having been frightened by lightning

- Marble Arch was once the venue for public hangings, at Tyburn gallows, where the crowds paid high prices for ringside seats

- Only members of the royal family are allowed to drive through Marble Arch

- Britain's smallest police station is built inside a lamp-post in the south-east corner of Trafalgar Square.

- Author Charles Dickens wished to be buried in the Dickens family tomb in Highgate Cemetery. This wish was overruled by Queen Victoria who insisted he should be buried in Westminster Abbey.

- There is a ghostly driverless bus in Notting Hill which has been blamed for numerous accidents (some fatal) over the past 40 years.

- Bow has historically been connected with women's rights. In 1888, the Bryant & May match factory was the scene of a brave and bitter strike by nearly 700 match-girls protesting conditions, especially 'phossy jaw', a weakening of the jawbone brought on by overexposure to the phosphorus used for matchheads. Socialist and feminist Annie Besant helped to organise the strike. Twenty five years later Sylvia Pankhurst used Bow as the base for her East London Federation of Suffragettes.

- Spencer Perceval is the only British Prime Minister to have been assassinated. In 1812, he was shot in the lobby of the House of Commons by John Bellingham, a bankrupt Liverpool broker.

- London's first aerial bombing took place in September 1915 when German Zeppelins dropped a bomb near the Guildhall.

- The first phase of Germany's blitzkrieg lasted for 57 nights. 7 September 1940 was the first night of bombing. 2,000 were killed without warning.

🦁 The first public radio broadcast was from the roof of Marconi House in the Strand in 1922.

🦁 The first BBC TV broadcast came from Alexandra Palace on 26 August 1936.

🦁 Buckingham Palace took 20 years to build and even then had faulty drains, doors that wouldn't open and windows that wouldn't shut.

🦁 The manuscript of *The French Revolution*, Thomas Carlyle's massive tome, was erroneously used by a friend's maid to light the fire, and he had to start again from scratch.

🦁 Newgate Prison (now the Old Bailey) has had some famous inmates. Casanova, Sir Thomas Malory, Daniel Defoe and Ben Jonson all did time here.

(Above): St Paul's Cathedral as it appeared in the 1880s.

🦁 The first London Underground line opened in 1863. It joined Paddington and Farringdon Road and attracted over 30,000 passengers on the first day.

🦁 Old pennies are used to adjust the weight of Big Ben's mighty pendulum

🦁 It was discovered that James Barry, Inspector General of the Army Medical Department, who died in 1865 and is buried in Kensal Green Cemetery, was actually a woman.

🦁 The giant Christmas tree in Trafalgar Square is an annual donation by Norway, in thanks for the Allied liberation of the country from Nazi occupation.

🦁 In the 18th and 19th centuries public executions at Newgate attracted crowds of up to 100,000. The riotous behaviour of these crowds prompted the executions to go indoors from 1868.

🦁 St Paul's Cathedral became a symbol of British determination to survive the Nazi blitz, when it survived intensive bombing. On one night 28 incendiary devices fell around it, but the dome remained unscathed.

🦁 Some of the British Museum's most interesting galleries are best reached via the back door, along Montague Place.

🦁 The Lamb & Flag pub in Covent Garden was once known as the 'Bucket of Blood' because of the bare-knuckle fights that took place there.

🦁 London's first Chinatown was in Limehouse, a notorious spot for opium dens and gambling parlours.

🦁 The Mayflower pub on Rotherhithe Street is the only pub licensed to sell postage stamps.

🦁 Legend has it that if any of the eight ravens who live at the Tower of London fly away the Tower will collapse. It is to prevent this that their wings are pinioned to prevent them from flying away.

🦁 The Imperial War Museum is built on the site of Bedlam, a hospital for the mentally ill, where visitors were allowed to watch the patients who were placed in cages like animals in a zoo.

🦁 Many people run in the London Marathon for charity and wear fancy dress.

Above: A police marksman prepares to take aim during the Seige of Sidney Street, 1911

🦁 Frith Street and Jermyn Street are named after their respective self-important property developers

🦁 Piccadilly is named after Piccadilly House, built by Robert Baker, a wealthy 17th-century tailor which was in turn named after the 'picadils', or stiff collars, that he made

🦁 In 1813 the Thames froze over for the last time. The demolition of Old London Bridge in 1831 increased the flow of the river and ended the chance of it freezing again

🦁 Although the BBC's Broadcasting House was hit by a bomb on 15 October 1940, the newscaster continued to read the news

🦁 In 1948, London hosted the Olympic Games.

🦁 In 1911 anarchists battled police in the Seige of Sidney Street. Following a shootout that left one Russian anarchist and three policemen dead, the gang were cornered in a building on Sidney Street. By the end of the seige, that left two charred bodies in the ruins, a

detachment of Scots Guards, two cannons, and Home Secretary Winston Churchill had put in an appearance.

🦁 When it was built in 1973, Trellick Tower was the highest block of flats in England. The building was so despised by local resident Ian Fleming, that he named the villain of one of his James Bond novels after the architect. The architect's name? Ernö Goldfinger.

🦁 In 1969 the Rolling Stones played for free to 500,000 people in Hyde Park

🦁 Pop songs with London connections have included '*Waterloo Sunset*' by The Kinks, '*Down in the Tube Station at Midnight*' by The Jam, '*London Calling*' by The Clash, '*The Old Main Drag*' by The Pogues, and '*Brompton Oratory*' by Nick Cave and The Bad Seeds.

🦁 The first Grand Lodge of Freemasonry was founded in London in1717, and the city is still at the heart of Masonry. Freemason's Hall in Great Queen Street houses the impressive Grand Temple and co-ordinates the rituals of nearly 9,000 British Lodges.

LONDON'S HAUNTED PUBS

BY ELIZABETH CARTER

THE TOWER OF LONDON HEADS THE LIST OF THE
CAPITAL'S MOST HAUNTED PLACES WITH AN IMPRESSIVE
ARRAY OF ROYAL AND NOBLE GHOSTS. BUT LONDON'S
PUBS, SUCH PERFECT MICROCOSMS OF HUMANITY, HAVE
ALWAYS BEEN A RICH BREEDING GROUND FOR SPOOKS,
AND WE LIST HERE SOME OF THE BEST PUB HAUNTS
LONDON HAS TO OFFER.

SW1

GRENADIER,
Wilton Row, SW1

(turning off Wilton Crescent). Nearest tube - Knightsbridge

An engaging, if rather compact place, a survivor of the London of the early 1800s. It was once used by King George IV as his local, a fact that caused *The Times* to comment indignantly, but is nowadays noted for being the most famous haunted pub in the world.

In the early 19th century the pub was called The Guardsman and acted as a Mess for the officers of the Duke of Wellington's regiment - most of the buildings around had something to do with the army. The public drank below stairs in what is now the cellar, while the officers ate, drank and gambled above. The gambling often led to cheating, the cheating led to brawls and, on one such occasion, a young officer was killed.

The story goes that the subaltern was flogged to death after being tried by a kangaroo court and 'sentenced' to be stripped and thrashed. Presumably this happened in September, since this is when his ghost walks - successive landlords have reported unusual happenings and the pub now makes much off this yearly haunting - the apparition either appearing as a shapeless blob, or making its presence felt through poltergeist activity.

Whether it's September or not, the Bloody Marys are recommended.

NW3

WILLIAM IV,
Hampstead High Street, NW3.

Nearest tube - Hampstead

A girl committed suicide in the dentist's surgery that once stood opposite the William IV . Her ghost now stares in at pub customers, who are able to see that her hair is plaited and that she wears a white shift like a shroud. No one has any explanation as to why she should do this but curiosity could be an explanation - The William IV is a gay pub, although not exclusively.

THE SPANIARDS,
Spaniards Lane, Hampstead NW3.

Nearest tube- Hampstead, but quite a walk.

Wonderfully old fashioned former toll

Above: The Grenadier

house, complete with snug little alcoves, open fires, oak panelling, and a very pretty sheltered garden. No one knows how The Spaniards got its name, the stories vary: it could be that the place was built in the year of the Spanish Armada, or the Spanish Ambassador to James I stayed there, or that two Spanish brothers, who were landlords of the inn, fought a duel over a girl with fatal consequences to one of them.

What is not disputed is the connection with Dick Turpin; he used the inn as a headquarters for the London end of the York road. Leading from the cellar of The Spaniards are concealed passages that the highwayman used to dodge the Bow Street runners.

Dick Turpin has left a number of ghosts behind him in various parts of the country, most of them riding a phantom Black Bess. It is this apparition that has been reported galloping over Hampstead Heath towards The Spaniards. Past landlords have also heard the sound of horses' hoof beats - and found nothing to account for them.

N6

THE GATEHOUSE,
North Road, Highgate Hill, Highgate, N6.
Nearest tube - Highgate/Archway

Toll gates did not come into general use until the passing of the Turnpikes Act in 1663. But in 1364 King Edward III authorised William Phillipe, a hermit, to set up a toll-bar on Highgate Hill. With the money collected from travellers, mainly drovers and graziers on their way to Smithfield, he was ordered to keep the road in good repair. The toll-gate, eventually a solidly high gate across the road, remained until 1890. It was from this that The Gatehouse, and the area, took its name. At the inn the drovers would make their final stopover (see entry for The Horns). The original licence was granted by the then Bishop of London in 1310, making this the site of one of the oldest pubs in London.

The present building has a solid Edwardian look with very recent and extensive refurbishment blurring any features from an earlier time. There used to be a fairly modern ballroom overlooked by a minstrels' gallery - the oldest part of the pub. In this gallery, described by one medium as a 'cold and evil place', walked the ghost of Mother Marnes, a widow who, with her cat, was murdered for her money. The ghost, a black-robed figure, was said to appear only when there were no children or animals on the premises. And, some thirty years ago, members of staff reported that when they looked into a particular mirror, they did not see their own reflections, but a blurred and cloudy image that was not recognisable.

N1

OLD QUEEN'S HEAD,
44 Essex Road, Islington N1.
Nearest tube - Angel

As a favourite of Queen Elizabeth I, Sir Walter Raleigh received many perks. One of them was the authority 'to make lycences for the keeping of taverns and retayling of wynes throughout England'. The Old Queen's Head is one of the pubs he licensed, not surprisingly, since it is said that he had the house built in the first place. At the time many courtiers found Islington a pleasant place from which to commute to the Court. Although Raleigh never lived here, preferring the Pied Bull Inn nearby, Lord Burleigh, the Lord Treasurer, stayed at the inn for a time, as did the Earl of Essex, another favourite of the Queen, who herself made the inn an occasional stopping place.

This is not the original building, that was pulled down in 1829. Nevertheless, the massive Tudor fireplace was incorporated into the present pub, and may account for why the place is haunted by a lady in Tudor dress and by a sad little girl whose long dress has been heard rustling and swishing as she moves. And on the first Sunday of the month doors are opened and closed by unseen hands and feet heard tap-tapping up the stairs.

Below: Black Bess is reputed to gallop over Hampstead Heath.

Nowadays the place attracts a young, trendy crowd, and the music and bustle make ghost hunting nigh impossible, although during the day the clientele is more varied and the atmosphere quieter.

SE1

THE HORNS,
Crucifix Lane, SE1.

Nearest tube - London Bridge

Hidden beneath the arches of London Bridge Station, The Horns is a curiously named pub in a curiously named street. Nearly two hundred years ago, this part of Bermondsey had as its nearest neighbour Jacob's Island, a festering rookery of slum dwellings perched on rotting platforms above black mud, open sewers and tidal ditches spanned by plank bridges. In the foul water of the adjacent creek, ironically named St Saviours, witches and whores were ducked to purge their souls. The Holy Rood, from the old Bermondsey Abbey of St Saviours, set up at the junction of Bermondsey Street and Crucifix Lane, gave the lane its name.

The Horns was a common name for a pub frequented by drovers, graziers, and shepherds. It is thought that by 1824 the Kent drovers were using Crucifix Lane as a short cut to the new bridge at Southwark, which led directly to the markets of Eastcheap and Smithfield. The Horns would have been a final stopping place.

Nearly every inn of this name used to keep a magnificent pair of horns, sometimes silver tipped, for the curious custom of 'swearing on the horns', a kind of initiation ceremony. This originated as the swearing-in of drovers or graziers to their favourite pub but by the 19th century had such a romantic appeal that even the poet Byron took the oath of allegiance on the horns kept at The Gatehouse in Highgate (see entry) and summed it all up thus:

And many to the steep Highgate hie,
Ask ye, Boeotian shades! the reason why
'tis to the worship of the solemn horn,
Grasp'd in the holy hand of mystery,
In whose dread name both men and maids are
sworn,
And consecrate the oath with draught and dance
till morn.

It was in the early 1960s that reports of a haunting occured. The then landlords started to hear the voice of a young girl of about eight crying, sometimes screaming, for her mother. The cries became more and more frequent until it was decided that as she seemed so desperately unhappy they should do something. A letter was sent to the Bishop of Southwark who passed it on to a Canon of Southwark Cathedral who arrived with a medium.

According to the medium two ghosts were haunting The Horns - the little girl and a very old lady. The little girl was exorcised, but the old lady is still in one of the upper rooms, perfectly happy - there was no point in making her go against her will.

NW1

THE VOLUNTEER,
Baker Street NW1.

Nearest tube - Baker Street

The Volunteer stands on the site of a medieval manor house belonging to the Nevill family. In 1654 the entire family perished in a fire that razed the house to the ground. It is Rupert Nevill who haunts the pub. Dressed in surcoat, breeches and fancy stockings, he lurks in the dark recesses of the cellar.

Below: Victorian drovers on their way to The Horns.

QUICK REFERENCE
ACCOMMODATION LISTS

QUICK REFERENCE LISTS

BUDGET ACCOMMODATION

These establishments provide single rooms that are £35 a night or less. They are listed in alphabetical order.

ABER HOTEL ♦ ♦
89 Crouch Hill N8 9EG
☎ 020 8340 2847

ANCHOR HOTEL ♦ ♦
10 West Heath Dr, Golders Green
NW11 7QH
☎ 020 8458 8764

BEDKNOBS ♦ ♦ ♦ ♦
58 Glengarry Rd, East Dulwich SE22 8QD
☎ 020 8299 2004

GROVE HILL HOTEL ♦ ♦ ♦
38 Grove Hill, South Woodford E18 2JG
☎ 020 8989 3344 & 8530 5286

GROSVENOR ♦ ♦ ♦
18 Grosvenor Rd, Muswell Hill N10 2DS
☎ 020 8883 0487

MELBOURNE HOUSE HOTEL ♦ ♦ ♦
79 Belgrave Rd, Victoria SW1V 2BG
☎ 020 7828 3516

MOUNT VIEW ♦ ♦ ♦ ♦
31 Mount View Rd N4 4SS
☎ 020 8340 9222

THE PILOT INN ♦ ♦
68 Riverway, Greenwich SE10 0BE
☎ 020 8858 5910

PREMIER WEST HOTEL ♦ ♦ ♦
28-34 Glenthorne Rd,
Hammersmith W6 0LS
☎ 020 8748 6181

WESTON HOUSE HOTEL ♦ ♦
8 Eltham Green, Eltham SE9 5LB
☎ 020 8850 5191

CHILDREN'S FACILITIES

Some establishments provide special facilities for children, which may include drawing materials, a play area, toys and supervision.

ATHENAEUM ★ ★ ★ ★
116 Piccadilly W1V 0BJ
☎ 020 7499 3464

THE BEAUFORT ♦
33 Beaufort Gardens SW3 1PP
☎ 020 7584 5252

THE DORCHESTER ★ ★ ★ ★ ★
Park Lane W1A 2HJ
☎ 020 7629 8888

ACCOMMODATION WITH PARKING

Many establishments have their own car parking reserved solely for use by residents. In London this can be an indispensible facility for many visitors.

BED & BREAKFASTS

ANCHOR HOTEL ♦ ♦
10 West Heath Rd, Golders Green NW11 7QH
☎ 020 8458 8764

CENTRAL HOTEL ♦ ♦ ♦
35 Hoop Lane, Golders Green NW11 8BS
☎ 020 8458 5636

CRYSTAL PALACE TOWER HOTEL ♦ ♦ ♦
114 Church Rd, Crystal Palace SE19 2UB
☎ 020 8653 0176

THE EXECUTIVE HOTEL ♦ ♦ ♦
57 Pont St, Knightsbridge SW1X 0BD
☎ 020 7581 2424

LA GAFFE
107-111 Heath St NW3 6SS
☎ 020 7435 4941 & 435 8965

THE GARTH HOTEL ♦ ♦ ♦
64-76 Hendon Way, Cricklewood NW2 2NL
☎ 020 8455 4742 & 8209 1511

GROVE HILL HOTEL ♦ ♦ ♦
38 Grove Hill, South Woodford E18 2JG
☎ 020 8989 3344 & 8530 5286

KINGS LODGE HOTEL ♦ ♦ ♦
5 Kings Rd, Wimbledon SW19 8PL
☎ 020 8545 0191

LAKESIDE ♦ ♦ ♦ ♦ ♦
51 Snaresbrook Rd, Wanstead E11 1PQ
☎ 020 8989 6100

THE LANGDORF HOTEL ♦ ♦ ♦
20 Frognal, Hampstead NW3 6AG
☎ 020 7794 4483

LONDON CONTINENTAL HOTEL ♦ ♦
88 Gloucester Place W1H 3HN
☎ 020 7486 8670

MELROSE HOUSE HOTEL ♦ ♦ ♦
89 Lennard Rd SE20 7LY
☎ 020 8776 8884

MITRE HOUSE HOTEL ♦ ♦ ♦
178-184 Sussex Gardens, Hyde Park W2 1TU
☎ 020 7723 8040

PEACEHAVEN HOTEL ♦ ♦ ♦
94 Audley Rd, Hendon Central NW4 3HB
☎ 020 8202 9758 & 1225

THE PILOT INN ♦ ♦
68 Riverway, Greenwich SE10 0BE
☎ 020 8858 5910

PREMIER WEST HOTEL ♦ ♦ ♦
28-34 Glenthorne Rd,
Hammersmith W6 0LS
☎ 020 8748 6181

RHODES HOTEL ♦ ♦
195 Sussex Gardens W2 2RJ
☎ 020 7262 5617 & 0537

RIDGEWAY HOTEL ♦ ♦ ♦
115/117 The Ridgeway,
North Chingford E4 6QU
☎ 020 8529 1964

SANDRINGHAM HOTEL ♦ ♦ ♦ ♦
3 Holford Rd, Hampstead NW3 1AD
☎ 020 7435 1569

SWISS COTTAGE HOTEL ♦ ♦ ♦
4 Adamson Rd, Swiss Cottage NW3 3HP
☎ 020 7722 2281

TROCHEE HOTEL ♦ ♦
21 Malcolm Rd, Wimbledon SW19 4AS
☎ 020 8946 1579 & 3924

VANBURGH HOTEL ♦ ♦ ♦
St Johns Park, Blackheath SE3 7TD
☎ 020 8858 7000

WESTON HOUSE HOTEL ♦ ♦
8 Eltham Green, Eltham SE9 5LB
☎ 020 8850 5191

WIMBLEDON HOTEL ♦ ♦
78 Worple Rd, Wimbledon SW19 4HZ
☎ 020 8946 9265 & 1581

WORCESTER HOUSE HOTEL ♦ ♦
38 Alwyne Rd, Wimbledon SW19 7AE
☎ 020 8946 1300

YARDLEY COURT ♦ ♦ ♦
18 Court Rd, Eltham SE9 5PZ
☎020 8850 1850

THE BARBICAN ★ ★ ★
Central St, Clerkenwell EC1V 8DS
☎020 7251 1565

BARDON LODGE ★ ★ ★
15-17 Stratheden Rd SE3 7TH
☎020 8853 4051

BASIL STREET ★ ★ ★
Basil St, Knightsbridge SW3 1AH
☎020 7581 3311

THE BERKELEY ★ ★ ★ ★ ★
Wilton Place, Knightsbridge SW1X 7RL
☎020 7235 6000

CANNIZARO HOUSE ★ ★ ★ ★
West Side, Wimbledon Common SW19 4UE
☎020 8879 1464

CAPITAL ★ ★ ★ ★
Basil St, Knightsbridge SW3 1AT
☎020 7589 5171

THE CAVENDISH ST JAMES'S ★ ★ ★ ★
81 Jermyn St SW1Y 6JF
☎020 7930 2111

CENTRAL PARK ★ ★ ★
Queensborough Terrace W2 3SS
☎020 7229 2424

CHELSEA VILLAGE ★ ★ ★ ★
Stamford Bridge, Fulham Rd SW6 1HS
☎020 7565 1400

CHURCHILL INTER-CONTINENTAL
★ ★ ★ ★ ★
30 Portman Square W1A 4ZX
☎020 7486 5800

CLARENDON ★ ★
8-16 Montpelier Row, Blackheath SE3 0RW
☎020 8318 4321

CLIFTON-FORD ★ ★ ★ ★
47 Welbeck St W1M 8DN
☎020 7486 6600

CONRAD INTERNATIONAL LONDON
★ ★ ★ ★ ★
Chelsea Harbour SW10 0XG
☎020 7823 3000

COPTHORNE TARA ★ ★ ★ ★
Scarsdale Place, Wrights Lane W8 5SR
☎020 7937 7211

DELMERE ★ ★
130 Sussex Gardens, Hyde Park W2 1UB
☎020 7706 3344

THE DORCHESTER ★ ★ ★ ★ ★
Park Lane W1A 2HJ
☎ 020 7629 8888

DRURY LANE MOAT HOUSE ★ ★ ★ ★
10 Drury Lane WC2B 5RE
☎020 7208 9988

FORUM ★ ★ ★ ★
97 Cromwell Rd SW7 4DN
☎020 7370 5757

FOUR SEASONS ★ ★ ★ ★ ★
Hamilton Place, Park Lane W1A 1AZ
☎020 7499 0888

GORING ★ ★ ★ ★
Beeston Place, Grosvenor Gardens
SW1W 0JW
☎020 7396 9000

GREAT NORTHERN ★ ★ ★
Kings Cross N1 9AN
☎020 7837 5454

GROSVENOR HOUSE ★ ★ ★ ★ ★
Park Lane W1A 3AA
☎020 7499 6363

THE HALKIN HOTEL ★ ★ ★ ★
Halkin St, Belgravia SW1X 7DJ
☎020 7333 1000

THE HOGARTH ★ ★ ★
33 Hogarth Rd, Kensington SW5 0QQ
☎020 7370 6831

**HOLIDAY INN KINGS CROSS /
BLOOMSBURY** ★ ★ ★ ★
1 Kings Cross Rd WC1X 9HX
☎020 7833 3900

HOTEL IBIS ★ ★
30 Stockwell St SE10 9JN
☎020 8305 1177

HOTEL IBIS EUSTON ★ ★
3 Cardington NW1 2LW
☎020 7388 7777

HOTEL INTER-CONTINENTAL ★ ★ ★ ★ ★
1 Hamilton Place, Hyde Park Corner
W1V 0QY
☎020 7409 3131

HYATT CARLTON TOWER ★ ★ ★ ★ ★
Cadogan Place SW1X 9PY
☎020 7235 1234

THE KENNEDY ★ ★ ★
Cardington St NW1 2LP
☎020 7387 4400

LANDMARK ★ ★ ★ ★ ★
222 Marylebone Rd NW1 6JQ
☎020 7631 8000

LANESBOROUGH ★ ★ ★ ★ ★
Hyde Park Corner SW1X 7TA
☎020 7259 5599

**LONDON MARRIOTT GROSVENOR
SQUARE** ★ ★ ★ ★
Grosvenor Square W1A 4AW
☎020 7493 1232

**LONDON MARRIOTT HOTEL
MARBLE ARCH** ★ ★ ★ ★
134 George St W1H 6DN
☎020 7723 1277

LONDON MARRIOTT HOTEL REGENTS PARK ★ ★ ★
128 King Henry's Rd, NW3 3ST
☎020 7722 7711

THE LONDON RYAN ★ ★ ★
Gwynne Place, Kings Cross Rd WC1X 9QN
☎020 7278 2480

MANDARIN ORIENTAL HYDE PARK
★ ★ ★ ★ ★
66 Knightsbridge SW1X 7LA
☎020 7235 2000

THE MILLENNIUM BAILEYS HOTEL
★ ★ ★ ★
140 Gloucester Rd SW7 4QH
☎020 7373 6000

MILLENNIUM BRITANNIA MAYFAIR
★ ★ ★ ★
Grosvenor Square W1A 3AN
☎020 7629 9400

THE MILLENNIUM CHELSEA ★ ★ ★ ★
17 Sloane St, Knightsbridge SW1X 9NU
☎020 7235 4377

THE MILLENNIUM GLOUCESTER HOTEL ★ ★ ★ ★
4-18 Harrington Gardens SW7 4LH
☎020 7373 6030

THE MONTCALM-HOTEL NIKKO LONDON ★ ★ ★ ★
Great Cumberland Place W1A 2LF
☎020 7402 4288

NOVOTEL LONDON WATERLOO ★ ★ ★
113 Lambeth Rd SE1 7LS
☎020 7793 1010

NOVOTEL LONDON WEST ★ ★ ★
Hammersmith Int Centre, 1 Shortlands
W6 8DR
☎020 8741 1555

PARAGON HOTEL ★ ★ ★
47 Lillie Rd SW6 1UD
☎020 7385 1255

PARK LANE ★ ★ ★ ★ ★
Piccadilly W1Y 8BX
☎020 7499 6321

PEMBRIDGE COURT
34 Pembridge Gardens W2 4DX
☎020 7229 9977

POSTHOUSE BLOOMSBURY ★ ★ ★
Coram St WC1N 1HT
☎020 7837 1200

POSTHOUSE HAMPSTEAD ★ ★ ★
215 Haverstock Hill NW3 4RB
☎020 7794 8121

POSTHOUSE KENSINGTON ★ ★ ★
Wright's Lane, Kensington W8 5SP
☎020 7937 8170

POSTHOUSE REGENTS PARK ★ ★ ★
Carburton St, Regents Park W1P 8EE
☎020 7388 2300

RADISSON SAS PORTMAN ★ ★ ★ ★
22 Portman Square W1H 9FL
☎020 7208 6000

RAGLAN HALL ★ ★ ★
8-12 Queens Ave, Muswell Hill N10 3NR
☎020 8883 9836

ROYAL LANCASTER ★ ★ ★ ★
Lancaster Terrace W2 2TY
☎020 7262 6737

THE ROYAL SCOT ★ ★ ★
100 Kings Cross Rd WC1X 9DT
☎020 7278 2434

ST GEORGE'S
Langham Place, Regent St W1N 8QS
☎020 7580 0111

THE SAVOY ★ ★ ★ ★ ★
Strand WC2R 0EU
☎020 7836 4343

THE SELFRIDGE ★ ★ ★ ★
Orchard St W1H 0JS
☎020 7408 2080

SHERATON PARK TOWER ★ ★ ★ ★ ★
101 Knightsbridge SW1X 7RN
☎020 7235 8050

SWALLOW INTERNATIONAL ★ ★ ★ ★
Cromwell Rd SW5 0TH
☎020 7973 1000

THISTLE HYDE PARK ★ ★ ★ ★
90-92 Lancaster Gate W2 3NR
☎020 7262 2711

THISTLE KENSINGTON GARDENS ★ ★ ★
104 Bayswater Rd W2 3HL
☎020 7262 4461

THISTLE MARBLE ARCH ★ ★ ★ ★
Bryanston St, Marble Arch W1A 4UR
☎020 7629 8040

THISTLE TOWER ★ ★ ★ ★
St Katherine's Way E1 9LD
☎020 7481 2575

22 JERMYN STREET
St James's SW1Y 6HL
☎020 7734 2353

VENCOURT ★ ★ ★
255 King St, Hammersmith W6 9LU
☎020 8563 8855

THE WHITE HOUSE ★ ★ ★ ★
Albany St NW1 3UP
☎020 7387 1200

THE WINDMILL ON THE COMMON
★ ★ ★
Southside, Clapham Common SW4 9DE
☎020 8673 4578

GOLF COURSES

A list of golf courses in London and Greater London. Further information on these courses can be obtained from the AA Guide to Golf Courses, which is published annually by the AA.
Some courses may want advance notice of any visit, and possibly a letter of introduction from your own club. They may also require a handicap certificate. It is always a good idea to check with any course in advance to find out how they operate.

GREATER LONDON

ADDINGTON

THE ADDINGTON
205 Shirley Church Rd, CR0 5AB
☎020 8777 1055

ADDINGTON COURT
Featherbed Lane CR0 9AA
☎020 8657 0281
📠020 8651 0282

ADDINGTON PALACE
Addington Park, Gravel Hill CR0 5BB
☎020 8654 3061
📠020 8655 3632

BARNEHURST

BARNEHURST GOLF COURSE
Mayplace Rd East DA7 6JU
☎01322 523746
📠01322 554612

BARNET

ARKLEY GOLF CLUB
Rowley Green Rd EN5 3HL
☎020 8449 0394
📠020 8440 5214

OLD FOLD MANOR GOLF CLUB
Old Ford Lane, Hadley Green EN5 4QN
☎020 8440 9185
📠020 8441 4863

DYRHAM PARK COUNTRY CLUB
Galley Lane EN5 4RA
☎020 8440 3361
📠020 8441 9836

BECKENHAM

LANGLEY PARK GOLF CLUB
Barnfield Wood Rd BR3 6SZ
☎020 8658 6849
📠020 8658 6310

BECKENHAM PLACE PARK
The Mansion,
Beckenham Place Park BR3 2BP
☎020 8650 2292
📠020 8663 1201

BEXLEYHEATH

BEXLEYHEATH GOLF CLUB
Mount Rd DA6 8JS
☎020 8303 6951

BIGGIN HILL

CHERRY LODGE GOLF CLUB
Jail Lane TN16 3AX
☎01959 572250
📠01959 540672

BROMLEY

SUNDRIDGE PARK GOLF CLUB
Garden Rd BR1 3NE
☎020 8460 0278

SHORTLANDS GOLF CLUB
Meadow Rd, Shortlands BR2 0PB
☎020 8460 8828

BROMLEY GOLF COURSE
Magpie Hall Ln BR2 8JF
☎020 8462 7014

CARSHALTON

OAKS SPORTS CENTRE
Woodmansterne Rd SM5 4AN
☎020 8643 8363
📠020 8770 7303

CHESSINGTON

CHESSINGTON GOLF CLUB
Garrison Ln KT9 2LW
☎020 8391 0948
📠020 8397 2068

CHISLEHURST

CHISLEHURST GOLF CLUB
Camden Park Rd BR7 5HJ
☎020 8467 2782
📠020 8295 0974

COULSDON

COULSDON MANOR HOTEL
Coulsdon Court Rd CR5 2LL
☎020 8660 6083

WOODCOTE PARK GOLF CLUB
Meadow Hill, Bridle Way CR5 2QQ
☎020 8668 2788
📠020 8668 2788

CROYDON

SHIRLEY PARK GOLF CLUB
194 Addiscombe Rd CR0 7LB
☎020 8654 1143

CROHAM HURST GOLF CLUB
Croham Rd CR2 7HJ
☎020 8657 5581
📠020 8657 3229

SELSDON PARK HOTEL GOLF COURSE
Addington Rd, Sanderstead CR2 8YA
☎020 8657 8811
📠020 8651 6171

DOWNE

WEST KENT GOLF CLUB
West Hill BR6 7JJ
☎01689 851323
📠01689 858693

HIGH ELMS GOLF CLUB
High Elms Rd BR6 7JL
☎01689 853232

ENFIELD

ENFIELD GOLF CLUB
Old Park Rd South EN2 7DA
☎020 8363 3970
📠020 8342 0381

WHITEWEBBS MUNICIPAL GOLF CLUB
Whitewebbs Lane EN2 9JN
☎020 8363 4454
📠020 8363 4454

CREWS HILL GOLF CLUB
Cattlegate Rd, Crews Hill EN2 8AZ
☎020 8363 6674
📠020 8364 5641

GREENFORD

PERIVALE PARK GOLF COURSE
Stockdove Way UB6 8TJ
☎020 8575 7116

235

LIME TREES PARK GOLF CLUB
Ruislip Rd, Northolt UB5 6QZ
☎0120 8842 0442

C & L GOLF & COUNTRY CLUB
Westend Rd, Northolt UB5 6RD
☎020 8845 5662

HORSENDEN HILL GOLF CLUB
Whitten Ave, Woodland Rise UB6 0RD
☎020 8902 4555

EALING GOLF CLUB
Perivale Lane UB6 8SS
☎020 8997 0937
📠020 8998 0756

HADLEY WOOD
Hadley Wood Golf Club
☎020 8449 4328
📠020 8364 8633

HAMPTON

FULWELL GOLF CLUB
Wellington Rd, Hampton Hill TW12 1JY
☎0181 977 3844

HAMPTON WICK

HOME PARK GOLF CLUB
KT1 4AD
☎020 8977 2423

HILLINGDON

HILLINGDON GOLF CLUB
18 Dorset Way UB10 0JR
☎01895 233956
📠01895 233956

HOUNSLOW

AIRLINKS GOLF CLUB
Southall Lane TW5 9PE
☎020 8561 1418

HOUNSLOW HEATH MUNICIPAL
Staines Rd Tw4 5DS
☎020 8570 5271

ILFORD

ILFORD GOLF CLUB
Wanstead Park Rd IG1 3TR
☎020 8554 2930
📠020 8554 0822

ISLEWORTH

WYKE GREEN GOLF CLUB
Syon Lane TW7 5PT
☎020 8847 0685
📠020 8569 8392

KINGSTON UPON THAMES

COOMBE WOOD GOLF CLUB
George Rd, Kingston Hill KT2 7NS
☎020 8942 0388
📠020 8942 0388

COOMBE HILL GOLF CLUB
Golf Club Dr, Coombe Ln West KT2 7DF
☎020 8336 7600
📠020 8336 7601

MITCHAM

MITCHAM GOLF CLUB
Carshalton Rd CR4 4HN
☎020 8648 4280
📠020 8647 4197

NEW MALDEN

MALDEN GOLF CLUB
Traps Ln KT3 4RS
☎020 8942 0654
📠020 8336 2219

NORTHWOOD

HASTE HILL
The Drive HA6 1HN
☎01923 822877
📠01923 824683

SANDY LODGE GOLF CLUB
Sandy Lodge Ln HA6 2JD
☎01923 825429
📠01923 824319

NORTHWOOD GOLF CLUB
Rickmansworth Rd HA6 2QW
☎01923 821384
📠01923 840150

ORPINGTON

LULLINGSTONE PARK GOLF COURSE
Parkgate Rd, Chelsfield BR6 7PX
☎01959 533793 & 533794
📠01959 533795

CRAY VALLEY GOLF CLUB
Sandy Ln, St Paul's Cray BR5 3HY
☎01689 837909 & 871490
📠01689 891428

RUXLEY PARK GOLF CENTRE
Sandy Ln, St Paul's Cray BR5 3HY
☎01689 871490
📠01689 891428

CHELSFIELD LAKES GOLF CENTRE
Court Rd BR6 9BX
☎01689 896266
📠01689 824577

PINNER

GRIMS DYKE GOLF CLUB
Oxhey Lane, Hatch End HA5 4AL
☎020 8428 4539
📠020 8421 5494

PINNER HILL GOLF CLUB
Southview Rd, Pinner Hill HA5 3YA
☎020 8866 0963
📠020 8868 4817

PURLEY DOWNS

PURLEY DOWNS GOLF CLUB
106 Purley Downs Rd CR2 0RB
☎020 8657 8347
📠020 8651 5044

RICHMOND UPON THAMES

ROYAL MID-SURREY GOLF CLUB
Old Deer Park TW9 2SB
☎020 8940 1894
📠020 8332 2957

THE RICHMOND GOLF CLUB
Sudbrook Park, Petersham TW10 7AS
☎020 8940 4351

ROMFORD

ROMFORD GOLF CLUB
Heath Drive, Gidea Park RM2 5QB
☎01708 740986

RISEBRIDGE GOLF CENTRE
Risebridge Chase,
Lower Bedfords Rd RM1 4DG
☎01708 741429
📠01708 741429

MAYLANDS GOLF & COUNTRY CLUB
Colchester Rd, Harold Park RM3 0AZ
☎01708 346466
📠01708 373080

RUISLIP

RUISLIP GOLF CLUB
Ickenham Rd, HA4 7DQ
☎01895 638081
📠01895 635780

Coombewood Golf Club, Kingston

SIDCUP

SIDCUP GOLF CLUB 1926 LTD
7 Hurst Rd, DA15 9AE
☎ 020 8300 2150

SOUTHALL

WEST MIDDLESEX GOLF CLUB
Greenford Rd, UB1 3EE
☎ 020 8574 3450
📠 020 8574 2383

STANMORE

STANMORE GOLF CLUB
29 Gordon Ave, HA7 2RL
☎ 020 8954 2599

SURBITON

SURBITON GOLF CLUB
Woodstock Lane KT9 1UG
☎ 020 8398 3101
📠 020 8339 0992

TWICKENHAM

TWICKENHAM GOLF CENTRE
Staines Rd TW2 5JD
☎ 020 8783 1748 & 1698
📠 020 8941 9134

STRAWBERRY HILL GOLF CLUB
Wellesley Rd, Strawberry Hill TW2 5SD
☎ 020 8894 0165

UPMINSTER

UPMINSTER GOLF CLUB
114 Hall Lane RM14 1AU
☎ 01708 222788
📠 01708 222788

UXBRIDGE

STOCKLEY PARK GOLF CLUB
Stockley Park UB11 1AQ
☎ 020 8813 5700
📠 020 8813 5655

UXBRIDGE GOLF COURSE
The Drive, Harefield Place UB10 8AQ
☎ 01895 237287
📠 01895 813539

WEMBLEY

SUDBURY GOLF CLUB
Bridgewater Rd HA0 1AL
☎ 020 8902 3713
📠 020 8903 2966

WEST DRAYTON

HEATHPARK GOLF CLUB
Stockley Rd UB7 9NA
☎ 01895 444232
📠 01895 445122

WOODFORD GREEN

WOODFORD GOLF CLUB
Sunset Av IG8 0ST
☎ 0181 504 3330
📠 020 8559 0504

LONDON

E4

ROYAL EPPING FOREST GOLF CLUB
Forest Approach, Chingford E4 7AZ
☎ 020 8529 2195

WEST ESSEX GOLF CLUB
Bury Rd, Sewardstonebury, Chingford E4 7QL
☎ 020 8529 7558
📠 020 8524 7870

E11

WANSTEAD GOLF CLUB
Overton Dr, Wanstead E11 2LW
☎ 020 8989 3938
📠 020 8532 9138

N2

HAMPSTEAD GOLF CLUB
Winnington Rd N2 0TU
☎ 020 8455 0203
📠 020 8731 6194

N6

HIGHGATE GOLF CLUB
Denewood Rd N6 4AH
☎ 020 8340 5467
📠 020 8348 9152

N9

LEE VALLEY LEISURE GOLF COURSE
Picketts Lock Sports Centre, Meridian Way, Edmonton N9 0AS
☎ 020 8803 3611

N14

TRENT PARK GOLF CLUB
Bramley Rd, Oakwood N14 4UW
☎ 020 8366 7432

N20

NORTH MIDDLESEX GOLF CLUB
The Manor House, Friern Barnet Ln, Whetstone N20 0NL
☎ 020 8445 1604 &3060
📠 020 8445 5023

SOUTH HERTS GOLF CLUB
Links Dr, Totteridge N20 8QU
☎ 020 8445 2035
📠 020 8445 7569

N21

BUSH HILL PARK GOLF CLUB
Bush Hill, Winchmore Hill N21 2BU
☎ 020 8360 5738
📠 020 8360 5583

N22

MUSWELL HILL GOLF CLUB
Rhodes Av, Wood Green N22 4UT
☎ 020 8888 1764
📠 020 8889 9380

NW4

THE METRO GOLF CENTRE
Barnet Copthall Sports Centre, Gt North Way
NW4 1PF
t020 8202 1202
020 8203 1203

NW7

FINCHLEY GOLF CLUB
Nether Court, Frith Lane, Mill Hill NW7 1PU
020 8346 2436 & 5036
020 8343 4205

HENDON GOLF CLUB
Ashley Walk, Devonshire Rd, Mill Hill
NW7 1DG
020 8346 6023
020 8343 1974

MILL HILL GOLF CLUB
100 Barnet Way, Mill Hill NW7 3AL
020 8959 2339
020 8906 0731

SE9

ELTHAM WARREN GOLF CLUB
Bexley Rd, Eltham SE9 2PE
020 8850 4477 & 1166

ROYAL BLACKHEATH GOLF CLUB
Court Rd SE9 5AF
020 8850 1795
020 8859 0150

SE18

SHOOTERS HILL GOLF CLUB
Eaglesfield Rd, Shooters Hill SE18 3DA
020 8854 6368
020 8854 0469

Mill Hill Golf Club, NW7

SE21

DULWICH & SYDENHAM HILL GOLF CLUB
Grange Ln, College Rd SE21 7LH
020 8693 3961 & 8491

SE22

AQUARIUS GOLF CLUB
Marmora Rd, Honor Oak, Off Forest Rd
SE22 0RY
020 8693 1626

SE28

RIVERSIDE GOLF COURSE
Summerton Way, Thamesmead SE28 8PP
020 8310 7975

SW15

RICHMOND PARK GOLF COURSE
Roehampton Gate, Priory Lane SW15 5JR
020 8876 1795
020 8878 1354

SW18

CENTRAL LONDON GOLF CENTRE
Burntwood Ln, Wandsworth SW17 0AT
020 8871 2468
020 8874 7447

SW19

WIMBLEDON PARK GOLF CLUB
Home Park Rd, Wimbledon SW19 7HR
020 8946 1250
020 8944 8688

ROYAL WIMBLEDON GOLF CLUB
29 Camp Rd SW19 4UW
020 8946 2125
020 8944 8652

WIMBLEDON COMMON GOLF CLUB
Camp Rd SW19 4UW
020 8946 0294
020 8946 7571

W7

BRENT VALLEY GOLF CLUB
138 Church Rd, Hanwell W7 3BE
020 8567 1287

Percival David Foundation, WC1 100
Peter Jones, SW1 63
Petrie Museum of Egyptian Archaeology, WC1 100-1
Pétrus, SW1 33
Pharmacy Restaurant, W11 92
The Phene Arms, SW3 73
Phillips, W1 44
Phoenix, WC2 113
Phoenix Bar and Grill, SW15 186
Photographers' Gallery, WC2 112
Piccadilly, W1 35-6, 38
    see also Mayfair, Piccadilly and Oxford Street
Piccadilly Circus 35-6, 211
Piccadilly (theatre), W1 114
Pied à Terre, W1 53
Pied à Terre, W8 81
The Pilot Inn, SE10 172
Pineapple Dance Centre, WC2 118
Pizza Chelsea, SW7 93
Pizza Express, W1 118
Pizzeria Castello, SE1 143
The Place, WC1 101
Planet Hollywood, W1 43, 122
The Playhouse, N5 128
Playhouse, WC2 137
Plaza (cinema), W1 40
Plaza on Hyde Park, W2 85
Plaza Shopping Precinct, W1 41
Please Mum, W1 43
Pollock's Toy Museum, W1 102
The Popeseye, W14 92
Portobello Road Market, W10 78
post codes 14
Posthouse Bloomsbury, WC1 105
Posthouse Gatwick Airpoert, Gatwick Airport 182
Posthouse Kensington, W8 86
Posthouse Regents Park, W1 105
Prada, SW3 64
Premier West Hotel, W6 188
Primrose Hill, NW1 99
The Prince Bonaparte, W2 94
Prince Charles, WC2 113

Prince Edward, W1 114
The Prince of Teck, SW5 93
Prince of Wales, WC2 122
Prinstead, Gatwick Airport 184
Prospect of Whitby, E1 163
Public Record Office Museum, Kew, Middx 194
public transport 14
Puppet Theatre Barge, W9 102
Purple Sage, W1 53
Purves & Purves, W1 102
Putney Bridge, SW15 190

Q
Quaglino's, SW1 33
Quality Chop House, EC1 142
Quality Eccleston, SW1 25
Quality Harrow Hotel, Harrow, Middx 198
Queen Victoria Memorial, SW1 30
The Queen's Chapel, SW1 31
Queen's Gallery, SW1 30
Queen's Ice Skating Club, W2 82
The Queens (pub), NW1 107
Queen's (theatre), WC2 114
Quincy's Restaurant, NW2 180
Quo Vadis, W1 121

R
Raceway, N1 128
Radisson Edwardian Berkshire Hotel, W1 47, 53
Radisson Edwardian Grafton, W1 105
Radisson Edwardian Hampshire, WC2 119
Radisson Edwardian Kenilworth, WC1 105
Radisson Edwardian Mountbatten, WC2 119
Radisson Edwardian Pastoria, WC2 119
Radisson Edwardian Vanderbilt, SW7 84
The Radisson SAS Portman Hotel, W1 47, 53
Raglan Hall, N10 185
Rain, W10 92
Rainforest Café, W1 43

Ramada, Heathrow Airport, Middx 181
Ranelagh Gardens, SW3 61
Rani, N3 189
Ransome's Dock, SW11 189
Rasa, N16 53
Rasa W1 53
Rathbone Books 128
Red or Dead, WC2 116
Red Lion (Crown Passage), SW1 33
Red Lion (Duke of York St), SW1 33
Red Pepper, W9 92
Redmond's, SW14 190
The Regency Hotel, W1 49
Regent Street 36
Regent's Canal 100
Regent's Park 96-7, 99, 102, 103
    see also Regent's Park and Bloomsbury
Regent's Park and Bloomsbury 96-107
    accommodation 104-6
    children's entertainment 102
    cinemas 101
    entertainment and nightlife 101-2
    literary Bloomsbury 103
    map 97-8
    museums 100-1
    places of worship 103
    pubs, inns and other eating places 107
    restaurants 106-7
    shopping 102
    sightseeing 99-100
    sport and leisure 103
    theatres and concert halls 101
Regent's Park Golf School, NW1 103
Regent's Park Open-Air Theatre 101
Rembrandt, SW7 84
Renoir, WC1 101
Restaurant Gordon Ramsay, SW3 71
restaurants 11
    see also individual areas
Rhodes Hotel, W2 88
Rhodes in the Square, SW1 71-2
Rhythm Records, NW1 128
RIBA, W1 101

The Automobile Assocation would like to thank the following photographers and libraries for their assistance in the preparation of this book:

MARY EVANS PICTURE LIBRARY 227; ILLUSTRATED LONDON NEWS 223b, 225, 226; LANCASTER HOTEL 188; RITZ HOTEL 204; PAUL SPENCER 205;

The remaining pictures in this guide are held in the Association's own library (AA PHOTOLIBRARY) and were taken by:

AA PHOTOLIBRARY Front Cover (d), 42a, 59a, 60b,. 62a, 62b, 82b, 99c, 135b, 138b, 151b, 159a, 219b; PETER BAKER Front Cover (b); PETE BENNETT 221; THEO COHEN 30b; ROGER DAY 59c; STEPHEN GIBSON 145, 150b, 152b; CAROLINE JONES 236, 238; PAUL KENWARD Back Cover (b), 23b, 30a, 31b, 42b, 43, 44a, 44b, 58, 59b, 63a, 63c, 64b, 77, 79a, 81c, 98, 101b, 103a, 114b, 116a, 117a, 127c, 134a, 135a, 136a, 139a, 148b, 159b, 168c, 169b 209b, 234; JENNY McMILLAN Front Cover (I), Back Cover (a), 24a, 29a, 30c, 35, 213; S & O MATHEWS Front Cover (f), 160b, 176a; ROBERT MORT 11, 63b, 82a, 96, 99b, 100a, 103b, 112b, 118a, 128a, 128b, 149c, 158a; BARRIE SMITH 41b, 101c, 110, 113b, 115b, 115c, 126b, 134b, 138a, 139c, 159c, 161b, 168b, 224, 232; RICK STRANGE Front Cover (a), 19, 23c, 37, 39c, 42c, 56, 60a, 60c, 61b, 61c, 75, 78a, 78b, 99a, 100b, 102a, 102b, 103c, 109, 115a, 116b, 118a, 150a, 155, 160c, 208a, 209a, 210b, 210c, 211a, 212a, 212b, 214, 217a, 217b, 218a, 218b, 219a, 223a; RICHARD SURMAN 170a; JAMES TIMS 8, 22a, 23a, 39b, 61a, 78c, 80a, 112a, 117b, 123, 125, 126a, 137b, 149b, 168a, 177a, 211b; MARTIN TRELAWNY Front Cover (e), 24b, 79c, 126c, 127b, 131, 135a, 139b, 176b, 176c, 215a; RICHARD TURPIN 39a, 81b, 127a, 151c, 152a, 177b; ROY VICTOR Front Cover (c), 1, 31a, 40, 101a, 113a, 160a, 161a, 166, 167, 228, 231; WYN VOYSEY 21, 38, 114a, 116c, 136b, 136c, 158b, 165, 170b, 215b, 222; PETER WILSON 41a, 80c, 133, 210a, 233; TIM WOODCOCK Front Cover (g), Front Cover (h), 22b, 27, 29b, 29c, 64a, 79b, 81a, 137a, 149a, 151a, 169a, 169c, 206, 207, 208b; GREGORY WRONA 7, 80b, 174